Playing the Game

To Islwyn Morris Williams

PLAYING
THE GAME

The Story of
Western Women
in Arabia

Penelope Tuson

I.B. TAURIS

LONDON · NEW YORK

Published in 2003 by I.B.Tauris & Co Ltd
6 Salem Road, London W2 4BU
175 Fifth Avenue, New York NY 10010
www.ibtauris.com

In the United States and Canada distributed by Palgrave
Macmillan, a division of St. Martin's Press
175 Fifth Avenue, New York NY 10010

ISBN 1 86064 933 5

A full CIP record for this book is available from the British
Library

Typeset in Sabon by Dexter Haven Associates, London
Printed and bound in Great Britain by MPG Books, Bodmin

Contents

Illustrations

The author and publisher would like to thank the following for their kind permission to reproduce photographs: 1: British Library Oriental and India Office Collections; 2: Dr Omar Zawawi; 3, 4 and 5: Dr Marjorie Gillespie; 6, 7 and 8: Gardner A. Sage Library, New Brunswick Theological Seminary, New Jersey; 9, 10, 11 and 12: St Antony's College, Oxford, Middle East Centre.

Preface

This book is about Western women who lived, worked and travelled in the Arabian Peninsula and the Gulf region between the 1890s and the 1930s. In particular, it maps their changing and complex involvement with the British Empire from its high point at the end of the nineteenth century to its twilight, on the eve of the Second World War. Sometimes flamboyant and unconventional, sometimes conservative and conformist, these women and their stories are largely unknown. With the exception of a handful of famous travellers such as Gertrude Bell and Freya Stark, their histories have not been excavated from the archives, let alone brought to a wider readership. Almost all of them wanted in some way to be a part of British imperial life. Some were prepared to conform and 'play the game' and others decidedly were not. Some were allowed to play the game; others were not. As well as reconstructing their lives, therefore, this book also looks at the ways in which women negotiated, or tried to negotiate, power and position in the imperial enterprise, and how this negotiated power and involvement changed over time; it examines the ways in which the conventional roles of Western women were determined and defined by the masculine perspectives and hierarchies of imperial culture and authority; and it considers the extent to which women themselves actively participated in, passively colluded with, or deliberately subverted these roles, both in their day-to-day activities and in their own representations of their lives.

In the introduction to a collection of writings on gender and imperialism published in 1998, the feminist historian, Clare Midgley, noted the ways in which gender history and traditional imperial history have developed separately, with imperial history being regarded and written as 'the history of the exploits of male policy-makers, military commanders, explorers and missionaries', while the history of women and imperialism has, until recently, been seen as of marginal significance, 'a special interest area which can be safely left to female historians'.[1] Midgley's comment still holds true in relation to the Arabian Peninsula. Although major inroads are now being made into the study of gender in the context of imperial India and colonial Africa, the story of Western involvement in Arabia and the Gulf has been, and still is being, studied almost exclusively from the traditional perspectives of political and international relations. Titles such as *Britain and the Persian Gulf*; *Britain, India and the Arabs*; *The*

Struggle for Power in Arabia and *Politics in an Arabian Oasis* have dominated the market since the 1970s and continue to do so.[2] The current academic viewpoint can perhaps be best illustrated by the example of a recent, scholarly, and detailed account of British relations with the Lower Gulf maritime shaikhdoms in the early-nineteenth century, in which the author implicitly categorises and dismisses the female presence by his use of one monolithic index entry: 'women'.[3] In short, the participation of Western women in the late-nineteenth and early-twentieth century European and American imperial enterprise in the region has received almost no attention from historians, other than in the context of the literary-historical subject area of travel, travel-writing and Orientalism. On this topic, at least, there have been some innovative and challenging books on women's lives and perspectives, although perhaps not surprisingly they have concentrated predominantly on the famous few.[4]

Women have been silenced in varying degrees by traditional imperial and colonial history writing. In relation to the British presence in Arabia, the silence can to some extent be blamed on the fact that the region was on the periphery of imperial administration in India, an important stage on the route to the Subcontinent and in the maintenance of British power there, but nevertheless part of the so-called 'borderlands' of empire. The small political posts which the British created to maintain their influence and protect their interests were never the focus of large British communities as they were in some areas of India itself, or in the white settler colonial societies in Africa, but they were strategic outposts, generally thought of as masculine preserves and 'unsuitable places for women'. There was no established network of memsahibs, or social round of tea and tennis. In comparison with India, the Gulf, where most of the British posts were located, was regarded as a hard and lonely posting, totally lacking the supportive domestic infrastructure of British 'Raj' society. In the years before the First World War there were very few Western women in the region. The first American female missionary, Amy Wilkes Zwemer, arrived in Basra in 1896. The wives of the half dozen or so British political agents stationed at Bushire, Bahrain, Kuwait and Muscat were not encouraged to live permanently with their husbands but tended to retreat to India during the stiflingly hot Gulf summers. Gradually, however, as British strategic and economic interests in the region increased, more political and military officials, administrators and, subsequently, business and professional men and women began to arrive and to construct small Western communities in the coastal Gulf shaikhdoms. With the development of the oil industry and the Arabian Gulf air routes in the 1930s, the area began to be seen from the Western perspective as finally being 'opened up', although even in 1939 the expatriate Gulf communities were still tiny, both in an absolute sense, and by comparison with those in India.

In terms of historical evidence, the problems for research on women in this geographical and political context are enormous. Because of the nature of the part-settled and part-bedouin society in the Gulf before the development of the oil economies, and because of the predominance of an oral rather than a written history tradition, there are not many relevant written indigenous sources. Direct evidence from regional sources is therefore sparse, at least for the early part of the period. As a result, British imperial and colonial archives remain the major source available for Gulf history and they also, at first sight, appear to contain very little information on women, either imperial or colonial, colonising or colonised. Their content, classification and arrangement reflect the political and economic priorities and perspectives of the men who first created and subsequently preserved them. Women in general in the Arabian Peninsula region are simply absent from this archival mainstream of imperial history, unless they were among the handful of individuals who were actually employed for a short time in government service as, for example, were Gertrude Bell and Freya Stark, or unless they and their activities were viewed as likely to undermine or ruffle the surface of imperial diplomacy, as were Rosita Forbes and some of the American women missionaries. Research into their lives and perspectives is therefore a daunting struggle involving detective work, perseverance, frustration, anger and occasional delight. It is both physically and intellectually 'groping in the margins of history'.[5]

Fortunately, government archives are not the only Western sources. A surprising number of diaries, letters and published memoirs and autobiographies by Western women travellers, missionaries, doctors and 'memsahibs' are now also available in British and American libraries, archives and private collections. Many of them are only just being discovered and exploited but they have the potential to fill some of the gaps and to bring new and refreshing perspectives to the story of women and empire. The accounts in this book are drawn not just from the official government archives of the British administrations in the Gulf but also from the personal papers and published works of British women who lived or travelled in the region and from the reports and accounts of American missionaries in the area.

The most familiar women's writings on this part of the Middle East are the correspondence and books of Gertrude Bell and Freya Stark. Another irrepressible and independent traveller, Rosita Forbes, was also a prolific letter writer and journalist and she published numerous books recounting her experiences in Arabia and North Africa. However, the lives of so-called 'ordinary' women, in particular the appropriately styled 'incorporated wives', whose outward identity in empire was largely defined by the position and status of their husbands, are still frustratingly hidden from history.[6] Some of the most exciting primary source materials, therefore, for the history of Western women in the Gulf and surrounding region, are the previously unexplored and unpublished papers of Emily Overend Lorimer, which are now in the British Library. Emily Lorimer was the wife of a British Political Officer who was posted to Bahrain in 1911. She wrote detailed and regular letters to her family for almost thirty years, from her early life at Oxford University through her subsequent experiences in Bahrain, Basra, the North West Frontier of India, and in retirement in Welwyn Garden City. Her papers are a mass of factual information on her day-to-day activities and on her attitudes and perspectives as a 'memsahib'. They also present in extraordinary detail her changing views, both of the countries and people around her and of her own role and identity in the imperial world-picture. Other memsahibs, for example Belle Cox, whose husband's career as Political Resident in the Gulf and, subsequently, as High Commissioner in Iraq, spanned the period from the 1890s to the 1920s, appear to have left no record of their own lives. Belle Cox's story can only be pieced together from accounts by her contemporaries and friends. Yet she was clearly a powerful and much-admired figure in the Cox household and in the domestic and social epicentre of British authority in the Gulf.

While going a long way to make up for the silence of the official archives, and while presenting an alternative, and often subversive, non-official viewpoint, personal papers and travel writings of course bring with them their own particular cultural baggage and there is a substantial amount of academic theory about the self-production of identity or the 'story of the self'.[7] Autobiographical materials are, by definition, self-representational and they inevitably suppress or emphasise, either consciously or unconsciously, events and opinions, depending on the author's immediate perspective and the intended audience. As one critic has commented, in auto/biographical writings identities are not discovered but are 'actively constructed' by individuals.[8] Furthermore, as feminist academics have shown, many 'biographers' or recorders of women's lives, including women themselves, have suppressed the truth about female experience in order to make the 'written life' conform to society's expectations of what that life should be.[9] The contents of unpublished personal letters reflect a conscious decision on the part of the author to verbalise an opinion and to make selective information available, even to a restricted readership. In this book I have looked at the ways in which different groups of women (for example, British memsahibs and American missionaries) and different individuals (for example, Emily Lorimer, Gertrude Bell, Rosita Forbes, Violet Dickson) actively set about constructing their own identities, in distinct and often conflicting ways from each other and in widely varying relationships with empire, but all nevertheless informed by their knowledge of the imperial project and their aspirations to play some part in it.

Alongside the writings of British women are the memoirs and reports produced by the men and women of the American Arabian Mission during their small but long-lasting presence in the Gulf. In particular, the field reports prepared for the Mission's supporters back home contain distinct and detailed information on daily life in the Gulf. The writers' commitment to the missionary cause clearly influenced their style of reporting and the manner in which they recorded facts and events. Their general bias and perspective, their American and Protestant, proactively religious, standpoint, is immediately obvious to the reader. The very title of the field reports, *Neglected Arabia*, is itself the most telling indication of their general cultural approach to the region. Nevertheless they provide a discrete and vital counterbalance to the British versions of imperial involvement, a much more immediate account of local history and, in particular, a unique narrative of women's history, of Western (in this case American) women's perceptions of their domestic and public roles, and of the social and cultural hierarchies of relationship between different groups of Western and of Arab women.

In the last two decades historians and literary critics have begun to re-examine, re-appraise and re-write imperial and colonial history and historiography. Feminist historians, for example, have attempted to confront the silences in traditional Western history by locating and researching previously unexplored materials on individuals and groups of women outside the centres of political and economic power. More generally, historians and post-colonial theorists have addressed the problems of bias and exclusion in the mainstream archival and literary sources for the history of imperialism and colonialism.[10]

Work on Western women's participation in imperial and colonial life has developed from the 1970s and 1980s when the first, so-called, 'Raj revival' writings of authors such as Pat Barr and Margaret MacMillan set out to rescue or recover Western women from either oblivion or from the stereotype of what feminist historians have called 'the myth of the destructive female in colonial society'.[11] These early writings were followed by an explosion of research and more 'recuperative' work, which pointed to a diversity of female involvement which had been stifled by the conventional masculine discourses of empire.[12] They also opened up the way for further examination of alternative female-authored sources. At the same time, however, they generated historical controversy and stimulated a lively debate on the relationship between gender and imperialism, or colonialism. In particular, the apparent focus only on white, middle-class women, drew criticism from writers such as, for example, Jane Haggis who, in a seminal 1990 review article, provoked academic debate with her assertion that 'centering white women…actually serves to ungender the colonised people and contribute to silencing colonised women'.[13] Nupur Chaudhuri and Margaret Strobel's 1992 collection of essays, *Western Women and Imperialism: Complicity and Resistance*, encapsulated in its title the dilemmas facing current and future researchers on the subject of Western Women and Imperialism.[14]

During over twenty years as Curator of Middle East Archives in the British Library's Oriental and India Office Collections, I became only too aware of the predominantly imperial and masculine discourses of Arabian Gulf archives and history and the corresponding difficulties of researching the hidden histories of women. This book is an attempt to recover a small number of them. The focus of my research is not intended to be a history of Arab Gulf women, for the discovery of which I have only limited resources and linguistic skills. My standpoint and perspective is that of a white western-educated feminist historian and my subject is a history, or more accurately many diverse histories, of Western women in a small area of the Middle East over a half-century of time. By writing about Western women, however, I do not wish to collude in the 'silencing' of Arab women and my choice of subject is not intended to make any hierarchical judgment about the relative interest or value of Western women's stories in relation to those of Arab women. On the contrary, my intention is to show how much more evidence is waiting to be explored and how many more stories are still to be told.

The Western historical, literary and artistic perspective on the Middle East, which, for the sake of convenience, may be described by the term 'Orientalism', has been the subject of numerous studies since the publication of Edward Said's seminal work. In this book I have to some extent been interested in the ways in which Western women perceived the 'Orient'. However, I have not been attempting to study the history of the Gulf through Western women's eyes. My interest in their representation of it is related much more to the extent to which they measured and defined themselves through their construction of local society and how

they positioned themselves in the overall hierarchies of imperial administration and power. Again, this is not intended in any way to diminish or
ignore the regional and local history. But this study is not a history of
Arabia; it is an account of Western women in Arabia. There is a continuing need to unearth histories of women, both colonising and colonised,
without the stifling inhibitions of competing historical and political
hierarchies. As Clare Midgley persuasively argued, by shifting emphasis,
making connections, absorbing the insights of post-colonial and feminist
theory, but at the same time abandoning the false binary categories of
coloniser and colonised and recognising that neither were homogenous
groups, we should be able to 'aspire to tell the truth about the history of
imperialism'.[15]

NOTES ON PREFACE

1   Clare Midgley, 'Gender and imperialism: mapping the connections', in Midgley
    (ed.), *Gender and Imperialism* (Manchester: Manchester University Press,
    1998), pp. 1–2.
2   Traditional 'imperial' histories of the area, whose titles indicate their stand-
    point, include J. B. Kelly, *Britain and the Persian Gulf, 1795–1880* (Oxford:
    Oxford University Press, 1968), Briton Cooper Busch, *Britain and the Persian
    Gulf, 1894–1914* (Berkeley and Los Angeles: University of California Press,
    1967) and *Britain, India and the Arabs, 1914–1921* (Berkeley: University of
    California Press, 1971), and Mahdi Al-Tajir, *Bahrain 1920–1945: Britain,
    the Shaikh and the Administration* (London: Croom Helm, 1987). Recently
    published national and regional histories, many of them by female academic
    historians, have been similarly political and 'masculine' in perspective, for
    example: Madawi Al Rasheed, *Politics in an Arabian Oasis: the Rashidi
    Tribal Dynasty* (London: I. B. Tauris, 1991); Moudi M. Abdul-Aziz, *King
    Abdul-Aziz and the Kuwait Conference, 1923–1924* (London: Echoes, 1993);
    Haifa Alangari, *The Struggle for Power in Arabia: Ibn Saud, Hussein and
    Great Britain, 1914–1924* (Reading: Ithaca Press, 1998); Salwa Alghanim,
    The Reign of Mubarak Al-Sabah, Shaikh of Kuwait, 1896–1915 (London:
    I. B. Tauris, 1998).
3   Charles L. Davies, *The Blood-Red Flag: An Investigation into Qasimi Piracy,
    1797–1820* (Exeter: University of Exeter Press, 1997).
4   Academic interest in Western women in the Arabian Peninsula and Gulf has
    focused and continues to focus on 'Orientalism', travel and travel writing.
    See, for example: Sara Mills, *Discourses of Difference: an Analysis of Women's
    Travel Writing and Colonialism* (London and New York: Routledge, 1991);
    Mary Louise Pratt, *Imperial Eyes: Travel Writing and Transculturation*

(London and New York: Routledge, 1992); Billie Melman, *Women's Orients: English Women and the Middle East, 1718–1918* (Basingstoke: Macmillan, 1992). The most famous twentieth-century travellers in the region are Gertrude Bell and Freya Stark, whose lives have been described and re-evaluated in several biographies, the most recent of which are Janet Wallach's *Desert Queen: The Extraordinary Life of Gertrude Bell* (New York: Doubleday, 1996) and Jane Fletcher Geniesse's *Passionate Nomad: the Life of Freya Stark* (New York: Random House, 1999).

5   Gayatri Chakravorty Spivak, *A Critique of Postcolonial Reason: Toward a History of the Vanishing Present* (Cambridge MA and London: Harvard University Press, 1999), ch. 3. In this chapter Spivak revisits one of her earlier essays, 'The Rani of Sirmur' (1985) and describes the silences and 'fadeout points' in the India Office sources.

6   Hilary Callan and Shirley Ardener (eds), *The Incorporated Wife* (Beckenham: Croom Helm, 1984). See ch. 2.

7   On women's travel writing see note 4, above. On biography and auto/biography see, for example, the overview in Liz James, '"This is me!": Autobiography and the construction of identities' in Liz Stanley (ed.) 'Lives and Works: Auto/biographical occasions', *Auto/Biography*, no 3 (1994), pp. 71–82, and Liz Stanley, *The Auto/biographical I: The Theory and Practice of Feminist Auto/biography* (Manchester: Manchester University Press, 1992). More recent publications include Pauline Polkey (ed.), *Women's Lives into Print: the Theory, Practice and Writing of Feminist Auto/biography* (Basingstoke: Macmillan, 1999), and Alison Donnell and Pauline Polkey (eds), *Representing Lives: Women and Auto/biography* (Basingstoke: Macmillan, 2000).

8   James, '"This is me!"', p. 71.

9   This point was made by Carolyn Heilbrun in her ground-breaking 1988 volume, *Writing a Woman's Life* (New York: Ballantine Books).

10 The catalogue of contemporary research and writing on imperial and colonial history and post-colonial theory is extensive. The most relevant and illuminating publications are cited in the bibliography. Any book on the history of Western involvement in the modern Middle East must, however, acknowledge the work of Edward Said, whose seminal 1978 book, *Orientalism* (London and New York: Routledge & Kegan Paul Ltd) arguably launched the debate, and whose subsequent work continues to inform and influence it. Also influential, particularly in the area of women's studies, is the work of Spivak, most recently *A Critique of Postcolonial Reason*.

11 Midgley, 'Gender and Imperialism', p. 7. Margaret Strobel, *European Women and the Second British Empire* (Bloomington and Indianapolis: Indiana University Press, 1991), ch. 1. Pat Barr, *The Memsahibs* (London: Hamish Hamilton, 1976) Margaret MacMillan, *Women of the Raj* (London: Thames & Hudson, 1988).

12 Midgley, 'Gender and Imperialism', p. 7. See, for example: Callan and Ardener, *The Incorporated Wife*; Claudia Knapman, *White Women in Fiji, 1835–1930: The Ruin of Empire?* (Sydney: Allen & Unwin, 1986); Helen Callaway, *Gender, Culture and Empire: European Women in Colonial Nigeria* (London: Macmillan, 1987); Strobel, *European Women and the Second British Empire*.

13 Jane Haggis, 'Gendering colonialism or colonising gender? Recent women's studies approaches to white women and the history of British colonialism', *Women's Studies International Forum*, 13 (1990), pp. 105–15. In a more recent essay, Haggis has reasserted her view that primarily 'recuperative' histories of white women 'risk colonising gender for white men and women rather than gendering colonialism as a historical process': 'White women and colonialism: towards a non-recuperative history' in Midgley (ed.), *Gender and Imperialism*, pp. 45–75.

14 Nupur Chaudhuri and Margaret Strobel (eds), *Western Women and Imperialism: Complicity and Resistance* (Bloomington: Indiana University Press, 1992).

15 Midgley, 'Gender and imperialism', pp. 5–6.

Acknowledgements

Many people have contributed to the making of this book. Particular thanks go to Mary Evans, Anne Seller and students of the University of Kent's Women's Studies programme, who helped me clarify my ideas about women's history and its production, and whose encouragement and interest over many years provided reassurance when the project sometimes seemed impossible. Similar thanks go to Liz Stanley for her support and critical comments on the manuscript. I am also grateful to Philippa Brewster for her meticulous editing and invaluable suggestions.

For their assistance in libraries and archives I would like to thank Russell Gasero at the Gardner A. Sage Library, New Brunswick Theological Seminary; Debbie Usher at St Antony's College Oxford, Middle East Centre; Pauline Adams at Somerville College; Anthony Farrington, Graham Shaw and past and present members of staff at the Oriental and India Office Collections of the British Library; Anita Burdett for her discoveries at the Public Record Office.

Dr Marjorie Gillespie very kindly allowed me to quote from Emily Lorimer's papers and she and her husband Dr William Gillespie gave me encouragement and hospitality as well as personal reminiscences of her aunt. I would also like to thank Dr Omar Zawawi for his kind permission to allow me to use his photograph of Percy and Belle Cox, John Townsend for allowing me to quote from his unpublished biography of Sir Percy Cox, and Tam Dalyell for giving me some of his invaluable time to talk about his parents. David Wochner and Aimee Ibrahim, in Washington DC, provided fresh ideas about certain Arabian travellers, and were inspiring colleagues for several years.

For their consent to quote from material in their collections, or for which they hold the copyright, I am grateful to the following: the British Library Oriental Office Collections for the Curzon and Mary Curzon papers; St Antony's College Oxford, Middle East Centre for extracts from the Philby papers; John Murray for extracts from Freya Stark's letters in Caroline Moorehead's *Over the Rim of the World: Freya Stark Selected Letters* (1988); the Gardner A. Sage Library, New Brunswick Theological Seminary for extracts from *Neglected Arabia*; the *Contemporary Review* for Ernest Barker and Freya Stark's 1932 article on 'Women and the Service of Empire'. Every effort has been made to trace copyright holders, but in the event of any omissions the author would be glad to hear from them.

I owe most of all to my family. Without their constant patience, advice, support and focus on present-day reality, none of this would have been possible.

ARABIA
Districts and towns

based on a map taken from *Handbook of Arabia*,
Admiralty War Staff Intelligence Division, 1916
(British Library Oriental and India Office Collections)

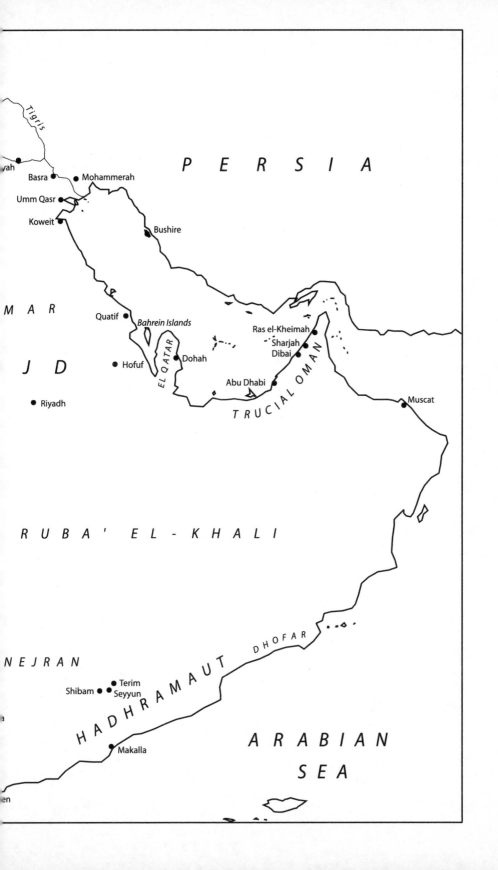

Introduction:
Claiming a Place: Women and Imperial Politics before the First World War

In March 1911 Emily Overend Lorimer arrived in Bahrain to begin a new career as wife of the recently appointed British Political Agent in the small Arabian Gulf shaikhdom. Married in December 1910, the Lorimers left Britain in the New Year and travelled, via Rome and Athens, to Egypt, the Red Sea, Aden and Bombay. From Bombay they sailed to the Gulf, stopping briefly at Muscat to meet other British officials, and, after a calm journey along the coast, they landed at Bahrain in bright, warm spring weather. Emily immediately sent a brief note to her mother: 'Arrived yesterday. Awfully pretty place, lots of green trees etc. Lovely and palatial quarters...Both delighted by surroundings and prospects.'[1] The Agency at Bahrain was a very small station on the edges of Britain's vast Indian Empire and would have seemed to many people a backwater, totally lacking in the splendour and civilisation of Delhi or Bombay. In the years before the First World War, however, the island state and the other neighbouring Arabian Gulf shaikhdoms were becoming more and more important places on the international stage, as Britain sought to protect her overseas economic and political interests from increasingly assertive European and Ottoman Turkish rivals.

Like many women of her generation, Emily Overend's interest in the empire began long before the voyage out. She met her future husband in 1909, in Oxford where she was tutor in Germanic Philology at Somerville College. Born in Dublin in 1881, she later described her own ancestry as 'Ulster non-conformist Scots and English stock'. Her father, Thomas George Overend, was 'a distinguished land and chancery lawyer' and Recorder and County Court Judge of Londonderry.[2] Emily was educated at Alexandra School and College, Dublin, and she took her first degree in 1904, in modern languages, at Trinity College, after which she

1

went on to Somerville to study German. She achieved a First Class mark in her final exams in 1906 although, as she recalled much later in life, Oxford women of her generation were not actually awarded their degrees until after the First World War.[3] She spent a year at the University of Munich, where she acquired a lifelong interest in Asian languages and culture, before returning to Somerville to teach. In 1910, aged 29, she resigned in order to marry the 34-year-old David Lockhart Robertson Lorimer ('Lock'), an army officer then assigned to the Indian Political Service and serving as British Consul at Ahwaz in southern Persia. Lorimer was born in 1876, the son of a Scottish Presbyterian minister, the Reverend Robert Lorimer of Mains and Strathmartine near Dundee, and a Scottish mother, Isabella Lockhart Robertson, whose family had served in India for five generations.[4] After military training at Sandhurst, he joined the Indian Army in 1898, and served on the North West Frontier. In 1903 he was selected for transfer to the Indian Political Service, and was subsequently posted to Ahwaz. His brother, Gordon, was Political Agent in Baghdad and another brother, Bert, was in the Indian Police. His sister, Hilda, was classical tutor at Somerville and a contemporary and colleague of Emily.

Soon after their arrival in Bahrain, Emily wrote long letters to her parents and to her sister, Edith, to tell them about her new home in the Arabian Gulf. She gave enthusiastic accounts of the British imperial presence in Bahrain, the pleasant social life of the tiny Western community and the impressive rituals of diplomatic meetings and receptions. She was, she told her sister, 'beginning to realise...the dignity of Her Britannic Majesty's Political Agent and, in consequence, of his wife'. With some trepidation, but enormous optimism, she added that she hoped she would be able 'to play the game well' and 'keep up the dignity of the Empire properly'. Anyhow, she said, 'I shall do my best. If the role is new, it is also interesting and amusing.'[5]

The Lorimers were a scholarly couple, and their lives overseas were eventually to develop along less conventional lines than those of most of their contemporaries. However, Emily Lorimer's explicit and active identification with the empire was typical of the attitudes and assumptions of middle- and upper-class women of her generation, increasing numbers of whom expected to take an interest or play a part in the imperial project. The exact nature of this involvement was fiercely argued over in the years before the First World War, and ideas about it were closely linked to the contemporary debate on female suffrage and women's changing roles in public life in Britain.[6] Educated women, like Emily Lorimer, who married civilian or military officials in the imperial services saw no inconsistency in progressing from independent academic or professional life to that of imperial or colonial memsahib. One of Emily's contemporaries, the wife of the future Governor-General of Nigeria, Lady Flora Lugard, had famously given up a successful independent career as a journalist when she married and first accompanied her husband to Africa. As Flora Shaw, she had been a successful novelist as well as special correspondent for *The Times* in South Africa, and subsequently head of the newspaper's Colonial Department. After her marriage she dedicated her formidable talents to the advancement of her husband's public life.[7] Flora Lugard, Emily Lorimer and other women like them saw themselves as taking on not only a domestic responsibility as wives and perhaps future mothers, but also a patriotic role. When they went overseas, they were expected to support and nurture their husbands in their professional duties and at the same time play their own separate parts in preserving the imperial social structure and helping to bring the European civilising mission to the rest of the world. With widening educational backgrounds, however, some of them were beginning to define this role more ambitiously. At the same time, women who perhaps never travelled abroad but remained at home in Britain were also claiming a right to participate more extensively in empire-building activities.

From the late-nineteenth century onwards, female involvement in the imperial mission was stimulated and debated more widely than ever before. After 1870, for example, several predominantly female, and overtly imperialist, associations were formed, the most prominent of which were the Girls' Friendly Society, the British Women's Emigration League and the Primrose League. They were followed in 1901 by the Victoria League, prompted by the South African War and dedicated to the memory of the late Queen, whose own knowledgeable interest in the administration of the empire had itself provided an inspiration and justification for increased female involvement.[8] Victoria had been particularly concerned about the lives of her female Indian subjects. In 1885, for example, she was closely involved in the setting up of the 'National Association for Supplying Female Medical Aid to the Women of India' in response to an appeal from the Maharani of Punna at Lucknow describing the lack of health care for Indian women. 'Something must be done for the poor creatures,' the Queen is reported to have declared.[9]

The Victoria League described itself as 'an association of women of the British Isles who are in sympathy with Imperial objects and desire a close union between the different parts of the Empire'.[10] The league and the other similar organisations sprang from a view that women had a special and vital contribution to make to the enterprise of empire. Although they

were mostly dominated by a socially privileged and politically conservative élite, the activities of the associations reflected a new sense of a special
female mission which, while never seriously challenging the masculine
leadership and hierarchy of politics and administration, nevertheless, by
their very existence challenged the male 'monopolization of imperial
power'.[11] Meanwhile, sometimes in parallel, sometimes in tandem and
sometimes in conflict, female supporters of the campaign for women's
suffrage were also staking a claim to a more active, but still specifically
female, identity within the empire, concentrating on imperial philan-
thropy to reinforce their own status as liberated and knowledgeable
participants in imperial and national politics. An essential part of their
argument for political power via the vote was a fervent and genuine
belief in the superiority of Western culture and the duty of Western
women to bring civilisation and comfort to their Eastern sisters. In 1895,
for example, the great social reformer Josephine Butler explicitly linked
the progress of the campaigns against the Contagious Diseases Acts of
the 1860s, and her subsequent work on behalf of prostitutes in India,
to the suffrage issue: 'How often,' she wrote, 'in the course of the
long crusade, we in England have wished that we had possessed the
suffrage. Its possession would have saved us from much painful agitation
in the past.'[12]

The public debate on women's suffrage in the years before the First
World War provided a battleground on which closely related ideas about
empire and gender were played out. In June 1889 an 'Appeal against
Female Suffrage' was published in the monthly review *The Nineteenth
Century*. It was organised by Mary Ward, better known as Mrs Humphry
Ward, novelist, social reformer and one of the founding secretaries of
Emily Lorimer's Oxford college, Somerville. It was signed by 104 women,
many of whom were members of the British aristocracy and a large number
of whom had close connections with imperial rule and 'Orientalist'
scholarship.[13] The appeal emphasised the desire to develop 'the powers,
energies and education of women', but argued that women's work for the
state should be different from that of men. While men's duties should
include national politics and relations with the external world, women
should be encouraged to work in the local community and involve themselves in traditional philanthropic activities such as education, the relief
of poverty and care of the sick. On questions of foreign or imperial
policy, women's normal experience could not generally be expected to
'provide them with such materials for sound judgement as are open to
men'. They should be allowed increasing participation in areas which
involved 'thought, conscience and moral influence', but not in the

traditional masculine areas such as administration, military or financial matters.[14]

In a rejoinder to the appeal, one month later Millicent Garrett Fawcett, the President of the National Union of Women's Suffrage Societies, argued that if women were to be thought of as incapable of forming a sound judgment in politics, they should not be invited to join such organisations as the Primrose League. She lambasted the signatories of the appeal, 'ladies to whom the lines of life have fallen in pleasant places', for not putting much of their own energy into the growing domestic movement for social reform.[15] However, she still felt obliged to emphasise that the 'friends of women's suffrage' valued 'the womanliness of women' as much as the signatories of the appeal did. Fawcett's own extensive knowledge of empire had been drawn from her experience as amanuensis to her husband, the blind radical Henry Fawcett MP, whose reforming interest in the Subcontinent had earned him the popular title of 'Member for India'. After his death in 1884 she continued to take an interest in imperial reform issues such as child marriage and female infanticide, and she was to be one of the early supporters of the Victoria League.[16] Citing Florence Nightingale and Mary Carpenter, both famously involved in social reform in India, as the highest examples of what women could and should be aspiring to, Fawcett concluded that she did not want women to be 'bad imitations of men'; nor did she wish to deny or minimise the differences between men and women. 'The claim of women to representation,' she argued, 'depends to a large extent on those differences. Women bring something to the service of the state different from that which can be brought by men. Let this fact be frankly recognised and let due weight be given to it in the representative system of the country.'[17] By August 1889, however, almost two thousand women had signed the appeal against female suffrage, including many more names with close links to imperial administration, and independent women with an interest in empire, such as the journalist Mary Frances Billington, who in 1890 joined the *Daily Graphic* as a special correspondent on 'matters of feminine interest' and subsequently toured India, producing a series of articles for the paper and later publishing them in a book, *Woman in India*.[18]

The arguments put forward in this 1889 exchange set the pattern for a continuing and increasingly acrimonious debate on women's emancipation and empire throughout the next two decades. They also illustrate the complexities and contradictions of feminist, or women's activist, politics at the turn of the century, which could encompass suffragists like Millicent Fawcett, with her unswerving belief in the superiority of English institutions and the efficacy of British legislative reform as the basis for eradicating injustice, and anti-suffragists like Mary Billington, who was highly critical of what she regarded as Western matronising attitudes towards Indian culture.[19] What united them, in spite of their widely differing views on the definition and scope of female involvement in the traditionally masculine arena of national or imperial politics, was a view that as women they carried a special burden and mission towards the empire, both (or either) as helpmates to its rulers and as sisters to its 'other' citizens.

One prominent supporter of female activism in imperial affairs was Margaret Child-Villiers, Countess of Jersey. Widely travelled, she had an extensive knowledge of the empire and, after a visit to India in 1888, she published an account of her travels in the same volume of *The Nineteenth Century* as the appeal had appeared. 'There is a charm in India,' she told her readers, 'which cannot be defined...You live amongst palaces, men, and manners which have remained unchanged for centuries, whilst you see the strong rule of a conquering modern race, not destroying but organising the empire to which it has succeeded.'[20] From 1891 to 1893 Lady Jersey lived in Australia after her husband was appointed as Governor of New South Wales. Back in England, in 1901 she was one of the founders of the Victoria League and remained its president for 26 years. She was also one of the leading female opponents of women's suffrage and a founder, a few years later, of the Women's National Anti-Suffrage League. At the league's inaugural meeting, chaired by Lady Jersey at the Westminster Palace Hotel on 21 July 1908, an executive committee was elected, including Mrs Humphry (Mary) Ward, Lady George Hamilton, wife of the former Secretary of State for India, and Gertrude Bell, one of the most well-known Western women travellers in the Middle East. Also on the committee was Janet Hogarth, one of Bell's close friends and sister of David Hogarth, Oxford Arabist and subsequently famous for his management of the Arab Bureau in First-World-War Cairo. The following day Gertrude Bell was appointed honorary Secretary. During the next few months, branches of the league were set up in provincial towns, including one in Oxford after a meeting held on 22 October at the house of another imperial scholar and traveller, Georgina Max-Müller. Whether or not Emily Overend was present is not recorded in her surviving letters. Somerville was known much more as a centre of pro-suffrage activity, in spite of the firmly and publicly held views of its benefactress, Mary Ward. Its principal, Edith Penrose was pro-suffrage, most of its tutors were supporters and, in 1910, 75 out of a total student body of 94 were members of the Somerville Women's Suffrage Society.[21] Nevertheless, like Gertrude Bell and other talented and academically successful women of her class and background, Emily Overend failed to see any underlying political injustice in the range of opportunities available to women. A few years later she certainly supported the view that the more militant women's suffrage campaign was subversive, anti-social and anti-imperial. In 1913 she wrote to her parents that the suffragettes were 'terrible': 'How they can persuade themselves that any cause, however holy, could justify blowing up post offices and setting fire to theatres and wantonly damaging property is hard to see'.[22]

In the first issue of the Women's National Anti-Suffrage League's journal, *The Anti-Suffrage Review*, an editorial by Mary Ward re-emphasised some of the assertions of the earlier 'Appeal against Female Suffrage', arguing that the parliamentary franchise for women would involve 'a kind of activity and responsibility for woman which is not compatible with her nature, and with her proper tasks in the world':

> Men who have built up the State, and whose physical strength protects it, must govern it, through the rough and ready machinery of party-politics. Women are citizens of the State no less than men, but in a more ideal and spiritual sense. The great advance of women during the last half-century, moral and intellectual, has been made without the vote; and the work now under their hands, for which the nation calls upon them, work with which the parliamentary vote and party-politics have nothing to do, is already more than they can accomplish. To plunge women into the strife of parties will only hinder that work, and injure their character.[23]

Referring to the 'scandalous behaviour' of the Women's Social and Political Union, led by the Pankhursts, Ward warned that increasingly militant suffragette activities were destroying all the support which Millicent Fawcett's more moderate campaigning had gained for their cause. The action also proved 'conclusively' that women were not fit for the 'ordinary struggle of politics'. Indeed, any widening of participation by women would increase 'the violent excitable element in politics...and a sex feeling and sex antagonism will be aroused, rendering the calm and practical discussion of great questions impossible; a feeling and antagonism disastrous to women, disastrous to England'. While the Women's National Anti-Suffrage League would continue to support an increase of women's powers in local government, it would do everything it could

> to prevent the spread of a movement, the success of which would weaken our country in the eyes of the civilised world, and fatally diminish those stores of English sanity, of English political wisdom, based on political experience, which have gone – through all vicissitude, failure and error – to the making of England, and the building up of the Empire.

The same sentiment was expressed at a meeting in Birmingham, by Lady Leigh, who argued that women had their own important work in the world and could not be called on to bear the additional burden of political life. More specifically, she thought it was 'impossible that they should also devote the time and thought necessary to study those great Imperial problems periodically laid before the voters of this country'.[24]

Lady Jersey's, and the Women's League's, views on the empire and separate imperial spheres were representative of a widely accepted establishment interpretation of the British imperial mission. They also reflected a growing anxiety, in the years leading up to the First World War, about the precariousness of empire and the need to maintain the very specific and separate direction of female involvement. Lady Jersey's 1889 article on India was echoed more famously by the Viceroy of India, Lord George Nathaniel Curzon, at the turn of the century. 'I do not see,' wrote Curzon to the Liberal politician and future Secretary of State for India, John Morley,

> how any Englishman, contrasting India as it now is with what it was, and would certainly have been under any other conditions than British rule, can fail to see that we came and have stayed here under no blind or capricious impulse, but in obedience to what some (of whom I am one) would call the decree of Providence, others the law of destiny – in any case for the lasting benefit of millions of the human race.[25]

Curzon was Viceroy from 1898 to 1905, and his career and opinions encompass the contemporary debates on gender, empire, India and the Gulf. Much travelled in the Middle East and Central Asia, and recognised as a knowledgeable and scholarly authority, Curzon toured the Gulf during his viceroyalty and was the architect of a more interventionist policy in the region. In the years between leaving India and the outbreak of the First World War, he became an equally outspoken opinion-former on women's issues. Five months after the inaugural meeting of Lady Jersey's Women's League, Curzon was one of the founding members, and a major fundraiser and propagandist for the 'Men's Committee for Opposing Female Suffrage', a collection of public figures many of whom, like their female counterparts, had strong, but in this case direct, experience of imperial rule. The committee's figureheads were the two men who most embodied the principles and practice of imperial rule: Curzon himself and the Earl of Cromer, British Agent and Consul-General in Egypt for the previous 20 years.[26] Other prominent supporters included Austen Chamberlain, Rudyard Kipling, Sir Edward Elgar, Sir Alfred Lyall and Sir Hugh Bell, northern industrialist and father of Gertrude. In 1910 the Men's Committee merged with the Women's League, in spite of some predictable and long-lasting disputes over leadership and policy, to form the National League for Opposing Woman Suffrage.

George Curzon's complicated views on women epitomised the perspective, and to some extent inconsistency, of the male opponents of female suffrage during these pre-war years. They also paralleled, although not exactly, the arguments of the women 'antis'. Just a year before the formation of the Men's Committee, Curzon was elected Chancellor of Oxford University, where he startled the academic community with his reforming zeal. Among a number of suggestions, he proposed that the university should put an end to the anomaly by which women were allowed to attend lectures and sit certain exams but were not able to be awarded a degree.[27] In a speech to mark the opening of a new building at Lady Margaret Hall in 1910, he put forward his own views on what educated women should aim for in life, suggesting to the lady students of Lady Margaret Hall that they might consider a rather motley collection of occupations including journalism, literary work, gardening, playing the organ, house decoration (one of Curzon's own passions), archaeology and historical research. Besides, he added, there were enormous openings in the colonies as secretaries, managers of households and so on:

> And in India, too, although it is only slowly awakening from the torpor of centuries, there is a movement towards the emancipation of the native women, even inside the walls of the *zenana*. As these ladies free themselves from the shackles of their old traditions and customs, they will want English teachers and English ladies to preside over their households and teach their children. I have known several English ladies who have rendered most valuable help in that direction, and I commend India to you as worthy of serious remembrance.[28]

Emphasising that Oxford was a place from which the British 'sound' should 'go out into all lands, and our words unto the ends of the world', Curzon told his audience that he could see no reason 'why women, as well as men, should not be bearers of the message'. However, he ended with a caution and a hope

> that the ladies of these Oxford Colleges, in their pursuit of vocations, in their attainment of academic success, in their possible triumphs in respect of degrees, will never forget the sublime truth that the highest ideal and the most perfect conception of womanhood are still to be found in the home.

Going out to the Gulf from Oxford a few months later, Emily Lorimer could not fail to have been influenced by such forceful words from the former Viceroy.

In advocating work towards the emancipation of Indian women, Curzon was at one with his otherwise implacable opponents in the women's suffrage movement, whose journals and newspapers had for several years emphasised the special mission of Western women to bring education and social reform to their less fortunate imperial sisters. In 1913 the editor of the suffrage journal *Common Cause*, Helena Swanwick, summed up their long-standing identification with the imperial project when she wrote that, if only for the sake of India, women in Great Britain 'would be bound to demand the vote'. 'The responsibilities of Empire rest on women as well as men,' she argued. It was not because suffragists underestimated these responsibilities that they wished to share in them; it was 'the consciousness of responsibility' which urged them on. Whether they liked it or not, women were 'members of an Empire which must leave a mark on human history, from the sheer size and glory of it'.[29]

On the same principles of female educational advancement, Curzon was also the moving force in the decision to admit women to the Royal Geographical Society after he became its president in 1911. He defended the decision on the grounds that the Society was one whose aims were 'nothing more formidable or contentious than the advancement of a particular department of human knowledge'. Admitting women, therefore, would not be the same as giving them a share in 'the Sovereignty of the country and the Empire'.[30] On women's role in political life he was adamant and unbending, and in a famous speech on female suffrage at a National League meeting in Glasgow in November 1912 he spelled out the reasons why, in the increasingly tense and dangerous international situation, women's roles in the state and empire should be limited to feminine, domestic and local issues:

> Issues sometimes arise in public affairs – you can see them on the horizon now – great issues of peace and war, of treaties and alliances, of the treatment to be adopted towards our Colonies and dependencies. An unwise, and still more an emotional decision of those issues might...lead to the disruption and even to the ruin of the Empire...[31]

The news of the female vote, Curzon continued, would be received in India not only with astonishment but also with dismay. For the governments of far-flung imperial dependencies the qualities of the masculine, not the feminine, mind were essential. India needed to be ruled with sympathy but not emotion, with sentiment but not sentimentality, and above all, with knowledge and experience. If a crisis, such as the Rebellion of 1857, were to occur again and the British were again forced to fight for their territory, and 'for the glory of our people and the blessing of the human race', what part would women play in the struggle? 'Would women hold India? No. By men was India won, by men alone can it be retained.'[32] In spite of this, Curzon told his audience not to assume that he wanted to deny women a suitable share in the empire. It was their heritage as well as men's; it was 'their joint acquisition and their joint glory'. Women could not only make a practical contribution in their feminine roles as wives, mothers, nurses and teachers, but they could also defend the ideals on which the empire existed. In rhetoric as sentimental as any of the classic Victorian and Edwardian romanticisations of women's lives, he linked the existence of female power to 'the universal conscience of mankind': 'You do not require the vote to defend the share in Empire which women already own. Instead they have something more important to guard even than Empire itself. They have to guard the womanhood of woman, with all its responsibilities, its ideals, its spiritual endowment.'[33]

In India, among the British community, the same arguments were being rehearsed. The following year a public suffragist meeting held at Mussoorie prompted the immediate formation of an 'All India Federation' of the National League for Opposing Woman Suffrage. Writing to the league's office in London, its president, Mrs Grace Walton, said that she and many of her acquaintances felt very strongly about the 'undesirability of introducing this "Woman's Movement" into India' and had 'begged people' to join the league and 'fight in this portion of the Empire against an evil which we consider is a peril to the British Empire'. Curzon drafted an encouraging reply, reiterating his views that female suffrage would 'lower rather than raise the conception of European womanhood in the East', would 'weaken the social fabric in India' and be 'injurious to the Empire', not least because 'Indians would never submit to be ruled by women'.[34]

Curzon's correspondence and the papers and propaganda of the anti-suffrage organisations show how closely the fate of the empire and the fabric of imperial society were seen by many of the imperial establishment to be linked to the preservation of rigidly hierarchical and strictly defined gender roles. That not everyone agreed with Curzon's views on suffrage and empire, however, was simultaneously apparent from the speeches, literature and activities of the suffrage organisations. The response to Curzon's public financial appeal, launched in the summer of 1910 on behalf of the anti-suffrage movement, was not uniformly positive, and among the many predictable responses from Establishment colleagues were some less-than-enthusiastic replies. From Lord Astor he received 'full sympathy' but a reminder that the socialist movement was a 'more imminent danger than the suffragist movement'; from Lord Lambton he received a cheque for £500 and a commitment that the 'male portion of the Lambton family can be relied on to give very candid opinions about women'. Other male colleagues were rather more circumspect and some, like Arthur Sassoon, admitted that their wives would not allow them to subscribe.[35] From a prominent suffragette, Maud Arncliffe-Sennett, Curzon received a closely argued letter, echoing Millicent Fawcett's reasoning in 1889 and pointing out that Curzon's 'Appeal', published in *The Times*, had been signed by an overwhelming and disproportionate number of the aristocracy. The anti-suffrage movement was, in Arncliffe-Sennett's view, undeniably based on class prejudice and, as the daughter of an Italian immigrant and an employer herself of over one hundred working people in the family confectionery factory, she was infuriated by the denial of their rights. Lady Jersey might claim to know about the empire but not about working-class women whose lives were 'unprotected, either by the hereditary protection of wealth and position, or the democratic one of the power of the Vote':

> You are right and women desire their human rights and dignities, which in the great industrial centres and among the poorer classes have been so shamefully plunged in the mire...I declare I see in the opposition of the aristocracy and such ladies as the Countess of Jersey whose lives and social status prevent them from only dimly perceiving the horrors of the submerged classes, action which may have a terrible retribution on their order.[36]

From the Baltic Shipping Exchange, the former Viceroy also received an unsigned letter castigating him in no uncertain terms for his views:

> Surrounded as you are by despicable flatterers, I am afraid it is very seldom indeed that you hear the truth, but I would just tell you that in connection with the women's movement, more men than you perhaps guess have nothing but pity left for the *rubbish you talk!* Your 15 points against womens votes are so illogical that one wonders how you ever managed to be Viceroy of India.[37]

By 1910, then, when Emily Overend made the decision to set off to the further reaches of the empire, the public debate on female participation in both national and imperial affairs had assumed an unprecedented intensity and increasingly ranged over wider issues of culture, class and politics. Moreover, the battles over suffrage and over the definition of women's roles in national and imperial life were inextricably linked to the increasingly turbulent background of national and international issues such as social reform, free trade, home rule, imperial defence and future self-government for imperial and colonial territories, international economic and military competition. In the sphere of women's activism, the battle lines were not always clearly drawn. As feminist historians have shown, there were female imperialists and imperial feminists; not all suffragists were in favour of imperial reform and not all anti-suffragists were imperialists.[38] George Curzon's voice and those of his female supporters represented one perspective in the arena of Indian imperial administration, where arguments for reform and eventual self-government had also begun to influence the political scene since the end of his viceroyalty. In the Gulf, however, his reputation and memories of his proactive involvement in regional affairs continued to have great influence among British officials, who still regularly recalled his interest and support for their diplomacy on the Arabian borderlands of empire.[39] Playing the game in the years before the First World War could mean different things to different people; and it encompassed a wide range of continually changing views on female participation in empire. Nevertheless, while the issues were wide-ranging and the responses not homogenous, there was still a common core. Feminists and anti-feminists, suffragists and anti-suffragists all staked their claim to participate in the imperial project, and they shared a belief in the benefits of British rule and the importance of 'practical' women's work for the empire. Emily Lorimer's aspirations to keep up the 'dignity of the Empire properly' were grounded in the collective self-confidence of a nation which fervently believed in its right and duty to guide, govern and administer, even if it did not always agree about the extent, the methods and the objectives of the mission.

NOTES ON INTRODUCTION

1   Emily Lorimer to her mother, 11 March 1911, Emily Overend Lorimer Collection, British Library (Oriental and India Office Collections), MSS Eur F177/4.

2   Emily Lorimer to her daughter's future parents-in-law, Mr and Mrs Munro, 6 August 1940, MSS Eur F177/46.

3   Degrees were finally conferred at Somerville in 1920. In a genealogical sketch of the Lorimer family, written by Emily Lorimer c.1947, she noted that she took Final Schools in 1906 ('no degrees for women in Oxford in 1906') and 20 years later took her Oxford MA. See 'The Family of James Overend of Tandragee, Co. Armagh, Northern Ireland', MSS Eur F177/92.

4   Emily Lorimer to Mr and Mrs Munro, 6 August 1940, MSS Eur F177/46.

5   Letter, undated, end March 1911, to her sister Edith: first 4 pages of letter missing but annotated by Emily Lorimer, 15 March 1948, MSS Eur F177/5.

6   Recent studies by feminist historians have shown just how closely women's attitudes towards Empire in the years before the First World War were linked to changing perceptions of their own domestic gender roles. See, for example,

Antoinette Burton, 'The white woman's burden: British feminists and "the Indian Woman", 1865–1915', in Nupur Chaudhuri and Margaret Strobel (eds), *Western Women and Imperialism: Complicity and Resistance* (Bloomington: Indiana University Press, 1992) and *Burdens of History: British Feminists, Indian Women and Imperial Culture, 1865–1915* (Chapel Hill and London: University of North Carolina, 1994); more recently, Julia Bush, *Edwardian Ladies and Imperial Power* (London: Leicester University Press, 2000).

7   Shaw married Sir Frederick Lugard in 1902 when he was High Commissioner for Northern Nigeria. See Helen Callaway and Dorothy O. Helly, 'Crusader for Empire: Flora Shaw/Lady Lugard', in Chaudhuri and Strobel, *Western Women and Imperialism*, pp. 79–97, and Helen Callaway, *Gender, Culture and Empire: European Women in Colonial Nigeria* (London: Macmillan, 1987), pp. 166–67, quoting E. M. Bell's description of Lady Lugard as having 'ceased to be a woman with a career' when she 'ceased to be Flora Shaw'. E. M. Bell, *Flora Shaw (Lady Lugard DBE)* (London: Constable, 1947), p. 250.

8   Bush, *Edwardian Ladies and Imperial Power*, and Bush, 'British Women's Imperial Politics and the South African War (1899–1902)', *Women's History Notebooks*, vol. 7, no 2, Summer 2000, pp. 2–9.

9   Frances Elizabeth Hoggan, *Medical Women for India* (Bristol, 1882), pp. 1–2, in Penelope Tuson, *The Queen's Daughters: an Anthology of Victorian Feminist Writings on India, 1857–1900* (Reading: Ithaca Press, 1995), p. 122.

10   Peter Gordon and David Doughan, *Dictionary of British Women's Organisations, 1825–1960* (London: Woburn Press, 2001), pp. 147–48.

11   Bush, *Edwardian Ladies and Imperial Power*, p. 80.

12   Letter to the editor of the *Auckland Star*, 3 May 1895, quoted by Antoinette Burton, *Burdens of History*, p. 168.

13   'An Appeal against Female Suffrage', *The Nineteenth Century: A Monthly Review*, vol. 25, January–June 1889, pp. 781–88. The signatories included, for example, Mrs Courtenay Ilbert, wife of a well-known barrister and member of the Governor-General of India's Council, and Georgina Max-Müller, traveller, author of *Letters from Constantinople* (London, 1897) and wife of Friedrich Max-Müller, Sanskritist and Taylorian Professor of Modern European Languages at Oxford. See also Brian Harrison, *Separate Spheres: the Opposition to Women's Suffrage in Britain* (London: Croom Helm, 1978), pp. 115–17.

14   'An Appeal against Female Suffrage', p. 782.

15   Millicent Garrett Fawcett, 'The Appeal against Female Suffrage: a Reply', *The Nineteenth Century*, vol. 26, July 1889, pp. 86–96.

16   Tuson, *The Queen's Daughters*, pp. 217–29; Bush, *Edwardian Ladies and Imperial Power*, pp. 171 ff.

17 Fawcett, 'The Appeal against Female Suffrage: a Reply', p.96.

18 Mary Frances Billington, *Woman in India* (London: Chapman & Hall, 1895). 'Signatures to Appeal against Female Suffrage', *The Nineteenth Century*, vol.26, July 1889, pp.86–96.

19 Tuson, *The Queen's Daughters*, pp.217–29, 289–319.

20 M.E.Jersey, 'The Hindu at Home', *The Nineteenth Century*, vol.25, January–June 1889, pp.653–66.

21 Pauline Adams, *Somerville for Women: An Oxford College, 1879–1993* (Oxford: Oxford University Press, 1996), pp.78–79. I am grateful to Pauline Adams, Somerville College Librarian, for searching Somerville archives for information on Emily Overend's suffrage views.

22 Emily Lorimer to her father and mother, 21 May 1913, MSS Eur F177/10.

23 Editorial by M.A.W. (Mary Ward), *Anti-Suffrage Review*, no 1, December 1908.

24 *Anti-Suffrage Review*, no 1, December 1908.

25 Curzon to Morley, 17 June 1900, Curzon Collection, British Library (Oriental and India Office Collections), F111/181, and David Gilmour, *Curzon* (London: John Murray, 1994), pp.165–66.

26 Evelyn Baring, 1st Earl of Cromer, was Consul-General in Egypt from 1883 to 1907. Cromer had also previously been Private Secretary to the Viceroy of India (1872–76).

27 Gilmour, *Curzon*, p.366.

28 'Women's Work': speech given by Curzon as Chancellor of the University, at Oxford, 22 October 1910, when opening new building at Lady Margaret Hall, in George Nathaniel, Marquis Curzon of Kedleston, *Subjects of the Day: Being a Selection of Speeches and Writings*, ed. Desmond M. Chapman-Huston, (London: George Allen & Unwin, 1915), pp.150–54.

29 Helena Swanwick, 'The New Imperialism', *Common Cause*, 30 May 1913, p.116, quoted by Burton, *Burdens of History*, p.172 ff.

30 Gilmour, *Curzon*, p.401. Curzon had, however, changed his mind on the Royal Geographical Society membership issue, and several years earlier had campaigned against the acceptance of women on the grounds that they would be out of place in a scientific body. Gilmour, *Curzon*, p.94.

31 'Woman Suffrage', speech at NLOWS meeting in Glasgow, 1 November 1912, in Curzon, *Subjects of the Day*, pp.296–308, p.302.

32 Ibid., p.303.

33 Ibid., pp.304–5.

34 Mrs Grace G.Walton, Mussoorie, to NLOWS, 1 July 1913, and draft reply from Curzon, 28 September 1913, MSS Eur F112/36.

35 Letters to Curzon from W.W.Astor, 9 July 1910, Earl of Lambton, 13 July 1910, and Arthur Sassoon, MSS Eur F112/32.

36 Letter to Curzon from Maud Arncliffe-Sennett, G.Sparagnapane & Company, 'the oldest established manufacturers of Christmas Crackers and

Wedding Cake ornaments in the United Kingdom', Ironmonger Row, Old Street, 21 July 1910, MSS Eur F112/33. Born Maud Sparagnapane, she and her husband ran the family confectionery firm: Elizabeth Crawford, *The Women's Suffrage Movement: A Reference Guide, 1866–1928* (London: Routledge, 1999), pp.623–26.

37 Letter to Curzon, signed only with initials, Baltic Shipping Exchange, 14 July 1910, MSS Eur F112/33.

38 Bush, *Edwardian Ladies and Imperial Power*, and Burton, *Burdens of History*. Bush has shown that among the predominantly conservative Edwardian ladies associated with imperialist organisations, roughly half were in favour of women's suffrage and half against (p.171 and Appendix 2).

39 In March 1912, for example, David Lorimer wrote to his father-in-law to thank him for a 'delightful present' of George Lovat Fraser's book, *India under Curzon and After* (London: William Heinemann, 1911), which he thought did 'more than justice to the wonderful "Human Dynamo"'. He added that 'The Gulf has lost a very good friend in Curzon. We are now fallen on lean years…its [government's] main idea is to cut down expenses. In order to save "not less than £3333/-" annually it appears to be prepared to reduce all the Gulf posts to a state of hopeless inefficiency'. Lorimer to Emily Lorimer's father, 3 March 1912, MSS Eur F177/7.

1 'Keeping up the Dignity of the Empire': The Viceregal Tour of the Gulf in 1903

Arriving in the Gulf today, travellers notice first of all the huge orange flares of offshore petroleum and gas installations. Passengers land in skyscraper cities of steel and glass. Western travel and holiday advertisements and brochures extol the luxury of the hotels, the beauty of the beaches and water sports, the golf, the desert safaris and the duty-free shopping. It is hard to imagine that only a hundred years ago Abu Dhabi, Dubai, Kuwait and the other modern state capitals of the region were small coastal villages, often no more than a single fort, which were regarded by the British as mere outposts of their Indian Empire. The modest economy of the area depended almost entirely on dates, fishing, small-scale cargo-carrying across the Gulf and pearling. Although a few wealthy Arab and foreign merchants made fortunes from the profits of the pearl industry, away from the coast the nomadic bedouin people often subsisted on very meagre produce from the barren desert.[1]

Almost exactly a century ago, in the winter of 1903, the Viceroy of India, Lord George Nathaniel Curzon, and his wife, Lady Mary Curzon, the Vicereine, toured the Gulf on a Royal Indian Marine ship, the *Hardinge*, together with a large naval escort, in a deliberately ostentatious demonstration of Britain's dominance of the Gulf coasts and waters. The Curzons were also accompanied by various officials of the British Political Service in India, including Emily Lorimer's brother-in-law John Gordon Lorimer, whose primary task was to record the events for posterity and at the same time collect information for a handbook on the region. Lorimer's research eventually resulted in one of the greatest works ever to be written about the Arabian Peninsula, the *Gazetteer of the Persian Gulf, Oman and Central Arabia*. In an appendix to the *Gazetteer* he described the viceregal tour and the British relationship with

Lord and Lady Curzon on deck during their tour of the Gulf, 1903.

the local rulers and their subjects. Lorimer's account is a vivid example of the traditional narrative of 'Imperial History', which at the same time unconsciously illustrates the narrow masculine perspective of British involvement in the Gulf.[2]

The first port of call on the tour was outside the Gulf, at the Indian Ocean town of Muscat, where a durbar, or reception, attended by the Sultan, Sayyid Faysal bin Turki Al Bu Sa'id, was held on board the most imposing cruiser, HMS *Argonaut*.[3] Sailing through the Straits of Hormuz, the party next visited the tiny Arabian coast shaikhdom of Sharjah, and then they crossed the Gulf to Bandar 'Abbas and other ports on the Persian side; finally they recrossed the sea to Bahrain and Kuwait. At each place, in Lorimer's description, the Viceroy received local rulers and merchants and made stirring speeches in which he emphasised the power and glory of the British Empire. At Muscat, Curzon also gave a dinner party on board ship. It was followed by fireworks, during which 'the magnificence of the spectacle' was enhanced by the sight of the British ships ablaze with colour 'against the deep blue sky, hulls and masts and funnels outlined in fiery relief by the electrician's magic wand'. It was 'a vision of stately beauty and power', wrote Lorimer, 'which startled even the stolid impassiveness of the Arabs into admiring awe'.[4]

During his visit to Sharjah, on 21 November, Curzon spoke to the assembled rulers of Abu Dhabi, Sharjah, Dubai, and the smaller Trucial States and described the history of their relations with Britain and the benefits he believed this relationship had brought them. 'I have come here,' he announced,

> as the representative, in the great Empire of India, of the British authority which you and your fathers have known and dealt with for more than a hundred years; and my object is to show you that though you live at some distance from the shores of India, you are not forgotten by the Government…
>
> We were here before any other Power, in modern times, had shown its face in these waters. We found strife and we have created order…The great Empire of India, which it is our duty to defend, lies almost at your gates. We saved you from extinction at the hands of your neighbours. We opened the seas to the ships of all nations and enabled their flags to fly in peace. We have not seized or held your territory. We have not destroyed your independence but have preserved it. We are not going to throw away this century of costly and triumphant enterprise; we shall not wipe out the most unselfish page in history. The peace of these waters must still be maintained; your independence will continue to be upheld, and the influence of the British Government must remain supreme.[5]

Each shaikh attending the ceremony at Sharjah was given a sword, a gold watch and chain and a sporting rifle. On 26 November the party arrived at Bahrain and the Viceroy received its ruler, Shaikh 'Isa bin 'Ali Al Khalifah, and his three sons. Two days later the procession reached Kuwait, where the same formal receptions took place and the Viceroy also attended a display of Arab camel-riding and horse-riding in which over two hundred horsemen, twenty camel riders and four thousand rifle-bearing men on foot took part. Lorimer continues his description in increasingly flamboyant language:

> It was a strikingly picturesque scene; the bright colours of the cavalcade, their flowing robes of orange and red and golden brown flung to the wind as they careered about on their spirited Arab steeds…the moving crowds of spectators shuffling along on foot; well-fed townsmen in their best dresses; Arabs from the desert, lean and hungry in their ragged 'Abas; veiled women with dark indigo cloaks thrown over their heads and long trailing skirts of gaudy cotton prints; black-eyed and brown-skinned children in every stage of undress; and in the back-ground, behind the black tents of a large Bedouin encampment, the white walls and flat roofs of the town gay with bunting, and far away across the pale blue waters of the bay, girt with the yellow desert, the fleet lying at anchor, grey and grim, with the *Hardinge* all in white, conspicuous in their midst…The Viceroy drove through the town to the Shaikh's residence on the sea front, where on his arrival a salute of 31 guns was fired. An interview followed in an upper chamber…ornamented,

on this occasion, with coloured portraits of the King and Queen of England and of Her late Majesty Queen Victoria.[6]

In private meetings such as these, Lorimer reports, the Viceroy lost no time in chastising the rulers for any faults or shortcomings. The ruler of Kuwait, Shaikh Mubarak Al Sabah, was warned not to meddle in the affairs of central Arabia. A few days earlier, the ruler of Bahrain had been advised in no uncertain terms to put his customs administration in order.[7] Nevertheless, Curzon proudly informed the British government that the Sultan of Muscat 'was quite pathetic in his trust of me, and in his readiness to do anything that I pleased', and that Shaikh Mubarak was 'unaffectedly flattered and rejoiced' at the visit. 'My entry into Koweit' he told the Secretary of State for India, 'in a carriage with the Sheikh (the only vehicle in the place) surrounded by a galloping and shouting cavalcade of Arab horsemen and camelmen, between lines of thousands of the inhabitants, and groups of women uttering shrill cries, was one of the most picturesque incidents of the tour.'[8]

The language, imagery and symbolism of Curzon's and Lorimer's descriptions of awe-inspiring – even magical – pageantry perfectly illustrate what has been described by historians as the 'invented tradition', or most recently the 'ornamentalism' of imperial rule at its most confident moment.[9] In contrast, their depictions of the loyal receptions offered by the waiting shaikhs, and their portrayal of the picturesque, but impassive and uncivilised, appearance of local men and women, articulate the perceived juxtaposition of disadvantaged and yet grateful people. The accounts also emphasise the almost exclusive masculinity of the political imperial enterprise. Lorimer mentions the Vicereine's part in the proceedings only once in his version. On 29 November, he writes, the Viceroy sailed off for an inspection of local ports, leaving behind some of his entourage who were able to explore the town and its outskirts, while Lady Curzon, with some of the staff, 'made a tour of the bay in a steam launch'.[10]

Mary Curzon's relationship with her husband has been explored both by her own and by Curzon's biographers.[11] Curzon's public views on women, and on their place and status within domestic life and the empire, are clearly stated in his speeches and writings, in particular those relating to female suffrage. However, his personal life was more complicated and his private letters reveal a deep love and an increasing reliance on Mary's friendship after his posting to India. The *Times* correspondent Valentine Chirol, who accompanied the Gulf tour, later recalled that Curzon had told him during the tour that he believed he could not bear the isolation of his position as Viceroy without Mary by his side to share all his 'thoughts and hopes and fears'.[12] Nevertheless, the reliance was firmly grounded in the old Victorian ideal of submissive and loyal woman-hood, unbesmirched by the rough and tumble of political life or business affairs and never getting in the way of male ambition and public duties. Curzon bizarrely insisted on a secret two-year engagement, during which the couple would hardly see each other while he continued his travels in Asia, and this set the tone for their future relationship.[13] After their marriage and his appointment to India, the Viceroy assumed his wife would occupy herself with domestic and social arrangements except on occasions when she had to appear with him publicly.[14] On those occasions, however, the Vicereine was expected to play a carefully defined, but strikingly visual role.

Mary Curzon was in some ways an unlikely candidate for this task. She was American, born Mary Leiter in Chicago in 1870, into a wealthy self-made business family. She married Curzon in 1895 and at first she found London society disconcerting. Soon after her marriage she told her parents that her path was 'strewn with roses' although the 'unforgiving women' were more like 'thorns'.[15] In 1898, when Lord Salisbury recom-mended to Queen Victoria that Curzon should be appointed as Viceroy, the Queen replied that she had only two reservations: first, that Curzon would treat the Indians well, since 'they must of course *feel* that we are masters but it should be done kindly and not offensively'; secondly, would 'Mrs Curzon, who is an American, do to represent a Vice Queen?'[16] Mary Curzon's own excited anticipation, tinged with private doubt, was expressed in a letter telling her father, and asking him to keep secret for the time being, the fact that George was to be made 'Vice Roy of India as soon as the House of Commons rises'. It took her breath away, she admitted:

> for it is the greatest position in the English world next to the Queen and the Prime Minister...the greatest place ever held by an American abroad. Heaven only knows how I shall do it, but I shall do my best to be a help to George and an honour to you and Mamma, and I shall put my trust in Providence and hope to learn how to be a ready made Queen.[17]

In fact, Lady Curzon seems to have risen to the occasion and played her part enthusiastically. While confined to bed after the birth of her second child, Cynthia, in September 1898, she studied the history and geography of India, and in December she set off with the baby and her two-year old daughter, Irene, for the three-week voyage to the Subcontinent. By the time she arrived she had prepared herself for the public performance ahead and, very much like Emily Lorimer in Bahrain a decade later, Mary, the wife, was overwhelmed by the dignity and power of her husband's role. Soon after her arrival in Calcutta, she wrote from Government House to her mother and her sisters to tell them that George had been proclaimed Viceroy. The previous Sunday they had been to the cathedral, which she found 'rather an ordeal'. The Viceroy's seat was 'an odd box with two large Gothic chairs in full view of the whole congregation' and, since everyone there had spent their time 'gazing' at the Curzons, 'it was pretty trying'. The service had consisted of 'long anthems and every sort of elaborate music', which tired both the Viceroy and Vicereine. Mary was so glad to get out that she 'nearly committed the awful crime of climbing into the carriage before George'. She said that she found it difficult to remember always to allow him to go through the door first, particularly as he never thought of it himself, but she was managing. She added that it was also the custom for the Viceroy and his wife to walk side by side, but she thought that when they marched through big crowded rooms he should go first.[18] A week later she wrote to her father to tell him that she was

> getting used to the new life – and it is all very wonderful. George is treated *exactly* like a reigning sovereign. Everyone bows and curtseys – ADCs [aides de camp] precede him – the only difference is that he has a great deal more power than most kings, and ruling India is no sinecure – and Vice Roy has it in his power to be a *very* great force, or he can be a cypher. Great things are expected of G.[19]

In a passage in Nigel Nicolson's 1977 biography of Mary Curzon, the author reproduces some of the stereotypes of Orientalism and of Victorian domestic gender roles, but gives an apt description of the contemporary public imagery of imperial ruling-class partnerships:

> She took immense pains with her trousseau, knowing that she must match the magnificent jewels, uniforms, turbans and saris of her host and hostess, and how much importance an oriental people attach to outward appearance. She must be ultra-feminine when the men were ultra-masculine. She must not give offence by adopting Indian style, but pay tribute to it by discreet reminders that she knew what it was…She was a success. She knew instinctively that she had two main roles in India: to comfort and support her husband; and to compensate for the fear and awe that he inspired.[20]

There was no doubt in the minds of the British rulers and administrators of empire that outward appearances were of vital importance in the maintenance of power, even though officials tended sometimes to justify this 'dressing up for empire' with the argument that it was in some way an 'Oriental' perversion. Curzon himself was characteristically open in his belief that dressing up mattered. Before he set off on a trip to Afghanistan in 1894, he had prepared for his meeting with the Amir of Kabul by visiting a theatrical costumier in London and hiring an enormous pair of gold epaulettes, together with several glittering foreign decorations. On arrival in Bombay, he completed his costume by borrowing a very large sword from the Commander-in Chief.[21] Women played a distinct, but supporting, role in these displays of pageantry and, a few months before her departure for the Gulf tour, Mary Curzon presented the feminine face of imperial power to the world in the Delhi Coronation Durbar celebrations of January 1903.[22] Gertrude Bell, in India on a world tour with her brother, described the opulence of the Viceregal procession which lasted for nearly an hour. First came the soldiers, she wrote, then the Viceroy's bodyguard, native cavalry and Cadet Corps, then the Viceroy and Lady Curzon, followed by Edward VII's brother, the Duke of Connaught, all on elephants. After them came 'a troop of some hundred Rajas on elephants, a glittering mass of gold and jewels. The Rajas were roped in pearls and emeralds from the neck to the waist, with cords of pearls strung over their shoulders, and tassels of pearls hanging from their turbans'. Their costumes were shot-gold cloth, or gold-embroidered velvet, and the elephants 'had tassels of jewels hanging from their ears'. Bell thought it was 'the most gorgeous show that can possibly be imagined' although, with a flash of the political radicalism which would later bring her into conflict with the British imperial establishment, she reflected that 'whether the Durbar is wise or not is an open question. I hear all the Rajas are grumbling over the tremendous expense to which they have been put...And no doubt some of them don't think they receive the respect they deserve.'[23]

In India, Mary Curzon's attendance at state functions was 'obligatory'.[24] She was expected to play hostess at garden parties, official dinners, lunches and dances for the British ruling and administrative classes and visiting dignitaries. She was also expected to accompany the Viceroy on his tours of the Princely States, where she would meet both the princes themselves and, usually separately, their wives and other women of the royal families. In her diary for winter 1902, she recorded a visit to Jodhpur where she was received by the Maharani, who had come up to one of the beautiful marble halls of the palace 'from her house in the sand below'. Mary found her a handsome woman, 'more gorgeously dressed' than anyone she had ever seen: 'her velvet and cloth of gold dress was a mass of embroidery, and jewels hung from her neck to her feet; anklets of great weight dangled over her insteps and emeralds the size of eggs were in chains round her neck'. She also had great power with the Maharajah, as she had 'plenty of wits and a son besides'. While the meeting took place,

George sat on a 'beautiful marble balcony' waiting for his wife. 'The contrast', Mary reflected,

> he and I standing side by side looking over the battlements, and that painted jewelled female prisoner inside covered with emeralds, who has to receive her horrid little husband on the rare occasions he comes near her by placing her face to his feet – is really the contrast and dividing line between East and West. We were rather saddened by our visit to the Fort, and trundled across the desert in our carriage full of thought.[25]

Like many of her female compatriots, for example the Protestant women missionaries who were beginning to travel to the Gulf at the turn of the century, Mary enunciated very powerfully her identity as a liberated American woman, in partnership with her husband, and she reinforced this representation by comparing her position with the perceived fetters of the Princely States wives. During the Gulf tour, however, in contrast to her enforced official visibility in India, Mary Curzon stayed on board ship for most of the time, while local rulers and dignitaries made speeches to her husband and sent formal greetings to her in her absence. Pregnant for the third time, she told her mother that she sat in her chair and read while the party went ashore to see the sights. It was too difficult to climb in and out of launches, but in Kuwait the air was 'divine – a mixture of sea and desert' and she was 'very well indeed'.[26]

The Vicereine's role and status, her outward identity in the imperial ruling hierarchy, was primarily defined by her relationship to her husband and to his position as the British monarch's deputy ruler of India. She was, to all outward appearances, the archetypal example of what Hilary Callan and Shirley Ardener have so appropriately described as the 'incorporated wife', a woman whose ascribed 'social characteristics' are 'the intimate function of her husband's occupational identity and culture' and whose own personality and character is consequently silenced or under-recognised.[27] In relation to Mary Curzon, this ascription was all the more striking because of her American nationality and upbringing and her, only belated and actively managed, assimilation into the British imperial ruling class. At the same time, her very Americanness, her 'outsider' background, may have given her the means and perspective to preserve, at least privately, a separate and more unconventional identity. In Mary Curzon's case, as in the case of many wives of senior imperial and colonial officials, it is often difficult to distinguish between the representation of female identity and the 'reality'. Historians seeking to recover women's lives are frequently faced with the dilemma that women appear in imperial historical narratives only as adjuncts to their husbands. More often than not there are no alternative versions with which to work, and there is no way of distinguishing between public and private, male-authored and female-authored stories.

In mainstream political histories of British relations with the Gulf, Curzon's tour has always been cited in the context and language of imperial expansionism, and Lorimer's *Gazetteer* and Curzon's own correspondence have been the main sources for subsequent descriptions of the events.[28] Mary Curzon, however, kept her own journal and, although not previously explored by historians of the region, it provides a reinforcing and yet subtly subversive version of the party's progress up the Gulf.[29] Most of the time the Vicereine, arguably the most powerful woman in the empire, was excluded, or excluded herself, from public events. When, for example, the Sultan of Muscat came on board ship, she 'peeped through the fringes of the golden hangings from an unseen corner at the rear'.[30] Much of the journal is a second-hand account of events described to Mary by Curzon, in which she repeats the details of each piece of ritual imperial diplomacy, and reports occasional references to her own absent but symbolic figure. While still in Muscat, she wrote that the Sultan made a speech in which he referred to her as a pearl, and George replied 'gently laying down the important fact that Great Britain meant to retain her paramount position in these parts in order to protect her trade and her many Indian subjects trading in the Gulf and in Muscat'.[31] Moving on to the Sharjah durbar, however, the Vicereine's account unconsciously parodies Lorimer's with an almost pantomimic quality:

A sea got up in the night and was running quite high when we got to Shargah, where George was to hold a Durbar for the Arabian Sheikhs. These had been collected together by Colonel Kemball and were all aboard a small ship and reported to be very seasick: a good many of our party were very feeble, and as it looked impossible to get boats off to the *Argonaut*, it was settled to postpone the Durbar until afternoon in the hope that the sea would calm and the Sheikhs revive. A certain number of brave men got into boats and launches and went over to the *Argonaut*, but no-one was enthusiastic about the prospect of getting into full dress and holding a seasick Durbar. Watching the gymnastics of people boarding boats and getting very wet kept us fairly cheerful, and when 3.30 o'clock came and the sea had not calmed, Mouche [Mary Curzon's lady-in-waiting] and I had a most amusing time watching the distress of the Staff in red tunics at the bottom of the companion ladder, waiting for the magic moment in which to spring into the dancing launch. It took forty minutes to get one boat off, and pitiful screams rose as waves dashed over Captain Keighley and Captain Wigram's uniformed legs, and feathered hats flew off as they leapt in the air in the hope of landing in the launch. Launch loads of green-faced soldiers danced on the waves, and presently two barge loads of Sheikhs were seen appearing and I got a good photo of them as they went by. George was the last to start, and his full dress and gold collar of the Star of India contrasted oddly with his efforts to board the wobbling launch. Fortunately there were no *contre-temps*, and only one Sheikh's retainer fell into the sea; and the *Argonaut* was fairly steady, and George made a speech to the Sheikhs (one of whom was sick over the side)…The Shargah Durbar will remain unique for sick Sheikhs, high sea, and a pea-green staff.[32]

At Bahrain, the diary records similar transport difficulties when George's launch struck a reef and his party had to land in the surf and ride through the waves on the backs of donkeys, during which several officials fell off. So much time was taken in reaching the shore that 'they saw very little' of the shaikhdom.[33] Finally, there is a light-hearted description of the Kuwait camel-riding display, which again undermines Lorimer's writing, and in which the dignity of the British appears as severely diminished. The British Minister in Tehran, Sir Arthur Hardinge, who was present at the occasion, rode 'a flea-bitten gray, with a rope round its nose, caracoled along, and was almost instantly shot off, as an Arab fired off his musket in his face, and George saw the gaitered legs of the Minister disappear into the rabble'. Louis Dane, the Foreign Secretary to the Government of India, who was also accompanying the tour, 'in full dress, was hauling in vain with a rope at the nose of his pony, while an immense camel, ridden by a shooting Bedouin in chain armour, was biting off the top of his head'. The Viceroy told his wife that:

> never in his many comic experiences had he seen anything approaching this ballyrag, which was prolonged for two miles through desert and bazaar until the Sheikh's house was reached, by some miracle without an accident; but no sooner had George left the carriage than the horses set to and kicked the vehicle to matchwood!

The party returned 'quite enchanted with their adventures', and laughed for the rest of the day at each one's account of his particular escapade 'on horse, or camel, or foot'.[34]

These private accounts of what was intended to be a very dignified and impressive official occasion have a tone of *lèse-majesté* about them which could only, perhaps, have been provided by an outsider, in this case an American. In Mary Curzon's descriptions, both Arab and British male dignitaries are frequently portrayed as figures of fun. At the same time, her journal, much of which can only have been based on Curzon's own account of events, presents a less pompous view of the Viceroy than the official versions.[35] It also hints at a less pretentious domestic relationship between George Curzon and his wife and evokes exchanges between human beings rather than imperial stereotypes. Most importantly, it reveals Mary Curzon as an individual who managed to preserve for herself at least some separateness and vitality beyond official duty and the bejewelled passivity of the imperial figurehead. This does not mean, however, that either George or Mary Curzon thought of the empire as a light-hearted game. They certainly do not appear to have doubted their right to rule and, while they may have been willing to laugh at themselves, this would have been done strictly in the privacy of their own family and social group. Curzon was a firm believer in the benefits and responsibilities of British imperial rule, and Mary Curzon's journal does not in any way undermine this interpretation of him, or her commitment and support for him as husband and Viceroy. She played her part with outward enthusiasm. But the journal does rather startlingly illustrate the narrow line between pomp and pomposity, public and private, and the extent to which the imperial project depended on the written official accounts of its spin doctors and journalists.[36]

After the Gulf tour, Mary Curzon returned to England for the birth of her daughter Alexandra in March 1904. After a long subsequent period of serious ill health, during which she suffered a miscarriage followed by peritonitis, she finally recovered enough to go back to India in the spring of 1905, for the remaining turbulent period of her husband's viceroyalty.[37] She died, aged 36, on 18 July 1906, from a heart attack brought on by influenza, only a few months after the couple's final return to England and Curzon's temporary exile to the political wilderness. In the sense that she visited the Gulf for only one very brief period, and then merely as a mostly silent figurehead, her story is marginal to the story of Western women in the region. As an American, she could hardly be described as the archetypal British memsahib. The most prominent imperial identity had been thrust upon her by marriage and, although her wealthy background allowed her to assimilate relatively easily into the British ruling class, she always remained, to some extent, an outsider. She learned and outwardly performed her role with the required grace and dignity, while at the same time a separate, female, and distinctly American, voice recorded the show from the perspective of a former colonial, and now proudly independent national, identity. Apparently the female and feminine embodiment of 'Empire', Mary Curzon's life in India, and her own and other representations of it, illustrates the contradictions and dangers of traditional readings of the imperial feminine. However, as first lady of the empire, she set publicly the tone and style for the social behaviour and attitudes of other wives in the higher social ranks of British imperial administration in India and beyond.

The Curzons' visit to the Gulf was the first ever made by any Viceroy and it was designed to encourage international acceptance of Britain's special position in the area. J.G. Lorimer concluded that the 'memorable cruise made by Lord Curzon in the Persian Gulf at the end of 1903 was undertaken for the purpose of…testifying to the paramount political and commercial ascendancy exercised in the Persian Gulf waters' and, as such, it was 'an effectual demonstration of British power and influence'.[38] Curzon, with his forward policy for the Gulf, was not without his critics in the British Government and his visit had only been agreed by the Cabinet after he proposed the tour for the second time.[39] Nevertheless, his speeches, and the manner of his travelling, were in keeping with the overall pre-war British confidence in their wide-ranging imperial enterprise. The tour, with its pomp and pageantry, and the carefully orchestrated visits to each shaikhdom, were part of an operation in which the British Government of India set out to create a local and international perception of Arabian Gulf membership of the British imperial world, embellished by honours and rewards and reinforced by the threat of isolation as a penalty for non-co-operation. Curzon's speeches in the Gulf, his awesome escort of British warships and naval officers, and his deliberate and careful inclusion of local shaikhs in the ceremony and ritual of empire, all served to define and publicly reaffirm the Gulf as an integral and active part of the Indian Empire. Furthermore, the formalised ceremonies followed a well-established practice of organised viceregal and royal progresses and durbars around India, which had been increasingly used since the Rebellion of 1857 to establish the British crown as the centre of authority and to 'incorporate' the Indian Princes and local dignitaries into the British administration.[40] Mary Curzon's role as 'Deputy Queen', the female representative and representation of the highest formal imperial power, confirmed the inclusion of women in the imperial hierarchy and, at the same time, defined and demarcated their public status.

The Gulf tour was a serious political initiative designed to enhance British prestige in the region, and it was also a reflection of the long-established British position there. When the Viceroy told the local rulers at Sharjah that the British 'were here before any other Power, in modern times', he was referring to much more than a merely invented past. Curzon's speech made a certain assumption about the definition of 'Power' as meaning 'European Power', and he conveniently forgot about earlier Portuguese and Dutch economic activity in the region in the sixteenth and seventeenth centuries. Nevertheless, he was correct in referring to a long history of British involvement and pre-eminence. The story of this involvement is an important key to understanding the British position and perspective in the Gulf at the turn of the century and, in spite of Mary Curzon's Viceregal appearance in 1903, the predominantly masculine nature of the enterprise.

The British had first arrived in the Gulf and Arabian Peninsula in the early seventeenth century, when the East India Company, looking for new markets, opened offices (known as 'factories') at Mokha on the Red Sea in 1618, at Bandar 'Abbas, on the southern Persian coast of the Gulf, in 1623 and at Basra in 1635. By the late eighteenth century the purely economic motivation for British activity in the Arabian Peninsula had acquired a political dimension. With the consolidation of the empire in India, the British became less concerned with the pursuit of local trade and more concerned with the strategic importance of the Gulf as one of the major routes to India. Offices and contacts outside India, which had at first been established by the East India Company merely for trading purposes, now took on a political and diplomatic role that was directly related to the preservation of British fortunes in the Subcontinent. This imperial link was to last until Indian Independence in 1947, and it had a major impact on the attitudes, backgrounds and perspectives of the British men and women who passed through, and who lived and worked in, the Arabian Gulf. Until the First World War, Britain preserved its increasingly dominant position in the Gulf area through a combination of sea power and treaty relations with the coastal Arab states, such as Bahrain and Muscat. Because inland Arabia was perceived as economically barren, there was never any suggestion that the area should be technically colonised, as long as the Gulf waters were kept safe for British shipping. However, in order to achieve maritime supremacy the British set up a network of political 'Residencies' and 'Agencies' around the Gulf, beginning in the mid-eighteenth century with an office at Bushehr (better known to the British as Bushire) on the Persian coast, where they appointed an official, known as a Resident, to look after British interests and to conduct diplomatic relations with the regional powers.[41] In southern Iraq (then known as Turkish Arabia), the East India Company's original factory at Basra was upgraded to a Political Agency, and between 1800 and 1904 British officials were posted to Muscat, Bahrain, Kuwait and Sharjah. Often they were the only Europeans in their particular area, working with a few locally engaged Arabs or, more often, Indian, translators and clerical staff and supported by regular visits from the British Indian naval patrols. Outside the Gulf, in southern Yemen, a fuelling station for shipping was established at Aden in 1839.

This British presence, and relations with the local Arabian Gulf shaikh-doms, were underpinned by a series of cleverly constructed treaties that offered the rulers British protection against local rivals in return for acceptance of British predominance as the international power in the area.[42] In theory the shaikhs retained their independence and in practice the British refrained from interfering in internal affairs. Nevertheless, when any of the shaikhs were thought to have backtracked on their under-takings, their towns and villages were bombarded into submission by British frigates, and local shipping was continuously regulated and dominated by the overwhelming power of the British Indian Navy. Local attempts by individual coastal Arab shaikhdoms to assert themselves as maritime powers were regarded as acts of piracy, particularly when they involved aggression towards British shipping. For almost half a century, for example, between 1800 and 1853, the people of the lower Gulf shaikh-doms were described by the British as 'pirates' and the area now comprising most of the United Arab Emirates continued to be known as the 'Pirate Coast' until well into the twentieth century. After the signing of the 1853 treaties, or truces, the shaikhdoms became known as the 'Trucial Coast', a quasi-colonial label which also stuck until the final British withdrawal from the Gulf region in 1971.[43]

By 1903, therefore, when the Curzons began their progress up the Gulf, all the small shaikhdoms on the Arabian coast were to some extent under the protection of the British and each of them had a resident British or Indian representative, giving them advice and preserving British and British Indian political, strategic and commercial interests. In spite of this, Curzon and his supporters in the Foreign Office and the India Office believed they needed an even better knowledge of the region, particularly during the pre-World War I period of increased international tension. Gordon Lorimer's project to produce a *Gazetteer* that would give officials a 'convenient and portable handbook' to the places with which the British were likely to be concerned was viewed as an essential prerequisite to the strengthening of British influence in the region.[44] Like the ceremonial and pageantry of the viceregal tour, it was a useful political tool dev-eloped and imported from India, where for over a century the British rulers had been consciously applying the belief that 'knowledge is power' to their increasingly sophisticated administration.[45] In the Gulf, the in-formation gathered by Lorimer and his assistants could be added to a body of European knowledge acquired during three centuries of Arabian travel and literary studies. In an appendix to his *Gazetteer*, Lorimer produced a 35-page list of published works, including travel writing and history, and unpublished government studies relating to the Arabian

Peninsula and Gulf region which might be of use to officials in the future.[46]

This history of British political relations with the Gulf, and its literary and scholarly Orientalist fringes, is significant for its almost exclusively male perspective. With one or two exceptions, before the twentieth century women are simply not present in the primary sources and records of the story of imperial trade, politics and gun-boat diplomacy, or in scholarly societies and Orientalist travel and teaching. Perhaps the most famous Western female intrusion into the narrative is that of the aristocratic explorer and Arabic scholar, Lady Anne Blunt, the granddaughter of Byron, whose famous journey from Aleppo to the Gulf with her husband, Wilfred Scawen Blunt, in 1878 to 1879 was recorded in her *Pilgrimage to Nejd*, published in 1881. The Blunts travelled extensively in Arabia and were increasingly sympathetic to Arab, in particular Egyptian, nationalism. Lady Anne's other contribution to Western knowledge of Arabia is *Bedouin Tribes of the Euphrates*, published in 1879.[47] Less well known, but author of an important contribution to the late nineteenth-century European study of the region, is Mabel Virginia Bent. The daughter of an Irish landowner, she married the explorer and archaeologist James Theodore Bent in 1877, and travelled with him on several explorations in the Gulf and East Africa. In 1889 the couple carried out excavations in Bahrain, and in the 1890s they made pioneering journeys inland from Muscat to Dhufar and also to the southern Arabian region of Hadhramaut and the island of Socotra. After Theodore died from malaria in 1897, Mabel, who had taken the photographs of their travels, began to put together her husband's notes and her own diaries and eventually published them in *Southern Arabia*. The book's significance was acknowledged the following year by the Government of India Foreign Department, when it recommended that the British Agent at Muscat, Percy Cox, should read it before travelling around Oman on a political mission to assess the extent of the Sultan's territorial authority.[48]

Both Anne Blunt and Mabel Bent wrote themselves into the story of British involvement in the Arabian Peninsula with these accounts of their own exploits. Away from the Orientalist tradition of travel and literature, however, the picture is more fragmented. Before 1900, some women accompanied male officials to the region, but their stories are almost completely hidden from history. In spring 1809, for example, in one of the controversial piratical incidents of the period, the Armenian wife of a British officer at Bushire, Lieutenant Robert Taylor, was captured with her baby son during an attack on a British boat, the *Minerva*. The vessel, with its surviving crew and passengers, was taken to Ras al-Khaimah where it was stripped of its cargo. The contemporary British accounts of the incident are somewhat inconsistent.[49] However, most of the passengers seem to have been released by the local Al Qasimi Shaikh, after some of the men were said to have been 'forcibly' converted to Islam. The immediate fate of Mrs Taylor and two other women on the boat was later hinted at, with slightly prurient reticence, in the *Annual Asiatic Register*. The Register reported that 'the pirates mitigated something of their usual ferocity; and no lives were lost, except in the gallant defence which was made by the unfortunate captives.' Some men however, were forcibly circumcised. Much as the men must have suffered, the account continued, it was

> comparatively nothing to the distress of the three ladies who were on board; and who, consequently, fell into the hands of these lawless and unprincipled violators. The subject is too painful to enlarge on. The indignities they were compelled to undergo can be easily conceived; and must excite the strongest emotions of pity in every feeling and delicate mind.[50]

In October, the Acting British Resident at Bushire, William Bruce, received a letter from Mrs Taylor in Bahrain, where she had been taken by an Arab who had 'purchased her'. She asked Bruce if he could find a way of paying the thousand-dollar ransom demanded by the man who had taken her to Bahrain. Bruce also received a letter from the man himself, saying that 'he had been induced to purchase her, to prevent her from falling into other hands who would never have parted with her', and that the price he had paid the Al Qasimi Shaikh, together with subsequent expenses, amounted to $1000. On receiving these communications, Bruce told the Bombay Government that 'the dictates of humanity, as also the national character, urged me instantly to adopt some means of extricating this unfortunate woman and infant from the hands of such barbarians as she had fallen into'. After some difficulty, and with a sum of money, he persuaded the captain of the dhow which had brought the letters to deliver the ransom and also a 'trifling present for the person in whose possession she was in, as Mrs Taylor had wrote that he had been as kind to her as a person in his situation of life, could be expected'. The Bombay authorities were not in the least moved, and told Bruce to pass the bill on to Lieutenant Taylor and ask him to reimburse the government.[51] Mrs Taylor just about surfaces in the archives because she was caught up in a maritime skirmish and then became the subject of a monetary transaction on the part of local British agents. Her plight, however, was evidently not regarded as an official responsibility or a suitable cause for government spending.

Another woman who appears in the archives at around the same time and in the same place is Anne Thompson, also the wife of an army officer, the flamboyant Captain Thomas Perronet Thompson. A Cambridge mathematics graduate and the son of a Methodist lay preacher, Thompson was a determined opponent of slavery. He had been Governor of Sierra Leone at the age of 25, and in 1819 was serving in the Gulf with the 17th Light Dragoons, as interpreter to the commander of a British expedition put together to subdue and negotiate treaties with the 'Pirate Ports'. Anne, who had run away from home to marry Thompson against her parent's wishes, accompanied him to Ras al-Khaimah and played a significant part in the production of the important 1820 'General Treaty' between the British and the local shaikhs. In a letter to her family she described 'the office' she held in the expedition:

> I beg leave to inform you that it was that of Political Secretary. I used to think it was rather hard that the Military Secretary should wear a cocked hat and Saxon plume, and get 400 rupees a month to boot, while I had nothing – but thus is merit rewarded. All the copies of the Treaty signed, sealed and delivered to the different chiefs were in my hand-writing.[52]

Not many women, then, accompanied husbands, fathers or brothers to the Gulf before the late nineteenth century, and if they did, very few of them made it into the archives unless they created trouble for the authorities. Even when, like Anne Thompson, they appear to have contributed significantly to British administration and diplomacy, they have been largely ignored. Mary Curzon's arrival might, therefore, conveniently be regarded as a symbol of the formal entry of women into the story of twentieth-century British involvement in the region. When she sailed with her husband into the Gulf, in November 1903, she was arriving in an area which was then generally thought of as being unsuitable for women and where British interests were mostly represented by single, or unaccompanied, male officials in places defined as 'hardship' postings. One of the strongest deterrents, for example, for men and not just for women, was the harsh climate, and the fear of it was based on a genuine history of illness and early death among British political officers stationed in the Gulf. In 1890 the British Admiralty described the environment as 'one of the most trying imaginable':

> The intense heat of the summer is aggravated by the humidity of the atmosphere, and the dust raised by every wind…In the winter the winds are cold and cutting…In the cold weather fevers are most prevalent; the so-called gulf-fever of the remittent type is very dangerous and convalescence is often only possible after leaving the Gulf.[53]

In such harsh conditions officials were required to have physical stamina as well as political acumen, and by 1903 a tradition had grown up of a special service made up of exceptional talent. Reporting to the Viceroy and the British Government of India, male officials in the Gulf were members of the Indian Political or Military Services, usually trained in the Subcontinent, and confident, with their education and fluent linguistic ability and the collective memory of three hundred years as imperial rulers, of their mission and their ability to bring the skills of modern European diplomacy to the area. They have traditionally been described as 'picked men, picked from picked men', part of a service which presented, according to Lord Curzon, the possibility of a career 'as fascinating as any the history of the world could offer'.[54] In a speech delivered at Simla in 1905, Curzon himself defined the ideal political officer:

> A good Political is a type of officer difficult to train. Indeed training itself will never produce him. For there are required in addition qualities of tact and flexibility, of moral fibre and gentlemanly bearing, which are an instinct rather than an acquisition. The public at large hardly realises what the Political may be called upon to do. At one moment he may be grinding in the Foreign Office, at another he may be required to stiffen the administration of a backward Native State, at a third he may be presiding over a jirga of unruly tribesmen on the frontier, at a fourth he may be demarcating a boundary amid the wilds of Tibet or the sands of Seistan. There is no more varied or responsible service in the world than the Political Department of the Government of India...I commend [it] to all who like to know the splendid and varied work of which Englishmen are capable.[55]

In the Gulf, freed from the large bureaucracies of Indian central and regional government in Delhi, Calcutta or Bombay, these officials were able to exercise even more personal power, and indulge in more creative policy-making, than they might have done in previous postings. When, for example, Emily and David Lorimer arrived in Bahrain in 1911, on Lock's appointment to the post of Political Agent, Emily thought her parents would be wondering what exactly his duties were and what he would be doing. Both of them, she said were 'still rather vague', Emily 'some shades vaguer than Lock'. The 'first obvious thing' was to protect British trade and British shipping, but it seemed that somehow the British had 'gradually adopted a sort of tacit protectorate footing', although whether it was 'a "veiled" protectorate' she was not sure.[56] In any case, they not only engaged in political and diplomatic activities, but also involved themselves in the administration of justice to the many Persians, Indians and Arabs drawn to the islands by the local fishing and pearl-fishing industries, which generated a large amount of litigation, 'sometimes involving vast sums of money'. With an interesting use of the personal 'we', implicitly claiming her own inclusion in imperial administration, Emily continued with an account of the Bahrain courts:

> A proportion of these cases we refer to native sheikhs, some for civil and some for religious disputes (sending some of our staff to attend and hear the evidence and see that all is in order and general fair play is observed), the sheikh sends in his finding and the P.A. [Political Agent] here gives judgement or precedents or potential appeals, free to do justice and love mercy.

In addition to all of this, David Lorimer's predecessor in Bahrain, Major Stuart George Knox, had told the Lorimers that the post was 'one of the most responsible and important posts in the Political Service'.[57] Emily told her sister Edith that it was important not to have 'rotters' posted to the Gulf, because while in India there was always an immediate superior 'to keep things straight' and there were 'no big international questions', in the Gulf 'all sorts of things turn up and each man has far wider powers and far more responsibility'. She later told her parents that she was glad they had not been posted to India; 'as Julius Caesar said (à la Longfellow): better be first in a little Iberian village than second in Rome!'[58] For the following half-century, Gulf officials came to think of themselves more and more as special and specialist, closely connected with India but part of a unique foreign service of their own.[59]

While free from some of the bureaucratic red tape which constrained their colleagues in India, Gulf officials were obliged to endure living and working conditions that contrasted strikingly with the comfortable social and domestic expatriate life in most parts of the Subcontinent. Before moving to Bahrain, Major S.G. Knox had been the first Political Agent appointed to Kuwait, in 1904, where he had complained that the house selected for him by the ruler was 'quite unfitted for a European to live'. Moreover, his allowance was inadequate because he had been compelled to send his wife home to England and was now 'committed to the expense of a double establishment – one in England – for some time to come'.[60] On the establishment of the Agency in Bahrain, also in 1904, the first Political Agent there drew up a 'Memorandum of Instructions' for the guidance of officers posted to Bahrain, which advised that:

> all in-door servants should be brought from India – more particularly, cooks, sweepers and washermen. Persian table-waiters, house-bearers and valets, cooks' mates and horse-attendants can sometimes be got locally, but they are hardly as good as the servants procurable in India, though possibly a little cheaper.[61]

The notion that Indian servants could and should be transported into the Gulf illustrates more clearly the close connection, both political and social, between the Subcontinent and the Gulf. The Gulf was seen as part of the same geographical entity as India, but rather as an unruly outpost, to which British Indian imperial tradition and society could be, if not duplicated, at least used as a guide to ways of doing business and living. The British men and women who came to the region all came with the same social 'baggage', and, even though their relative remoteness allowed them more freedom, their political and social positions and attitudes were nevertheless still influenced by rigid hierarchies of rank and status.

The Curzons were the top of the social and political order, and their rank and power was made visible when they sailed into Muscat harbour, in November 1903, on their ship, the *Hardinge*, with the accompanying vessels from the East Indies Squadron 'specially strengthened' for the occasion by the addition of HMS *Argonaut*.[62] Mary Curzon described the four largest warships as 'four grey monsters', echoing J.G. Lorimer's use of the contrasting symbolism and obvious visual message of the '*Harding* all in white' and the fleet 'grey and grim'.[63] 'We fell back', she wrote, 'and followed the four grey monsters all night and the next day and the next night; and when Muscat was sighted, we glided between the quartet and sailed into harbour at Muscat, our great white ship leading, and the four iron grey ones following behind.'[64] The Vicereine's diary, for all its light-hearted subversiveness, draws an accurate sketch of both the British community in the Gulf and the British position in the various states and shaikhdoms. On arrival, the viceregal party was joined by Colonel Arnold Kemball, the British Resident in the Gulf, normally stationed in the Persian town of Bushire. Also present were Sir Arthur Hardinge, the British Minister in Tehran, and Major Percy Cox, the British Agent in Muscat. Although none of the standard accounts mentions them, Mary Curzon's journal records that Kemball's wife and Cox's wife, Belle, were also present and came to dinner on board ship.[65] Cox was the senior Political Officer, under the British Resident, on the Arabian side of the Gulf. The Muscat Agency had been established in 1800, and although it had been closed down for several periods, mainly because of the climate, and the frequent illness and deaths of agents, by 1903 its active presence symbolised the status of the Sultanate as a predominantly British sphere of influence. In the early twentieth century the British presence was 'by far the most imposing foreign representation' in Muscat, with a medical officer, interpreter, clerical staff and even an occasional Assistant Political Agent.[66] Furthermore, the Agency building, reconstructed at vast expense in 1890, was one of the most impressive buildings in the town, completely overshadowing the residences of the French and American consuls. The Sultan, Sayyid Faysal bin Turki, described by Mary Curzon as 'a fine-looking man with much grace of manner', was sympathetic to the British and reliant on them for protection against the political ambitions of rivals in inland Oman.[67]

The British representative in Muscat, Percy Cox was born in Essex in 1864 and educated at Harrow and Sandhurst. He joined the Indian Political Department in 1890, and in 1893 was appointed Vice-Consul at Zayla, in British Somaliland. He was British Consul and Agent at Muscat from 1899 to 1904, after which he was gradually promoted through the posts of Political Resident in the Gulf, Chief Political Officer and Civil Commissioner in Mesopotamia, and finally British High Commissioner in Iraq. He was one of the most important figures in British imperial history in the Gulf in the years before and immediately after the First World War, and in 1903 he was the local representative of Curzon's proactive viceroyalty. Cox was an accomplished linguist and, like many of his contemporaries in the political service, a traveller, making time during his postings in Somaliland and Muscat to explore the country outside his immediate locality.

In November 1889 Cox married Louisa Belle Hamilton, daughter of a surgeon-general in the Royal Army Medical Corps. Her father was Irish and her mother Scottish. The couple were immediately posted to Peshawar and then to Jhelum where their first child, a daughter, was born and died.[68] In 1895, when their second child, this time a son, was born, the Coxes made the decision to leave him in the care of Cox's mother in England, rather than arrange for Belle to return to India or England. After this they saw him rarely, and when Cox's mother died in 1908, neither of them had seen their son for four years.[69] Unlike most political wives, Belle instead accompanied Cox on his postings, and on some of his travels, and she rarely left Muscat for India, even during the hottest summer months. Cox's first biographer, Philip Graves, admiringly noted that Belle bore the climate courageously, and he concluded that, in spite of the scorching summers, the Coxes liked Muscat and enjoyed their life there, giving the occasional dinner party for visiting warships and making use of the billiard table 'thoughtfully' provided by the India Office.[70]

After the Vicereine, whose presence was in any case symbolic and brief, Belle Cox was arguably the most important Western woman in the Gulf in the period before the First World War. Yet she is an enigmatic and elusive figure. She is hardly ever mentioned in official papers and, if she kept a diary of her own or any correspondence, it has not become publicly available. In some ways she was the archetypal memsahib, frequently

Percy Cox, British Political Agent at Muscat, and his wife Belle, together with the ruler of Muscat, Sayyid Taymur bin Faysal Al Sa'id, and Muscat notables including Sayyid Yusuf Zawawi (on the right). The photograph was taken to mark the Delhi Coronation Durbar celebrations in January 1903.

referred to as a 'motherly' person and the provider of social life for the many characters who passed through the Cox household, in Muscat, Bushire, Basra and, finally, Baghdad. In 1909, after Percy Cox had been promoted to the post of Political Resident at Bushire, Arnold Wilson, like Cox a future Civil Commissioner in Mesopotamia, wrote to his family that 'what social life there is centres around the Residency and Mrs Cox, a stately person, but the quintessence of kindness… She treated me like a mother and clearly spares no pains to make life tolerable for all Europeans in the social sphere.'[71] In 1912 Emily Lorimer wrote to her mother and father that Cox never saw his wife alone at Bushire because of all the guests.[72] Furthermore, and again unusually, this social role was extended into a quasi-diplomatic arena when Belle accompanied Cox to some of his meetings with local rulers and dignitaries. A 1903 durbar photograph, taken in Muscat, shows Belle with Percy Cox, seated on either side of the Sultan's young son, Sayyid Taymur bin Faysal, and surrounded by 12 Omani and Muscati notables.[73] Throughout Cox's career, Belle would be present as the homemaker but, in comparison with the strict social and domestic codes of British memsahib life in India, these Gulf homes and the 'home life' of Gulf families stood out as rather idiosyncratic and unconventional. Referring to the Coxes' short postings in India itself, a more recent biographer, John Townsend, commented that, in society there:

> the Persian Gulf would conceivably have been regarded as no more than a distant outpost of the empire and the Coxes, equally conceivably, may have been thought to be rather quaint colonials. The homely and motherly qualities

which Belle had demonstrated throughout their marriage would have counted for little in a society of smart memsahibs, exquisitely attuned to the cutting remark.[74]

After Muscat the Viceroy and Vicereine had sailed, via Sharjah and some ports on the Persian side of the Gulf, to Bahrain, 'the great pearl island, which yearly produces half a million in revenue from pearl fishing'. While George was 'lecturing the Sheikh', Mary sampled the actual goods, 'surrounded by pearl merchants, looking at the most heavenly pearls', for which her 'mouth watered' but which were 'quite prohibitive in price'.[75] When the American missionary Samuel Zwemer visited Bahrain ten years earlier in 1892, he reported that its population was about fifty thousand and that, although its main industry was pearl fishing, it also exported dates and was a centre for the import of goods for other towns along the coast and inland.[76] By 1919, according to a later missionary report, the population had risen to seventy-five thousand:

> Bahrein is a group of islands of which the largest is about twenty-six miles long by twelve miles wide, and the total population is about seventy-five thousand. These live in about one hundred and sixty-five villages and towns, most of which are in the northern half of the island. There are two other islands in the group, of rather large size. The one is called Moharrek, and it is here that the ruling sheikh lives. Sitra is the other island and is situated to the southeast of the largest one, and on it is the summer home of the brother of the ruling sheikh.[77]

Emily Lorimer's descriptions of Bahrain, written a few years later for her father and mother, were characteristically detailed. They illustrate the contrasting attraction and harshness of the region, even though the narrative is overlaid with Lorimer's own Western, imperial, middle-class and 'Orientalist' perception of this part of the Arab world:

> But now you are longing to know about conditions of life here. First water, there is an excellent quantity of water on the island, wells upon wells, it is slightly blackish and a little hard but does for washing and baths while for drinking we get water specially distilled for our use by the steam launch... The food, fish, prawns and crabs in every sort and variety, good eggs and fowl and a fair supply of mutton. Vegetables and fruit are not very plentiful locally but one gets weekly supplies of potatoes, bananas, oranges and whatever else is going, from the ships.[78]
>
> When you leave the Agency...there is a flat, sandy-stony common...Here and there native houses are dotted over it, sometimes singly, sometimes in groups of four to ten or more, paled in with a rude (but apparently strong and effective) fence of dead palm-leaves. The individual houses are rather

like rough hay-stacks to look at. A coarse, straw matting thrown over them forms roof and walls and a hole in the side acts as door window and chimney all in one...if you turned to the right and walked off parallel to the sea-front, you would go thro the town of Manama itself and the crowded smelly bazaar...I haven't been thro it yet. It seems it isn't a place one would make a habit of going thro oftener than one could help! But if you avoid this turn and strike out towards the south-west, the world indeed lies before you and a most attractive world it is. The main ingredient in it is a flat stretch of beautiful clean sand, covered still with sea-shells and occasionally inter-rupted by small dips with water standing in them...Eastward the horizon is bounded by the sound of three miles or so which divides us from Muharrak, but as the plain is scarcely above sea-level the sound seems merely to form a tiny blue ribbon on your left, behind that the buildings of the Muharrak sea-front form a little greyish-white streak and beautiful white-sailed boats race past continually. Straight ahead and on the right the horizon is broken by little date-palm groves at varying distances which look wonderfully fairy-like in the evening light.[79]

Emily's 'fairy-like' light description recalls her brother-in-law John Gordon Lorimer's account of the fireworks at Muscat and the 'electrician's magic wand' which symbolised the notion of British grandeur and civilisation imported into the barren desert. Almost a century later, Emily and Gordon would both have been impressed, although perhaps at the same time astonished, by the grander visual 'fireworks' of the oil industry, and the fairy-like lights of the modern city, both symbols and evidence of the independent wealth and power of the region.

The Curzons ended their tour of the Arabian side of the Gulf in Kuwait, whose ruler, Shaikh Mubarak Al Sabah, was later described by one missionary doctor as 'the maker of modern Kuwait, a man of long vision and great ability' who was 'a generation ahead of any of his subjects and had a grasp of world affairs that was amazing at that time'.[80] Kuwait was another great pearl-diving centre, with a pre-war population of about 40,000 people.[81] In the early 1900s, however, its strategic importance at the head of the Gulf brought it to prominence in the international arena. Mary Curzon alluded to this growing political importance in her diary:

So much ink has been expended on descriptions of Kuwait and the political importance of the place that I won't write reams about the Baghdad Railway having its outlet here, or the great question of England establishing a protectorate over the place. At present the Sheikh is fighting the Amir of Nejd and has just won a victory, so he is particularly cheerful.[82]

Towards the end of the nineteenth century, the notion of the Gulf as a British lake was beginning to be challenged by other European powers, and Kuwait was the focus of increasing imperial rivalry. In the 1870s, the Ottomans, who since the sixteenth century had maintained a fluctuating presence in the area, especially in the southwest corner of the peninsula and along the Red Sea coast, began a major expansion in the Gulf and into the interior. In addition, both the Russians and the Germans were showing commercial and strategic interest in the region, and the Germans in particular had established business contacts in the northern Gulf. Kuwait was regarded by the British as being especially vulnerable to German influence, especially after 1899 when the German Government obtained a concession from Sultan Abdul Hamid to build a railway from Constantinople to the Gulf with Kuwait as the terminus (the Baghdad Railway). Furthermore, German friendship with local Turkish authorities had paved the way for the establishment of the German firm Wönckhaus as a rival to British commerce in the region. The 1899 British Protectorate treaty with Kuwait was a direct response to the threat of German influence in Kuwait.[83] As a result of this international interest in the area, by the early twentieth century there were a few non-British Europeans living in, or visiting, the main Gulf ports.

In addition to the Europeans there were also small numbers of American missionaries beginning to establish themselves at Bahrain, Basra and Muscat. The activities of the missionaries are described in later chapters of this book, but their interests and motivations were, in the early years at least, very different from those of the British. In her reference to Kuwait, Mary Curzon also mentioned 'Nejd', the central Arabian region regarded as the most coveted prize of the American missionary activity and now the heartland of modern Saudi Arabia.[84] One well-known missionary, Stanley Mylrea, later recalled that the first missionaries in the area had recognised the great strategic importance of Kuwait as 'the gateway' to Najd and the interior of the Peninsula.[85] At the beginning of the century Najd was the focus of a power struggle from which the Amir 'Abd al-'Aziz bin Rahman bin Faysal Al Sa'ud (usually referred to in Western writings as 'Ibn Saud'), the future king of Saudi Arabia, was to emerge as the dominant authority. The origins of the Saudi state, however, may be traced back to the alliance made in 1744 between Muhammad bin Sa'ud Al Sa'ud, head of a powerful central Arabian family, and an Islamic reformer, Muhammad bin 'Abd al-Wahhab.[86] In the late eighteenth century the combination of religion and the sword was brilliantly exploited by successive Saudi rulers to construct the infrastructure of a central government authority and to spread influence over a very large area of the Arabian Peninsula, from Baghdad and Damascus in the north to the Red Sea and Gulf shores in the south. Although during the nineteenth century this territorial expansion was curtailed by successive Ottoman and Egyptian invasions, as well as by local and internal family rivalries, the basis of an emerging regional authority had been laid. The nadir of Saudi influence was reached in 1891 when the Saudi capital, Riyadh, was captured by the rival Al Rashid family and the head of the Saudi dynasty, 'Abd al-Rahman bin Faysal, was exiled to Kuwait. The re-capture of Riyadh and with it control over Najd, over ten years later, by 'Abd al-Rahman's 20-year-old son, 'Abd al-'Aziz, was one of the major turning points in Arabian history.[87] During three centuries of European and Ottoman imperial involvement in the Arabian Peninsula, central Arabia had been largely left alone by the international powers, and in 1902 the Sultanate of Najd was, together with the Imamate of Yemen, free from formal colonial or imperial ties. The British were consistent in their belief that, while maintaining the necessary diplomatic contacts, they should keep out of the affairs of inland Arabia, and their future relations with the Americans were to be influenced by their continual attempts to prevent the latter from establishing closer relations with the Saudi ruler.

In the meantime, the British reigned supreme in the Gulf, confident overall in their continuing ability and mission to bring security and protection to the small Gulf shaikhdoms. In a passage which encapsulates the British attitudes, perceptions and representation of the region's rulers as grateful, naive and childlike, Mary Curzon, like Lorimer, recorded that at the durbar in Kuwait George presented Shaikh Mubarak with 'several rifles, a gold watch with a gigantic chain, and a sword of honour in a scarlet velvet case':

> This greatly excited him, and he bounded to his feet and said he desired to be considered a fighting subject of England and tried instantly to put on the sword. The sword had no belt, so he cried loudly for one, but none was forthcoming so George suggested his postponing wearing the sword until tomorrow, to which the Sheikh reluctantly agreed. But he was quite an altered being, and sat literally beaming with delight, hugging his tawdry sword like a huge child.[88]

The following day Shaikh Mubarak, the ruler described by Stanley Mylrea as 'the maker of modern Kuwait' and who, a century later, is acknowledged as one of the great Arabian Gulf statesmen, came for a private interview with the Viceroy. He brought his two small sons, aged eight and ten, and Mary tried to give them chocolates and cherries, which they 'did not take to'. One of their attendants, 'fearing their lukewarm reception of British sweets might be interpreted as rudeness, forced open the boys' mouths and pushed the sweets in'. Mary thought this so cruel that she stopped him and offered sherbet instead, which was similarly rejected. Later the boys went to see the Admiral on his flagship and 'altogether had a thrilling afternoon'.[89]

With this small glimpse of the rather more universal pleasures of childhood, Mary Curzon concluded her diary of the Gulf Tour. The dignity of the empire had been upheld, confidence in British cultural and political superiority had been asserted and Western imperial gender roles had been displayed and reinforced.

NOTES ON CHAPTER 1

1   In his memoirs of a life in the Emirates and Oman, Edward Henderson recalled that even in the late 1940s the bedouin in very remote areas relied on dates and camel's milk for food, and that rice and meat were sometimes a great rarity. *This Strange Eventful History: Memoirs of Earlier Days in the UAE and Oman* (London: Quartet Books, 1988), chs 1–2.

2   John Gordon Lorimer was David Lorimer's brother. He was an official in the Indian Political Service who had been placed on special duty to compile the gazetteer which would provide the British Indian Government with better knowledge of the Gulf region. The finished work, *Gazetteer of the Persian Gulf, Oman and Central Arabia* (Calcutta: Superintendent Government Printing, 1908–15), ran into over 5000 pages. It was an enormous achievement which, in spite of its overtly political purpose and perspective, provided a compendium of detailed information on the region which has never been superseded. The account of the tour is in vol. 1 pt II, pp. 2626–62, Appendix P: 'Cruise of His Excellency Lord Curzon, Viceroy and Governor-General of India, in the Persian Gulf'.

3   'Durbar' is a Persian word meaning a court or 'levee'. It was one of many words and traditions adopted or adapted by the British from the local languages and customs of Indian imperial, and other colonial, territories.

4   Lorimer, *Gazetteer of the Persian Gulf, Oman and Central Arabia*, p. 2632.

5   Ibid., pp. 2638–39, and *Lord Curzon in India: Being a Selection from His Speeches as Viceroy and Governor-General of India, 1898–1905* (London: Macmillan & Co., 1906), pp. 500–3.

6   Lorimer, *Gazetteer of the Persian Gulf, Oman and Central Arabia*, p. 2647.

7   Ibid., pp. 2645–7

8   Curzon to Sir Charles Hardinge, Foreign Office, 21 November 1903, MSS Eur F111/182; Curzon to William St. J. Brodrick, Secretary of State for India, 17 December 1903, IOR:R/15/1/508.

9   Eric Hobsbawm and Terence Ranger (eds), *The Invention of Tradition* (Cambridge: Cambridge University Press, 1983); Bernard S. Cohn, 'Representing Authority in Victorian India', in Hobsbawm and Ranger, *The Invention of*

Tradition, pp. 165–210; David Cannadine, *Ornamentalism: How the British Saw their Empire* (London: Allen Lane, 2001).

10 Lorimer, *Gazetteer of the Persian Gulf, Oman and Central Arabia*, p. 2648.

11 Nigel Nicolson, *Mary Curzon* (London: Weidenfeld & Nicolson, 1977) and David Gilmour, *Curzon* (London: John Murray, 1994).

12 Gilmour, *Curzon*, p. 360.

13 Ibid., pp. 114–16.

14 Nicolson, *Mary Curzon*, pp. 93–94.

15 Ibid., p. 89. Nicolson notes that Curzon's marriage to an American was frowned on by his social circle.

16 Queen Victoria to Salisbury, Balmoral, 29 May 1898, enclosed in letter from Salisbury to Curzon, 24 June 1898, MSS Eur F112/1, and Nicolson, *Mary Curzon*, p. 103.

17 Mary Curzon to her father, undated (July 1898), Mary Curzon Collection, British Library (Oriental and India Office Collections), MSS Eur F306/8, and Nicolson, *Mary Curzon*, pp. 103–4.

18 Mary Curzon to her mother and her sisters, Daisy and Nancy, 12 January 1899, MSS Eur F306/43.

19 Mary Curzon to her father, 17 January 1899, MSS Eur F306/9.

20 Nicolson, *Mary Curzon*, pp. 138–39.

21 Gilmour, *Curzon*, pp. 97–98.

22 The 1903 Delhi Durbar was a public celebration of the accession of Edward VII, at which the King was represented by his brother, the Duke of Connaught, and the Viceroy.

23 Elizabeth Burgoyne, *Gertrude Bell: From her Personal Papers, 1889–1914* (London: Ernest Benn, 1958), pp. 139–141.

24 Nicolson, *Mary Curzon*, pp. 117–120.

25 Mary Curzon to her father, sister Nancy and brother Joe, 22 November 1902, written in diary form, MSS Eur F306/43.

26 Mary Curzon to her mother and father, 1 December 1903, MSS Eur F306/43, and letter to her mother, 25 November 1903, in John Bradley (ed.), *Lady Curzon's India: Letters of a Vicereine* (London: Weidenfeld & Nicolson, 1985), p. 144.

27 Hilary Callan and Shirley Ardener (eds), *The Incorporated Wife* (Beckenham: Croom Helm, 1984), Introduction by Callan.

28 See, for example, Rosemary Said Zahlan, *The Origins of the United Arab Emirates: a Political and Social History of the Trucial States* (London: Macmillan, 1978), p. 18, and Briton Cooper Busch, *Britain and the Persian Gulf, 1894–1914* (Berkeley and Los Angeles: University of California Press, 1967), pp. 257–62.

29 Letter-Diaries from Mary Curzon to her family, November 1903, MSS Eur F306/43. Also published as 'Mary Curzon's Persian Gulf Journal' in Bradley, *Lady Curzon's India*, pp. 145–53.

30 Ibid., 16 November 1903.

31 Ibid., 19 November 1903.

32 Ibid., 19 November 1903.

33 Ibid., 26 November 1903.

34 Ibid., 29 November 1903.

35 More than a decade later Curzon himself also wrote a rather humorous account of his entry into Kuwait in his *Tales of Travel* (London: Hodder and Stoughton, 1923), ch. 7, pp. 247–50.

36 As well as J. G. Lorimer, the Viceroy and Vicereine were accompanied on the Gulf tour by the Special Correspondent of the London *Times*, Valentine Chirol, who was ostensibly in the party as a friend of Curzon but who was also one of the most influential and experienced of British journalists, with extensive Middle East and Asian experience.

37 For a detailed account of the political infighting surrounding Curzon's last year in India, see Gilmour, *Curzon*, ch. 21.

38 Lorimer, *Gazetteer of the Persian Gulf, Oman and Central Arabia*, pp. 2626, 2662.

39 Gilmour, *Curzon*, p. 268, and Busch, *Britain and the Persian Gulf*, pp. 257–62. In 1902 and 1903 there was extensive public debate on Gulf policy, and Curzon's personal papers include numerous press cuttings on the subject, for example MSS Eur F111/351.

40 Cohn, 'Representing Authority in Victorian India', pp. 167 ff. At these gatherings the British had increasingly formalised the outward representations of imperial hierarchy with strictly defined forms of address, tables of precedence, gun salutes, dress codes, speeches and military parades, all depending on imperial rank. In the Gulf a system of forms of address was worked out for oral and written correspondence with the various ruling shaikhs, and it was amended regularly and carefully worded to reflect the status accorded by the British to each shaikhdom. These tables of address also included the size of gun salutes to be accorded and the form of Arabic greeting to be used in correspondence with the rulers. See, for example, IOR:R/15/1/237. The rituals were not confined to the Indian Empire. For an account of the ways in which this 'Theatre of Empire' was also transported to colonial Nigeria, see Helen Callaway, *Gender, Culture and Empire: European Women in Colonial Nigeria* (London: Macmillan, 1987), ch. 3, 'Power and Rank made visible'.

41 The 'Persian Gulf Residency' at Bushehr (always spelt in British archives as 'Bushire') was established in 1763. It remained there until 1948, when it was transferred to Bahrain. For a more detailed description of British imperial administration in the Gulf, see Penelope Tuson, *The Records of the British Residency and Agencies in the Persian Gulf* (London: Foreign and Commonwealth Office, 1979).

42 The main basis of British diplomatic relations with the Gulf states were the 1820 Preliminary and General Treaties and the 1853 Treaties of Maritime

Peace in Perpetuity. Between 1892 and 1899 'exclusive agreements' were signed with Bahrain, Kuwait, Abu Dhabi, Sharjah, Dubai and the smaller states of the present-day United Arab Emirates, by which the rulers agreed not to enter into any agreement with other foreign powers, not to admit the agents of any foreign powers into their territory and not to cede, sell or mortgage any part of their territory to other foreign powers except with British permission. P. Tuson and E. Quick, *Arabian Treaties, 1600–1960*, 4 vols (Farnham Common: Archive Editions, 1992).

43   The idea of widespread piracy was unquestioned until well into the late twentieth century, when it was re-examined by Shaikh Muhammad Al-Qasimi in his book, *The Myth of Arab Piracy in the Gulf* (London: Croom Helm, c. 1986). A more recent review of the events and their historiography is Charles L. Davies, *The Blood-Red Flag: An Investigation into Qasimi Piracy, 1797–1820* (Exeter: University of Exeter Press, 1997).

44   Government of India to Secretary of State for India, 30 June 1904, Government of India Foreign Department (External) Proceedings, IOR: P/6886.

45   Bernard S. Cohn, 'The Command of Language and the Language of Command', in Bernard S. Cohn (ed.), *Colonialism and its Forms of Knowledge: The British in India* (Princeton: Princeton University Press, 1996), pp. 16–56. First published in *Subaltern Studies: Writings on South Asian History and Society*, ed. Ranajit Guha, 4 (1985), pp. 276–329.

46   Lorimer, *Gazetteer of the Persian Gulf, Oman and Central Arabia*, vol. 1, pt II, Appendix R, pp. 2701–36.

47   Lady Anne Blunt, *A Pilgrimage to Nejd, the Cradle of the Arab Race*, 2 vols (London: John Murray, 1881) and *Bedouin Tribes of the Euphrates* (London: John Murray, 1879).

48   James Theodore and Mabel Virginia Bent, *Southern Arabia* (London: Smith Elder & Co., 1900). H. Daly, Foreign Department, Calcutta, to Arnold Kemball, Political Resident, 19 February 1901: 'Have you seen *Southern Arabia*, a book recently published by Theodore Bent's widow? It contains a good deal of interesting matter... which Cox might like to know.' IOR:R/15/6/28.

49   See Al-Qasimi, *The Myth of Arab Piracy in the Gulf*, pp. 93–94, and Davies, *The Blood-Red Flag*, pp. 104–7.

50   Asiatic Annual Register, 1809, quoted by Al-Qasimi, Al-Qasimi, *The Myth of Arab Piracy in the Gulf*, p. 97.

51   William Bruce, Acting Resident Bushire, to GOB, 17 October 1809, Bombay Political Consultations, IOR: P/383/11, Consultation 6 December 1809.

52   Anne Thompson letter to her family quoted by H. Moyse-Bartlett, *The Pirates of Trucial Oman* (London: Macdonald, 1966), p. 112. The Thompson papers are at the University of Hull, Brynmor Jones Library.

53   *Persian Gulf Pilot* (Admiralty, Hydrographic Office, 1890), reproduced in *Arabian Mission Field Report*, no 25, January–March 1898.

54 Philip Woodruff (pseudonym), *The Men who Ruled India: The Guardians* (London: Jonathan Cape, 1954), p. 270, quoted by Said Zahlan, *The Origins of the United Arab Emirates*, p. 231. Woodruff was also an Indian Civil Servant for many years. *The Men who Ruled India* was published in an abridged version under his real name, Philip Mason, in 1985 (London: Guild Publishing).

55 Speech by Lord Curzon, Simla, 30 September 1905, IOR:R/15/2/51.

56 In 1898 the Government of India admitted that 'Politically we virtually have a "Protectorate" already' but when the Political Resident, Percy Cox, suggested, in 1905, that the position should be formalised, the Government responded that any such plans would be 'distasteful' and 'foreign' to British policy in the Gulf. Curzon himself thought there should be no formal protectorate but merely a 'steady but unobtrusive increase' in influence. Busch, *Britain and the Persian Gulf*, pp. 139, 146–52.

57 Emily Lorimer to her father and mother, 13 March 1911, MSS Eur F177/5.

58 Emily Lorimer to her sister Edith (end March 1911), MSS Eur F177/5, and to her father and mother, 19 June 1913, MSS Eur F177/10.

59 Paul Rich, *The Invasions of the Gulf: Radicalism, Ritualism and the Shaikhs* (Cambridge: Allborough Press, 1991), p. 14. Rich quotes from an interview with Arnold Galloway, Political Agent in Bahrain from 1945 to 1947, in which Galloway told him, 'Yes, I was thought of as a Gulfite…Certainly some of us regarded ourselves as Gulf specialists…'.

60 Knox to Political Resident Bushire, 7 August 1904 and 11 February 1905, IOR:R/15/5/1.

61 Memorandum by Captain Francis Prideaux, 28 October 1904, IOR:R/15/2/51.

62 Lorimer, *Gazetteer of the Persian Gulf, Oman and Central Arabia*, p. 2626.

63 Ibid., p. 2647. See above, p. 19

64 'Persian Gulf Diary', 16 November 1903, MSS Eur F306/43.

65 Ibid., 16 November 1903.

66 Busch, *Britain and the Persian Gulf*, p. 21. By 1901 the establishment consisted of a Head Clerk/Accountant, Correspondence/Confidential Clerk, Treasury Clerk, Munshi, two peons and seven domestic staff as well as the surgeon (J. A. Saldanha, Précis of Maskat Affairs, 1892–1905, Simla, 1906, IOR:L/PS/20/C245).

67 'Persian Gulf Diary', 16 November 1903, MSS Eur F306/43. For an account of Omani politics in this period, see Busch, *Britain and the Persian Gulf*, ch. 6.

68 Philip Graves, *The Life of Sir Percy Cox* (London: Hutchison & Co., 1941).

69 John Townsend, unpublished manuscript of the life of Sir Percy Cox, St Antony's College Middle East Centre (MEC), Oxford, Private Papers Collection, GB 165-0286.

70 Graves, *The Life of Sir Percy Cox*, p. 76.

71 Arnold Wilson, *S. W. Persia: Letters and Diary of a Young Political Officer, 1907–1914* (London: Oxford University Press and Readers Union Limited, 1942), p. 100.

72 Emily Lorimer to her father and mother, 17 June 1912, MSS Eur F177/7.

73 Collection of Dr Omar Zawawi.

74 Townsend, unpublished manuscript of the life of Sir Percy Cox, p. 208.

75 'Persian Gulf Diary', 26 November 1903, MSS Eur F306/43.

76 *Arabian Mission Fourth Quarterly Report*, October–December 1892.

77 Mrs Dirk Dykstra, 'A letter from Bahrein', *Neglected Arabia*, no 111, October–December 1919, pp. 13.

78 Emily Lorimer to her father and mother, 13 March 1911, MSS Eur F177/5.

79 Emily Lorimer to her father, 1 April 1911, MSS Eur F177/5.

80 C. Stanley Mylrea, 'Kuwait before Oil: Memoirs of a Pioneer Medical Missionary of the Reformed Church in America, written between 1945 and 1951', St Antony's College, Oxford, MEC, GB 165-0214, pp. 37–38. Mylrea was an English doctor, educated in Philadelphia and appointed to Kuwait by the American Mission.

81 Mylrea, 'Kuwait before Oil', p. 37.

82 'Persian Gulf Diary', 28 November 1903, MSS Eur F306/43.

83 Agreement between the British Government and the Shaikh of Kuwait, 23 January 1899, in Tuson and Quick, *Arabian Treaties, 1600–1960*, vol. 1, pp. 557–61. An Anglo–Russian convention, in 1907, settled spheres of influence with Russia and left Germany and Turkey as Britain's most serious rivals in the years before World War I. In the early 1900s Wönckhaus opened offices in Bahrain and Basra, and in 1906 the German Hamburg–Amerika shipping line started a steamer service to the Gulf with an office in Basra.

84 Modern Saudi Arabia grew out of the central Arabian region of Najd, which today forms a province of the Kingdom of Saudi Arabia.

85 Mylrea, 'Kuwait before Oil', p. 37.

86 The followers of Muhammad b. 'Abd al-Wahhab were referred to by European contemporaries as 'Wahhabis', a name which was first used by opponents of the movement, but which is still often used today to describe the Saudi interpretation of Islam. The more correct term is 'muwahhidin' or 'unitarians'.

87 There are a great many studies of the creation and history of the Saudi state. They include: Gary Troeller, *The Birth of Saudi Arabia: Britain and the Rise of the House of Sa'ud* (London: Frank Cass, 1967); Alexei Vassiliev, *The History of Saudi Arabia* (London: Saqi Books, 1998); R. Bayley Winder, *Saudi Arabia in the Nineteenth Century* (London: Macmillan, 1985).

88 'Persian Gulf Diary', 28 November 1903, MSS Eur F306/43.

89 Ibid., 29 November 1903.

2 The Wife of the Political Agent: Emily Overend Lorimer in Bahrain, 1911–12

Emily Overend Lorimer and David Lockhart Lorimer began their posting in Bahrain in March 1911 and stayed for almost two years until October 1912, when David Lorimer was posted to Kerman in southern Persia. The Lorimers had left England in January 1911, immediately after their honeymoon, still unsure where they were to be posted but assuming they would be going either to India or to Persia, probably to Ahwaz, where David Lorimer had previously been British Vice-Consul for six years.

Even before leaving England, both Emily and Lock seem to have enjoyed the prospect of a posting outside the Subcontinent, but at the same time both of them felt slightly apprehensive about the reaction of Emily's parents. In October 1910 Lock wrote to his future mother-in-law to reassure her that Ahwaz would be much nicer than India because the climate was better, and they would not have to make friends because he already knew the people there.[1] They would also be within travelling distance of his brother Gordon, of *Gazetteer* fame, now Political Resident in Baghdad and living there with his wife Nesta. Lorimer told Emily's mother that work and pleasure at Ahwaz would be 'very integrated because you live in the office' and Emily would not, therefore, be left alone. It never seems to have occurred to him that work and pleasure might be better separated, and from the very beginning of their marriage Lock acted on the assumption that Emily would wish to be involved in his career. He continued, in the same letter, to bolster the arguments for a posting outside India, even referring to the advantages of the Gulf itself, although long before knowing that they would actually be going there:

Left: Emily Overend, photographed in Oxford, 1909. Right: Captain David Lockhart Robertson Lorimer in his uniform, 1909.

Persia is freer than India from custom and social convention...I haven't seen a great number of women in Persia but I cannot remember ever having met one who was unhappy in it. Even in the Persian Gulf itself, which is in many respects deservedly reviled, Mrs Cox has I think always spent at least the cold weather with her husband, at first at Maskat and then at Bushire. Mrs Knox apparently enjoyed the unmitigated society of her husband at Koweit; and Major Gray's mother and sisters used to spend the cold weather with him at Maskat – and even the cold weather at Maskat is not paradise... Emily has worked herself up into quite an enthusiasm for Persia and I think she will be quite cross now if fate takes us to such a hackneyed place as India.[2]

When the Lorimers arrived in Bombay at the end of February they were surprised to find that they were to be posted to Bahrain. Emily immediately sent off a letter to her father to re-emphasise the advantages and to dispel any fears her parents might have about the atmosphere of the place and its status in the social and political hierarchy. First, she said, they were particularly pleased because Lock would be working under Percy Cox, who had been his chief in Ahwaz and with whom he had got on well. They were also pleased because he would be working among Persians and Arabs in a more-or-less familiar atmosphere and using his special knowledge and linguistic skills. Most importantly, as in Ahwaz, he would be 'practically his own master', whereas 'any Indian job would have meant at first a less responsible and less important position and an entire re-adjustment of mental vision'.[3] Emily repeated Lock's earlier assurances to her mother that the climate must be good because the women were not obliged to retreat for the hot weather. As far as the smallness of the European community at Bahrain was concerned, it was a relief to know that they would not be drawn into 'a vortex of social duties' but would have some time for themselves 'and each other and our pet pursuits'. Finally, she hoped her parents would not mind about her not going to India. Lock was not at all sorry to miss the bureaucracy, 'with its red-tape', and would be happy to resume the more independent Gulf work, but he was concerned that Emily's mother and father would think he had 'deceived' them 'about his prospects of an Indian billet!' Emily reminded them that Bahrain was not nearly so cut off from home as a place in the Indian interior. For independent, educated women like her there were many attractions in a posting free from some of the boring social constraints of India and having the potential for rather more exotic intellectual stimu-lation. There was still, however, a nagging doubt that being outside India was in some way socially inferior and off the main career path.

From the moment she arrived in Bahrain, Emily Lorimer wrote regularly and extensively to her parents and family. Her long and voluminous cor-respondence is now deposited in the British Library and presents a unique and detailed Western female perspective on life in an early twentieth century Gulf state.[4] The entire collection, however, together with literary papers, covers a much longer period, from 1908 to 1949, and describes the much broader story of one woman's participation in the empire and her personal representation of her social, cultural and political develop-ment and identity, from the Edwardian decade of imperial confidence to the gradual acceptance of Indian Independence in 1947.[5] Emily Lorimer consciously and overtly 'produced' and edited her life story for a very specific audience. During the period she was in Bahrain, her letters were addressed mainly to her mother and her father. At first they were hand-written; later they were separated into two different styles. The first, typescript letter-diaries, were intended to be circulated to other family members and are very similar to the letter-diaries written by the Vicereine, Mary Curzon, to her family in the US; the second, handwritten private

and personal letters addressed to Emily's father and mother, either separately or together, were intended only for the recipients.[6] The very fact that
the overwhelming majority of the letters were addressed to her mother
and father gives the narrative a consistency and momentum, but it also
raises some issues of interpretation. The self-imposed limitations of writing
for this particular audience are apparent from the earliest correspondence
and are most obvious in the ways the author divides her subject-matter
and presents her information to her parents. In letters addressed only to
her mother, for example, she tends to describe questions of household
management, clothes, servants and health; in her letters addressed only
to her father, and also those addressed to her parents jointly, she writes
about politics and intellectual life. Emily Lorimer's early political views
were clearly moulded by her upbringing, and many of the opinions
expressed in letters to her father and mother reflect a confident family
outlook assimilated by Emily without any apparent personal self-doubt
or questioning. There is, however, a certain sense that, as a daughter, she
is telling the parents what they want to hear. Furthermore, in the early
years at least, there is also a feeling of the daughter trying to impress the
parents with the success of her life.

The papers were edited by Emily Lorimer herself in the year before her
death in 1949. Some of the most disappointing omissions relate to personal matters, such as her courtship with her future husband, her father's
death and the Lorimers' eventual adoption of a daughter.[7] Although there
are a few letters in the collection from David Lorimer to his and to her
parents, the papers contain hardly any correspondence received by either
David or Emily, so that the story is, literally, almost always one-sided.[8]

Emily Martha Overend was born in Dublin in 1881, the daughter of
a very successful barrister, Queen's Counsel and judge who, according to
Emily's own notes on her family history, was one of the first three non-
conformist students to be admitted to Oxford, where he read law and
history.[9] In his final examinations, Thomas George Overend was awarded
a first-class degree but, because non-conformist students were not accepted
in lodgings or given tutors, he was unaware that to obtain anything above
a third-class degree the candidate had to offer a 'special subject'. The
examiners stretched a point and gave him a second. Emily proudly thought
it was 'very characteristic of a most magnanimous man that he never
betrayed any bitterness over the avoidable loss of the First to which
he was fully entitled by the quality of his work'. In 1876 he married 19-
year-old Hannah Kingsbury, and Emily was their second child, with a
younger sister, Edith, and elder and younger brothers, Andrew Kingsbury
and George Acheson. Emily's paternal grandfather, James Overend, was

a Methodist builder who, in 1831 and against the wishes of her parents, married Martha Best, the daughter of a 'well-to-do county family, very Church of England'. Emily later described how Martha's parents 'in the most extreme Puritan tradition of savagery, cut the girl completely out of their lives. Her name was erased from the family Bible and to the day of her death, 37 years later, she had no communication with her parents'. Emily described her grandmother as a 'stern woman with high principles and a strong sense of duty', fiercely determined to do her best for her children and not to spoil them, but convinced that the family's hard life and privations were 'the just judgment of her Puritan God, wreaking vengeance on a daughter who had disobeyed her parents'.[10] In this tradition of Protestant industriousness, Emily took her first degree, in modern languages, at Trinity College Dublin in 1904, and then obtained her own first class in final schools, at Somerville, in 1906.[11] In 1907, after her year at the University of Munich, she returned to Somerville as tutor in Germanic Philology.

Emily Overend's letters to her parents from Oxford portray the life of an archetypal, almost a caricature, bluestocking. She describes cycling to meetings at the Indian Institute or the German Literary Society, attending lectures by public figures such as A.J. Balfour and George Bernard Shaw, and tea parties in the company of learned and eccentric professors. By her own admission she preferred the company of men and, in March 1909, wrote to her mother that two of her professors, one accompanied by his wife, had been to tea with her. While the two professors talked, Emily 'entertained the Mrs', who was very nice, but the situation frustrated her. She admitted to her mother that she would much prefer 'men's talk', but she wanted the two professors to 'have their fling', and she thought they enjoyed it.[12] This 'woman in a man's world' posture was partly a result of the lack of many female peers at Oxford but it was an attitude which also permeated her later relationships, even though mellowed slightly by friendships with educated and independent female and feminist contemporaries. At the same time, at Oxford she displayed the seemingly boundless appetite for learning which was to last for the rest of her life. She read around every subject in which she was involved, and underlying all her activities was a determination, inherited from her father and grandmother, to do things well and thoroughly. Enthusiasm and energy spill out from her writing and give her letters a vitality which sets them above most personal correspondence. Everything new was taken on as an active project rather than a passive experience. In her spare time at Somerville, for example, she learned Sanskrit, and later, when she became a player in the imperial pageant, she acquired languages as other memsahibs acquired social etiquette. When describing her Sanskrit lessons to her mother, she commented rather disingenuously that it was

> really a wonderful pleasure to learn to do anything well: I have no snobbish feeling that my sort of work is in any way superior to other work; I believe I would get a similar pleasure from cooking or trimming hats or carpentering though of course as a matter of taste I do prefer my own job.[13]

This enthusiasm and intellectual energy are both endearing and impressive. Yet although she claimed not to be a snob, and although her relationship with her students at Somerville was by her own account sympathetic and caring, she was, as a young woman, very easily bored and brutally critical of people she regarded as dull – men as well as women. In November 1909 she wrote to her sister Edith about a lunch party at which she met two men from Cooper's Hill Engineering College and their wives. The wives, she complained, talked solidly for an hour about Cooper's Hill people and one of the men, Mr Minchin, seemed interesting but was 'a little discouraged-looking, like an anchovy'. Emily could not get a word in edgeways.[14] Even the bursar at Balliol was not above criticism, both for his own demeanour and for the intellectual failings of his wife. A week earlier Emily had written about a Sunday afternoon outing:

> It was bright and cold so I donned my new coat and skirt which is very smart and set out on my bicycle for a regular raid!…I started with the Minchins, gave thanks to find they were away for the week end, went on to the Hilliards. Mr H. is a nice effeminate curly-haired young elderly man who is Bursar at Balliol. His wife is a pretty well-dressed doll-woman with nothing special in her head…[15]

While Oxford women and men who did not measure up to Emily's exacting expectations were dismissed without a second thought, her perspectives on the wider world of national and international politics and society were equally firmly rooted in her own unquestioned conservative family values. She seems not to have been interested in female political activism and suffrage while at Somerville, although she certainly perceived the injustice of not being awarded a university degree.[16] Her attitude to national and imperial politics was demonstrated in January 1910, when she told her father and mother that she found the Liberal election defeats 'just spiffing', especially when North Oxford 'kicked out its Liberal'. Most people, she said, were 'wildly elated'. He was 'an utter cad who had gone out to Egypt as journalist and lied and libelled our soldiers and our work out there, a brute called Bennett, fellow of Hertford'.[17] This blunt and authoritarian attitude also epitomised her views on Ireland and on Irish home rule, to which, like many actively imperialist women, she was consistently and virulently hostile, regarding it as a threat to the cohesion and security of the wider British Empire.[18] In her letters, she frequently described and identified herself as 'white' and British, and, much later, in her 1940 family genealogy, she proudly referred to her brother as 'an unrepentant Protestant Unionist'.[19]

Perhaps it is not so surprising, then, that suddenly, in 1910, this apparently independent, academic, single woman decided to marry. Her first meeting with her future husband seems to have taken place in Oxford in September 1909. Emily told her mother that she was going to tea with Hilda Lorimer to meet Hilda's brother, whose immediate attraction in Emily's mind seems to have been that he had spent time in the East and knew a number of Oriental languages.[20] Hilda Lorimer was classical tutor at Somerville and had been a friend and companion to Emily during the previous year. Like Emily, an outstanding academic, Hilda had arrived at Somerville from Girton in 1896, the college's first appointment from Cambridge.[21] Later described by Vera Brittain as 'one of the most brilliantly eccentric of women dons', Hilda was also an ornithologist whose 'solitary Saturday cycling expeditions with binoculars to the remoter fastnesses of Oxfordshire became a College legend in her picturesque and dauntless prime'.[22] During Emily's time at Somerville, she and Hilda undertook various outings together, including an excursion to London in May 1910 to hear a Royal Geographical Society lecture at the Albert Hall given by the American explorer Robert Peary, who had reached the North Pole in 1909. Before the lecture Emily and Hilda met up in the nearby Vienna Café with another of the academic Lorimer sisters, Floss, who was working at the British Museum as secretary to the explorer and archaeologist, Aurel Stein, 'sorting his "finds"'. Afterwards they went to the zoo and then dined at an Italian restaurant, Pagani's, which Emily said was 'the place' to eat.[23] The Albert Hall took her breath away with its size and wonderful acoustics, but Peary was disappointing. Although his lecture was interesting she found his personality unattractive: 'The whole thing was so well worked out and planned and the wheels so well oiled, so to speak that the voyage sounded more like a very successful well-directored commercial venture than a dangerous and toilsome voyage of discovery.'[24] Nevertheless, Peary was awarded the Royal Geographical Society's gold medal. Unimpressed, the two women returned to Oxford early the next day to give lectures before lunch.

Emily Overend and David Lorimer's relationship unfortunately remains unrecorded until July 1910 when, in a letter to Emily's parents, Lock thanked them for their hospitality during a fortnight in Dublin and told them he would try to 'deserve' Emily.[25] The following year, in September

1911, writing to her parents from Bahrain and reassuring them of her continuing happiness, Emily referred back to Lock's arrival in Oxford exactly two years earlier and his subsequent 'startling proposal' followed by her own 'more startling proposal' to accept him.[26] In 1909 and 1910 Lorimer was between tours and in England on leave. Emily was clearly much taken by his military masculinity and in October 1910 wrote to her mother about the splendour of his appearance:

> Lock put on his uniform the other day to show Em and me. It is awfully pretty. There is the mess kit, the undress uniform and full-dress. They all suit him especially the full-dress. It is dark navy beautifully fitting with broad gold lace band down trousers, narrow gold lace on velvet collar and cuffs and gold embossed buttons and a lovely sword patent boots and spurs.

Em Lorimer was another of Lock's sisters, also in Oxford and recruited by Lock and Emily to act as chaperone for their meetings, some of which must have been more taxing than others.[27] When not showing off his uniforms, Lock was an intellectual soulmate with whom Emily immediately settled down to learn more languages. She told her mother that they were taking Vedic classes together, which were 'a great sport'. It was 'so much more fun', she said, 'having someone else to work with. When we come in from our walk to have tea, we hear each other's paradigms and run through the translation together and the result is that we now know an amazing quantity of grammar, for neither quite likes to be caught out by the other.' Lorimer seemed 'nicer and nicer every day! I don't believe you could find anywhere a more unselfish or considerate boy nor one who could learn Sanskrit paradigms half so quick.'[28] Whether or not she felt a great loss at abandoning her academic career is unclear, although she later recalled that the Principal of Somerville, Edith Penrose, had kept her 'berth' open 'in case I don't find matrimony to my taste'.[29] Certainly, neither she nor her husband expected her to confine herself to domestic household chores. Two weeks before their wedding, after having a last tea in Emily's room and saying 'goodbye to it together', Lorimer saw her off on the train from Oxford. He wrote a touching letter to her mother, to tell her that he understood how much her daughter was giving up to leave Oxford in order to marry him and how clearly he recognised 'the full force of the break with a happy and a full and a useful past, which this goodbye meant' and 'all that she is giving up in exchange for what she believes I can give her, and what I hope and, without arrogance, now almost believe that I may be able to give her'.[30]

Emily Lorimer never seems to have regretted her choice, either of husband or career. Although her views modified during the following decades, along with the changing political environment, she never seems to have questioned the basis and purpose of British rule, or her own position and her duty towards the imperial hierarchy. Once having made the decision to leave Oxford, she threw herself into marriage and diverted all her energy into supporting her husband and country and preparing for the tasks ahead. From the model of the Oxford bluestocking, she swiftly and efficiently reinvented herself as an actively engaged memsahib, and when she later edited her own papers and correspondence for posterity, in her late sixties, she labelled her correspondence from the period of her wedding and journey to the Gulf as the 'First Joint Adventure of DL and EOL'.[31] Clearly influenced by her family and her educational background, Emily's attitude to British imperial rule in the wider world was largely unquestioning but she brought to her new career as memsahib a formidable intellectual knowledge of the empire, its history and its languages and she continued to build on that knowledge throughout her life. While Mary Curzon, the American-born Vicereine, had learned a role and been absorbed into a culture and class, Emily Lorimer learned about a 'culture' almost as an academic product in a lifelong continuation of her Oxford education.

The couple were married on 16 December 1910 and spent their honeymoon in Killarney in Ireland. Four days after the wedding Emily told her parents that she found 'each twenty four hours far too short for all we want to do and say...We are as happy as the day is long, happier because we could wish the day longer while we can't think how we could wish ourselves improved.'[32] Still uncertain where they would finally be posted, in January 1911 the Lorimers set off, calling at Rome to see Lock's parents and Athens to meet up again with Hilda, who was on leave from Somerville and working in Greece on archaeological excavations. When the sea was rough in the Mediterranean, Emily stayed in her bunk while Lock read Gibbon to her. When they were bored on the latter stages of the voyage, she worked at Hindustani while he read 'a ponderous German book of Mohammedan Studies'.[33] On arrival in Bombay they heard that Lock had been posted to Bahrain and Emily wrote proudly to her parents that she would be the wife of 'His Britannic Majesty's Political Agent'.[34] Lock would again be working under Colonel Percy Cox, now Political Resident in the Gulf, who had appreciated his work so much at Ahwaz that he had recommended him for a C.I.E. (Commander of the Indian Empire). Furthermore, Lorimer had received a 'very kind and cordial letter' from Cox, inviting them to stay with him and Mrs Cox at the Residency in Bushire while en route to Bahrain. Lock would be able to see all the files there, and also receive a briefing from Cox, for whom he had a great liking and respect. As the senior imperial couple in the Gulf until after World War I, the Coxes set the tone of local expatriate life, and their influence on the Lorimers was to be significant.

After a few days in Bombay, the Lorimers sailed for the Gulf, calling at Bandar 'Abbas, where they met the local Political Agent, Captain Biscoe, and his 'pretty little vivacious' wife, and at Muscat, which Emily described, in language remarkably similar to that used eight years earlier by Mary Curzon, as 'one of the most picturesque places' she had ever seen. The Portuguese forts in Muscat harbour reminded her of the castles on the Rhine:

> The coast comes out in wild, jagged promontories, high and steep and seared, forming several most inhospitable looking bays. One of these forms Muscat harbour. The rocks are a sort of grey black which is eminently sinister and picturesque (nearer the colour of the Lorelei rock than any other I remember) without a trace of vegetation past, present or to come. On a couple of the most inaccessible-looking jags quaint old Portuguese forts are perched, which again remind one of the castles on the Rhine...On a few hundred square yards of rock and at the bottom of this bay lies Muscat. Its whole sea-front is not many yards and consists of the British Consulate, the I.M.S. [Indian Medical Service] Doctor's house, the 'Palace' of the Sultan of Muscat and Oman and five or six other buildings...In behind these, clusters a native town and up all round on every side rise the black rocks. It is a place you could never forget.[35]

She was further comforted, and also amused, to find that the unmarried Political Agent, Major Trevor, was competent enough to have provided a very familiar domestic environment for their lunch at the British Consulate. It was a pleasant change to be able to eat onshore and she was impressed that men like Trevor seemed to manage their household affairs so well that they had 'no excuse for a wife! Everything was nicely cooked and daintily served; table-centres, finger bowls, dessert dishes, nice table-linen, "balls" of butter, everything as civilized as could be; tea in the same way, home made cakes, Scotch shortbread etc etc. It is really amazing.' Trevor himself was a 'middle-sized man, active and healthy-looking though a shade stout, with bright quick eyes, a preposterous eye-glass, and slow-coming speech'. He took them ashore in his boat rowed by 'four natives in red fezes and red dressing jackets over white night-shirts'. However, in spite of the fact that he had pleasant manners and 'made you feel quite at home for the whole day in his house', he gave Emily the curious impression 'of a man whose work is too important and too absorbing to leave him leisure to talk unless he has definitely something to say and a man who has lived too much alone to have any conversational change':

When I thanked him as he handed me into the boat for the pleasant day etc etc. he looked at me, curiously puzzled, yet without any embarrassment or awkwardness, as if reflecting 'Now there is some sort of reply one makes; I wonder what it is', evidently decided it wasn't worth racking one's brains about, gravely shook hands and lifted his hat. He is just going home on leave; he may find a wife – and his tongue. He seemed a thoroughly nice and a most interesting man.'[36]

While they were at Muscat the Lorimers heard that Major Stuart Knox, who they were to take over from at Bahrain, had been taken ill, and so they cancelled their planned trip to meet the Coxes in Bushire and headed to Bahrain direct. They arrived in early March, in bright and warm weather, the clear atmosphere producing 'wonderful lights and shade and a greater variety of colour than at home'.[37] On arrival they were welcomed by Knox and his wife, 'a nice little woman about forty' with 'slightly faded reddish golden hair' that was 'evidently her very own', who was 'really a brick'. Mrs Knox took endless trouble to explain the 'mysteries of water tanks and "go-downs" (store-rooms) and "dhobies" (washermen) who take a donkey and the soiled clothes and go out and camp for two or three days beside a well and wash the things and come back to iron them'. She also outlined the 'distribution of work between the various household servants'; and she guided Emily through the stores catalogue to see what she would need for the next few months.[38] Among her many pieces of advice and information before leaving, Mrs Knox provided Emily with a detailed account of the Political Agent's house in 'full working order' so that she would know 'what to aim at and not relapse too readily into picnic style':

> Indeed there will be little enough of that, if you saw the dinner table with table centre a silver bowl of bulbs and four flower glasses with violets (artificial of course) nicely made up table linen (the dhobi and the donkey and the well produce most creditable results) menu-cards and silver plate and the excellent meals you would never guess that this was the 'Persian Gulf'. Only the plaster and white-washed walls, the curious arched window spaces with deep window seats quaint little French windows and semi-circular fan-lights remind one that it is not Dublin nor even Europe.

One of Emily's first worries was whether the house would be big enough to entertain visitors. The ground floor contained the office, kitchen and wash-house and was built round a square courtyard open to the sea-front and 'out-lined by heavy square stone pillars' which supported the verandah above and formed 'a sort of rude cloister'. Upstairs there was a large, bright drawing-room, furnished with solid, comfortable government furniture,

Emily Lorimer photographed by her husband in her sitting-room in Bahrain, 1911.

including chesterfield sofas, easy chairs, good steady tables, a 'revolving' bookcase and a fine big carpet.[39] There was also a large dining-room, with sideboard, table and chairs and a huge butlers' pantry opening off it and leading to side stairs which ran down to the kitchen. In addition, there was a main bedroom and a guest room, each with dressing-rooms attached, and three bathrooms. The verandah almost completely surrounded the first floor, and in one direction had a beautiful view out to sea 'with steamers and fishing boats and strand stretching off uninterrupted as far as one can see'; in the other direction it looked across a strait of two or three miles to the smaller Bahrain island of Muharraq. It was 'extremely spacious', although the actual number of rooms was 'not great'. Emily told her sister, Edith, they would probably need to put up a partition because it was 'ridiculous to have only one spare room when we are supposed to be able to put up anyone who comes along'. Thinking also, as usual, of her own intellectual life, she added that it was 'worse than ridiculous to have no second sitting-room for a study'.[40] Furthermore, under the present arrangement, local shaikhs calling on Major Knox had to be shown into the drawing-room 'on top of European visitors to Mrs K':

and a good deal of difficulty and confusion ensue; they have to be offered tea which they don't care for and we have our tea spoiled by the smell of incense which is brought in for them. And there is no recognised etiquette as to how they should salute a lady and altogether it is a little awkward, whereas we could beat a hasty retreat if there were some place to fly to.

Having only been in Bahrain for a couple of weeks she nevertheless told Edith that, 'seeing the Arab view of woman kind', Lock was probably right in deciding that it would be 'more dignified for the ladies not to be in the room where natives are received except on very special occasions and on these rare occasions to be treated with a good deal of ceremony'.[41] Two months later, Lock wrote officially to Cox to complain about the defects in their accommodation and to ask for some urgent alterations to keep out the winter winds, which he said had made life almost intolerable for the Knoxes and given both himself and Emily colds and neuralgia. Turning 'with some diffidence' to what was clearly the real purpose of his letter he then raised the thorny issue of the 'memsahib and the native' and the fact that the Agency had only one room to be used both as a private living-room and a public reception-room. Lock thought this issue had probably not been raised before, because the first two British agents in Bahrain had been single and because his own predecessor, Knox, had been temporary and, although married, 'doubtless did not think it worthwhile to expend his energies on such an unwelcome subject'. However, on regular occasions the one room had to serve as 'a sitting room for the Political Agent's wife, a reception room for the Arabs and Persians on pleasure or business and a reception room for European visitors of either sex'. This situation was inconvenient and undesirable, 'no less from the Native than from the European point of view'. Lock thought that the ruler of Bahrain, Shaikh 'Isa bin 'Ali Al Khalifah, would prefer not to have ladies in the room when he called on the Political Agent. An additional sitting-room 'to which neither Europeans nor Natives would feel insulted by being asked to come' would, therefore, be a great advantage. Furthermore it would 'secure the Political Agent's wife, when he has one, in always having one place or another besides the bedroom where she could sit or work without the possibility of having Natives shown in on her at any moment'.[42]

The accommodation situation was eventually resolved when the Government of India authorised the Lorimers to carry out renovation work on the Agency building. However, the episode illustrated the tensions which surfaced when the first Western women arrived in these small outposts. Cultural and sexual separation were thought by most British imperial administrators and their wives to be vital to the preservation of both male and female, and British and Arab, dignity and position. In the early 1900s the British were consciously and carefully preserving and reinforcing their power and influence in the region and were not about to undermine it by any social embarrassments, misadventures or apparent lapses in hierarchy and protocol.

Emily Lorimer's own sense of the protocol of the empire, and of her husband's and her own roles in it, was reinforced by the long-awaited meeting with the Resident, Lieutenant-Colonel Cox, who appeared unexpectedly in Bahrain a few days after the Lorimers' arrival. As soon as Cox's cruiser was sighted 'Major Knox climbed into his uniform, then on to a horse, then into a punt, on to a dinghy, on to a sailing boat, on to the steam launch and out to greet him'. He returned later from Cox's ship, accompanied by an eleven-gun salute. 'Just think', Emily said to her sister, 'of Lock getting eleven-gun salutes whenever he goes out to a man of war – isn't it fine?!'[43] When Cox himself finally came ashore he was greeted by a guard of honour from the sepoy battalion:

> At ten a.m. on Sunday Lock and Major K. in uniform, the whole office staff in its best clothes, the chaprassies in scarlet and gold, filed down the narrow pier as Colonel Cox was rowed up to it. (Mercifully it was high tide which eliminates the ponies, dinghies etc). It was a wonderful sight from the verandah…Inside the compound the whole sepoy battalion except the sentries was drawn up in two rows of six looking very spick and span and it presented arms and was inspected and much elated. After a few minutes' chat with us in the drawing-room Colonel Cox went down to inspect files and papers etc in the office and only reappeared for lunch. He is a tall beautifully-built man, clean shaven and with clear-cut features, every inch a great man and very pleasant though a little alarming to talk to.[44]

It was at this time that Emily told her family that she was 'beginning to realise…the dignity of Her Britannic Majesty's Political Agent and, in consequence, of his wife'. Unconsciously echoing Mary Curzon's words on her husband's appointment to the viceroyalty, she added that she hoped she would be able 'to play the game well and…keep up the dignity of the Empire properly. Anyhow I shall do my best.'[45] As Mary Curzon's words and her short role in the British imperial project in the Gulf have already illustrated, appearance, protocol and ritual were both the outward emblems and subtle reinforcements of imperial power and authority. Uniform, pageantry, correct forms of address and precedence all had huge symbolic significance and played an important part in maintaining hierarchy and authority throughout the British overseas territories. Like George and Mary Curzon, Emily Lorimer was an enthusiastic actor in this theatre of empire. One of the most unexpected aspects of her personality, given her apparent preference for the life of the mind, was an obsession with clothes, revealed even in her earliest correspondence from Oxford. One of her first letters to her mother, in March 1909, describes her views on how to wear a fox fur over the shoulder; her earliest account of David Lorimer, as we have seen, focused on the attraction of his uniform and sword.[46] Throughout her years in India and the Gulf she continued to write in great detail about clothes in her separate letters to her mother. In July 1911, for example, she devoted six pages entirely to the question of clothes, many of which were purchased and sent out to the Gulf by her mother, and to the question of what she should be ordering for the winter. In this case, she thought she would need a little felt hat and an everyday winter coat and skirt, so that she could keep her pale green tweed for extra best, her navy one for Sundays and visits and an old black one for donkey rides. Meanwhile, she was grateful to her mother for having selected a suitable trousseau on her behalf, and she was particularly pleased about a pair of pyjamas in which she could sprawl on the verandah.[47] These continual references to the needs of her wardrobe were partly a reflection of the unquestioned assumption that suitable European dresses, coats and hats needed to be ordered from dressmakers at home. The almost obsessive interest in fashion and outward appearance, which is also present in both Mary Curzon's and Gertrude Bell's correspondence, reflects a continuing interest and concern to preserve the visual symbolism of confident and affluent European womanhood. However, it also illustrates the individualism and flamboyance of these somewhat unusual and striking women.

Dressing up for the empire and acting the part of the British Political Agent's wife certainly came naturally to Emily and she admitted very early on that it was 'fun' to have numbers of servants who stood to attention. The Agency steam launch was also 'fun':

> It sails along majestically with a union jack at its stern and a little flag at its mast-head…indicating that no less a person than His Britannic Majesty's Political Agent is aboard. And it solemnly ducks its little flag to the B.I. [British India] steamer and they solemnly duck back and the P.A.'s wife, who hasn't yet the sense of her 29 years, is much elated.[48]

She described to her mother another boat trip in which she 'had a ripping time', adding that she and Lock were 'splendidly well and I love Bahrein and am awfully happy to be here. Lock takes Orientals and deserts and flags and sepoys all rather as a matter of course – which is of course not unnatural – but my interest and amusement afford him a lot of pleasure at second hand'.[49] While absorbing the exoticism of the Orient, however, the Lorimers at the same time managed to follow the British Indian example and create a domestic environment which closely resembled England. 'The really curious thing,' Emily wrote to her father, 'is the absolute civilisation that insulates the Agency from the general atmosphere. Except for the barefooted, white-clad beturbaned servants, one might be living in Britain anywhere and you pinch yourself in vain to try to realise that this is really Arabia'.[50]

Nevertheless, Emily, in spite of her attraction to etiquette and hierarchy, professed to prefer the Gulf life to that of an Indian station, 'free from the eternal Club, the rival dinner-parties, the calls, and the social claims of an ordinary station, which in anticipation were just the one fly in my ointment'.[51] Part of the attraction seems to have been the scope such a small community gave to her for a more prominent social and even political role but it was also a genuine realisation that in Bahrain the Western community was well educated and engaging:

> Here we have society enough and really interesting society at that, cultivated literary people round us. The missionary's point of view may be one sided on some questions, but still it is the point of people who have work to do in life and as such much more stimulating than the gossip of people who only kill time. Moreover I shall here be able to get into touch with Lock's work in a way that would be impossible in India. Much of the most interesting part will of course be confidential and I must not even write of it in my letters home but if I am sufficiently discreet – and I think I have had enough training at home to secure that – there will be very little that need be kept from me. Perhaps as time goes on I may even be able to help in typewriting files or letters or despatches which could not be entrusted to clerks and and would have otherwise to be done by Locks own hand.[52]

By May 1911 she had defined a small administrative role for herself and told her parents that the experiment of her typing Lock's private business letters and keeping the files seemed as if it would work quite well, so that she might in fact develop into 'some kind of private secretary if not into an accomplished house-keeper!'[53] By October she was still typing urgent correspondence when there were secretarial crises in the office, and she told her mother that she had offered to go in as clerk and let Lock look for a wife, 'which would I think at the moment be just as easy to find!' Lock was reluctant to let her help on principle, 'if Government cripples itself by economy to help it out by "unpaid labour"'.[54] She, however, loved doing 'serious work' and it was typical of her attitude to household responsibilities that she also encouraged her sister in Dublin to employ a housekeeper to free her for more intellectual activities:

> If people can't afford such things, why that settles it and I don't think either Edith or I would shirk or funk the heavy life, if, to use Lock's pet phrase, 'it

would serve any useful purpose'. But when it can be helped it would be a pity, both for the sake of Ed [Edith's husband] and the babies, if Edith should let herself sink into the mere 'Hausfrau' and had no leisure for reading or thinking or enjoying her life. She used to be so fond of books, and good books, that it would be a wicked waste of good material.[55]

The small 'interesting society' in Bahrain in 1911 consisted of only 14 Europeans, mainly merchants, and the American 'missionary colony' whom the Lorimers met on their first Sunday at church.[56] Samuel Zwemer, the head of the mission, was 'an intellectual, ascetic looking man … reported to be a first rate Arabic scholar and to have one of the best libraries in this part of the world'. Emily thought he preached well enough, although unconvincingly, and the 'regular Methodist Presbyterian service' was 'homely and sincere and mercifully brief'. Mrs Zwemer, 'American, Dutch extraction', was 'a contrast to her husband, a stout hearty healthy motherly woman very kindly and pleasant', and the other missionaries included a Danish woman doctor (Miss Iverson), a German-speaking Swiss woman (Miss Spaeth) and an American 'college-girl' (Miss Firman). The Mission Hospital doctor was an Englishman, accompanied by his American wife (Dr and Mrs Mylrea) and there was a Dutch doctor and his wife (Dr and Mrs Dykstra). All the women were aged between 30 and 35. There were other English and German merchants whom they had yet to meet but, in the meantime, Emily thought the women all looked cheery, and exceptionally healthy, and they seemed very glad that another memsahib had arrived. She thought all of them seemed 'friendly and kind hearted and I don't doubt that our relations will be pleasant'.[57] The American missionary community in Bahrain provided a perfect intellectual foil for Emily's cultural and class-based certainties. Although broad-minded enough to recognise that the missionaries, both men and women, would be interesting companions, the Lorimers also showed the same mixture of grudging respect, suspicion, superiority, and even ridicule, which British political officers in the Gulf were to adopt towards the Americans right up to the Second World War. One of Emily's first reactions to Samuel Zwemer was a rather surprised and pained complaint that he failed to recognise the seriousness of her reading habits and she was relieved to find that he was not at a dinner party given by Mrs Knox in March 1911:

> He is too Johnsonian, in his liking for monologue, to inspire general conversation round him and is probably best without other guests when you can give him your whole attention. Alone he is most interesting though not just great enough to be free from vanity. His unconscious attitude to the lay female mind is lovely. Our first conversation ran something like this 'Your husband seems to be a great reader'. 'Yes, he is very fond of books, indeed we both

are'. 'You are fond of reading too? Novels and story books I presume'. I was too much amused at the unconscious superiority to do more than smile and say I thoroughly enjoyed a good story.[58]

In the same letter she told her father that Mrs Zwemer was a 'nice healthy round motherly woman with two merry little girls of about four and six (others at home) who was a trained hospital nurse and is a sane, practical-minded corrective to her husband.' Even so, she wrote separately to her mother on the same day to tell her that she had ordered her a copy of Zwemer's book, *Arabia, the Cradle of Islam* from Blackwell, because she thought it would interest her. Emily had not read it herself, but according to Lock it had 'a lot of interesting stuff in it though the missionary point of view obtrudes itself sometimes a little out of place'.[59] She later complained that Zwemer tried to pretend he was more learned than British officials. By this time she had decided that he really was 'a nice man' and 'very good company', amusing them 'by his invincible American desire to bluff'. But he had 'no more idea of real scholarship than the man in the moon, or even real serious accurate reading', and he was simply unable to stop 'posing' and talking about books he had not actually read. She thought it odd because he had no need for it: 'one is perfectly willing to give him credit for his real knowledge of colloquial Arabic and to believe that a Missionary's life is pretty full without original research. However, I suppose the humbug germ is in his blood.'[60] By the following year she was sufficiently comfortable with him to allow him to accompany her when they happened to be in Karachi at the same time. Zwemer took her round the shops. 'Failing Lock,' she wrote, 'I could not have had a better companion; he knows his way about Eastern places and has any amount of American bluff to carry him through.'[61]

The women missionaries provided Emily with some intellectual companionship. She read the Quran with Mrs Mylrea and when the Mylreas went on leave in February 1912 she wrote, grudgingly, that she would miss them – 'even though they are dull'.[62] Somehow, however, the 'Americans', as a group, always failed the etiquette test. In November 1911 Emily reported the imminent gathering in Bahrain of over thirty missionaries from all over the Gulf (Basra, Bushire, Muscat and Kuwait) for their annual conference. Just before the conference she invited one couple, Dr and Mrs Bennett (formerly Dr Iverson) to dinner. The dinner seemed to go reasonably well, although Emily was disappointed that neither of her guests liked Thackeray.[63] However, their greatest misdemeanour was that they did not call back afterwards:

which is probably only slackness; but I am a little annoyed as I had waived ceremony in asking them promptly on their arrival instead of waiting till they called formally – as I should have done. I wanted to be friendly, but it was perhaps foolish to waive etiquette. The big batch of Missionaries arrive today for their conference; I certainly shan't issue any invitations to a monster tea till I see whether they call or not. I feel sure they will but it is better to be punctilious. And if they don't I shall be saved the fag of getting things ready.

In fact only one of the missionaries called which 'seemed pretty rude – even for Americans and Missionaries! – and we were a little piqued'.[64]

The underlying concern of the British was that the Americans would somehow bypass their authority and establish direct relations with local rulers, although this idea was always presented rather as a warning that inexperienced newcomers could create diplomatic incidents without realising what they were doing. The assumption, of course, was that the British knew better than anyone else how to deal with the Arabs. As Emily explained to her mother:

> I feared my diatribes against Mission manners would alarm you! – but there is no fear of our being either quarrelsome or tactless and of course we would not think of allowing any coolness to spring up between us and those whom we have been friendly with, like M's [Mylreas] and Zwemer, just because a lot of the rest are rude, uneducated boors. In the east (out of India) where all Europeans are more or less on sufferance the movements of anyone may make international trouble, and it is a recognised thing that you do not think of travelling about on your own without informing your consul if there is one, or whatever European authority there is at hand, from whom you would claim protection or assistance if in trouble...[65]

Moreover, the British were sceptical about the wisdom of attempting to convert Muslims in the Gulf. In July 1912 Emily heard that one of her former Somerville friends had decided to take up missionary work in Africa. Her comment to her mother summed up one strand of opposition to missionary activity:

> Hilda Barham doesn't look strong enough for a missionary. However, if she is going, Uganda is a sensible place to go. One gets woefully out of sympathy with these good missionaries to the Muhammadans who knock their wooden heads up against the solid rock of Islam year after year. The same effort might do real good somewhere, but when after twenty years you have confessedly done *none* one would think you had Scripture warrant for shaking the dust of that desert off your feet.[66]

In this she was reflecting a view of the British Indian establishment of the time. The former Viceroy, Lord Curzon, was known to have little sympathy for missionary activity, which he believed was harmful, both to the local people and to imperial power. In 1901 he had written to the Anglican Bishop of Calcutta commenting that he was 'not at all in accord with the policy (however morally or spiritually exalted) of flooding India with thousands of missionaries. I do not think that India will become Christian: and I am not at all convinced that its loyalty would be increased or assured even if it did.'[67] The missionaries, their critics thought, should stick to providing much-needed medical and nursing services, which not only had a practical use but also raised the status of Europeans in the eyes of the locals. Emily Lorimer concluded that, although the American Mission had been in Bahrain for twenty years 'without making a single convert':

> ...it has done an immense service to all other Europeans by merely being here. For this group of high-minded, clean-living people, quietly living on year after year, doing good and doling out medicine and good advice, without fear or favour, to anyone who wants it, has set a new standard before people who could probably never have otherwise conceived it and has no doubt increased immensely the respect instinctively offered to Europeans.[68]

Unlike some of her contemporaries, Emily also had some grudging sympathy for Islam. In November 1911, after sitting through a particularly boring and unconvincing sermon from a visiting missionary preacher, she wrote to her parents that she was not surprised that the Arabian Mission had made so little progress. 'An astute Muhammadan is not going to be "had" by that sort of stuff; and one can only respect his reasoning'. It was to both Lock and herself 'a grave question whether Missionary effort would not be fifty times better directed to the real heathen who have no conception of a higher life and no standard of morality than to the Muhammadan who has so much that is lofty at his own door': 'Of course it may be urged that the Mohammedan does not live up to his religion, but on that principle the most urgent need for Missions would be to the Christians at home'.[69]

Several years later, her views unchanged, she told her mother that she could never 'see how people can set off to teach "heathens" while we have our own slums and our own social problems unsettled':

> Think of the filthiness of the white slave traffic in London or Dublin or even just the poverty and misery of the unemployed or the sweated. No heathen country has anything half so horrible or half so 'dark'. I'd like to see them get a move on to 'lighten' that. And as you say, even China can tackle her opium better than our Christians their drink.[70]

For Christmas 1911 Lock gave her a historical atlas and a translation of the Quran.[71]

A sympathetic interest in, and knowledge of, Islam, together with an 'Orientalist' literary background, and a skill and enthusiasm for languages, should perhaps have given the Lorimers a receptive and empathetic attitude to Arabian Gulf society. They certainly thought of themselves as caring and benevolent. They read voraciously, both together and separately, and one of Emily's first self-imposed tasks, on arrival in Bahrain, was to prepare for herself a booklist and a language programme. In April she told her father that she had 'begun a little Arabic... finished Hogarth's *Penetration of Arabia* – a very dull, purely geographical account of all explorations, but good as an introduction to others', and she was now 'at Lady Anne Blunt's *Pilgrimage to Nejd*', which she took next because it was 'lighter than Palgrave's *Travels* or the great classic Doughty's *Arabia Deserta* but these are all on my program'.[72] She was also reading the *Arabian Nights*, Alexandre Dumas (in order to keep up her French); and in their constant thirst for knowledge, the Lorimers had also decided to spend some of their wedding present money on the new, lightweight edition of the *Encyclopaedia Britannica*.[73] Its total weight was to be only 80 pounds and it required only 28 inches of shelf-room so it would be 'a very different business from trying to travel about with the old one'. In a place like Bahrain, far away from libraries, they thought it would be convenient to have reliable information at hand 'on any subject under heaven that may turn up', and Emily could not think of a better way to spend the money. By early July she had finished Doughty, an author she thought her father would love, and also Kaye's *Sepoy War*, a 'ripping book' which, she said, she could hardly put down and which made her proud to be compatriot of the Lawrences and Nicholson.[74] At the same time her reading list included Malory's *Morte d'Arthur*, read under the shade of some date palms, Malcolm's *Sketches of Persia*, 'a jolly little book', and 'Muir's *Life of Mahomet*'. She found it 'just jolly having time to read anything and everything' as a result of the forced indolence imposed by the heat and humidity. On her thirtieth birthday Lock gave her a tennis racquet but ordered Chamberlain's *Foundations of the Nineteenth Century*, 'for a real birthday present'. Light reading in the evening or at bed time tended to be Trollope, George Eliot or Sir Walter Scott.[75]

In her classic study of 'Orientalist' travellers and travel writing, published in 1986, Rana Kabbani emphasised the notion of a recapitulation of inherited ideas, and she persuasively argued that, in the late nineteenth and early twentieth centuries, British travellers had intellectually commenced their voyage long before the actual physical embarkation: 'They had absorbed from their education, from the readings of their youth, a great many of the qualities with which they were predestined to endow the East'.[76] The Lorimers, in many ways, illustrate Kabbani's cultural and literary imperial world picture. However, their educational and intellectual backgrounds also prepared them in a much wider manner for the practicalities of imperial rule. In the sense argued by Bernard Cohn, in his study of imperial forms of language and authority, the Lorimers set about acquiring the local knowledge necessary for strengthening British authority in the Gulf.[77] Languages, for example, were a vital skill for successful imperial rule and, for Emily and Lock, they were also a challenge and a joint hobby. On their arrival in Bahrain, David Lorimer wrote to his mother-in-law about his need to brush up his Arabic, and about his expectation that Emily would also learn the language. 'At present,' he wrote, 'Emily regards Semitic with a tinge of Indo-Germanic prejudice; but what else could you expect with her upbringing? When she has got Sanskrit and modern and old Persian off her mind, she'll probably be quite hungry for Arabic.'[78] By May 1911 Emily was spending two hours each day on Arabic language study. She was also progressing slowly, with the help of Lock, in Hindustani. He, meanwhile, began to brush up his Pashtu in case they were posted next to the North West Frontier. Emily was disappointed that she could not be 'a lot of use to him – owing to the disgraceful omission of Pashtu from the curriculum of elementary schools at home', but Lock managed to find a local Pathan to help him with his grammar. Lock, however, had become a great convert to the fascinations of philology, and they both had 'great fun' talking about language. Not to be outdone, when the Lorimers hired a new Persian servant in February 1912, Emily decided to learn Persian. It was, she thought, 'a respectable language with a decent literature of its own' and 'really worth learning both to read and talk, whereas Hindustani is only a sort of servants' esperanto and seems never to be anyone's real tongue'.[79] With this 'wonderful opportunity' to develop her cultural studies, she felt she had no need to miss the intellectual life of Oxford: 'Granted lots of well-chosen books, I recommend an Arabian desert island for anyone really seeking Culture – with a capital C'.[80] Dinner parties with the Lorimers must have challenged even the most erudite minds and bewildered most people. Many of their colleagues and acquaintances were given secret or open nicknames and in December 1911 Emily explained to her father why they referred to Major Knox as 'the Professor':

> Major Knox is called the 'Professor' 'because one evening at dinner my mind switched back unconsciously to Oxford or Munich and without thinking I addressed the older gentleman beside me as 'Professor'. This caused much merriment, and then the name stuck, making a convenient form of address sufficiently reverent and courteous and yet less stiff than 'Major Knox'. The

same sort of need for a less formal address than Mrs Lorimer and less familiar than Christian names, made them hit on 'Hypatia'...[81]

The classic Orientalist texts, such as Doughty's *Arabia Deserta*, portray a mixture of admiration for exotic landscapes and the supposed moral virtues of desert life, together with a perception of Islam as superstitious, and Arabs as backward and childlike. In many ways Emily Lorimer's views sit perfectly in this tradition, although her own personal attitude towards Islam was also coloured by an intense dislike of both Catholicism and Catholic ritual, as well as Presbyterianism. Her religious beliefs and prejudices were grounded not only in her education and her religious upbringing as a Protestant Christian, but also, perhaps much more importantly and certainly more evidently from her own writings, in her Irish Unionist political background. One of the most visual and sensual reminders of Catholicism, burning incense, became a frequent literary symbol for her aversion to the outward forms of Muslim, or Arab, religious and secular behaviour. Her earliest problems with domestic management in Bahrain had, as we have seen, involved a desire to avoid having her tea spoiled by the smell of incense from visiting shaikhs, and her reports of subsequent contacts with local dignitaries frequently included similar remarks.[82] In a letter to Edith, written very shortly after the Lorimers arrived in Bahrain, Emily described how visiting shaikhs were received by Major Knox and Lock at the Political Agency:

A sheikh comes in, in beautiful flowing robes of gorgeous colours with a golden embroidered cloth over his head held there by a double golden rope-fillet, followed by three or four attendant people. The great man puts his hand on his heart and says (almost chants) some slow impressive greeting in which Salaam and Al-l-lah are the only words I can understand...Then they converse a little and then sit impressively silent (which is more polite than talking hurriedly) and then off again. Then a servant brings poisonous black coffee and all drink slowly, in a few minutes he brings a yet more poisonous sweet drink of melted sugar and cinnamon and spices (awful filth!) and then lastly a funny little censer with native incense (which smells very like the R.C. stuff) The Sheikh bends his head over it, holds out his headdress over it to catch the fumes and wafts them into his nose by using both hands like fans. Then Major K. and L in turn bend over it and wave it on their faces with their hands and don't look in the least as if they liked it. Then after sufficient pause they rise to go and the same sort of graces-after-meat are exchanged. It is very impressive and dignified, but disturbing to an ordinary tea party. Lock goes through the performance awfully well and contrives to catch the solemn manner and the dignified silence to perfection.[83]

This passage, with its romantic Orientalist suggestion of decadence and sexuality, reducing the shaikhs to stereotypes and distancing the British from the ritual 'otherness', encapsulates the contradictions of Emily Lorimer's determination to engage with Arab 'culture', through the study of language, literature and politics, and her failure to immerse herself, or connect physically, with the everyday 'culture' of Arab life. A description of the 'Id al-Adha festival, sent to her father and mother towards the end of her stay in Bahrain, shows no sign of any real understanding of Islam, or more particularly, of Muslim life and religious practice. She reported that the previous Sunday had been 'the great day of the pilgrimage (on which they run round and round their sacred stone, or something) and it is observed as a holiday all over the Muhammadan world'. For Emily, this simply meant that Lock had to make huge numbers of calls and suffer the 'grave physical discomfort of the interminable cups of highly spiced coffee, the sweet sherbets, the douches of rosewater and the fumes of the terrible incense'.[84] With 'the usual humour of Fate', in the same week she faced one of the most serious challenges to her organisational skills in making the arrangements for the Coronation (of George V) Durbar celebrations in Bahrain. Her letter continues with a vivid and illuminating account of the formal interracial social etiquette of the occasion, which included receiving representatives of the various communities. On the first day, she wrote, the 'game' would start with receiving the Europeans and Americans. Then, two days later, 'the fun really begins':

> In the morning, probably before breakfast, Lock receives the Sheikh. At noon all the British subjects (there are only six white ones in all), all British Indian subjects, and people who are in any way reckoned as subjects of King George, are summoned to hear the King's proclamation read – in English and Hindustani...While the public is assembling, native drinks and smells and scents and fumes will be handed and squirted about...That evening the rest of the White Community comes to dinner...
>
> But what is really causing me heart-searchings is the native dinner party. I am striving to produce a menu of things they will be sure to like even if they have not tasted them before. Lock laughs at my anxieties on this account; he says happily not everyone shares my dread of the unknown edible! I do hope they will feel fairly comfortable, though I don't know how many of them are very expert with knives and forks. Anyhow we shall do our best to put them at their ease. Fortunately most of them talk English quite well...

In a postscript she added that the day went off splendidly and she described the various deputations arriving in their ethnic groups:

The forenoon meant for [Lock] first a huge deputation of Arabs, thirty or so, a long and very flowery Arabic address…then the two deputations of Indians at which I was also present, for they were British subjects. We stood in the middle of the room and shook hands with each person as he came in – and Oh, how clammy their hands are!…Then nuts and the few things that can be offered to Hindus were handed round; they were plentifully watered with rose-water, and be-incensed and then took their leave. We rushed off to wash our hands and have a breath of unincensed air while the next deputation was being marshalled…And finally our dinner was a success… [The native guests] were more or less familiar with the implements [knives and forks] but nothing could describe the extraordinarily funny way they handled them. First of all they would not pull in their chairs, and sat several feet from the table, and then between whiles would recline back with a knife vertically in one hand and the fork in the other. And their efforts to deal with peas and potatoes were a study…However it really went well and I think they felt at their ease and were gratified…

Lock acted the miniature Viceroy with great *éclat* with a very happy blend of dignity and graciousness and his speeches were excellent.

Apart from the more absurd elements of the middle-class code of social manners described, the letter expresses, in vivid physical terms, the sense of cultural separateness which runs through Emily Lorimer's letters from this period and this posting. Furthermore, the negative representation of Arab rulers and dignitaries, and their communities of Indian merchants and civil servants, was both an added justification for, and a reflection of, the British conviction that the local shaikhdoms were in need of imperial protection and education. The political realities of relations with local rulers and officials produced a stark contrast to the colours and scents of formal occasions. The British were in no doubt about the inability of the Arabs to manage their small states effectively and about the imperial mission to guide and educate. In Bahrain, for example, fruit and vegetables were rare but, according to Emily, needlessly so. The Arabs were 'a godless race' who could grow nearly anything 'if they would lay their minds to it, for there is tons of water, but they are too slack, especially as it pays better to pearl fish for four months and then idle for the rest of the year'.[85] The ruler, Shaikh 'Isa bin 'Ali Al Khalifah, was 'nice but incapable', with a frustrating tendency to procrastinate. Emily thought the British would eventually, and inevitably, have to take over, in order to knock things into shape. She told her parents that aspects of the ruler's administration were growing 'more and more hopeless':

And we sit still and protest, and expostulate, and complain to the worthy old shuffling Sheikh who 'rules' Bahrein, and conscientiously try to stave off

the evil day, when we shall have to say to him 'Look here, you either can't
or won't run this show right, it doesn't matter much which, and as it has to
be done we shall have to do it ourselves'. It is awfully characteristic of our
queer English methods that we have for ten years or more acquiesced in
trying to run things in spite of the most hopelessly incompetent or non-
existent machinery, instead of taking over the place at once. It is the Egyptian
problem on an infinitesimal scale. Of course the status quo may continue for
many a year to come but the end is nonetheless inevitable; it is only a
question of how many P.A.s' nervous systems they intend to wreck in the
futile endeavour to postpone that end. Lock says, however, that it is what
he is paid for!

   You can't help feeling sorry for the poor old man, who keeps his temper,
and meets every new complaint smiling, hopeful and incompetent as ever.
He really seems to try, but whatever power or influence he may once have
had, he is evidently quite incapable now of organising things and managing
men; the material he has to deal with would puzzle an abler man than he to
handle.[86]

In September 1911 Emily wrote to her father that Lock had made a visit to
neighbouring Qatar, on the mainland, and had called on its ruler, Shaikh
Qasim bin Muhammad Al Thani. Even further removed from British
influence, at least until 1916 when the first Anglo–Qatar treaty was signed,
the Qatari shaikhs were regarded by the political agents in Bahrain as less
of a responsibility but at the same time more untutored. Reporting Lock's
trip to her father, Emily described the Al Thanis as intelligent and interesting but 'wild'. The ruler had made Lock very welcome but had startled
him by trying to give him by 'two sheep, and a "school" of hens and a
gazelle'.[87]

   While Lock was in Qatar, Emily reassured her mother that she was
not alone and was, in fact, safer than when 'alone in a house in any town
at home'. Lock had put on an extra sentry and she had four guards, 'any
one of whom would have laid down his life to keep his trust, as Sepoys
and native Indian servants have so often proved'.[88] It was, perhaps, ironic
that away from the Subcontinent, the Indian sepoy, the feared protago-
nist of the so-called 'Indian Mutiny' or 'Sepoy Revolt' of 1857, now became
a guard against potentially dangerous, or at least unreliable, Arabs. Earlier,
in June, Emily had written to her mother and father about a fire which
had broken out in the huts and which the sepoys, with Lock's assistance,
had put out, since the 'Arabs have no public spirit'.[89] As far as other
servants and the household were concerned, the area where memsahibs
were most likely to meet local 'culture' and establish closer relationships
with local women and men, Emily was forced, to some extent, to confront

Bahraini society. However, even in household matters, 'the Arab' seems to have been regarded as not very reliable and certainly lower in the domestic hierarchy than Indian staff. On arrival in Bahrain, in March 1911, Emily wrote to her parents that Goanese cooks were very popular and that the American missionaries, who all had them, were helping the Lorimers to find one. Mrs Knox was taking her own cook, whom she had trained since he was a boy, to Muscat with her.[90] Overcoming, in this environment at least, her distaste for Catholicism and Catholics, a month later Emily reported to her father and mother that her new servants were Goanese and Roman Catholic, so that at least they brought 'no caste or food complications with them'.[91]

In practice, Emily Lorimer seems to have had very little contact with the local Arab population. Her domestic, housekeeping, business with merchants and traders was dealt with entirely by her Indian or Persian servants. The dark bazaars, with their 'hot narrow lanes, were full of dirty Arabs and Persians smoking and spitting and jostling', to which only the servants could be sent.[92] Except for the formal visits and official receptions, she kept out of the way of the shaikhs and their officials, while frequently praising Lock for his patience, tact and ability to handle Arab food, Arab ritual and Arab politics. Furthermore, local women and their everyday lives seem to have been entirely outside her experience and of no interest to her. Far from 'penetrating the harem', she was content to allow her most superficial impressions to count as knowledge and, in one of her very few references to women, to reproduce a strangely stereotypical description of the ugly–beautiful extremes of Orientalist representation:

> the women with their varying types of veils, some with thick black muslin screens, some with little stiff masks just like what you wear with a domino, all drawing over their cloaks in addition when they saw our cavalcade; some were the ugliest old withered hags you can conceive, and one felt the precaution a little superfluous; some on the other hand were extremely pretty and they usually contrived to let you have a good peep before they quite hid themselves with a coquettish gesture.[93]

It is significant that this paragraph was taken from a description of impressions and sights gathered on a picnic outing during which, as long as five months after arriving in Bahrain, Emily saw the town for the first time. In the meantime, however, the island itself was an exotic combination of light and dark, which Lock was photographing with his Kodak camera. Away from the centres of habitation, or viewed from the safety of the Agency, there were brilliant landscapes, blue seas, sunshine and night skies full of stars.[94] Furthermore, their personal domestic lives seemed remarkably untouched. In her Christmas letter to her parents she reminded them that a third of the Bahrain posting had already gone by. It had been full of new experiences, but the 'amazing thing' was:

> [how] superficial is the difference in one's life which surroundings make. Arabian deserts & black servants, and queer-shaped houses, and extra-ordinary bath-rooms, leave your habits and tastes fundamentally the same, and your life goes on for all serious purposes much as if your tent was pitched in Leeson St or Banbury Road.[95]

In her 1987 study of European women in colonial Nigeria, Helen Callaway found an inconsistency between traditional colonial images of memsahibs and other white, Western women and those women's own understanding of the reality of their lives. She showed that women often overcame the constraints imposed on them by the masculine social and political environment of colonial rule and forged satisfying and often compassionate relationships with local women.[96] Emily Lorimer's representation of her 'self', and her consciously constructed imperial identity, do not in any way conform to this theory of the 'ameliorating memsahib'. During her two years in Bahrain Lorimer 'flew the flag', and never questioned her role or position in the imperial hierarchy. Far from feminising imperialism, she played her part with almost masculine pride and energy, determinedly identifying herself as different from other women, as the self-confessed bluestocking and the rational and active participant in the politics and administration of empire. Her views of Arab and 'Oriental' culture and society were informed by her educational and social background and were typical of her class and of the political structure of early-twentieth-century imperialism. Furthermore, to a surprising extent, she relied on and recycled her husband's, and her husband's male colleagues', perceptions and accounts of local politics and local life, absorbing these second-hand opinions while distancing herself from personal involvement. The semi-isolation of the Gulf environment from British Indian society, however, provided her with an opportunity, unusual for imperial or colonial wives, to develop or retreat back into her academic, intellectual life. While this served to reinforce a sense of racial separateness, it nevertheless under-mined the conventional boundaries of gender and femininity.

Emily Lorimer's life in Bahrain, represented as it is through layers of inherited and acquired perceptions of her 'self' and her colonial 'others', illustrates both the consistency and the instability of traditional inter-pretations of the 'memsahib' or the 'white woman in the colonies'. In her determination to participate in the intellectual debate on imperialism she undermines the stereotypical myth of the politically ignorant memsahib, the mere housekeeper, wife/mother and social hostess. On the other hand, her views and perceptions of the British imperial mission and her clearly defined and firmly held views of the gendered boundaries of imperial intercourse conform to all the traditional images of the turn-of-the-century overseas official's wife.

Lorimer was a complicated and fascinating woman, and her voluminous letters present an opportunity to examine the shifts and subtleties of women's imperial responses over a much longer period. Her experiences during the First World War, for example, changed many of her attitudes to the wider world, as did those of many other women. Later, as a mature traveller, she was to become more open-minded and responsive to cultural diversity. In 1911 she was not young, but she had not yet completely emerged from a background of academic and political 'knowledge', inherited and learned remotely rather than through actual contact and experience. In the post-colonial world of the twenty-first century we are not comfortable with Emily Lorimer's pre-World War I perceptions of imperialism and of the interplay between the British imperial objectives and local and regional perspectives. Historians, in particular feminist historians, would perhaps prefer to find Emily Lorimer subversive and capable of bringing to imperialism a distinct and more congenial voice. In a recent paper on the problems of writing and researching women's lives, Dorothy Sheridan records her reactions to a long period of research on a woman for whom she found she had mixed sympathies but of whose life her interpretation developed over time, as both her own and her subject's standpoints changed. She emphasised the need to value other women's accounts without necessarily identifying with them, concluding that 'We cannot find common cause with all women and…we should not expect to'.[97]

When Emily Lorimer died in 1949, after a long and varied career as memsahib, journalist, traveller and translator, her obituary in the Somerville annual report accurately summarised her strengths and her weaknesses, but also acknowledged the changes in her perceptions and attitudes over time:

> Her energy and vigour seemed boundless; whether on the river, on the tennis court, or in widening the scope of her academic work, she seemed to excel without effort and to enjoy every side of life. As a Tutor she was immensely stimulating, though the pace she set might leave her pupils somewhat breathless. Blurred edges, sloppy scholarship and insincerity of thought or feeling she would not endure. Mere stupidity she accepted as one of the 'ills the flesh is heir to', 'the poor thing!', she would say. But with maturity and experience came a deeper sympathy and understanding, and an unfailing kindness…

Emily Lorimer's life was packed full of achievement and adventure in the fields of scholarship and exploration. She was indeed brilliant: only that term truly describes the many facets of her richly gifted and clear-cut mind. Yet the most vivid memory that remains with her friends is of her gallant courage and of the warmth and steadfastness of her affection.[98]

Emily Lorimer's accounts of her experiences in Bahrain reflect one particular woman's representation of her own imperial identity during a short and specific period before the First World War. Her letters are suffused with the imperial and racial attitudes and the social and domestic conventions of her time. However, she had an enormous enthusiasm for adventure and challenge, a sharp sense of humour and, in spite of her prejudices, a kindness and humanity. She was also an exceptionally talented writer, and in the details of daily life and the observations of people and places her letters are a unique record of one Western woman's involvement in the Gulf region in the early twentieth century.

NOTES ON CHAPTER 2

1   D.L.R.Lorimer to Hannah Overend, 24 October 1910, MSS Eur F177/3.
2   Ibid. Knox was Political Agent at Bahrain before Lorimer and had previously been the first British Political Agent at Kuwait, where he had originally lived alone (see ch.1 above); William George Grey (incorrectly referred to by Lorimer as Gray) was Political Agent at Muscat from 1904 to 1908, after the departure of Cox to the Residency at Bushire.
3   Emily Lorimer to her father, 24 February 1911, MSS Eur F177/4.
4   The papers, located in the 'European Manuscripts' section of the Library's Oriental and India Office Collections, MSS Eur F177, consist of 106 folders of papers in 15 boxes and 4 bundles, covering the period 1908–49. None of the letters have ever been published. The family letters use a number of standard abbreviations for words such as 'wh' or 'cd' ('which'/'could'), as well as for titles of officials, eg 'H.B.M.' ('Her Britannic Majesty'). These have generally been extended in the quotations.
5   This chapter describes Emily Lorimer's life in Bahrain before World War I. Aspects of her subsequent career and intellectual development during the First World War, and afterwards, are discussed in chs 4 and 5, although much of her later life is outside the geographical scope of this book.
6   'Circular' letters were a common practice in expatriate imperial and colonial life, and were an effective way of keeping in touch with family and friends back home. Most of the letters in the Emily Lorimer collection are addressed to her parents and, after the death of her father in February 1915, to her

mother. There are a small number of letters addressed to Emily's brothers and sisters and to David Lorimer's parents.

7   It is not clear whether these omissions are a result of the author's subsequent editing or because she simply did not write to her parents on these matters. The adoption of Dorothy appears in the letters as a sudden event, in 1920, and only much later does Emily describe the 'deep distress' of trying, and failing, for 10 years, to have a child (letter from Emily Lorimer to Dorothy's prospective parents-in-law, Mr and Mrs Munro, 6 August 1940, MSS Eur F177/46).

8   The small D.L.R.Lorimer collections in the British Library (Oriental and India Office Collections), MSS Eur D922 and D1168, also contains mainly literary papers and very few letters.

9   'The Family of James Overend of Tandragee, Co. Armagh, Northern Ireland', compiled by Emily Lorimer, c.1947, MSS Eur F177/92.

10 Ibid.

11 See Introduction, above. Like her father, but for different reasons, she was not actually awarded her degree at the time.

12 Emily Overend to her mother, 21 March 1909, MSS Eur F177/2.

13 Letter to her mother, 31 October 1909, MSS Eur F177/2.

14 Letter to Edith Overend, 21 November 1909, MSS Eur F177/2. The Royal Indian Engineering College at Cooper's Hill was opened in 1872 to provide a training for civil engineers in the Indian Public Works Department. It later began to take in students of forestry as well as engineers who did not intend to work in India.

15 Letter to her mother, 13 November 1909, MSS Eur F177/2.

16 See Introduction, above.

17 Letter to her father and mother, 23 January 1910, MSS Eur F177/3.

18 For example, letter to her mother, 2 August 1917, MSS Eur F177/22: 'I could put Ireland right myself within about three weeks if I could be given a really free hand and the necessary executive power. Recipe collect all celibate priests and nuns and children at present attending their schools; add all Irish politicians of all parties and all political speakers, place on one large ship, take out to sea and scuttle in mid-Atlantic: Secondly collect all Sinn Feiners and anti-British Home Rulers or Nationalists and exile them in perpetuity outside the Empire, preferably to Prussia...'. On the links between hostility to Irish Home Rule and female imperialist attitudes, see Julia Bush, *Edwardian Ladies and Imperial Power* (London: Leicester University Press, 2000).

19 For example, letter to her mother, 4 April 1920, MSS Eur F177/27: 'I quite agree with Mother that for the last 50 years the only people in Ireland with legitimate grievances against the British Govt. have been the "white people" like ourselves'. Emily's brother, A.K.Lorimer, was a barrister and a King's Counsel. In her genealogy she notes that he became a High Court Judge in Eire in spite of 'remaining an unrepentant Protestant Unionist who refused to take the oath in Gaelic...': 'The Family of James Overend of Tandragee'.

20   Emily Overend to her father, 19 September 1909, MSS Eur F177/2.

21   Pauline Adams, *Somerville for Women: An Oxford College, 1879–1993* (Oxford: Oxford University Press, 1996), p. 54.

22   Vera Brittain, *The Women at Oxford: A Fragment of History* (London: George G. Harrap & Co., 1960), p. 91, quoted in Adams, *Somerville for Women*, p. 54.

23   Emily Overend to her father and mother, 8 May 1910, MSS Eur F177/3. Aurel (later Sir) Stein (1862–1943) was an official of the Indian Education Service, but most famous for his work with the Indian Archaeological Survey and his explorations in Central Asia and China.

24   Emily Overend to her father and mother, 8 May 1910.

25   D. L. R. Lorimer to Emily Lorimer's mother, 29 July 1910, MSS Eur F177/3.

26   Emily Lorimer to her father, 29 September 1911, MSS Eur F177/6.

27   Emily Overend to her mother, 15 October 1910, MSS Eur F177/3, and to her mother, 16 November 1910, MSS Eur F177/3: 'Em is really a very jolly girl and I am getting very fond of her. She never thinks it a bore to come with us and chaperone us though it probably often inconveniences her and she is just thoroughly nice'.

28   Emily Overend to her mother, (10?) October 1910, MSS Eur F177/3, and letter to her mother, 21 October 1910, MSS Eur F177/3.

29   Emily Lorimer to her father, 5 August 1911, MSS Eur F177/6.

30   David Lorimer to Emily's mother, 30 November 1910, MSS Eur F177/3.

31   MSS Eur F177/4.

32   Emily Lorimer to her father and mother, 20 December 1910, MSS Eur F177/4.

33   Emily Lorimer to her mother, 13–21 February 1911, MSS Eur F177/4.

34   Emily Lorimer to her father, 24 February 1911, MSS Eur F177/4.

35   Emily Lorimer to her mother and father, 6–9 March 1911 on board SS *Waroonga*, MSS Eur F177/4.

36   Ibid.

37   Ibid.

38   Emily Lorimer to her mother and father, 13 March 1911, MSS Eur F177/5.

39   Ibid.

40   Emily Lorimer, (end March 1911?: first four pages of letter missing but annotated by EOL, 15/3/48 with suggested date) to her sister Edith, MSS Eur F177/5.

41   Ibid.

42   Lorimer to Cox, 26 May 1911, IOR:R/15/2/52.

43   Emily Lorimer, to her sister Edith (end March 1911?), MSS Eur F177/5.

44   Ibid.

45   Ibid.

46   Emily Lorimer to her mother, 21 March 1909, MSS Eur F177/2, and 15 October 1910, MSS Eur F177/3.

47   Emily Lorimer to her mother, 24 July 1911, MSS Eur F177/6.

48   Emily Lorimer to her mother, 1–2 April 1911, MSS Eur F177/5.

49   Emily Lorimer to her mother, 3 April 1911, MSS Eur F177/5.

50   Emily Lorimer to her father, 1 April 1911, MSS Eur F177/5.

51   Emily Lorimer to her father, 15 April 1911, MSS Eur F177/5; see also letter to her father, 1/2 April 1911, MSS Eur F177/5.

52   Letter to her father, 15 April 1911, MSS Eur F177/5.

53   Emily Lorimer to her father and mother, 5 May 1911, MSS F177/5.

54   Emily Lorimer to her mother, 14 October 1911, MSS Eur F177/6.

55   Ibid.

56   Emily Lorimer to her mother, 18 May 1911, and to her father and mother, 13 March 1911, MSS F177/5.

57   Emily Lorimer to her father and mother, 13 March 1911, and to her father, 1 April 1911, MSS Eur F177/5.

58   Emily Lorimer to her father, 1 April 1911, MSS Eur F177/5. This was a slightly strange mis-reading of Zwemer, whose wife, Amy, was the first woman American missionary to work in the Gulf (see ch. 3).

59   Emily Lorimer to her mother, 1–2 April 1911, MSS Eur F177/5. Samuel Zwemer's *Arabia, the Cradle of Islam* was published in 1900 (Edinburgh, London and New York: Oliphant, Anderson & Ferrier).

60   Emily Lorimer to her father and mother, 26 October 1911, MSS Eur F177/6.

61   Emily Lorimer to her mother, 4 and 6 April 1912, MSS Eur F177/7.

62   Emily Lorimer to her father and mother, 1 February 1912, MSS Eur F177/7.

63   A reference to the English author of *Vanity Fair*, William Makepeace Thackeray (1811–63), who was born in Calcutta.

64   Emily Lorimer to her father and mother, 26 October, and 9 and 19 November 1911; and to her mother, 11–12 November 1911, MSS Eur F177/6.

65   Emily Lorimer to her mother, 13 January 1912, MSS Eur F177/7.

66   Emily Lorimer to her mother, 9 July 1912, MSS Eur F177/8.

67   Curzon to the Bishop of Calcutta, 17 November 1901, Curzon Papers, MSS Eur F111/182.

68   Emily Lorimer to her sister Edith (end March 1911?), MSS Eur F177/5.

69   Emily Lorimer to her father and mother, 19 November 1911, MSS Eur 177/6.

70   Emily Lorimer to her mother, 19 June 1917, MSS Eur F177/22.

71   Emily Lorimer to her father and mother, 26 December 1911, MSS Eur F177/6.

72   Emily Lorimer to her father, 5 May 1911, MSS Eur 177/5. David George Hogarth, *The Penetration of Arabia: a Record of the Development of Western Knowledge Concerning the Arabian Peninsula* (London: Lawrence and Bullen, 1904); Lady Anne Blunt, *A Pilgrimage to Nejd, the Cradle of the Arab Race*, 2 vols (London: John Murray, 1881); William G. Palgrave, *Narrative of a Year's Journey through Central and Eastern Arabia (1862–1863)*, 2 vols (London: Macmillan, 1865); Charles Doughty, *Travels in Arabia Deserta*, 2 vols (Cambridge: Cambridge University Press, 1881).

73   Emily Lorimer to her father, 30 April and 5 May 1911, MSS Eur F177/5.

74 Emily Lorimer to her father, 25 May 1911, MSS Eur F177/5, and 3 July 1911, MSS Eur F177/6. Sir John Kaye, *A History of the Sepoy War in India, 1857–1858*, 3 vols (London: W.H.Allen, 1864–76). Sir Henry Lawrence was in charge of the British Indian army in Oudh during the Rebellion of 1857 and was killed at the siege of Lucknow; General John Nicholson led, and was killed at, the British storming of Delhi.

75 Emily Lorimer to her father, 3 July 1911, her father and mother, 18 July, 16 August and 26 December 1911, and her mother, 24 July and 16 September 1911, MSS Eur F177/6. Sir John Malcolm, *Sketches of Persia, from the Journals of a Traveller in the East*, 2 vols (London: John Murray, 1828); Sir William Muir, *The Life of Mahomet and History of Islam, to the Era of the Hegira*, 4 vols (London, 1858–61); Houston Stewart Chamberlain, *The Foundations of the Nineteenth Century*, 2 vols (London and New York: John Lane, 1911).

76 Rana Kabbani, *Europe's Myths of the Orient: Devise and Rule* (London: Macmillan, 1986), p.87.

77 Bernard S.Cohn, 'The Command of Language and the Language of Command', in Bernard S.Cohn (ed.), *Colonialism and its Forms of Knowledge: The British in India* (Princeton: Princeton University Press, 1996), pp.282–83. See ch.1 above.

78 David Lorimer to Emily's mother, 9 March 1911, MSS Eur F177/4.

79 Emily Lorimer to her mother, 18 May 1911, MSS Eur F177/5; letter to her father and mother, 4 August 1911, MSS Eur F177/6; letter to her father and mother, 1 February 1912, MSS Eur F177/7.

80 Emily Lorimer to her father and mother, 11 October 1911, MSS Eur F177/6.

81 Emily Lorimer to her father, 23 December 1911, MSS Eur F177/6. The name was remarkably appropriate and has resonance with feminist academics today. Hypatia was a teacher, philosopher, mathematician and astronomer, leader of the Neoplatonic school in Alexandria in the fourth century AD. She has a journal of feminist philosophy named after her.

82 Emily Lorimer to her sister Edith (end March 1911?), MSS Eur F177/5.

83 Ibid.

84 Emily Lorimer to her father and mother, 6 December 1911, MSS Eur F177/6.

85 Emily Lorimer to her brother Archie, 29 April 1911, MSS Eur F177/5.

86 Emily Lorimer to her father and mother, 27 September 1911, MSS Eur F177/6.

87 Emily Lorimer to her father, 12 September 1911, MSS Eur F177/6.

88 Emily Lorimer to her mother, 18 September 1911, MSS Eur F177/6.

89 Emily Lorimer to her mother and father, 20 June 1911, MSS Eur F177/5.

90 Emily Lorimer to her mother and father, 13 March 1911, MSS Eur F177/5.

91 Emily Lorimer to her father, 30 April 1911, MSS Eur F177/5.

92 Emily Lorimer to her father, 25 May 1911, MSS Eur F177/5.

93 Emily Lorimer to her father and mother, 18 July 1911, MSS F177/6.

94 Emily Lorimer to her father, 27 September 1911, MSS Eur F177/6.

95 Emily Lorimer to her father and mother, 19 November 1911, MSS Eur F177/6.

96 Helen Callaway, *Gender, Culture and Empire: European Women in Colonial Nigeria* (London: Macmillan, 1987).

97 Dorothy Sheridan, 'Getting on with Nella Last at the Barrow-in-Furness Red Cross Centre: romanticism and ambivalence in working with women's stories', *Women's History Notebooks*, 5 (1998), p. 3.

98 Obituary of Emily Overend Lorimer, 1881–1949, Somerville College Association of Senior Members, Twenty-Fourth Annual Supplement to the Report of the College, 1948–1949, MSS Eur F177/92.

3 Rival Narratives: American Missionaries in the Gulf, 1892–1914

Emily Lorimer's accounts of her experiences in Bahrain vividly illustrate the public formalities and private prejudices of British imperial life before the First World War. In spite of Emily's academic background and independent spirit, and in spite of the relative freedom provided by their out-of-the-way Arabian posting, the Lorimers, and their handful of British compatriots, strove to preserve the hierarchical and cultural boundaries of European imperial society. During the same period, however, an equally small group of American missionaries established themselves in the Gulf and challenged the British with their non-conformist attitudes to local people and their own relations with them and with each other.

The American Arabian Mission opened its first permanent station in Basra in August 1891, followed by bases in Bahrain in 1892 and Muscat in 1893.[1] In Kuwait a dispensary was set up in 1910, after several unsuccessful attempts to send workers there from 1894 onwards. On the Trucial Coast, regarded by Europeans and Americans as the most inaccessible area of the Gulf, the first of the Mission's bible sellers, or *colporteurs*, arrived in 1896, but although missionaries made increasingly regular visits, they did not maintain a permanent presence in any of the Trucial shaikhdoms before the Second World War.[2] However, with contingents at the head of the Gulf (in Basra and Kuwait), on the island of Bahrain, and on the Indian Ocean at Muscat, missionaries were soon able to make forays both inland and all along the Arabian coast of the Gulf.

The idea for the Mission originated in New Brunswick, New Jersey, in 1889. It was the brainchild of James Cantine, Philip Phelps and Samuel Zwemer, who was later to become Emily and David Lorimer's contemporary in Bahrain. All three were students at the Theological Seminary of the Reformed (Dutch) Church in America, and were supported in the project by their tutor, Dr John Lansing, Professor of Old Testament Language and Exegesis at the seminary. Following the late nineteenth-century expansion of American protestant missionary activity in Asia and Africa, the challenge of Arabia, the 'Cradle of Islam', attracted the men as the ultimate goal for Christian reformers.[3] Although sympathetically received by senior members of the Reformed Church, the proposal for an Arabian campaign, in territory traditionally regarded as inaccessible and unknown, was at first rejected by the church's Board of Foreign Missions. The official historians of the Arabian Mission, Alfred DeWitt Mason and Frederick J. Barny, later recalled that most people at the time believed the task to be hopeless because of the unfamiliarity of the region and because of the difficulty of attempting to subordinate the 'Crescent' to the 'Cross'.[4] More importantly, the board simply did not have the finances for a new undertaking on this scale. However, Lansing, who was born in the Middle East, in Damascus, and his three students remained determined and decided to carry on independently in the hope that the board would take up the project later. They wrote a plan, in August 1889, at Cantine's home where Lansing also composed the new, six-verse, Arabian Mission hymn, whose imagery of 'bondage', 'slavery' and 'neglect' provided a continuing justification and validation for urgent action on the part of both missionary workers and their financial supporters:

> There's a land long since neglected,
> There's a people still rejected,
> But of truth and grace elected,
> In His love for them.
> …To the host of Islam's leading.
> For the slave in bondage bleeding,
> To the desert dweller pleading,
> Bring His love to them…[5]

In October 1889 Cantine departed for Beirut to study Arabic, followed eight months later by Zwemer. Back in the US, Lansing and other supporters of the project eventually managed to raise money for the work and, in January 1891 the Mission was incorporated into the Reformed Church of America, eventually becoming a fully fledged Mission of the Church in 1894. Its aim was to 'crusade against Islam in Arabia' and the long-term objective, as set by its charter, was 'the evangelisation of Arabia', to be achieved by the 'occupation' of the interior, using the coast as a base.[6] In his 'Historical Sketch of the Arabian Mission', published in 1914, the Reverend J.E. Moerdyk later recalled that the 'first thought, and always the thought of those who belong to this Mission is to occupy

The Arabian Mission hymn

ESTHER CHALLIS

There's a land long since neglected,
There's a people still rejected
But of truth and grace elected,
  In His love for them.

Softer than their night winds fleeting,
Richer than their starry tenting,
Stronger than their sands protecting,
  Is His love for them.

To the host of Islams leading,
To the slave in bondage bleeding,
To the desert dweller pleading,
  Bring His love to them.

Through the promise on God's pages,
Through His work in history's stages
Through the Cross that crowns the ages,
  Show His love to them.

With the prayer that still availeth,
With the power that prevaileth,
With the love that never faileth,
  Tell His love to them.

Till the desert's sons now aliens,
Till its tribes and their dominions,
Till Arabia's raptured millions,
  Praise His love of them.

Prof. J. G. Lansing, 1889.

The Arabian Mission hymn, published in *Neglected Arabia*, 1915.

and hold Arabia with the purpose of remaining there until the people shall have received the Gospel and shall have Christ as their Saviour'.[7] Mason and Barny noted that the missionaries 'were never forgetful of this purpose'.[8] The military vocabulary and symbolism of the early years of the missionary 'campaign' were to be maintained throughout the Mission's

history, and aptly illustrated both male and female missionaries' own perspectives of themselves and the crusading nature of their activities.[9]

The aims and objectives of missionary work, and the methods of
working adopted by the missionaries themselves, inevitably gave rise to a
strikingly different colonial standpoint from that of the British officials
and their wives. The underlying motivation for the British presence in
Arabia and the Gulf was, for almost 350 years, economic and strategic.
It was concerned with protecting the Indian Empire and ensuring the
uninterrupted movement of men and materials between the metropolitan
government in London and the Government of India administrations in
Bengal, Bombay and Madras. As far as the British were concerned, until
the development of the oil industry in the early twentieth century, Gulf
policy was firmly limited to establishing and maintaining friendly diplomatic relations with the coastal rulers (backed up where necessary with
naval power) and avoiding any interference with internal local politics,
religion and culture, or any expansion into inland Arabia. In contrast,
missionary work was by definition a 'hands-on' activity, a quest to win
the hearts and minds of others, not simply by treaties and agreements expressing mutual self-interest, but by persuading converts of the superiority
of the missionaries' religion and way of life. Although in missionary circles
there was a continuing debate and a tension between the relative values
and priorities of the twin aims of exporting religion and culture, by the
early twentieth century the term 'evangelisation' had come to mean both
spreading the Gospel and the 'civilizing mission'. Like British imperialists,
the Americans believed themselves to be privileged, and duty-bound to
liberate the rest of the world by sharing, or imposing, their own religion
and culture on it.[10] In its own way, this world view, which the missionaries were to bring to Arabia, was just as inflexible and narrow-minded
as that of the British imperial and colonial administrators but it was
based on a different self-image, it produced a different way of living, and it
generated a different representation of Arabia and an alternative discourse,
or 'rival narrative' of colonial experience.

The most fundamental difference between the Americans and the British
was that, once up and running, American missionary operations came to
depend on the participation of women, both as active workers and as
passive examples of the cultural and social values being exported. In
Arabia this attitude contrasted sharply with the British view of the region
as a hard and unsuitable place for a woman, and it inevitably produced
tensions between the Americans and the local British administrators, the
latter fearful of upsetting the delicate balance, as they perceived it, of
British political and economic interests and local customs. The first four

years of the Arabian Mission, however, were a deliberately all-male pioneering reconnaissance. Women were not regarded as suitable candidates for forays into unknown territory, particularly before any of the Mission Boards had sanctioned women's work in Arabia.

By April 1892, and with the publication of their first official quarterly report, Cantine and Zwemer had established themselves at Basra, working with the help of locally appointed male *colporteurs*, selling bibles, conducting bible readings and visiting ships docked in the busy cosmopolitan port.[11] They had also set up a dispensary, which not only enabled them to fulfil their missionary commitment to bring concrete social change to the local population, but at the same time had provided a neutral environment in which to carry out religious teaching. Faced with hostility from the local Turkish authorities in Ottoman-administered Mesopotamia, Zwemer and Cantine readily admitted that medical work was 'the one phase of mission effort which is accepted on all sides without question'.[12] Three years later, in March 1895, with the help of Zwemer's brother, Reverend Peter J. Zwemer, the men were operating additional missionary stations and employing more *colporteurs* to work in Bahrain and Muscat. The *colporteurs*, entrusted with the basic work of selling bibles and scriptures, were usually set up in shops that also sold 'educational' books as a way of enticing customers inside.[13] However, the men were seriously stretched in coping with bases so far apart. Zwemer constantly harangued the board to send out a doctor to Bahrain, and complained that he was compelled, because of the lack of any doctor on the island, to act as a pseudo-medical practitioner himself, even though he had no qualifications. It was a confession which would have amused Emily Lorimer and confirmed her view of him as an intellectual poser but at the same time a basically humane and well-intentioned person.[14]

The trustees responded by sending out a doctor for the Basra station in the spring of 1895 and, gradually, with the support of subscribers in the US, they raised the funds for a cautious but determined expansion of the Arabian Mission's religious and medical activities. By 1897 Cantine was able to report that:

> our mission and its workers are known by name or sight in many a town between Baghdad and Aden…Now, not to speak of other stations, we have at Muscat a school, a printing-press, a Bible-shop and an accessible 'hinterland' large enough to satisfy the most ambitious. The hand of the Lord has indeed gone before us![15]

Nevertheless, a year later, reporting on the Arabian Mission's annual meeting, Fred Barny newly arrived at Basra, noted that the meeting numbered only four men, while the Mission 'has a field with over a thousand miles of coast line, with millions of dying souls to be reached'.[16] Given the perceived urgency of the need for 'reinforcements' and given the wider history of the Reformed Church's female missionary activities, there was never any serious doubt that ultimately women would be involved in the work and, more particularly, in the development of a specific mission for women. As in India and China and the African missions, women's activities in the Gulf were required to be channelled in three main directions: teaching, the provision of Western medical care and visiting and socialising, all three of which activities would be imbued equally with an unabashed evangelism.

American missionaries accepted and encouraged women to join in the missionary project for a variety of reasons. Primarily women were needed for 'women's work', that is, for work with women, and in particular, for work with women in the secluded environment of their own homes, which, especially in Muslim countries, were often inaccessible to men. Missionary women were also recognised as having a softening effect on the appearance of missionary 'armies', helping to give the impression of 'peaceful intent' rather than aggression.[17] Finally, and not least, simply by accompanying their male husbands and colleagues, women could be displayed as living examples of Western, Christian, domestic harmony and modernity. In the years after the American Civil War, missionary activities had became increasingly feminised, with the founding of new female agencies and the growth of women's participation in the general missionary boards (itself a reflection of the influence of the earliest generation of college graduates). By the 1890s the married women attached to the general missionary boards and the single women sponsored by the women's boards together composed 60 percent of the mission force.[18]

The career opportunities provided by missionary work for middle-class women in Britain and the US have been widely examined.[19] The work primarily offered an intellectual and physical outlet for both independent single women and independently minded married women. Without threatening domestic family values, it offered them opportunities to travel, study new languages and establish and participate in women's groups. In particular, it widened the scope of teaching opportunities and opened up medical work for women when possibilities at home were still severely limited. Moreover, Christianity itself was seen by American Protestants to be empowering for women, providing them with a self-confidence and separate identity outside the home. At a time when British missionary organisations, for example the London Missionary Society, were still firmly defining women as mere adjuncts to a masculine activity,

American female missionaries appear to have regarded themselves, and certainly publicised themselves, as equals. Publicly, at least, they were described as such by their male partners and colleagues.[20] Dr Marion Wells Thoms, for example, the first female doctor in Bahrain, was described, on her early death in 1905, as 'not merely a missionary's wife, but herself a heroic and strong and self-denying missionary'.[21]

The Protestant American missionary enterprise was grounded in New England non-conformity. Both men and women shared a common, non-establishment social and educational background. To a certain extent they were outsiders in relation to the American 'ruling class' and this gave them all a flexibility and readiness to disregard colonial, and imperial, social conventions when they worked out in the field. Generally brought up in small-town, middle-class families, most women, as well as men, were, by the late nineteenth century, college educated, and many had trained as teachers, nurses or doctors. Furthermore, although the missionary project was originally an East Coast movement, by the 1890s there was a large number of women from farming families in the Mid-West who person-ified the 'pioneering spirit' of their upbringing and who often cited the freedom of their growing up as a reason for their calling.[22] Often there was a strong family precedent of missionary work, which offered women modest economic security and opportunity for achievement abroad and renown at home:

> Missionary work offered the independence, status and opportunity for achievement associated with a profession, but it was not a profession. As a calling it was characterized by a rhetoric of self-denial rather than of personal ambition. Unlike the 'professional woman', who in popular turn-of-the-century parlance had cast off her feminine nature to adopt the hard competitiveness of the world of men, the missionary woman placed feminine qualities of empathy at the center of her lifework. Rather than withdrawing into herself, she identified with all humanity. Missionary women…shared many of the needs that led women into the professions; but they had one unique need – to clothe their ambition in a garb which did no violence to their sense of feminine Christian virtue.[23]

Of the most active women missionaries in Arabia before the First World War, over half were either born or educated in the Mid-West. Dr Elizabeth DePree Cantine was born in Iowa; Dr Marion Wells Thoms was born Summitt, Minnesota, and Jessie Vail Bennett was born in Michigan. Thoms and Bennett were educated at the University of Michigan, as was Dr Anna Christine Iverson Bennett, although the latter was born in Denmark.[24] In 1911, through work with the Student Volunteer Movement, Samuel Zwemer persuaded the University of Michigan to establish the 'University of Michigan Scheme for Medical and Industrial Work at Basrah', which subsequently sponsored both male and female medical missionaries in the Arabian field.[25]

In keeping with their educational backgrounds and their determination and sense of purpose, American Protestant missionaries in Asia and Africa were generally expected to follow an additional training programme before they were allowed to practise in the field. In the Middle East this programme included thorough language training. A good working knowledge of Arabic was recognised as a prerequisite for missionary activity and, once the Mission had been firmly established, every new arrival, male or female, was expected not only to study the language but also to pass a set of rigorous exams, often taken at the missionaries' annual regional conference.[26] Mason and Barny described a two-year course of study that included spoken and written Arabic and 'Islamics', and they noted that the missionaries, however short of new recruits, always avoided the temptation to put new arrivals to work at once.[27] Dr Eleanor T. Calverley, for example, with a degree from the Women's Medical College of Pennsylvania in Philadelphia, arrived in Arabia with her husband, the Reverend Edwin Calverley, in 1909. In her autobiography she describes spending their first year of language study in Bahrain and the second year in Basra, after which they returned to Bahrain in the autumn of 1911 for the Annual Meeting of the Arabian Mission. There, together with a few other new missionaries, they both passed their language examinations and were then appointed to the newly opened Mission in Kuwait.[28]

The first 'American' woman missionary in the Gulf was in fact a British woman, Amy Elizabeth Wilkes Zwemer. Born in Wolverhampton, she was a trained nurse and worked for the Church Missionary Society in Baghdad where she met Samuel Zwemer, whom she married in May 1896. Emily Lorimer later described her as a 'sane practical-minded corrective to her husband'.[29] On their marriage, Mrs Zwemer was appointed to the Arabian Mission, having been released from her contract with the English Society after the Americans had refunded her travel costs. Mason and Barny recalled that 'it became a joke among the missionaries to say that "Mr Zwemer had obtained a wife in true Oriental fashion by buying her from her former people"'.[30] Eleanor Calverley regarded it as a 'great day for the Arabian Mission when the first woman missionary took her place among its membership':

> There were to be no women in the mission, our pioneers had decided. They thought that the field was not ready for women and that the Arabian living conditions were too hard for them. Cupid smiled when he heard that decision, for he was not of the same opinion. And then, suddenly, one of our

pioneers changed his mind (though he was a man, or, perhaps, because he was a man), and he realized that the work needed nothing so much as the life of a certain young lady now known to you all as Mrs Zwemer.[31]

On her move to Basra shortly after her marriage, Amy Zwemer assisted Dr Henry Worrall in the local dispensary and she also launched the Mission's programme of 'work among women'. She reported to the trustees on the particular urgency of the task ahead:

> And so we are praying for and expecting that this awful mountain of Islam will be removed soon; and especially for the sake of our Muslim sisters, who suffer many things, not knowing the pure, perfect liberty in Christ Jesus our Lord. We can only speak of the *possibilities* of work amongst women in these parts, because of our recent arrival among them. The vista is a wide one, and needs to supply its need the army of women spoken of in Ps[alm] 68...The ground is very hard and full of weeds, both of their own superstitions, and those of the Eastern Churches. But they are grateful for kindness shown them; and even a kind word will draw out most of them. At the dispensary many were roused and touched by the Word spoken, and by the demonstration of its teaching in good deeds done to their bodies...As the medical work progresses there may be a possibility of gathering the women into a separate room, and having separate Bible lessons with them. Such an audience is shifting and uncertain, as some of them are never seen again... My difficulty just at present is my limited knowledge of Arabic, and I ask most heartily the prayers of my sisters in America, that I may soon have this gift of the Holy Spirit, so that I may tell with no uncertain sound the love of God, revealed in Christ. There are open doors and the work is great...[32]

The first day of June 1896, said Mason and Barny, should surely be 'a red-letter day in the calendar of this Mission and indeed of all Christian Missions in Arabia, as the date whereon the first systematic and prolonged effort for the evangelization of the women of Arabia by the women of America was begun by Mrs Zwemer'.[33] Back home in the US, the Woman's Board of Foreign Missions, originally doubtful and reluctant to support women's work in Arabia, gradually increased its interest and, by 1918, had assumed support of the work of the Mission for women as a whole.[34]

The background of the late-nineteenth-century health-reform movement in the US, and middle-class women's involvement in it, provided the context for the concerned reforming attitudes of women missionaries, with their emphasis on public health, personal cleanliness and family hygiene. In the Protestant missionary catechism, cleanliness was close to Godliness, and the perceived uncleanliness (in both a moral and a physical sense) of uncivilised 'other' lands provided a compelling justification for humanitarian as well as evangelising efforts. Women missionaries were convinced of the superiority of Western medicine and were also influenced by American health-reform attitudes, which encouraged individual responsibility for personal health and hygiene.[35] The inevitable corollary of this crusading confidence was of course a criticism of traditional local, in this case Muslim, family life and medicine and what the missionaries saw as religious fatalism and acceptance of barbaric practices. The dispensary, with its captive audience, was therefore unequivocally regarded as a site for education as well as medicine, and for the simultaneous dispensation of religious as well as social advice and exhortation. After the appointment of Henry Worrall as the first doctor at Basra in 1895, Samuel Zwemer commented that by opening the dispensary for a few hours a day 'we gain an audience for the Gospel'.[36] Women, he believed, were an essential part of the Christian mission because they would be welcomed everywhere, 'with or without medical qualifications'. Lady Anne Blunt and Mabel Bent had proved what women could do in Arabia 'for the sake of science'; surely, then, there would be Christian women who would 'penetrate as far inland for the sake of their Saviour'.[37] Thirty years later, in their book on *Moslem Women*, the Zwemers reflected on the early, and continuing, need for medical work to combat what they still saw as the ignorance and cruelties of Muslim life and, at the same time, described the work as a powerful evangelising agency: it was 'a means of influencing individuals at the time when they are grateful for physical benefits received and kindness shown, and hearts are particularly open to receive the Gospel'. It was aptly called 'the entering wedge'.[38] Even Eleanor Calverley, much more of a practical and tolerant professional than either of the Zwemers, noted that it was fortunate that Amy Zwemer, 'whose privilege it was to take the Word of Life to the Arab women, for the first time', was a medical missionary, because without her nurse's training she would never have been able to break down the wall of prejudice and hatred.[39]

After moving to Bahrain in 1897, Amy Zwemer assisted in dispensary work there until the arrival of Dr Marion Wells Thoms and her husband, Dr Sharon Thoms, in the autumn of 1900. The Thoms had worked at Basra for the previous year, but had been waiting for permission from the Shaikh of Bahrain to acquire premises for a doctor's house and hospital on the island. By the end of 1901, after eight months of regular medical work for women, Marion Wells Thoms had treated 1631 women and children, mostly in the dispensary but including a handful of in-patient surgical cases and numerous house visits. At the same time, repeated visits from many women had given Dr Wells Thoms, assisted by Amy Zwemer, opportunities to read the Gospel to a captive audience.[40] Aside from the evangelising, however, there is no doubt that, because of their policy of employing qualified and well-trained doctors and nurses, the first missionaries were very soon able to provide an effective medical programme to combat some of the most prevalent diseases in the area. Eye infections were common, malaria was endemic throughout the Gulf, as was tuberculosis, and, in Bahrain, large numbers of pearl divers suffered from ear problems and emphysema caused by their long dives under water.[41] Missionary doctors and nurses were always well-educated and, in keeping with their confidence and pride in Western science and technology, the board and its supporters actively encouraged field-workers to keep abreast of new medical advances. When the two doctors Thoms and their children returned to Basra from furlough, in 1904, they were described in the *Quarterly Report* as having been 'wisely engaged in such medical study as they needed to keep themselves in touch with the thought and practice of the day…'.[42]

In Muscat, medical work for women was begun between 1904 and 1907 by Elizabeth DePree Cantine, the first single woman to be appointed to the Mission before her marriage to one of its founders, James Cantine. A women's dispensary was finally built in Muscat in 1913 and the following year the first woman doctor, Sarah Hosman, was appointed. Meanwhile Dr Emma Hodge Worrall, whose husband Amy Zwemer had worked with on her arrival at Basra, was appointed for women's medical work there in 1904, and began work on the ground floor of the Basra Mission building. Soon afterwards a 'Bible Woman' was employed to read to patients and lead prayers in the waiting area. There were no nurses and no facilities for in-patients, but Dr Henry Worrall carried out emergency cases such as amputation of the arm after shark bites, the treatment of stab wounds and cancer operations, while Emma Worrall was relegated to nursing patients as his assistant.[43] Later, an Indian Christian nurse was appointed and new premises acquired. A large bequest from America eventually subsidised the completion of the Lansing Hospital in 1911. Although the hospital at first contained only a very small space for women, in the first year the Worralls treated 93 female in-patients and provided over seven thousand treatments for women in the dispensary. Emma Worrall reported the improvement since the years before the hospital opened, when, because of their inadequate finances, the two doctors had been forced to make utensils out of oil tins.[44]

In 1911, Worrall described the Basra dispensary as the 'place of a thousand sorrows' encompassing diseases and injuries ranging from eye and ear infections, skin diseases and dog bites, to consumption and post-puerperal septicaemia, and including, not least, the ignorance of mothers about how to care for their children.[45] While there is no doubt that the missionaries provided much-needed and effective medical care, they continued to blame what they regarded as the dismal state of local health care on fatalism and isolation encouraged by Islam, in particular criticising Muslim women's ignorance of 'modern' health care management. Furthermore they linked their own ability to provide competent treatment as much to Christ as to their own medical training. Caring for the patients was seen as a preliminary to bringing them to God. As Worrall concluded: '…as each day dawns we cannot help but think, another day of privilege, of opportunity to relieve poor sick ones of the intolerable burden of suffering, and point them to Christ':

> So much for their ailing bodies. How about their poor sin-sick souls, so dark with lives so full of jealousy, envy and strife! Of the peace of God they Know not nor understand what it is. How can we explain it to them? How can we raise the curtain and let the light shine in?[46]

Back in Bahrain, the Mason Memorial Hospital was opened in 1903. Eventually, women's medical work began in Kuwait with the arrival there of Eleanor Calverley, Kuwait's first woman doctor, in 1912. Between 1910 and 1914 the medical work undertaken by both male and female missionaries more than doubled, with 31,355 treatments carried out in 1910, and twice as many in 1914, with 23,709 new cases reported.[47]

While Western-style learning was seen to be a fundamental part of medical and health care, traditional education in the wider sense was also a prime objective of the Arabian Mission. Mason and Barny noted that school education should ideally achieve a golden mean between what is wanted by prospective pupils and 'what ought to be'; they defined 'what ought to be' as a high standard of scholastic attainment and also as character-building.[48] By 1901 the Zwemers had set up a girls' school in Bahrain, and its curriculum consisted of classes in Bible, arithmetic, reading, writing and geography (taught in Arabic), classes in English conversation and reading, arts, crafts, physical exercises and sewing. Amy Zwemer described her pupils' dress as ranging 'from rag-tag to velvet gowns embroidered with gold braid'.[49] The school opened at eight o'clock in the morning with a hymn and a prayer, followed by writing, spelling, composition and arithmetic. After the scripture lesson the older girls wrote out 'portions of Scripture from memory, like the Lord's Prayer in Arabic or the order of the day's work in creation'. They also learned to hem and over-sew 'neatly, a thing unheard of before in this country'. The Arab women and girls did 'fancy work, gold lace and braid, and silk needle-work for their dresses' but, Zwemer added, 'their plain sewing is very bad and careless'. Discussions of sewing evoked potent visual images of tawdry Oriental opulence and Western modernity and fastidiousness.

In Muscat, Elizabeth DePree Cantine, as well as setting up the daily clinic, also opened a sewing school for girls and began a programme of house visits. Of these three areas of work, the house visitation was accorded at least equal status by the missionaries. House visitation, in its broadest sense, included also receiving visitors 'at home', conducting prayer meetings and opening Sunday schools. Personal contacts and friendship were thought to be the most important ways to win hearts, and the missionaries convinced themselves that Arab women were inspired simply by seeing and mixing with women who were 'happy and free and secure'.[50] The female missionaries' reports of their visits to Arab women's homes consistently described to their audiences and financial supporters in America the sadness and brutality of Arab life and the missionary belief in the power of the Gospel to bring light into those homes. An 1899 field report printed a 'diary' of Amy Zwemer, which subtly reproduced these contrasting images:

> Jan. 24, visited two houses and saw and talked with seven woman and many children. They are all fasting and so I had a conversation about the true fast. Fasting from sin is more pleasing to God than to fast for a month from food.
>
> Jan.25, visited three new huts. The owner of the house and of the women came in while I was there, such a gruff man, they seemed very much afraid of him and of having me there. I talked cheerfully to the gentleman in answer to his questions, but was half afraid of him myself. In these three huts I met ten women, none of whom could read. Attended to one sick woman, fever and eye-disease, and she seemed most grateful.
>
> Jan. 26–28, five women came; visited six others. Had an open-air meeting on the desert sand, sitting on the low wall of a small mosque. About ten women and half a dozen children. Spoke of the evils of the veil and the love of God.
>
> Mar. 17, in the last few days some thirty-three women and children came. Most of them cannot read. Some of the women asked me why I left my native land if it was as good as I told them? They cannot understand our motive. There is no all-overpowering love in their religion. Unselfishness is not found in Islam.[51]

In contrast to the British imperial view of the unsuitability for women of 'hardship' posts, missionaries, once the first forays into unknown territory had been made, regarded visible Christian family life, and the mutual support and comfort of wives and children, as a central pillar of their work, particularly in harsh and difficult circumstances. The fact that fieldwork and related studies might conflict with wives' domestic duties was openly recognised, and added a double burden, as well as glory, to their calling. After settling in Bahrain in 1898, Samuel Zwemer lost no time in reporting to the American trustees and supporters that 'Woman's work for Women' was extremely demanding, especially in places such as

Bahrain 'where civilization is so primitive [and] a hundred household cares, which in India can be delegated to servants, take up a woman's time and strength'.[52] Nevertheless, missionary wives were fully prepared to take on such a burden. Many of them were deeply religious women who chose their husbands, or whose husbands chose them, as marriage partners on the basis of a shared belief in their religious calling. Eleanor Calverley, for example, recalled in detail in her autobiography the steps she took in making her decision to become a medical missionary: first she decided she wanted to be a doctor, then, when she was at medical school, she met returnee missionary doctors who talked of their experiences.[53] Calverley realised there were opportunities for women doctors in 'countries where women were secluded', but she hesitated, waiting for a message from God. Once she had 'felt the Presence of God' she then had to pray for guidance on whether it would be acceptable to marry and have children because she could not imagine having to do without. Meeting her husband, Edwin, who was already preparing to go to the Arabian Gulf, was a further 'calling'. In September 1909 she married him, and in October they sailed together from Philadelphia, via Europe, to Bombay and the Gulf.

Married missionary women, like Eleanor Calverley, pursued apparently fulfilling careers at the same time as running the home, but without ever questioning the differences between their professional lives and their domestic relationships. Calverley, for example, also admitted that before she and her husband left America her father had told her: 'Have your ambition for him and not for yourself'; but, she added, it was 'not at all because of any personal ambition that he [Edwin] was coming to Kuwait. He was coming now to serve among Muslims for what he could give, not to get anything for himself'.[54] Paradoxically, as Jane Hunter has pointed out, the fact that so many women were working in the missionary field in the last decades of the nineteenth century had led the male missionary hierarchies in America to feel the need to remind women of their place. Hunter quotes an 1888 conference speech made by the Secretary of the American Baptist Missionary Union:

> Woman's work in the foreign field must be careful to recognize the headship of man in ordering the affairs of the Kingdom of God. We must not allow the major vote of the better sex, nor the ability and efficiency of so many of our female helpers, nor even the exceptional faculty for leadership and organization which some of them have displayed in their work, to discredit the natural and predestined headship of man in Missions, as well as in the Church of God: and 'the head of woman is the man'.[55]

This 'headship of man' was accepted largely without question by missionary couples. In spite of their encouragement of missionary 'woman's work', they still regarded the domestic role as the primary one for women, and they did not advocate any radical social change in their private, domestic relationships. On the contrary, they repeatedly offered their own marital status, and the late-Victorian glorification of motherhood, as the ideal to which other religions and cultures should aspire. Mason and Barny described the centrality of the Christian female, and her dual function as activist and passive role-model in the missionary project:

> It is the custom in missionary literature to accord separate treatment to work among women and there is ample reason for so doing. However, should this be carried too far, some may fall into the habit of regarding it as a department or feature of a mission's activity. Certainly in the Arabian Mission it is neither, but is of the very essence of its work. It is possible that the Mission may some day decide to give up all medical work or all educational work, but so long as its objective is the evangelization of the people of Arabia, so long must its work for women and men go parallel. This fact is here recognized. In its councils as in its practice, this parity or rather oneness of its work has always been recognized and further, since no people can rise above the condition of its motherhood, it is also recognized that until the Gospel gets into the harems no movement towards Christianity can be expected.[56]

At the same time, however, the burden of the workload on married women, and the need to recruit single women for certain areas of work, was eventually recognised, in spite of some early reluctance both at home and in the field. In 1902 the report of the missionaries' annual meeting discussed the subject of 'reinforcements' for Arabia and emphasised the need for single women:

> The married ladies of the Mission have done what they could (some of them hazarding health in doing more than they should) to meet opportunities golden and direct calls of necessity for help. Hitherto and now we have not had any one who could devote all her time to work among women. Conditions in Arabia are less hard for single ladies than for those who are married. Socially and morally we who are on the ground can see no objection whatever to their work among Moslem women, and there is every prospect of blessing. We know we have lost golden opportunities in the past ten years by not having a staff of single lady missionaries such as is working in many other Moslem lands under similar conditions as face us in Arabia.[57]

The report also noted the fact that the trustees had withdrawn earlier objections to the sending out of unmarried women and that the Woman's Board had agreed to bear the cost of supporting one and possibly more female missionaries.[58]

The first single female missionary appointed to the Arabian Mission was Elizabeth DePree (later Cantine), who arrived in Basra in 1902. By the eve of World War I, in September 1914, there were fifteen women working in the Gulf area, of whom eleven were married and four were single: three wives (Cantine, Barny and Dykstra) were carrying out 'Evangelistic Work'; two single women (Scardefield and Lutton) were responsible for 'Women's Evangelical Work'; one wife (Amy Zwemer, studying with her husband in Cairo) was described as doing 'Literary Work'; three wives were listed as doing 'General Medical Work' (Worrall, Bennett and Mylrea), and one wife and one single woman (Calverley and Hosmon) as doing 'Women's Medical Work'; one wife (Van Peursem) was Superintendent of the Mason Memorial Hospital in Bahrain; one wife (Van Ess) was engaged in 'Educational Work'; one wife and one single woman (Van Vlack and Schaftheitlin) were on language study.[59]

Even so, missionary work for women had never been, and was still not, easy to get into. In areas like the Arabian Peninsula the work required physical fitness, courage and stamina. The training, including proficiency in local languages, was as exacting for women as it was for men, and the work itself was presented as both physically and intellectually demanding. As Jessie Vail Bennett, in Bahrain, described it in 1905, the 'religion of Islam, which we have come to combat, has been aptly compared to a mountain [which]...looms up before us'; and the language training, she noted, had a wider importance than the technical ability to understand mere words:

> One of the first difficulties which the new missionary must face in any foreign country is, naturally, the native language, and it is doubtless a great advantage to the work that one cannot rush into service immediately upon entering the field, for two years of language study give the missionary time and opportunity to learn the peculiar mind and customs of the people among whom he is to spend his life.[60]

Bennett was a graduate of the Literary Department of the University of Michigan, and had taught in Michigan schools. She volunteered for the Arabian Mission together with her husband, and subsequently taught English in the small Bahrain school and visited women in their homes. In January 1906, however, she died of typhoid, one of the early victims of the harsh physical circumstances of missionary life in the Gulf.[61]

The physical cost of the work was undoubtedly high. However, although maintaining good health was a major problem, the women missionaries, like the men, exhibited great physical strength and tenacity, often succumbing to illness but never considering the possibility of a retreat. Mrs Bennett's dying words were recorded in the *Quarterly Report* as 'Tell the

Board I am going to be a missionary up yonder and to send someone in my place'.[62] A few months earlier, Dr Marion Wells Thoms, who had worked in Bahrain since 1899, also died, having 'worked above her strength for her Arabian sisters' and having always displayed 'skill and patience as a physician, her faithfulness in language study' and 'her self-effacement and humility'. Wells Thoms was also reported as uttering, among her last words, the plea for more missionaries to take the place of those who fall by the way.[63] That the Missionary Boards were continually able to find women to take the place of their predecessors was not just a consequence of the usefulness of the career choice for independent-minded but socially conformist women. It was also a reflection of deeply held beliefs about the rightness and righteousness of the cause. Missionary women all fervently believed that Christianity and woman's emancipation were inextricably linked and that, with their help, Christ could bring Arab women to the light.

In a 1903 article pleading for more women workers for Arabia, Marion Wells Thoms provided her readers back home with a harsh description of Islam's subjection of women, contrasted with the Christian Gospel of Jesus, 'the One who honored women'.[64] Thoms's article captured the missionaries' continuing attitude to Muslim women, ranging over the 'living death of thousands of Arab women', the 'ignorance, superstition and sensuality' of the harem, the 'absolute dominion' of men in relation to divorce, and the consequent need to teach them that there is a 'higher and better life'. Month by month and year by year, from Amy Zwemer onwards, missionary women sent back to America a growing catalogue of misery and bondage, which they invariably contrasted to the Christian way of life. In Josephine E. Spaeth's 1911 description of 'Arab Home Life' in Bahrain, for example, the author drew a complacent comparison between domestic life in Arabia and 'home life' in America:

> Home life has such sacred and holy memories that to us it can only be associated with the highest virtues and the purest morals. Without them it is no more home life. Home life associates one's thoughts immediately with a place where peace and love reign. Father, mother, or children are bound together by these holy ties...Our Christian home spells 'Union and Unity.' The Arab home spells 'Division and Separation'.
>
> Upon visiting an Arab home the first thing we notice after getting inside the dead, windowless walls, is division. A special place, the harem, is reserved for the women. No matter how much luxury we find in the harem, we may be certain that it is inferior to the men's quarter...
>
> ...Few Arab women I have met seem happy. When one visits them at first, they often appear content; they will entertain cheerfully and are always

hospitable. It is sometimes only after a series of visits, and after they are convinced of the sincerity of our friendship and love for them, that they have confidence enough to unburden their hearts.[65]

In the same year Samuel Zwemer acted as convener and chairman of the second international and interdenominational 'Conference on Missions to Moslems' held in India at Lucknow.[66] The conference was attended by over three hundred delegates from missions in India, Central Asia, Africa, China and the Middle East, including Persia, Turkey, Egypt, Palestine, Syria and the Arabian Peninsula, and it laid particular emphasis on work among Muslim women. Among the conference resolutions was a call for the urgent help of Christian women for the 'evangelisation and uplifting of Moham-medan women who, with their little children, constitute the larger part of the Moslem world'.[67] The conference recommended that Missionary Boards sending out both men and women should take steps to ensure that 'both sexes are reached in every mission station through the fullest co-operation between the workers', and that training colleges for women missionaries should lay particular stress on training for work among women.

Amy Zwemer was fired with the same evangelical zeal as her husband and their beliefs, as a missionary couple, which seem to have remained consistent throughout their lives, were described in their many publi-cations and reports, including their book, *Moslem Women*, which was published later in their lives, in 1926, while they were both living and working in Cairo.[68] *Moslem Women*, which summarises the Zwemers' lifetime crusade, described the 'plight' of Muslim women as a 'tragic story' and one which the Zwemers and their colleagues regarded as encapsulated by the wearing of the 'veil'. In the foreword to the book, the all-female group from the Committee on the United Study of Foreign Missions urged their readers to redouble their efforts against the rapid expansion of Islam in the world: 'We think with pity and sorrow of the veiled women of Islam. Is there not equal tragedy in the veil which hangs before our eyes, preventing us from realization or understanding of the vast need?'[69] The symbolism of the veil as a vehicle for, and outward badge of, oppression permeates the literature of the missionaries, and was fuelled by the continuing and fervently held belief that their own lives and social relations, elevated both by Christianity and also by Western (American) culture, were unquestionably preferable and fulfilling by comparison. Islam was described in no uncertain terms as a religion of darkness and oppression, a system which 'puts God's sanction on slavery, warfare, cruelty, polygamy, concubinage, unrestricted divorce, the seclusion and oppression of women'.[70] In contrast, Christianity was perceived as a religion of light.

Throughout the pre-World War I and post-war years, missionaries continued to regard the liberation of Muslim women as one of their most important missions and they firmly believed in the power of the Gospel to stimulate Muslim women to change. At the same time, by continually comparing and contrasting themselves with the 'lesser and inferior femininity' of native women, female missionaries were able constantly to redefine, elevate and reinforce their own status in both the colonial project and domestic society.[71] In pursuit of these objectives, the American missionaries, unlike the British, felt very little sense of distance, contamination, or danger in making direct contact with local people. The missionary men, at least in their published reports, did not express fears or hesitation about their women being alone with local Arab men, and the women themselves rarely expressed the sense of revulsion evident from some of the memsahibs' writings. On the contrary, direct contact was absolutely necessary to enable them to carry out their work, and they always felt themselves protected by their strong sense of God's presence. Amy Zwemer's 1899 diary recorded her everyday activities in Bahrain which included visiting Bahraini families and walking out with her young daughter:

> Jan. 1st, four women called; talked to them about Christianity and played the little organ. Jan. 5th, I visited the house of Sheikh S-; had a good time reading and talking to the crowd of women about Christ. May the Holy Spirit use His own word. Jan. 6th, took Katharina for a walk. Some rough boys and men followed and tried to throw stones at us, but by skillful manoeuvring I avoided their missiles. Jan. 8–18th, women came in numbers day by day, some to visit, others for medicine…Feb. 8, visited the girls school (Moslem) and had another talk with the children…Visited two houses, several women in each…Feb. 22, visited eight houses and saw forty women and children as well as some of the men. Had a most interesting time…Feb. 23, seven women came this morning. Visited a village in the afternoon…[72]

Eleanor Calverley's autobiographical descriptions of her relationships with local Arabs, although undoubtedly recounted with the benefit of hindsight, display a concern about 'doing the right thing', which contrasts starkly with Emily Lorimer's distaste at the social habits of her guests. When the Calverleys moved into their own house, for example, Eleanor planned her first dinner party for Arab women, and she describes details about cooking Arab food, how she made sure that her male servant, Hassan, waited outside to avoid the women having to meet him, and how she had to be careful to eat with her fingers and her right hand. She also describes trying to emulate her guest, Laila, rather than the other way round, and she makes a seemingly unquestioning assumption that she should show respect for local social habits.[73] Calverley also brought up her children in Kuwait, as did many of her missionary contemporaries. Two of the Zwemers' four young children died in Bahrain, within a week of each other, in 1904, and the dangers of sickness were always balanced against the unhappiness of family separations.[74] Calverley wrote that her children 'had a happy and normal childhood in Kuwait':

> As soon as they were old enough they had roller skates and skated from end to end of our long veranda … Socially we had many good times. Our family seized upon every opportunity for having a party … When the children grew older Dr Mylrea took them to his roof and taught them about the stars … [75]

Calverley went on to describe the special pleasures of springtime when the flowers bloomed. Arab families went out into the desert and women 'reveled in the freedom of going about unveiled'.[76] Sometimes the Calverleys would be invited to spend the day, and their children would enjoy camel rides and playing with the Arab children. Afterwards (after dinner) they would visit the women's tents. 'It never took long for us women to get acquainted,' she wrote; 'we had so much in common – especially those of us who were mothers.'[77] As well as family outings, Calverley was also invited to women's picnics and indoor gatherings:

> It pleased us greatly to find ourselves accepted as among those to be invited to such gatherings of Arab women. The outward circumstances of our lives differed in many ways from those of our Muslim friends. But friendship was gradually surmounting any barriers that the strangeness of our customs might have raised.[78]

Calverley concluded that she and her husband had made the right decision to bring up their children with them in the Gulf:

> Edwin and I may have wondered in earlier years whether our children might find themselves handicapped later in life because of long separation from the land of their heritage. It seems to us now, as we think back, that the advantages they enjoyed far outweighed any possible disadvantages. They themselves now speak with loving nostalgia of their childhood spent among the Arabs. For them, as for us, those were years of rich privilege.[79]

This proximity to the Arab population, and in particular to the ruling élite, gave rise to initial difficulties with the British imperial administrators in the Gulf and was eventually to produce serious political rifts.[80] At the beginning of the missionary enterprise, the missionaries, at least, felt comfortable and, to a certain extent protected, by the presence of the British agents on the Gulf coast. The British, however, were immediately suspicious of the Americans' intentions and doubtful about their political sensitivity. One of the major conflicts with the British arose from the missionaries' early and ongoing objective to 'occupy Arabia'.[81] The military metaphor aptly described the seriousness of this objective and helps to explain the hostility it aroused in the local British officials, who continued to pursue a long-term policy of non-interference with inland politics. While staying on the edge themselves, the British were unhappy when other people waded into forbidden territory. The activities of American missionary women, who were able to reach into parts of Arab society completely unknown to the British and their own socially segregated memsahibs, were later seen to be particularly threatening.[82]

In the early years, however, the British regarded their transatlantic rivals with a certain amount of condescension, and they professed to be neutral as to the missionaries' activities, while at the same time continuing to be paternally protective of the local shaikhs. In 1910 the Political Resident at Bushire wrote to the Agent at Kuwait, Captain Shakespear, about the invitation given to Dr Bennett by the Shaikh of Kuwait:

> Our attitude with regard to Missions is…one of neutrality – as a rule benevolent neutrality – but we don't try to force them on an unwilling Sheikh. If Sheikh Mubarek invites them it is his own look out, but when once the doctor is installed, no doubt others will follow…Let us hope the Sheikh won't fall out with them later and want us to help him to turn them out, for we shall not be able to help him. Once in they will always be with him like the poor.[83]

Shakespear's own opinion was that it would help to strengthen the British position in Kuwait:

> It will have a civilizing influence generally, and the reports of its work gradually spreading among the wild tribes of the desert cannot fail to enhance the existing English reputation for charity, justice and good Government, for even well-educated Arabs can hardly differentiate between the British and American nations.[84]

Furthermore, the fact that the Americans were able to penetrate local Arab society also made them useful to the British as unsuspecting political informants.[85]

Jane Hunter has argued that, for the Americans, the British represented a constant source of reference and a perpetual challenge in the early twentieth century when the former were struggling to acquire a sense of international stature:

> Troubled by feelings of social inadequacy in their dealings with the Old World, Americans built their case for their national culture on the superiority of

American democratic political instincts. Their critique of the British empha-
sized English authoritarianism, rigidity and arrogance – all results of the
British class system which Americans found so threatening.[86]

Most Americans thought the British were 'overly obedient to those above
them', and they were shocked by the British treatment of those below
them.[87] Certainly they failed to understand or sympathise with British
snobbishness and they found some of their local behaviour positively
curious. Eleanor Calverley's description of dinner with Captain Shakespear
expressed good humour but amazement:

> Social evenings at the consulate had been good for our morale. For one thing
> they gave us a chance to wear evening clothes…[Captain Shakespear's]
> household functioned with such smoothness and efficiency that seldom was
> a word from him needed, either to the cook, a native of Goa in South India,
> or to the North India butler. The latter in immaculate starched white
> uniform served the elaborate course dinners on a candle-lighted table,
> gleaming with damask, silver and crystal. Under an urbane and debonair
> exterior Captain Shakespear was determined not to permit the fact that he
> lived alone, in a place isolated from his fellow-countrymen, to make him
> careless and uncouth. It was said that even when touring in the desert, he
> always dressed for dinner and expected the butler to set his table with
> exactly the right kind of glass for each variety of drink.[88]

That the sympathy was not entirely reciprocated, however, can be seen
from Emily Lorimer's diaries and her accounts of the Americans' constant
failure to live up to British standards of imperial social etiquette.[89] Such
condescending behaviour was to be to some extent demolished by the
First World War, as were the political and social certainties of both British
and Americans and the political and social balance in their relations both
with each other and with local society.[90]

Recent academic work on missionary activities has demonstrated the
complex relationship between imperial or colonial administrators and
missionaries in both Africa and Asia.[91] In their preface to *Women and
Missions*, Deborah Kirkwood and Shirley Ardener argue that colonial
activities and missionary activities should not be treated as if one were a
branch of the other:

> Sometimes missionaries identified with local people and their traditions in
> opposition to Colonial Office policies; often missionary health and education
> programmes advanced colonial objectives; sometimes missionaries were critic-
> ised for tampering with traditional customs by administrators who wished
> to preserve them.[92]

In the same book, Fiona Bowie suggests that the related question of
whether the effect of missions on local populations was good or bad is

too simplistic.[93] The benefits of mission education and medicine were often seen by locals as good, while missionary attacks on cultural and social customs and practices were seen as bad. Furthermore, missionary groups differed in their attitudes towards local societies and these attitudes changed over time. The Arabian Mission reports suggest that same-generation individual missionaries also differed in their ability and willingness to 'empathise' with cultural difference and religious diversity.[94]

In a practical sense, in the Gulf, the missionaries brought in the newest Western scientific and technical developments in medical care. There is no doubt that the statistics for their treatments were impressive and the fact that, after the initial suspicion of the early years, they were conti-nually invited back and given money for medical facilities by local rulers, is itself an indication of the generally high local regard for the medical facilities they brought with them. The missionary doctors operated along-side local healers and offered alternative forms of treatment, which were sometimes accepted and sometimes rejected. That their medical methods were not always better than indigenous practices was later acknowledged by Eleanor Calverley, who admitted in her autobiography that some of her procedures for childbirth at the time were less sensible than those of local midwives:

> It never pays for a doctor to be too sure that his own theories about treat-ment are conclusive. Newly delivered mothers, in Arabia, were accustomed to sit up and walk about immediately after childbirth. I used to instruct my patients to stay in bed for a week. Nowadays, according to more modern concepts, it is generally accepted that ambulation should follow soon after delivery. In case any former patient of mine who was reluctant to stay in bed should read these words, I hereby confess that she was right![95]

At the same time, however, the Americans made very little progress in religious conversion and although they continually reported on the appa-rent sympathy of local people for their religious readings and prayer meetings, and gave extensive coverage to the few conversions they actually achieved, it seems more likely that the attendance at Gospel readings was a pragmatic decision to placate the missionaries and pay polite respect to them in return for their medical services; it may also reflect a willingness to take advantage of the ready-made environment for socialising. In a 1902 article, Amy Zwemer described her daily preaching and prayers in the women's room of the Bahrain dispensary. Between 12 and 30 women would attend, but only a few of them could read, and some of the scripture had to be put into 'village Arabic' because the words were too hard; although the women enjoyed being read to they did not join in the prayers. 'Some women,' Zwemer wrote, 'apparently think that if they do not approve they may not receive treatment, so they are fulsome in their agreement to all that is said, very often saying the wrong thing or agreeing in the wrong place, their too ready assent proving they have not understood.'[96]

In spite of the constant pressure in their reports to impress the board and their financial supporters, and to ensure the continuation of that support, as well as to justify their work to themselves, the missionaries were touchingly honest in their admission that they had hardly any real converts. Mason and Barny recorded that there were perhaps around five per year.[97] Emily Lorimer was scathing in her criticism of the futility of the religious aspects of the American missionary enterprise. Nevertheless, even she was willing to acknowledge the missionaries' successes, and admitted to her mother in July 1911 that the Mission Hospital was well staffed, well run and well funded'. In contrast, the Victoria Memorial Hospital, run by the British, who had 'plunged into it without counting cost of proper upkeep', was a 'fine large hospital with no kitchens, no accommodation for doctors and staff and insufficient income.' It was, she thought, 'awfully characteristic of Government. So when really bad cases come we have to ask the Mission Hospital to take them in'. Its head, Dr Manani, ran an excellent dispensary, so the people who mistrusted the missionaries were able to go there. And he did lots of visiting. 'But I always feel sorry for him when I see the big barrack standing there with rows of useless beds – especially as the comparison with the Mission must be galling.'[98]

Not surprisingly, the missionaries continued to remain optimistic about the value and likely future success of their work. In 1911, in a paper presented to the Lucknow Conference, Annie Van Sommer noted, with naive pleasure, the effect on women of the 1908 revolution in Turkey. When the constitution was proclaimed, she wrote, 'thousands of women streamed out into the streets with their husbands, to take part in the general cry of "Liberty". They discarded their veils and thought that a new era had begun.'[99] Turkish women, she went on, 'express their longing to be allowed to do what Christian women do without criticism, that is, to go about with their husbands, to meet people freely, and feel that the ordinary habits of a modest woman may be theirs'. Under the headings 'Light in Turkey', 'Light in Persia' and 'Light in Egypt', Sommer went on to discuss the progress made in the Middle East in female education and social customs – always, however, firmly linking the changes with Christian influence rather than national political developments or Islamic religious reform.

Like the British, American missionaries thought most Arabs were incapable of helping themselves. Both groups went to the Gulf with their own cultural baggage and with a pre-informed and prejudiced reading of what already existed; both set out to recreate Arabia in an image of their own society. In the case of the Americans, the Protestant (Reformed Church) Christian ideal of family and womanhood underpinned their entire project. They firmly believed that Christianity was responsible for the elevated status of Western women, and they failed to recognise the implicit inconsistency in their call for the liberation of Arab women and the gender imbalance in their own political and domestic backgrounds. Secure and comfortable with their status and identity as Protestant Christian and American women, they were, as Hunter points out, unwilling to challenge their own society and they were prepared to battle only against the male hierarchies of 'other' or 'lesser' cultures.[100] Moreover, like Victorian feminist social reformers, their concentration on the 'plight' of their Arab 'sisters' was an essential propaganda tool in their own struggle for recognition. Nevertheless, their active participation in the missionary project and their widely publicised self-representation as women workers in the field offered broadened possibilities for other Western women's lives. In her discussion of women in one of the other major targets of American activity, the Chinese Mission, Hunter concludes that '…the women who ventured alone overseas in ever-increasing numbers at the turn of the century took their place with their more rebellious sisters to constitute one of the most significant female generations in American history'.[101] The women of the Arabian Mission played a small but significant role in this revolution. At the same time they secured for themselves a participatory, and specifically female, position in the emerging American programme of involvement in the Arabian Peninsula.

NOTES ON CHAPTER 3

1   Alfred DeWitt Mason and Frederick J. Barny, *History of the Arabian Mission* (New York: Board of Foreign Missions Reformed Church in America, 1926).

2   Fatma al-Sayegh, 'American missionaries in the UAE region in the twentieth century', *Middle Eastern Studies*, no 32 (1996), pp. 120–39. Bible sellers were usually locally engaged Christians from the Subcontinent. They were also known as *colporteurs* (from the French, meaning 'pedlar' or seller of small items, books or newspapers).

3   In 1900 Zwemer published a book describing the geography, people and politics of the Arabian Peninsula, with accounts both of Islam and Christian missionary work to date. Its title (*Arabia, the Cradle of Islam*) and sub-title

(*The 'Neglected' Peninsula*) encapsulated the missionary view of the Arabian Peninsula. The *Arabian Mission Field Report* was renamed *Neglected Arabia* in 1902, and the title was retained until 1949 when, after discussion about the negative connotations of the phrase, it was finally abandoned and replaced by *Arabia Calling*. The complete run of field reports, from 1892 to 1962, was reprinted and published in eight volumes in 1988 (Farnham Common: Archive Editions).

4   Mason and Barny, *History of the Arabian Mission*, pp. 57–106.

5   The 'Arabian Mission Hymn' in Mason and Barny, *History of the Arabian Mission*, pp. 62–63. One of the earliest missionary projects was a school for freed slaves set up in Muscat by Peter Zwemer. The slippage between actual slavery and perceived slavery was always to be both an unconscious and conscious reference for missionary writing, particularly in relation to women.

6   Article 2 of the Rules of the Arabian Mission laid down the objectives as follows: 'The object of the Mission, in accordance of its original plan, is the evangelization of Arabia. Our effort should be exerted directly among and for Moslems, including the slave population; our main methods are preaching, Bible distribution, itinerating, medical work and school work. *Our aim is to occupy the interior of Arabia from the coast as a base.*' (italics in original text): Mason and Barny, *History of the Arabian Mission*, p. 196.

7   *Neglected Arabia: Missionary News and Letters*, October–December 1914, p. 11.

8   Mason and Barny, *History of the Arabian Mission*, p. 77.

9   As in the writings of other missionary literature, overt military terms pervade the reports of the Arabian Mission, for example 'News from the Front', the need for 'reinforcements', the 'battle cry' ('occupy the interior'), the 'army of women' etc.

10 William Hutchison, *Errand to the World* (Chicago: University of Chicago Press, 1987), summarised by Leslie A. Flemming, 'American Missionaries' ideals for women in North India, 1870–1930', in Nupur Chaudhuri and Margaret Strobel (eds), *Western Women and Imperialism: Complicity and Resistance* (Bloomington: Indiana University Press, 1992), p. 193.

11 *Arabian Mission Field Report*, no 1, January–March 1892.

12 *Arabian Mission Field Report*, no 5, January–March 1893, p. 4.

13 In 1895 Zwemer reported that 'our experience is that the sales of religious and educational books greatly aids the sale of Bibles. And this "mixed method" is often the only possible way to enter a new village or district. Only a few days ago a learned Moslem, after purchasing an Arabic Euclid and Astronomy, was persuaded to buy a large Bible as well.' *Arabian Mission Field Report*, no 15, July–September 1895, p. 4.

14 *Arabian Mission Field Report*, no 12, October–December 1894. See ch. 2.

15 *Arabian Mission Field Report*, no 21, January–March 1897, p. 9.

16 *Arabian Mission Field Report*, no 25, January–March 1898, pp. 6–7.
17 Jane Hunter, *The Gospel of Gentility: American Missionaries in Turn-of-the-Century China* (New Haven and London: Yale University Press, 1984), pp. 10–11.
18 Ibid., p. xiii.
19 For example, Hunter, *The Gospel of Gentility*, and Fiona Bowie, Deborah Kirkwood and Shirley Ardener (eds), *Women and Missions: Past and Present: Anthropological and Historical Perceptions* (Providence and Oxford: Berg Publishers, 1993).
20 American Arabian Mission reports, quoted passim below, include an increasingly substantial proportion of information both about women and by women. In contrast, in 'Reclaiming women's presence' (in Bowie, Kirkwood and Ardener [eds], *Women and Missions*), Fiona Bowie notes that British women's activities were edited out of reports before publication.
21 Samuel and Amy Zwemer, 'A tribute of love and admiration', *Neglected Arabia*, no 54, April–June 1905, p. 4. See pp. 99–100 above.
22 Hunter, *The Gospel of Gentility*, ch. 2, passim.
23 Ibid., p. 38.
24 A number of missionary women or their families had come originally to America from Protestant European countries including Denmark, Holland and Germany. Biographical information on missionaries in this study is taken from Mason and Barny, *History of the Arabian Mission*, Appendices, pp. 242–50.
25 Ibid., pp. 148–49, 246–47. Women missionaries at Basra sponsored by the scheme in 1911 included Mercy Van Vlack and Adele Shaw.
26 In 1903, for example, the Rev. John Van Ess, reporting on the missionaries' annual meeting at Bahrain, noted that the Rev. James Moerdyk passed 'very creditably' his second exam 'which required an accurate knowledge of the Arabic, written and spoken, and was topped by an extempore sermon in the vernacular': *Neglected Arabia*, no 45, January–March 1903, p. 3.
27 Mason and Barny, *History of the Arabian Mission*, pp. 108–9. They added, however, that it only became possible to 'put into operation the rules of the Mission relating to language study' in 1900, by which time the missionary 'force' consisted of six men and three women, of whom three (including one woman, Emma Worrall) were fully qualified physicians.
28 Eleanor T. Calverley, *My Arabian Days and Nights* (New York: Thomas Y. Crowell Company, 1958), pp. 12–13.
29 Emily Lorimer to her father, 1 April 1911, MSS Eur F177/5.
30 Mason and Barny, *History of the Arabian Mission*, p. 88.
31 Eleanor Calverley, 'In the steps of the Great Physician', *Neglected Arabia*, no 108, January–March 1919, p. 3.
32 Amy Zwemer, 'Work for Women', *Arabian Mission Field Report*, no 18, April–June 1896, pp. 4–5.
33 Mason and Barny, *History of the Arabian Mission*, p. 89.

34 Ibid., pp. 213–14. Mason and Barny noted that the first 10 years of mission-ary operations, or 'spying out the land', had, by 1899, 'proved that European and American men and women could live and work in East Arabia, even in the extremely unfavourable climate of the coast…' (p. 107). In the 1920s the Woman's Board was sufficiently involved to contribute money specifically for the Girls' School building in Basra and the Women and Children's Hospital in Bahrain.

35 Flemming, 'American Missionaries' ideals for women in North India, 1870–1930', pp. 197–99.

36 *Arabian Mission Field Report*, no 14, April–June 1895, p. 5.

37 Zwemer, *Arabia, the Cradle of Islam*, pp. 383–84.

38 'Findings of the Committee on Medical Work' at the Jerusalem Conference (1925) quoted by A. E. and S. M. Zwemer in *Moslem Women* (West Medford MA: Central Committee on the United Study of Foreign Missions, 1926), p. 201; 'the entering wedge', ibid., p. 206.

39 Calverley, 'In the steps of the Great Physician', p. 3.

40 *Arabian Mission Field Report*, no 40, October–December 1901, p. 7.

41 *Arabian Mission Field Report*, nos 10–11, April–September 1894.

42 *Neglected Arabia*, no 50, April–June 1904, pp. 14–15.

43 Emma Worrall, 'Sketches of Women's Medical Work in Arabia, I Busrah, 1895–1914', *Neglected Arabia*, no 90, July–September 1914, pp. 14–18.

44 Ibid., p. 17.

45 Emma Worrall, 'The Place of a Thousand Sorrows', *Neglected Arabia*, no 76, January–March 1911, pp. 8–14.

46 Worrall, 'Sketches of Women's Medical Work in Arabia, I Busrah, 1895–1914', p. 11.

47 Mason and Barny, *History of the Arabian Mission*, p. 160.

48 Ibid., p. 217.

49 'The Girls' School at Bahrein', *Neglected Arabia*, no 45, January–March 1903, pp. 10–12.

50 Mason and Barny, *History of the Arabian Mission*, pp. 219–20.

51 *Arabian Mission Field Report*, no 29, January–March 1899, pp. 13–14.

52 *Arabian Mission Field Report*, no 28, October–December 1898, p. 14.

53 Calverley, *My Arabian Days and Nights*, pp. 6–11.

54 Ibid., p. 14.

55 Hunter, *The Gospel of Gentility*, p. 14.

56 Mason and Barny, *History of the Arabian Mission*, pp. 211–12.

57 *Neglected Arabia*, no 42, April–June 1902, pp. 17–18.

58 *Ibid.*, p. 18.

59 *Neglected Arabia*, no 90, July–September 1914.

60 Mrs A.K. Bennett, 'In the shadow of Islam', *Neglected Arabia*, no 55, July–September 1905, p. 3.

61 *Neglected Arabia*, no 57, January–March 1906.

62 Ibid.

63 *Neglected Arabia*, no 54, April–June 1905.

64 'The need for women workers among the women of Arabia', *Neglected Arabia*, no 47, July–September 1903.

65 *Neglected Arabia*, no 79, October–December 1911, pp. 16–19.

66 January 1911. The First Conference, also chaired and convened by Zwemer, had been held in Cairo in 1906.

67 'Resolutions of the General Conference on Missions to Moslems held at Lucknow in 1911', in Annie Van Sommer and S. M. Zwemer (eds), *Daylight in the Harem: A New Era for Moslem Women: Papers on present-day reform movements, conditions and methods of work among Moslem women read at the Lucknow Conference, 1911* (Edinburgh and London: Oliphant, Anderson & Ferrier, 1911), pp. 213–14.

68 A. E. and S. M. Zwemer, *Moslem Women*: see note 41, above.

69 Ibid., Foreword. Later in the book the Zwemers described the 'march' of Islam in militaristic and doom-laden terms: 'The forces of Mohammed number now one-seventh of the entire population of the globe…The menace darkens the skies above the Dark Continent [Africa]' (p. 117).

70 A. E. and S. M. Zwemer, *Moslem Women*, p. 119.

71 In her introduction to a Special Issue of *Women's Studies International Forum* ('Women, Imperialism and Identity', 21, 1998), Penny Tinkler notes that the 'stereotype of the "native woman" produced in missionaries' reports was clearly implicated in the construction of a model of white British femininity (as physically and emotionally robust) through emphasis on the lesser and inferior femininity of native women' (p. 219).

72 *Arabian Mission Field Report*, no 29, January–March 1899, pp. 12–14.

73 Calverley, *My Arabian Days and Nights*, pp. 48–52. Compare Emily Lorimer's account of receptions and dinner parties with local people, ch. 2 above.

74 *Neglected Arabia*, no 51, July–September 1904. Ruth and Katharina Zwemer died in July 1904 from dysentery following measles. Katharina, the oldest, was seven.

75 Calverley, *My Arabian Days and Nights*, p. 107.

76 Ibid., pp. 110 ff.

77 Ibid., p. 112.

78 Ibid., p. 114.

79 Ibid., p. 128.

80 For a further discussion of Anglo-American relations and the role of women, see ch. 5.

81 The quest for influence in inland Arabia was an almost obsessive objective for Zwemer and the earliest American missionaries. In only their second quarterly *Arabian Mission Field Report* (April–June 1892) Cantine and Zwemer were already recommending to the Board of Trustees that Zwemer should be sent on a tour inland to 'open up Arabia to the Gospel' (p. 12); in the third

quarterly report (July–September 1892), they referred to their 'deep consciousness that our mission is called of God to carry the Gospel into the interior of Arabia' (p. 7).

82 See chs 5 and 6.

83 A. P. Trevor, Bushire, to W. H. I. Shakespear, Kuwait, 1 February 1910, IOR: R/15/5/313.

84 W. H. I. Shakespear to A. P. Trevor, 3 August 1910, IOR: R/15/5/313.

85 Al-Sayegh, 'American missionaries in the UAE region in the twentieth century', p. 133. See also ch. 5.

86 Hunter, *The Gospel of Gentility*, p. 152.

87 Ibid.

88 Calverley, *My Arabian Days and Nights*, p. 54.

89 See ch. 2.

90 See chs 4 and 5 for discussions of the effects of World War I on imperial politics and perspectives.

91 See, for example, Hunter, *The Gospel of Gentility*, and Bowie, Kirkwood and Ardener (eds), *Women and Missions*.

92 Bowie, Kirkwood and Ardener (eds), *Women and Missions*, Preface, p. xix.

93 Ibid., 'Introduction: Reclaiming Women's Presence', p. 3.

94 Compare, for example, the writings of Amy Zwemer and Eleanor Calverley, whose different attitudes were only partly generational.

95 Calverley, *My Arabian Days and Nights*, p. 150. For a more detailed account of the local response to American missionary medical practice, see Eleanor Abdella Doumato, *Getting God's Ear: Healing in Saudi Arabia and the Gulf* (New York: Columbia University Press, 2000).

96 'Lay-preaching in the women's dispensary', *Neglected Arabia*, no 43, July–September 1902.

97 Mason and Barny, *History of the Arabian Mission*, p. 207.

98 Emily Lorimer to her mother, 10 July 1911, MSS Eur F177/6.

99 Annie Van Sommer, 'A New Era for Moslem Womanhood', in Sommer and Zwemer (eds), *Daylight in the Harem*, pp. 23–24. See ch. 5 for further references to the perceived impact of American missionary work on Arab feminism.

100 Hunter, *The Gospel of Gentility*, pp. xv–xvi.

101 Ibid.

4 War Work for the Empire: Western Women in Mesopotamia and the Gulf, 1914–18

On 5 November 1914, three months after the outbreak of hostilities in Europe, Britain officially declared war on Germany's Eastern ally, Turkey. On 22 November a British Indian army, known as 'Indian Expeditionary Force "D"', occupied Basra. The events of the following four years were to have a profound effect on Britain's imperial relations with the Gulf territories and also on the activities and interrelationships of the men and women who were living and working in the area.

The 'Mesopotamia Campaign' was originally planned as a military holding operation to protect British trade, the routes to India and the economically important Persian oilfields. At the same time, it was intended to reaffirm to local Arab rulers and communities the supremacy of British power and prestige in the Gulf. The almost instant success of the invasion produced a semi-euphoric atmosphere of self-justification among British officials in both India and Mesopotamia, and plans rapidly expanded to encompass the idea of 'Pax Britannica' and conquest, with Baghdad as the ultimate objective. Imperial confidence was further stimulated by military successes at Qurna, fifty miles further up the Tigris, in December, and at 'Amara, another sixty miles north, in June 1915. In the following six months, however, the Turkish Army was gradually strengthened and at the end of the year, Force 'D', by now only twenty miles from Baghdad, was defeated at Ctesiphon and driven back downriver to Kut, leading to an infamous five-month siege and ultimate surrender in April 1916. In one of the most horrendous but less well-known episodes of the First World War, over ten thousand men, of whom 70 percent were Indian, were literally bogged down in the winter rains and spring floods of the southern Iraqi river plain. Two out of every three men perished in the campaign, many during the siege and the appalling conditions of subsequent captivity, from famine, dysentery, cholera and battle wounds.[1]

Meanwhile, in Basra, a local British Government was set up immediately after the occupation and, as the original objectives of the campaign widened, an increasingly sophisticated civil administration was planned for all the territories 'liberated' from Ottoman rule.[2] The post of British Resident in Baghdad had been vacant since February 1914, when its incumbent, J.G. Lorimer, the brother-in-law of Emily and author of the Gazetteer, had died prematurely at the age of 44.[3] Force 'D' was accompanied by Sir Percy Cox, Political Resident in the Gulf since 1904 and guide and mentor to David and Emily Lorimer during their posting in Bahrain. While still retaining his title as Political Resident, Cox was now appointed Chief Political Officer, on the staff of the General Officer Commanding, and was put in charge of the army's political relations in Mesopotamia. Together with his wife Belle, Cox moved from Bushire to Basra where, along with a small team of British Indian Foreign Service officials, he was responsible for solving the political, administrative and diplomatic problems which resulted from the slow progress of the army upriver to Baghdad. The Cox household was to be the social hub around which the small British political community circled.

Force 'D' had moored off Bahrain in October 1914 in response to reports of increasing Turkish military reinforcements in the northern Gulf area and the appearance of German naval vessels in the Indian Ocean. At the beginning of November, the Bahrain Agent, now Captain Terence Keyes, submitted a report to the government on the arrival of Force 'D', and commented on the inevitable anxiety in the local community but added that the ladies of the American Mission were doing 'good work' calming the fears of the female population of Bahrain's main town, Manama.[4] The American missionary, Reverend James Moerdyk, working in Bahrain at the time, described vividly the unease which had begun with the earlier declaration of war in Europe in August:

> When the reports of war in Europe began to arrive in Bahrein the people became first inquisitive and then interested. Men wanted to know what it was about and who were the fighting parties. Newspapers suddenly were in demand. Our Bible shop's reading room had many new visitors who carefully studied all the papers and magazines and men began to read with intelligence. Very many came to buy geographies and atlases of all kinds until the stock was exhausted. People who could not read would gather round men who had gathered their information from different sources and were proud to give it out, very frequently adding remarks and comments of their own. A few days before Turkey entered the war, Great Britain's first transports carrying troops

from India, and a few gunboats entered the harbor. This created a sensation and more talk followed. These troops never landed in Bahrein, but after a few days proceeded to Fao and Busrah in Turkish Arabia, so the excitement aroused by their appearance soon subsided.[5]

Moerdyk went on to describe a small amount of anti-British and pro-German, pro-Turkish sympathy but he thought that very few people in Bahrain would want a change from British protection. More important to Bahrainis were the potentially disastrous economic effects of the war. Within a month of the outbreak of hostilities, Bahrain's business as a distribution centre for smaller ports on the mainland coast had fallen by 50 percent. The ruler, Shaikh 'Isa bin 'Ali Al Khalifah, whose main income was from customs revenues, was unable to pay his employees, and all other businesses on the islands were suffering badly.[6] Most damaging was the collapse of the pearl trade and the departure of European pearl merchants, notably the French jeweller family, Rosenthal. Local traders were left with pearls on their hands, and the divers themselves, always the last people to receive their money, were left without wages. At the end of September, Emily Lorimer, now in the Persian city of Kerman, wrote to her father and mother that Bessie Mylrea, the American missionary whom the Lorimers had known in Bahrain, had told her of the imminent commercial crisis:

> Mrs Mylrea, writing from Kuweit, says they are anticipating great distress in the Gulf when there is no market for their £3,000,000 worth of pearls. It will be the same of course all over the world, but the brickfield in which one labours looms a good deal larger than France when viewed from Kerman.[7]

Keyes had already written to Stuart Knox, now Acting Resident at Bushire in the absence of Cox, to warn him of the likelihood of trouble after the outbreak of war, and he had begun to introduce emergency measures to ameliorate the situation. Keyes's letters put forward various plans to assist the Bahrain economy and the 15,000 divers likely to be without income, including arrangements for a ban on the export of foodstuffs and for the divers to be given advances to help them through the winter and keep them from starvation.[8] He also suggested that government building projects might provide an alternative source of work. In an interesting and rare sidelight on the power and influence of women in the Bahraini ruling family, and on the preconceived and somewhat uninformed contemporary British perspective on them, Keyes asked Knox whether the British Government in India would lend the ruler some money to reclaim land and build a new pier:

The ideal arrangement would be for the Shaikh's wife to do this out of her hoard. I gather from the missionary ladies and from Yusuf Kanoo that she is a very strong character – hard and avaricious and has more influence than anyone in Bahrein. She laughs at the missionary hospital, saying: let them die, what are they to you. It would be a great triumph to persuade her that relief works of the sort I have described would pay.[9]

By September Keyes was more optimistic and thought he had probably 'made Shaikh 'Isa realise his responsibilities as regards providing work for any destitute people there may be in the winter'. Furthermore, the Shaikh's son, 'Abdullah, had told him that his mother would not be 'found wanting' if relief measures became necessary.[10] 'Abdullah's mother, the unnamed wife of Shaikh 'Isa, was in fact 'Aisha bint Muhammad, a very powerful and influential member of the Al Khalifah family. She was never, however, referred to by name in British reports, only as the 'ruler's wife' or the 'wife of the shaikh'.[11] Knox passed on the information to the Government of India, reporting that a successful appeal had now been made 'to the cupidity of the Shaikhha, the millionaire of the Islands' and adding that the Shaikh himself had made a donation to the Prince of Wales' Fund for the relief of distress in England caused by the war. 'This,' Keyes wrote, 'is such a strikingly novel departure on the part of a Shaikh whom one has been accustomed for years to regard as avaricious, selfish and obstructive, that, to use a homely phrase, it took my breath away.'[12] In October Keyes was able to report that subscriptions were continuing 'to roll in to the Relief Fund', and that several ladies, 'principally Turkish Christians and Jewesses', were taking great interest in the Ladies League: 'I am almost ashamed to take their money in these hard times,' he concluded.[13] Shaikh 'Abdullah continued to help with the war effort, and the difficulties in fitting out the pearling fleet for the next fishing season were overcome largely with his help; it was, in fact, 'entirely through him and his mother, Shaikh 'Isa's only surviving wife, that Shaikh 'Isa was brought to see his responsibilities' towards the large numbers of divers who would otherwise have been 'hard put to it to weather the winter'. Overwhelmed by what he perceived to be such an astonishing change in attitude, Knox proposed that the ruler should be rewarded for his loyalty with the award of an honour, the CMG (Companion of St Michael and St George).[14]

In Basra, still in Turkish hands on the day after the declaration of war, Dr Arthur Bennett and the Reverend John Van Ess visited the Turkish Governor and offered the use of the American Mission's schools and hospitals for the accommodation of Turkish wounded. The Lansing Memorial Mission Hospital was subsequently used as a base for the Red Crescent

Society of Basra, and it was, according to the historians of the Mission, Mason and Barny, the only efficient unit the Turkish forces could rely on.[15] Within a very short time, the missionaries were treating over a hundred severely wounded Turks in a hospital designed to accommodate 45 patients. The missionaries' work not only earned them respect from the local Turkish authorities, but also enabled them, before the British occupation, to offer protection to the nervous local Christian community, some of whom were taken on as helpers.[16] After the arrival of British forces, the hospital continued to function, but under the auspices of the Red Cross rather than the Red Crescent, and it became the regular unit for Turkish and Arab wounded prisoners of war.

In their *History of the Arabian Mission*, Barny and Mason recalled that the missionaries felt a grateful sense of relief at the disappearance of all things Turkish and the restrictions of the old regime.[17] Although subsequent military reverses proved early optimism to have been premature, in his annual 'Report of the Arabian Mission for 1914', Paul Harrison, who was to become one of the most famous and successful of the medical missionaries in Arabia, rejoiced that the 'days of Turkish Medievalism' were over and that, under 'the British flag, Busrah and Mesopotamia face a new era and new opportunities, the extent of which we shall only realize as God shall unfold them'.[18] In a new drive for recruits, the Reverend Dirk Dykstra took the military symbolism of the Arabian 'campaign' to its ultimate conclusion by comparing recruitment for missionary work in Arabia with recruitment for the army in Europe and by illustrating it with an account of the 'white feather' movement:

> The story is told that in some parts of England young women go about with white feathers, which they pin on every able bodied man of military age who has not yet joined the army. Who among the able bodied and able minded young men and women in the Reformed Church is willing to receive the doubtful honor of being decorated with the white feather?...No Britisher has ever grudged the government the millions needed for the building of the effective fleet. And shall we not open hearts and hands to give ourselves and all we have so that reinforcements in abundance can be sent at once to those hard pressed on the far flung battle line.[19]

In attitude and principle, the missionaries quickly repositioned themselves and reaffirmed their roles and identities as soldiers of Christ, saviours of minds and bodies, and benign intermediaries between the British colonial administrators and the local communities. In practice, the Mission's activities were hampered by the fact that its financial situation was seriously unhealthy by the time of the outbreak of war, and for a while, recruitment was virtually abandoned. During 1915 only one new recruit, Charlotte

Dr Stanley and Mrs Bessie Mylrea in Arab dress. Published in *Neglected Arabia*, 1915.

B. Kellien, a former secretary of Samuel Zwemer and graduate of the University of Michigan, arrived in Basra to begin her language training.[20] Meanwhile the handful of men and women already qualified found themselves overwhelmed with the casualties and turmoil of the battlefield.

On the outbreak of war the missionaries had three well-equipped hospitals in the Gulf, treating over 25,000 patients in the previous year.[21] At Bahrain, the Mason Memorial Hospital was run by Mrs Josephine Spaeth Van Peursem, who was both hospital superintendent and also in charge of women's medical work. When she first arrived in Bahrain, Josephine Spaeth had been befriended by Emily Lorimer, after nursing Emily through a serious ear infection. Spaeth came from a devout Swiss Catholic family but had spent her teenage years in America living with her maternal grandmother. She then trained as a nurse at the German Hospital in New York, and at some point during her training she converted to Protestantism and joined the Dutch Reformed Church. After moving to Bahrain she was, according to Emily, 'persecuted' by letters from her old Catholic family priest in Switzerland, telling her that her parents were upset and then putting intolerable pressure on her by exaggerating their distress. Her engagement to the Reverend Gerrit Dirk Van Peursem had been the 'last straw for them and killed their last hope that she might turn Papist again'. Emily, however, had persuaded Josephine to return the priest's letters unopened. As for Van Peursem, he was a 'fat kindly good-natured fellow', rather dull but 'really nice'. He had neither 'her brains nor her education', but she seemed to like him and Emily therefore expected they would be happy, if only because they had work interests and religion in common.[22]

At Kuwait the new missionary hospital had just been completed and was to be supervised by Stanley Mylrea. Mylrea would eventually be assisted by Eleanor Calverley although, just before war broke out, the Calverleys had left for furlough in the US. In spite of the wartime dangers of travel, they returned in 1916, with their two young children and an eight-week-old baby, making a three-month journey via Japan, China, Singapore and India to avoid the Atlantic submarines. With no sense of reluctance, or doubt about the risks to themselves or their children, Eleanor Calverley recalled: 'How eager Edwin and I were to get back! We had been busy studying in America, but we had been away from our work and our people for a long time'.[23] At Muscat there was no hospital but there was a newly established and flourishing Women's Medical Dispensary, under Dr Sarah Hosman, which treated Muscat's cosmopolitan community, including local Arabs, and Muslims and Hindus from East Africa and the Subcontinent. In the first three months of the dispensary's activities, Hosman had treated just over two hundred patients and she was assisted by Emma Worrall, who reported that she had been vaccinating 90 patients a day against infectious diseases.[24]

Dorothy Van Ess, other teachers and pupils at the Basra Girls' School. Published in *Neglected Arabia*, 1916.

The 'banner' hospital, however, was the Lansing Memorial in Basra, from which institution, Harrison wrote, 'the reputation of Dr and Mrs Bennett extends far beyond the boundaries of our entire mission'.[25] Dr Christine Iverson Bennett was born in Denmark and emigrated to the US with her parents when she was 12 years old. Like many other medical missionaries, she was educated at the University of Michigan and she went out to Arabia in 1909 under the auspices of the University's Christian Association. After two years of language study she married Dr Arthur Bennett, and at the end of 1911 she joined him at the Lansing Memorial Hospital to take charge of women's medical work. The appointment as superintendent, in 1914, of Minnie C. Holzhauser, a trained nurse, also from the University of Michigan Christian Association, had made possible a great increase in the quality of work, and even after the outbreak of the war Mrs Bennett reported that women still continued to crowd the morning clinics. In September 1914 she recorded the highest daily number of women (440), but she admitted that already the scarcity of drugs was posing a serious problem and that the doctors were being forced to discriminate among patients in order to save medicine for the people most in need.[26] Nevertheless, the Bennetts, Miss Holzhauser and a small number of Indian nurses, struggled on for over a year, taking in Turkish and Arab wounded soldiers and also treating local general patients in separate clinics for men and women. When the numbers of wounded soldiers became too great for the hospital buildings, they set up tents in the compound grounds. Early in 1916 an outbreak of typhoid was brought into the hospital by Turkish prisoners and struck down the entire staff. The first to suffer were two Indian nurses, Minnie Holzhauser and then Arthur Bennett. Christine Bennett nursed all of them until she finally succumbed and died, aged 35, after her husband and colleagues were out of danger.[27] Christine Iverson was Arthur Bennett's second wife; the first, Jessie Vail, had also died of typhoid, in Bahrain in 1906.[28]

Christine Bennett's obituary, written by James Cantine, praised her medical and linguistic skills, but most of all her selfless devotion to duty and her 'quality of heart'.[29] Stanley Mylrea also added praise for her womanly fortitude:

> She had the knack of being able to run her hospital and her household work without either one or the other suffering unduly, and of course she was a woman of great energy. Everybody loved her, and at her funeral every bit of Busrah was represented, from the highest government officials down.[30]

Cantine wondered whether the mission was at fault for allowing her to remain in the field for a year longer than the usual term, since, he said,

'We can only surmise the physical strain of such a life upon one who was also a wife and a mother…She herself was one who held her bodily strength as the last factor to be considered when facing any call of duty'.[31] The requirement for women to combine, with womanly fortitude, the qualities and duties of wife, mother and ministering angel, was still much in evidence, and even more of an aspirational model, during the war years. After Christine Bennett's death, Arthur Bennett went home on furlough to the US with his small son Matthew. *Neglected Arabia* also published a letter from Sir Percy Cox, offering his sympathy to the Mission, acknowledging the loss of Christine Bennett's work and at the same time expressing general appreciation for the Mission's work.[32] In 1915 the British Indian Government gave the Lansing Memorial Hospital a grant of ten thousand rupees (US$3330) in response to its work in caring for wounded prisoners of war. Part of the sum, however, had been collected from the Muslim community in Bombay.[33]

While the Americans set about providing medical care and social welfare, the British concentrated on military tactics and wartime politics. With the army bogged down on the Tigris, Cox set up his administration in Basra. A civil service based on the British Indian model was created and a judicial department with a new penal code. Local provisions were made for sanitation and for medical care, including the services of the Missionary Hospital. In January 1915 a revenue commissioner, H.R.C. Dobbs, was appointed, and local political officers were placed in upriver towns as soon as they were occupied. In December 1915 David Lorimer was attached to Indian Expeditionary Force 'D' as an Assistant Political Officer, under Cox, and posted to Amara.

The Lorimers had left Bahrain in September 1912, unsure whether Lock would be posted to Kerman or Kashmir but surprisingly relieved to be away from the Gulf. 'We hardly knew how beastly Bahrein was till we found we were set free', Emily later wrote to her mother, 'but now we don't mind letting each other hear what we *really* think about it!'[34] In October they had finally heard they were to be posted to Kerman in southern Persia, the 'sugar-plum' of all the Gulf postings, where they stayed for the next two years, enjoying the climate, the opportunity to learn Persian and, not least, the social life, which, in spite of earlier anxieties, they thought contrasted favourably with that of Bahrain:

> It is nice to have some *English* ladies with one's own tastes and feelings. However nice the Americans were, they were always a foreign type… Somehow the house and servants all present a friendlier, kinder appearance than Bahrein. In our big garden we have complete privacy, instead of the mob of litigants always lurking round the Office doors in Bahrein, and

our servants are all cheery willing rascals, happily mono-lingual…I feel the greatest pleasure in being able to prowl around now into the kitchen now off to my store-room now backwards and forwards through the garden feeling myself mistress in my own domain and free from observation, whereas in Bahrein I could only move about freely upstairs…The exhilaration of the climate too is wonderful.[35]

En route to Kerman, in fact, Emily seems to have thrown off much of the social and cultural baggage of the Edwardian memsahib and discovered the more liberating attractions of travel. The Lorimers made the last part of the journey, from Bandar 'Abbas to Kerman, on horseback along mountain tracks, enjoying the scenery, camping or staying in caravanserai, and meeting and making contact with local people, an experience which Emily had either avoided or simply not been in a position to do in Bahrain. 'I cannot describe to you', she wrote to her parents, 'the exhilaration of the open-air life nor the fascination of following your route with maps and compasses and proudly identifying one land-mark or another…it is "travel" indeed, the *only* sort of travel and how you and Father would have enjoyed it!'[36]

Life in Kerman was only seriously marred for the Lorimers by the sudden and mysterious death of Lock's more famous brother, John Gordon, early in 1914. On top of years of hard work on the *Persian Gulf Gazetteer*, Gordon had also been Consul-General in Baghdad since May 1910 and in February 1914 was the latest temporary incumbent in Cox's vacant post at Bushire. While Emily and David were in Bahrain, the two Lorimer brothers and their wives had tried and failed on several occasions to make time to see each other. They had met up briefly in Basra in September 1912 when Lock and Emily were on their way from Bahrain to Kerman and Gordon, with his wife Nesta, was en route to Simla for briefings from the Government of India.[37] However, they had not seen each other again. In February 1914 David and Emily were devastated by the news of Gordon's sudden death from a gunshot wound from his own pistol. The *Times of India* on 28 February reported briefly that Lorimer had died at Bushire on 8 February 'from the accidental discharge of an automatic pistol which went off in his hand'. On 13 March the *Pioneer Mail*, published 'full particulars'. Lorimer, according to the report, after talking to the Governor of Bushire on the telephone, left his two assistants in his office and went upstairs to his dressing-room to check the exact calibre of his automatic pistol so that he could order some more cartridges from Bombay by the mail boat which was about to leave. When he failed to return the assistants went to look for him, and found him lying dead on the floor. It was 'evident that in examining the pistol he had pulled the trigger and discharged a last cartridge which had been overlooked in the magazine'. The residency surgeon found that the bullet had entered the stomach and passed right through the body to the spine. 'The shock, in Major Hunt's opinion, must have caused immediate loss of consciousness, for the expression of the face was calm and peaceful, and death speedily followed from syncope.' After a local enquiry a formal verdict was recorded that Lorimer died from wounds caused by the accidental discharge of an automatic pistol. The following May, Lord Curzon, with whom he had travelled to the Gulf in 1903, wrote to Nesta to express his condolences:

> I suppose in a sense that I was responsible for your husband's career, for I gave him the post in which he first so distinguished himself and took him with me to the Persian Gulf, which led to his subsequent service there. It is a deep grief to me therefore to contemplate such a career cut short – the career of a man who had a strong sense of duty, fine natural abilities, untiring perseverance, and a wonderful aptitude for dealing with the peoples and problems of the East. Such a man was a tower of strength to the cause of British prestige and good government wherever he went.[38]

After his brother's death, Lock, always plagued by indifferent health, succumbed to a fever and only slowly recovered during the spring. Emily continued to send spirited and fact-filled letters to her family, only occasionally alluding to their grief, until April, when she wrote to Lock's parents:

> I know and trust you too much to fear that you will misunderstand the trifling chatter of this and other letters as any lack of sympathy and loving participation in your sorrow and in Lock's, or any lightly laying aside of our own. But I have been trying to remember that all we write reaches you after six weeks and have purposely kept off the subject that is in all our minds all the day, so as not to stir up anew the first acuteness and vividness of grief that is mercifully subsiding. But indeed my heart is with you both. You would be proud of Lock's bravery and how he is going on with his work, but a great light and joy has gone from his life and he is recovering more slowly than he would have done, weighted as it were physically with his grief.[39]

When war in Europe broke out in August 1914 Emily reacted with characteristic 'gung-ho' enthusiasm. On 6 August she wrote to her parents about her shock and sorrow at the likelihood of bereavements and her hope that the war would change people from 'a herd of charity-children with our mouths open waiting to be state-fed, into men again, as our fathers were'.[40] A month later she was still feeling the same anxiety, but again, as so often in Emily's letters, it was expressed in masculine terminology and the fear was overlaid with the imagery of imperial pride:

We are stirred to every depth of our souls by this great war. But the terribleness of it is far outweighed by the discovery that we are still the men our grandfathers were and that the God of our Fathers need not blush to be the God of their succeeding race. One tried not to doubt it but really home politics had looked so grubby and sordid that it was hard not to doubt at times. Thank God 99% of the nation doesn't mess about in politics and so can keep itself clean; in peace one forgets this but in big crises it is the nation which counts and not our hireling politicians. And it can only do us good to show ourselves and our Colonies and the world what stuff we are made of still.[41]

Having been educated a Germanophile, she now reacted strongly against 'German aggression' as did many of her previously pro-German academic contemporaries, with a harsh and uncompromising hostility, telling her father that it was 'impossible not to feel profoundly sorry for the great bulk of the German nation. But for us it looks as if we should never have had a better chance to fight them and fight them we were bound to do sooner or later in spite of all Liberal talk and nonsense.'[42] By October 1914 David Lorimer was bemoaning the fact that being a political officer prevented him from being able to join up and fight, although Emily reminded him that 'there are many ways of serving and one has no right to want to choose one's own'. 'It is after all,' she thought, 'one of the great strengths of the Empire that we can count on everyone who is not actually able to help in more romantic ways going about his daily work without hustle and without rest. It is a glorious time to be alive.'[43] In December Lorimer was posted to Chitral, on the North West Frontier of India, as Assistant Political Agent.

Chitral was a remote and mountainous posting, thought by the Government of India to be too harsh a place for wives. Emily would not, therefore, be allowed to accompany her husband.[44] Back in England in 1915 she found work with the Red Cross and worked on the proofs of an article on a Persian dialect which Lock had submitted to the *Journal of the Royal Asiatic Society*. In July she was 'happy and proud' to be posted by the Red Cross to Alexandria, where she would be able to make use of her Arabic.[45] From Alexandria she was at last able to rejoin her husband, in November 1915, in the Gulf, where the couple spent 'three gloriously calm days and nights and a very jolly honeymoon', steaming up the Shatt al-'Arab. 'We are both splendidly well and fit and as happy as kings,' she told her mother, 'not looking unduly to the future and what it may bring forth.'[46] By early December, however, Lock had been moved to a different posting, at Amara, two-days' journey upriver, and Emily was billeted with Sir Percy and Lady Cox in Basra.[47]

Emily Lorimer had formed an immediate attachment to Belle Cox when the two women met in Bushire after the Lorimers' departure from Bahrain. She had described Mrs Cox then as 'a very handsome stately woman with a beautiful figure though distinctly stout. Her hair must have been a pretty brown but is now turning a most becoming grey; it is beautifully though simply dressed.'[48] Emily had admired Mrs Cox most of all because of the latter's ability to preside over a well-run imperial household. In July 1912 she had written to her parents that:

> Lock liked Lady Cox very much; she appears to be an exceptionally able and competent woman…Some people consider her rather over-masterful, but probably anything less would not avail to keep such a big establishment in good order, and as she is a dignified stately woman she can carry off a certain amount of imperativeness.[49]

In contrast to Mrs Haworth, the wife of the Consul at Muhammerah, whose servants were not told what to do and whose guest-room was filled with cobwebs, Lady Cox's house ran like clockwork, although under a benevolent despotism rather than a reign of terror. Furthermore, Emily liked Belle Cox because she saw her as a 'motherly' Irishwoman who would also talk about clothes, while Belle for her part was pleased to see that Emily was not just a 'blue-stocking'.[50] When both Emily and David had contracted malaria in Bushire, Belle had nursed them both and made soups, jellies and 'dainty dishes' to cater for their fevered appetites.[51] As soon as Emily was well again, Lady Cox had given her lessons in housekeeping:

> And as you can well imagine, with her 25 years experience, there was much that she could teach me. I drank it all in with gratitude and shall put it in practice – with discrimination. She talks wonderful Hindustani – all mem-sahibs do: a mongrel servant jargon that is terrible to think of – learnt as a girl in Lucknow. It seems a curious lapse for so exceptionally able a woman that in her eight years in Bushire she has not learnt a word of Persian. I could not help thinking that some of the awful shortcomings of the Persian race of which she complained from the mistress's point of view were perhaps due to their all being talked to in Hindustani. However, no one can do everything. Nothing could have exceeded her kindness in looking after us when we were ill…[52]

Now, three years later, in Basra, Emily again found Lady Cox to be 'a most kindly, natural, unaffected woman without any "nerves" or snobbishness; and as I have my own servant and my own sitting-room and can have my own guests I think there is no fear of my feeling myself thrown too much on her hands nor any fear of friction between us'. Sir Percy, meanwhile, in public the great administrator, inclined 'in his own house, whether from diffidence or slackness or over-weariness...to take a back seat!'[53]

In spite of the domestic comforts of the Cox household, Emily lost no time in getting down to some intellectual activity of her own, and she soon found a 14-year-old boy, educated by the American Mission school, to give her Arabic lessons.[54] In February 1916 she decided to widen her social circle by holding a tea party, to which she invited another female new arrival, 'wife of one of the Bank people'. In a complaint reminiscent of her Somerville days, Emily told her mother that she was relieved when the other woman left because, although she was 'pretty and pleasant...as an entertainer she wasn't exactly a success...However, after she was gone, the men still stayed on and we got some rational conversation; up to then it had been a monologue about servants and kitchen ranges and the price of fuel.'[55] In addition, Emily was able to help one of the officers with his Arabic. Still inclined to prefer the company of men to that of women, she found no lack of stimulus among the small group of political officers and Arabists gathered around Cox and his Mesopotamian administration. She told her mother there was 'certainly a larger choice of society' in Basra than in either Bahrain or Kerman, 'though I don't appreciate it fully without Lock, and would gladly swop the whole lot for him and a desert island – if that were possible without dereliction of duty'.[56] At the same time, although her letters were sometimes cut by the military censor, she managed to give her family back home a vivid description of life beyond the British civil administration and an increasingly depressing account of the conditions in which the army was bogged down. When the rains started in January the countryside turned into a swamp. Even the troops at the military base in Basra had found their huts flooded with thick mud and had been forced to find spades and literally dig out their blankets, while it was twenty times worse for the troops in the field. Conditions in Mesopotamia, she continued to believe, were far worse than in Europe, and many of the reinforcements coming from France, who were 'inclined beforehand to think they were coming to a picnic sort of warfare', now said that France was the picnic in comparison. Meanwhile, wounded Turkish prisoners being treated in the Mission Hospital had told the doctors about the massacres of Armenian people:

> some of them admit the most appalling Armenian atrocities; indeed it seems true, as many Muslims admit, that you may believe the very worst you hear about the massacres, for no one could conceive anything worse. In whole towns every single man has been murdered and all the women and children drowned or driven out into the desert to starve.[57]

Before long, Emily herself was occupied in war work. In February she wrote to her mother to tell her that Sir Percy Cox had 'electrified' her by asking if she would be willing to take on the editorship of the *Basra Times*. She had agreed immediately, while pointing out to him her lack of journalistic experience and privately reflecting on her 'own misgivings' afterwards.[58] The *Basra Times* was a daily newspaper started at the end of November 1914, under military auspices, and taken over by the civil administration about eighteen months later. It was distributed around the Gulf and the English circulation was 600–800 copies daily, with Arabic and Persian editions, printed together on the same sheet, running to about 600–700 copies.[59] Linked with the job of editor was that of temporary superintendent of the local government printing press. 'This paper I need hardly say is government-run and duly inspired from the Chief Political Officer's office,' Emily wrote. 'Today is my last day of liberty.'[60]

Working at the press immediately galvanised Emily Lorimer into energetic intellectual, and managerial, activity. She thought there was a fairly good staff of Persian and Arab translators, clerks and accountants, 'but all are natives of somewhere or other and so will need supervision'. As soon as Cox had appointed her she sent off to Karachi for an encyclopaedia and to Bombay for a good set of war maps. And she admitted that she had been 'most fearfully lazy about reading the home papers because Lock wasn't there to talk about things with'. The newspaper would add 'a huge interest to life' and she was 'just bursting with amusement and delight'. At the same time, however, she confessed to feeling a little anxious, because it would be 'so beastly for Lock' if she made a mess of things:

> I stipulated that I should be at first only on approval and should be allowed to retire gracefully if I did not give satisfaction...However I'm sure it is best to plunge first and think about one's own shortcomings afterwards!...But if they keep me on as Editor after a fair trial it will be fun to feel even a microscopic ephemeral insect on the wheel. I hope Lock will be pleased; there was of course no chance of consulting him, but I don't think he would have wished me to refuse. And apart from personal feelings altogether, I fancy I shall be the first woman to have held (even temporarily) the post of 'Superintendent of Govt. Printing' anywhere. So I must do my best that the wholesome precedent may not be an awful warning to those who would like to do the like again.[61]

In fact, she was to hold the post for over a year. While never losing sight of her identity as imperial memsahib, she easily recreated her former independent, intellectual and professional persona, this time as a woman war-worker, dismissing the household duties as essential but secondary, and revelling in being able to describe herself as on active service. She told her mother that she was enjoying every minute of her new life, happy to have a *raison d'être*, 'not to mention being entitled to frank her letters "ON FIELD SERVICE"'. There was, however, a hint in the letter that not everyone in the overwhelmingly masculine British administration in Basra approved of the inclusion of women in the workforce:

> You can't think how generous everybody is being about it, they all seem amused, and think it sporting of me to have accepted; Sporting is really another term for 'beastly cheek'! And I think perhaps it was rather cheek, but on the whole it seems silly not to have a shot at a thing; it is up to them to get rid of me if I can't manage it.[62]

The extraordinary circumstances created by the war precipitated both men and women into new roles and new identities. Ultimately, after 1918, there were to be public and private debates and disagreements about empire and imperialism and their purpose and justification. In the short term, however, the military conflict threw together men and women, career diplomats and amateur adventurers, Britons, Americans and Arabs, in new and unprecedented relationships and power struggles.

The Basra community in 1914 was a complex mix of imperial service and army officers, missionaries and Arabists. At the head of the group, Lieutenant-Colonel Sir Percy Zachariah Cox was the archetypal imperial officer. By 1914 he had served in the Gulf for over fourteen years, as Political Agent in Muscat and then as Political Resident, overseeing all British relations in the region. He worked long hours, spoke Arabic fluently and was said by contemporaries to be respected by both colleagues and local shaikhs.[63] Major Stuart Knox, who had been David Lorimer's predecessor at Bahrain, and whose wife had instructed Emily in household management on the Lorimers' arrival in the shaikhdom, was a barrister and also an Arabic scholar. In April 1915, after a period as British Consul in Muscat and subsequently Acting Resident at Bushire, he was appointed Senior Judicial Officer in Basra.[64] Of the younger officials, Emily Lorimer was most impressed by Arnold T. Wilson and Reader Bullard. 'These two are quite the most interesting of the younger men I have met,' she told her mother in January 1916.[65] Emily had been impressed by Wilson when he called to see the Lorimers in Bahrain in 1912, describing him then as 'by common consent, *the* coming man amongst the juniors'.[66]

However, she was to strike up a particular friendship with the young Bullard whom she regarded as well read and 'full of interesting talk', 'quite the most interesting and finest of the younger men I have met here; and his early days and struggles are not unlike Father's'.[67] Bullard had an unusual background for a colonial service officer, having been born into the family of an unemployed London dock worker and largely self-taught. A brilliant linguist, a fact which probably endeared him to Emily, Bullard had worked his way through correspondence courses to success in the Levant Service exams and then to Cambridge, after which he had been posted to Turkey, from 1908 to 1914. His languages included Arabic, Persian, Turkish and Russian, as well as French and German.[68] Among the missionaries, Emily regarded John Van Ess, 'though a bit of a rough diamond', as 'a more interesting man than the average missionary, and very much better read', a quality always likely to impress the bluestocking, Emily Overend. Furthermore, she also thought Dorothy Van Ess was 'an intelligent woman', and consequently admitted to enjoying their company more than that of other missionaries.[69]

Also in Basra was Harry St. John Bridger Philby, who, Emily thought, seemed 'a particularly nice fellow'. Philby had served in the Punjab as Assistant Commissioner. In 1910, in defiance of Government of India opposition to marriage in the first few years of service, he had married Dora Johnston, the daughter of a senior British railway engineer, whom he had met at a ball in Rawalpindi. Philby arrived in the Gulf in November 1915. Dora did not obtain permission to join her husband in Basra until the end of 1916.[70] Philby, although at this stage of his career an employee of the Indian Civil Service, was also an adventurer and an explorer, and he represented the link between the career diplomats and administrators of the British Indian civilian and military services and the rather more exotic Orientalists who have become known as the 'Arabists' and who were to have such a great influence on wartime policy and the post-war development of colonialism in the Middle East.

In her 1981 account of Orientalism and Arabian travel, Kathryn Tidrick remarks that the First World War was the Arabists' 'moment in history', when 'gifted amateurs of Arab history and psychology like Gertrude Bell, T. E. Lawrence and Sir Mark Sykes were precipitated by the fortunes of war into positions where they might hope to influence the course of events'.[71] Certainly, in the conditions of the First World War, the need for expert and enthusiastic amateurs to support and inform hard-pressed officials, provided a perfect opportunity for travellers and explorers to find a role in imperial politics. In January 1916 the Arab Bureau was set up in Cairo and it was responsible for intelligence-gathering on Arab affairs and for the co-ordination of British Middle East policy. It was the brainchild of Mark Sykes, and its first director was Gilbert Clayton, although in practice it was run by David Hogarth, an Oxford archaeologist and Arabist, serving as a wartime Naval Intelligence Officer.[72] A subordinate but semi-independent Basra branch was formed under the overall local supervision of the Chief Political Officer (Cox) for the collection and distribution of information relating to 'Near Eastern' questions in general and to the Turkish Empire in particular, and for the co-ordination of propaganda. The information was to be sent to London, Cairo and India, and was to include reports on relations with independent Arab rulers, for example the Saudi ruler, Amir 'Abd al-'Aziz b.Faysal Al Sa'ud, and on tribal politics.[73] In 1916 Gertrude Bell was appointed as Corresponding Officer to work under Cox's direction.

In the male environment of the imperial administration in Mesopotamia, Bell's arrival marked a significant new development. During the first years of the war, the locally based Western women had begun to create for themselves new identities and justifications for imperial service. The American missionary women took on much-needed welfare responsibilities; Belle Cox, in her own position as wife of the Chief Political Officer, also took on wider domestic and social responsibilities for the careworn and weary officials in the employment of the Government; Emily Lorimer accomplished a move from domestic service to 'field service', while never allowing the latter to obscure completely the importance of the former. Gertrude Bell, however, was entirely without the corporate imperial identity of political wife, memsahib or missionary. When she arrived in Basra, in her late forties, she was a much-travelled and well-respected explorer. She was also unmarried. Emily Lorimer commented to her mother on Bell's arrival: 'Miss Bell, the traveller, whom you remember I met in London at the Red Cross and who was my London chief while I was in Alex. has just rolled up here doing some gazetteer work for which her knowledge of Arabic and of the tribes fits her. She is most pleasant and friendly.'[74] Two weeks later she added that Bell was:

> An extremely interesting woman and without a trace of side. She knows all the Cabinet personally and was staying with the High Commissioner in Egypt and the Viceroy in Delhi on her way here, but she has no snobbery about her at all. I believe her father Sir Hugh Bell made his money in scrap iron or something, they have lots anyhow, however come by, but are model employers.[75]

Like Lorimer, Bell had spent the early months of the war working for the Red Cross, and she had been educated at Oxford. However, in spite of their similar intellectual and academic achievements, and, in the widest sense, a common belief in the duties and responsibilities of empire, they were, politically and culturally, very different personalities. Thirteen years older than Emily Lorimer, Gertrude Lowthian Bell was born in 1868.[76] Bell's grandfather, Isaac Lowthian Bell, was a wealthy Newcastle steel magnate and scientist. Her father, Hugh, was educated in chemistry and mathematics at the Sorbonne and in Germany and, although he joined his father's business, he also devoted time to Liberal causes, such as the promotion of education, public health and child-labour reform. Her mother, Mary, who died when Gertrude was two years old, came from a prominent Newcastle food-merchant family. Five years after Mary's death, Gertrude's father married Florence Olliffe, a playwright whose brother-in-law, Frank Lascelles, was a diplomat and, at the time, British Ambassador in Washington. Florence was to remain a close friend of Gertrude's throughout the latter's life.

Academically precocious, Gertrude went to Oxford, to Lady Margaret Hall, in 1886 and became the first woman to achieve first-class marks in modern history.[77] At Oxford, one of her closest companions, and eventually a lifelong friend, was Janet Hogarth, sister of the future Arab Bureau chief, David Hogarth. Janet Hogarth later described Bell's brilliance as a student:

> Gertrude Lowthian Bell, the most brilliant student we ever had at Lady Margaret Hall, or indeed I think at any of the women's colleges…She threw herself with untiring energy into every phase of college life, she swam, she rowed, she played tennis, and hockey, she acted, she danced, she spoke in debates; she kept up with modern literature, and told us tales of modern authors, most of whom were her childhood's friends. Yet all the time she put in seven hours of solid work, and at the end of two years, she won as brilliant a First Class in the School of Modern History as has ever been won at Oxford.[78]

After Oxford, Bell began a series of travels which took her around the world and established – or reinforced previously formed – social and diplomatic connections that were to provide her with the background and experience for her eventual appointment in Mesopotamia. In 1886 she went to Bucharest to stay with Lascelles, who was now British Minister in Romania, and his wife Mary. While there she also met Charles Hardinge who, as Viceroy of India, was to be responsible for sending her to Basra in 1916.[79] In 1892 she visited the Lascelles again, this time in Tehran, where she began to study Persian. A year later she was in Algiers, with her father, and learning Arabic. Between the Algiers trip and the end of the century she managed visits to Jerusalem and Damascus, a round-the-world trip with her brother Maurice, including San Francisco and Tokyo, and various interludes in Switzerland, where she became a proficient and courageous mountaineer. On her Middle East travels in 1899 she hired an Arabic teacher and by February 1900 she was reading from the *Arabian Nights* 'just for fun', and at the same time learning to read the Bible in Hebrew. She wrote to her father, from Jerusalem, that it was 'frightfully thrilling...It's extraordinarily near Arabic, much nearer than any two European languages I can think of'.[80]

In 1902 Bell went to India with her other brother, Hugo, and she was there for the Delhi Coronation Durbar celebrations in January 1903, which she recorded in detail for her stepmother.[81] At a lunch in the press camp with the *Times* correspondent, Valentine Chirol, she first met Percy Cox, from whom she heard 'the latest news of Central Arabia'.[82] For the next few years she travelled, published accounts of her travels, learned more languages and studied archaeology and the technical methodology of exploration. Before her 1911 travels to Mesopotamia, she prepared herself by visiting the Royal Geographical Society and learning the techniques of surveying, astronomical observation and map-making.

In 1913 Bell returned to Damascus to prepare for her most famous journey, to the central Arabian plateau of Najd, with the intention of visiting Riyadh and Ha'il, then the capitals, respectively, of the Al Sa'ud and the Al Rashid spheres of territorial influence in inland Arabia.[83] In spite of the opposition and the subsequent refusal of both the Foreign Office and the local Turkish administration to take responsibility for her safety, Bell travelled into the Nafud desert and reached Ha'il in February 1914. Before leaving Amman she had signed a note for the Turkish administration acknowledging that she travelled at her own risk.[84] She remained in Ha'il for two weeks, a virtual prisoner and unimpressed by the state of the Rashid regime. She later recalled that Ha'il gave her 'a sinister impression', and she accurately predicted the political future of central Arabia:

> I think the Rashids are moving towards their close...I should think the future lies with Ibn Sa'ud...I cannot find it in my heart to wish the Rashids much good. Their history is one long tale of treachery and murder...I do not know what Ibn Sa'ud is like, but worse he cannot be. So there! My next Arabian journey shall be to him. I have laid out all my plans for it.[85]

In the manner and tradition of independent women travellers of her culture and class, Bell finally left Ha'il, after demanding her impounded camels and money from the Rashidi authorities. She abandoned her plans to visit the Saudi capital, and went, instead, direct to Baghdad, Damascus and Constantinople, where she reported on her journey to the British Ambassador and the Foreign Office. On her return to London she was awarded the Royal Geographical Society's gold medal.[86] The Ha'il trip, however, was not simply an 'expedition'. It provided her and, through her, the British Government with important political intelligence at a crucially sensitive period at the beginning of the First World War. The cartographic material she collected was used by the War Office to produce a new map of the area.[87] At a meeting of the Royal Geographical Society shortly after Bell's death, her wartime colleague, David Hogarth, remarked on the wider achievements of the 1914 journey:

> To my thinking its interest and value lie by no means only or principally in its mere demonstration that a Christian Englishwoman could penetrate Nejd alone and return unscathed, but more in all sorts of gains that accrued to the geographical and archaeological sciences, and to our social and political knowledge of the Arabs…Her information proved of great value during the War…Miss Bell became, from 1915 onwards, the interpreter of all reports from Central Arabia.[88]

On her arrival in Constantinople, the British Ambassador, Sir Louis Mallet, reported to the Foreign Office that Bell's report on her journey would be 'of great interest and value', adding that 'Miss Bell's journey, which is in all respects a most remarkable exploit, has naturally excited the greatest interest here'.[89]

By the time of the outbreak of the war, Gertrude Bell had published several articles and two major books of her travels.[90] Her first book, *The Desert and the Sown*, published in 1907, had received very positive reviews, which firmly categorised her as a female 'explorer'. The *Times Literary Supplement*, for example, grudgingly declared that:

> Women perhaps make the best travellers, for when they have the true wanderer's spirit they are more enduring and, strange to say, more indifferent to hardship and discomfort than men. They are unquestionably more observant of details and quicker to receive impressions. Their sympathies are more alert, and they get into touch with strangers more readily.

The *New York Times*, however, thought that the 'ways of English women are strange. They are probably the greatest slaves to conventionality in the world, but when they break with it, they do it with a vengeance.'[91]

There was no doubt that Bell was willing and able to 'get in touch with strangers'. Unlike Emily Lorimer, and in stark contrast to the behaviour and code of conduct of the conventional memsahib, she travelled alone and, on her travels, she generally preferred the company of local people, stayed in their houses and acquired many close Arab friends. In *The Desert and the Sown* she had asserted that 'human nature does not undergo a complete change East of Suez, nor is it impossible to be on terms of friendship and sympathy with the dwellers of those regions. In some respects it is even easier than in Europe'.[92] In spite, however, of her obvious enjoyment of the excitement, danger and 'otherness' of the 'Oriental' travel experience, it is clear from some of Bell's more personal writing that she did not wholeheartedly identify herself as a female 'explorer'. Alongside Bell's Ha'il letters to her father and stepmother, there is also a parallel, private, diary, intended for Bell's friend and secret lover, Major Charles (Richard) Doughty-Wylie, the nephew of the nineteenth-century Arabian traveller, Charles Doughty. In it she reveals her doubts about the value of Arabian travel, particularly for a single woman, and hints at the attractions of the more disciplined intellectual activities of the political administrator she was eventually to become:

> I am suffering from a severe fit of depression today...The depression springs from a profound doubt as to whether the adventure is, after all, worth the candle...A compass traverse over country which was more or less known, a few names added to the map – names of stony mountains and barren plains, and a couple of deep wells – and probably that is all. It's nothing, the journey to Nejd, so far as any real advantage goes, or any real addition to knowledge, but I am beginning to see pretty clearly that it is all that I can do. There are two ways of profitable travel in Arabia. One is the Arabia Deserta way, to live with the people, and to live like them, for months and years. You can learn something thereby, as Doughty did...It's clear I can't take that way; the fact of my being a woman bars me from it. And the other is Leachman's way, to ride swiftly through the country with your compass in your hand, for the map's sake and nothing else. I might be able to do that over a limited space of time, but I am not sure. Anyway, it is not what I am doing now. The net result is that I think I should be more usefully employed in more civilised countries, where I know what to look for and how to record it...I fear, when I come to the end, I shall say: 'It was a waste of time'...It's a bore being a woman when you are in Arabia.[93]

As war threatened, the British Government asked Bell for an analysis of the political situation in the Middle East and, in 1915, as a result of her report, and her reputation as a knowledgeable and well-travelled expert, she was asked to work with Military Intelligence and joined Clayton, Hogarth and T.E. Lawrence in Cairo. In January 1916 she travelled to India to brief the Viceroy, Lord Hardinge, on the activities of the Arab Bureau, and in March 1916 she arrived in Basra, having been recommended by Hardinge as a 'remarkably clever woman with the brains of a man'.[94] In Basra she was to act as Liaison Officer between British Intelligence in Cairo and Government of India Intelligence in Delhi, to analyse and synthesise information about Arab personalities and tribes, and to prepare a political 'Gazetteer of Arabia'. In an India Office note the following May, the Permanent Under-Secretary, Arthur Hirtzel, commenting on the status and work of the Arab Bureau, predicted that 'the Bureau is expected to survive the war only as an intelligence dept. Miss Bell's knowledge is of course enormous'.[95] In spite of this, however, Bell was not given an official post until the following July when she was formally attached to the political staff of Indian Expeditionary Force 'D' as Liaison Officer, Correspondent to Cairo, and became the only female Political Officer in the British forces. She was to stay in Mesopotamia, and the newly created post-war state of Iraq, at the centre of political activity, until her death in 1926.

Sir Arnold Wilson later recalled that when Bell arrived in March 1916, her stay was originally intended to be a flying visit on her way back to Cairo from India. 'It was her destiny,' however, 'from the moment of her arrival, until her death in Baghdad ten years later, to devote the whole of her extraordinary talents and unbounded energies to the service of successive administrations in Mesopotamia.'[96] Bell's appearance in Basra introduced a radical and potentially disruptive element into the predominantly masculine, and overwhelmingly military, wartime environment. When Bell first arrived, Sir Percy Cox was away in Bushire but Lady Cox was there to meet her, and Bell at first lived in the Cox household. Unlike Emily Lorimer, Gertrude had little time for Belle Cox's motherly kindness, and she wrote to her stepmother that 'Lady Cox is absolutely no good to any mortal soul – she is so damned stupid... She is as kind as ever she can be but there's no possible subject on which you can converse with her.'[97]

Bell's life and work in Basra has been analysed by historians, most thoroughly by her male biographer, Victor Winstone. With Belle Cox firmly sidelined in the limited domestic sphere, and few other military or political wives allowed into Basra, Winstone's account suggests a cosy scenario in which Emily Lorimer and Gertrude Bell played dominatrix among the diverse and multi-talented officials of the Mesopotamia administration: 'The two women of this fraternity, Gertrude and Mrs Lorimer, took it upon themselves to maintain order among so many disparate and opinionated men, lecturing them like school-mistresses or surrogate mothers when the occasion arose'.[98] Winstone goes on to describe how Emily Lorimer delivered a reprimand to Philby after a disagreement Philby had with her husband at Amara. Characteristically, Emily wrote to Philby to complain that when a young man 'without very wide experience finds himself differing about practical policy from an older man and senior official acting in circumstances of which the former knows nothing, it is sound for him to assume that there may be two sides to a question'. Winstone also quotes Bell herself as having told Philby that he was 'too domineering and difficult'.[99]

If Emily Lorimer's papers had been available to him, Winstone would have been amused by her determined attempts to mother Reader Bullard and to find him 'the best sort of wife'. In August 1916 she even wrote to her own mother to elicit her help in a search for a suitable cultivated and educated girl.[100] Bell, however, does not seem to have been all that interested in surrogate motherhood or, for that matter, in other women's opinions. Surprisingly, given the fact that they were the only British women officials in the Basra administration, she rarely mentioned Emily Lorimer in her letters. She did, however, show strikingly similar opinions about the intellectual capacity of other women, and especially memsahibs, whom she regarded as boring and conformist. On an earlier visit to Baghdad, for example, Bell had been pleasantly entertained by Emily's brother-in-law, Gordon, and his wife, Nesta. On the same visit, however, Bell also reported dining with the British Consul in Baghdad, Colonel Ramsay, and his wife. She described the latter as 'a dull dog, a very stiff, narrow and formal Englishwoman, dreadfully afraid of giving herself away or of doing anything not entirely consistent with the duty and dignity of the wife and daughter of Indian officials'.[101]

Bell had no time for what she regarded as tedious female interests, and she usually openly preferred the company of men. Like Emily Lorimer, Bell was, at this time at least, firmly against women's suffrage, and she had been active in the anti-suffrage movement from its beginning.[102] However, she never seems to have allowed domestic politics get in the way of more compelling overseas interests. In November 1912, after working for the league in the north of England, interviewing the Archbishop of York and organising an anti-suffrage meeting in Middlesbrough, she had written to Valentine Chirol to complain that her life was 'nearly wrecked' by the work, which took an 'appalling amount of time' and was not nearly so congenial as her subsequent involvement in the international relief fund set up after the great fire and cholera outbreak in Constantinople.[103] At the same time, her strong personality sometimes intimidated even the worldly-wise and supremely confident male leaders of the anti-suffrage movement. Earlier in the same year, when discussing plans for public meetings and speakers, the Earl of Cromer had written to Lord Curzon to warn him off inviting Sir Hugh Bell:

> I strongly recommend you not to have Sir Hugh Bell. I know him well. He is the great Iron master at Middlesbrough, a strong Free Trader and a very clever man, with a phenomenal power of talking. He is a Liberal in politics, in so far that he votes Liberal, but like a good many other Liberals, all his ideas are strongly Conservative...he would not be regarded by the Liberals as a really representative man. This of itself is enough to rule him out. Moreover,

he would be entirely in the pocket of his daughter, Miss Gertrude Bell, who was present at the meeting yesterday. She is an extremely clever woman, who has travelled a great deal in the East, and written books, one of which she dedicated to me. She has not got much judgment and has a tongue.[104]

Victor Winstone commented that Bell was 'no early feminist' and that she 'did not regard her own liberated existence as anything more than a natural expression of her own ability and enterprise'. She was, Winstone concluded, lucky, because she came from an enlightened and affluent family; she disliked and distrusted women and she never missed an opportunity to criticise their ineptness or unfitness to engage in activities better left to men. She did not demand special rights but she did think that she 'merited the freedoms that were accorded her'.[105] This is perhaps too harsh and simplistic a judgment, and it fails to take into account the difficulties and prejudices faced by independent women with unconventional aspirations. Nevertheless, like Emily Lorimer, Bell certainly failed to acknowledge underlying political imbalances in the opportunities available for women. She was similarly uninterested in gender relations in the Arab world, although this was partly a consequence of her increasing lack of sympathy with the patronising (and matronising) attitudes of Western imperialism. Dorothy Van Ess, the only woman with whom Bell formed a friendship in Basra, later chided her for her lack of interest in the situation of Arab women and her refusal to spend time with them, as well as for her failure to sympathise with the American missionary point of view that Islam was responsible for the failure of Arab society to imitate the perceived freedoms of Western culture.[106] Bell, however, had no interest in Islam, or for that matter in Christianity. Once again like Emily Lorimer, she had no time for missionary proselytising in Arabia. Unlike Lorimer, however, she was a confirmed atheist and had been from a very early age. On 5 April 1902 she had written from Haifa that she visited the missionaries there: 'Heaven preserve us,' she said, 'what a set of scarecrows! It seems a pity that the Christian religion should be exclusively represented by ladies with wispy hair and spectacles. However, God is he who knows!'[107] Together with her Liberal family background, this perspective profoundly affected her views and interpretation of Victorian and imperial values and culture, and it separated her from Emily Lorimer and Dorothy Van Ess. Although she rarely mentions Lorimer in her writings, she does, however, like Lorimer, write about the respect and admiration she had for Dorothy Van Ess's intellect and compassion:

I get rather tired of seeing nothing but men…My great standby is Mrs. Van Ess, the wife of the American missionary. I like them both and she is particularly nice. He has an unexampled knowledge of the country and gives me a good deal of help. He speaks Arabic better than any foreigner I ever heard.[108]

Bell's views of other individual women, and her lack of sympathy for the gender inequalities in both domestic and imperial politics and society are difficult to reconcile with the single-mindedness and apparent self-confidence with which she pursued her own ambitions. That she had doubts about her own achievements and acceptance in the all-male hierarchies of the British Empire is clear from her 'Doughty-Wylie diary' and from occasional references, in her letters to her parents and friends, to her male colleagues in Basra. From the outset she faced opposition and suspicion. However, she countered it to a large extent by separating herself from her own sex and by constructing and representing herself as closely as possible to the masculine model of the imperial official. Bell's job description required her to prepare reports for the British military and political authorities in Cairo, India and London. Furthermore, the reports were to include information on relations with local Arab rulers and tribes.[109] These could only be produced with knowledge gathered partly by research and the reading of official reports, but also, and more importantly, through personal interaction with the rulers and tribes themselves. The expectation that a woman would be able to acquire this knowledge, as well as the techniques to present the information, reflects an outstanding ability on the part of Bell to adapt to the persona and style of a traditional male political officer. It has to be said, however, that it also reflects a unique and surprising sense of vision on the part of the senior officials who appointed her.

Locally, her colleagues were not so sympathetic to her activities. Wallach cites numerous instances of hostility from both military and political colleagues in Basra. Hubert Young, for example, another Political Officer, ignored her. Arnold Wilson, with whom Bell was to have a chequered relationship for many years, refused to give her access to all the office information going out and refused to give her codes for telegrams coming in.[110] In spite of this, Bell continued to produce lengthy and erudite reports, indistinguishable, in their government prose, from those of her male colleagues, and, in fact, only attributable to her from the marginal notes on the India Office files.[111] Through these official reports, she firmly asserted herself as an ungendered government official and staved off criticism by her relentless professionalism and competence. In January 1917, the British High Commissioner in Cairo, Sir Henry McMahon, reported to London on the work of the Arab Bureau, praising its work generally and concluding by 'calling attention to the valuable services rendered by Miss

Gertrude Bell under the direction of Sir P. Cox', stating that 'the manner in which this lady has so long devoted herself to the work of the Arab Bureau under most trying conditions of country and climate is deserving of special notice...her intimate knowledge of Arabia coupled with her ability and energy have rendered her services of great value'.[112] The Foreign Office suggested that Cox should be asked to convey the British Government's appreciation to Bell. In a handwritten note on the file, Arthur Hirtzel added:

> Miss Bell well deserves the commendation...Until she went to Basra the Irak branch of the Bureau was sterile, and no information reached either Cairo or us. On arrival she was treated with the utmost suspicion by the Basra political and military authorities under whose orders she was placed. They lectured her on the Indian Official Secrets Act and actually censored her letters. For a woman of her status the position must have been uncommonly galling; but she put up with it, and I imagine that the improvement in the political attitude of Basra to Cairo and HMG is largely due to her work. Her health has also suffered.[113]

On 11 March 1917 Baghdad was finally captured and Cox appointed Gertrude Bell as his 'Oriental Secretary', the key intelligence post. In spite of Bell's experience and success, General Maude, newly appointed as military commander of Mesopotamia, tried to block the appointment. In his biography of Sir Percy Cox, Philip Graves recalled that Maude 'at first "expressed considerable misgiving" at the news that a woman, however talented, was coming to join the Secretariat' because he was afraid that her arrival might be regarded as a precedent by officers who wanted to have their wives join them.[114] Emily Lorimer, meanwhile, was finally allowed to leave Basra in April 1917, and joined her husband in Kerman, where Lock had been reappointed to his former post. She had increased the circulation of the English edition of the *Basra Times* fourfold.[115] Arnold Wilson, in his memoirs, later chose to forget the difficulties of his relationship with Gertrude Bell and praised the contribution of both women to the war effort: 'Never was the paper better edited and less censored than under Mrs. Lorimer's regime, never were translations into Arabic better supervised; in her, as in Miss Gertrude Bell, the Administration had reason to congratulate itself on its feminine coadjutors'.[116]

Bell and Lorimer, together with the other British and American women in Mesopotamia – Belle Cox, Dora Philby and the military and civilian wives, Christine Bennett, Dorothy Van Ess and their missionary colleagues – created for themselves new, although often very different, roles and identities in the turmoil of the war. Each of them chose to represent themselves as active participants in the imperial war effort and each of them, in their separate ways, confronted and re-appraised their relationships with empire, its male hierarchies and its overseas subjects. The differences between the British and the American lives and aspirations were perhaps the most marked. In the winter of 1917 the Lorimers took leave because of Lock's poor health. As a result of the war they were unable to travel to Europe direct and went instead eastwards via India, Singapore and Canada. En route from Colombo to Singapore they met Mrs Eleanor Franklin Egan, a journalist from the *Chicago Saturday Evening Post* who had just visited Mesopotamia where she had spent six weeks 'to study what we are doing there and dish it up for American consumption'. Egan was much travelled, had been imprisoned in Constantinople and had been on a boat which was torpedoed, but she was still a cheerful and pleasant woman and 'not too noisy', unlike most Americans who were inclined to 'yell your head off'.[117] Eleanor Egan published an account of her experiences, and her views on the war and on imperialism, on her return to America in 1918. She found some of the most noticeable changes for women in the hospitals and medical services:

> They really are an amazing sisterhood. In the beginning it was thought there could be no nursing sisters in Mesopotamia because the conditions were such as no Englishman would ever ask a woman to endure. But the women had something to say about that, and eventually they began to arrive, small units now and then. And at once they began to demonstrate their astonishing powers of physical and spiritual resistance.[118]

The fundamental imperviousness of British imperial society to change, however, struck her most forcefully when she was away from the immediate theatre of war and staying in Bombay with the Governor, Lord Willingdon. She was disconcerted to find another female guest dressed for dinner 'in white satin with a rope of pearls and a tiara'. Accustomed to wartime simplicity, she expressed surprise to a male companion that this formality was still being kept up. 'But this is India,' he said, 'if we should let down an inch or give up a single item of our usual process, it would be taken at once by the Indians as a sign of weakness.'[119] Egan found such fears both picturesque and outdated. The war had begun to expose the differences between American and British attitudes to the Arab world and to imperialism and colonialism in the Middle East. In the immediate postwar years these differences, and their effects on women's roles, were to become more apparent.

NOTES ON CHAPTER 4

1   The principal secondary sources on the military aspects of the Mesopotamia campaign are A.J.Barker, *The Neglected War: Mesopotamia, 1914–1918* (London: Faber & Faber, 1967) and F.J.Moberley, *History of the Great War Based on Official Documents: The Campaign in Mesopotamia* (London: Committee of Imperial Defence Historical Section, 1923).

2   On the political and administrative developments of the wartime administration in Mesopotamia see Lt Colonel Sir Arnold T.Wilson, *Loyalties: Mesopotamia, 1914–1917, a Personal and Historical Record* (London: Oxford University Press, 1930), Briton C.Busch, *Britain, India and the Arabs, 1914–1921* (Berkeley: University of California, 1971), and P.Sluglett, *Britain in Iraq, 1914–1932* (London: Ithaca, 1976).

3   Lorimer shot himself, apparently accidentally, while emptying his pistol. See below, pp.123–24.

4   Keyes to Major S.G.Knox, acting Political Resident, 4 November 1914, IOR:L/PS/11/86, P.5020/14. Knox had moved from the Agency at Bahrain to Muscat in 1911, and was placed in charge of the Residency at Bushire in March 1914.

5   Rev. James E.Moerdyk, 'Bahrein since the War', *Neglected Arabia*, no 93, April–June 1915, p.3.

6   Ibid., p.4.

7   Emily Lorimer to her mother and father, 30 September 1914, MSS Eur F177/14. Before moving to Kuwait, Bessie Mylrea had been assisting in the women's section of the Mason Memorial Hospital in Bahrain, where her husband, Dr Stanley C.Mylrea, was in overall charge.

8   Keyes to Knox, 8 August 1914, and related file notes, IOR:R/15/2/67.

9   Keyes to Knox, 16 August 1914, IOR:R/15/2/67. Yusuf Kanoo was an eminent Bahraini merchant.

10   Keyes to Knox, 4 September 1914, IOR:R/15/2/67.

11   'Aisha bint Muhammad was the daughter of Muhammad bin Khalifah, who had been deported from Bahrain by the British in 1869: M.G.Rumaihi, *Bahrain: Social and Political Change since the First World War* (London: Bowker, 1976), p.186. A similar issue of naming and silencing in colonial women's history was discussed by Gayatri Chakravorty Spivak in her essay on 'The Rani of Sirmur', in *A Critique of Postcolonial Reason: Toward a History of the Vanishing Present* (Cambridge MA and London: Harvard University Press, 1999), ch.3. Spivak described the problems she encountered when researching the life of an early-nineteenth-century woman ruler of a northern Indian Princely State. Faced with the silences and 'fadeout points' in the archives of British imperial rule, Spivak found it difficult to piece together the life of the Rani, who, like Aisha bint Muhammad, was hardly ever even referred to by name.

12 Knox to the Government of India, 30 September 1914, IOR:R/15/2/67.

13 Keyes to Knox, 8 October 1914, IOR:R/15/2/67. The Ladies League was a relief fund organised in India under the patronage of the Vicereine.

14 Keyes to Knox, 5 November 1914, IOR:R/15/2/67.

15 Alfred DeWitt Mason and Frederick J. Barny, *History of the Arabian Mission* (New York: Board of Foreign Missions Reformed Church in America, 1926), pp. 173–74. Sir Arnold Wilson, in his memoirs, confirmed Mason and Barny's assessment and recalled the 'honourable part played at Basra' by the Mission under Dr Bennett and Rev. John Van Ess (who had earned during 15 years residence in the Gulf 'the respect of every class of the community'). Wilson also added that the Mission owned an excellent primary and secondary school at Basra which continued to function during the war. Wilson, *Loyalties*, p. 77.

16 Moerdyk, 'Bahrein since the War', pp. 7–8.

17 Mason and Barny, *History of the Arabian Mission*, pp. 174–75.

18 Paul Harrison 'Report of the Arabian Mission for 1914', *Neglected Arabia*, no 93, April–June 1915, p. 10. Paul Wilberforce Harrison was born in Scribner, Nebraska, and educated at the University of Nebraska and Johns Hopkins Medical School. He was appointed by the Arabian Mission in 1909, and arrived in Kuwait in 1912.

19 Dirk Dykstra, 'Recruits wanted – Who shows the White Feather?', *Neglected Arabia* no 93, January–March 1916, p. 6.

20 Ibid., p. 4.

21 Harrison 'Report of the Arabian Mission for 1914'.

22 Emily Lorimer to her mother, 17 June 1912 (postscript, 21 June), MSS Eur F177/7, and to her mother and father, 12 August 1912, MSS Eur F177/8.

23 Eleanor T. Calverley, *My Arabian Days and Nights* (New York: Thomas Y. Crowell Company, 1958), p. 65.

24 Harrison 'Report of the Arabian Mission for 1914'. Sarah Hosman was born in Kentucky and educated at the University of Illinois. She was appointed to the Arabian Mission in 1911.

25 Harrison 'Report of the Arabian Mission for 1914', p. 11.

26 Christine Bennett, quoted by Harrison in his 'Report of the Arabian Mission for 1914', p. 12.

27 Letter from C. Stanley Mylrea to the Rev. John A. Van Neste, Ridgewood, New Jersey, 27 April 1916, *Neglected Arabia*, no 98, July–September 1916, pp. 15–16. The Ridgewood Church was Mrs Bennett's financial sponsor.

28 See ch. 3.

29 James Cantine, 'Christine Iverson Bennett of the Arabian Mission', *Neglected Arabia*, no 97, April–June 1916.

30 Mylrea letter to the Rev. John A. Van Neste, 27 April 1916.

31 Cantine, 'Christine Iverson Bennett of the Arabian Mission', p. 8.

32 Letter from Sir Percy Cox to Rev. W.I.Chamberlain, Foreign Secretary of the Board of Foreign Missions, 6 May 1916, *Neglected Arabia*, no 97, July–August 1916.

33 'News and Notes from the Field', *Neglected Arabia*, no 94, July–September 1915, and Mason and Barny, *History of the Arabian Mission*, p.186.

34 Emily Lorimer to her mother, 14 October 1912, MSS Eur F177/8.

35 Emily Lorimer to her father, 9 February 1913, MSS Eur F177/10; 'sugar-plum', Emily Lorimer to her father and mother, 1 August 1912, MSS Eur F177/8.

36 Emily Lorimer to her father and mother, 20 December 1912, MSS Eur F177/9.

37 Emily Lorimer, at the British Consulate Muhammerah, to her father and mother, 13 September 1912, MSS Eur F177/8.

38 Newspaper cuttings and copy of letter from Curzon to Lorimer's widow, 21 May 1914, David Lorimer papers, MSS Eur D922.

39 Emily Lorimer to David Lorimer's parents, 2 April 1914, MSS Eur D922.

40 Emily Lorimer to her mother and father, 6 August 1914, IOR:F177/14.

41 Emily Lorimer to her father, 3 September 1914, MSS Eur F177/14.

42 Emily Lorimer to her father, 10 September 1914, and to her mother and father, 6 August 1914, MSS Eur F177/14.

43 Emily Lorimer to her mother and father, 29 October 1914, MSS Eur F177/15.

44 Emily Lorimer to her mother and father, 8 December 1914, MSS Eur F177/15.

45 Emily Lorimer to her mother, 13 July 1915, MSS Eur F177/16.

46 Emily Lorimer to her mother, 18 November 1915, from SS *Dwarka* in the Shatt al-'Arab, MSS Eur F177/18.

47 Emily Lorimer to her mother, 11 December 1915, MSS Eur F177/18.

48 Emily Lorimer to her mother, 20 September 1912, MSS Eur F177/8.

49 Emily Lorimer to her mother and father, 14 July 1912, postscript 18 July 1912, MSS Eur F177/8.

50 Emily Lorimer to her mother, 20 September 1912, MSS Eur F177/8. Emily condemned Mrs Haworth as '*the* most incompetent & ineffective person I ever saw'.

51 Emily Lorimer to her father, 28 September 1912, MSS Eur F177/8.

52 Emily Lorimer to her father and mother, 10 October 1912, MSS Eur F177/8.

53 Emily Lorimer to her mother, 4 November 1915, MSS Eur F177/18.

54 Emily Lorimer to her mother, 3 and 24 December 1915, MSS Eur F177/18.

55 Emily Lorimer to her mother, 5 February 1916, MSS Eur F177/18.

56 Emily Lorimer to her mother, 28 January 1916, MSS Eur F177/18.

57 Emily Lorimer to her mother, 13 and 22 January 1916, MSS Eur F177/18.

58 Emily Lorimer to her mother, 17 February 1916, MSS Eur F177/18.

59 Wilson, *Loyalties*, pp.72–73, and Emily Lorimer to her mother, 25 February 1916, MSS Eur F177/18.

60 Emily Lorimer to her mother, 17 February 1916.

61 Ibid.

62 Emily Lorimer to her mother, 25 February 1916, MSS Eur F177/18.

63 Wilson, *Loyalties*, p. 65, and the India Office List. Cox had been knighted in 1911.

64 Ibid., pp. 67–68, and the India Office List.

65 Emily Lorimer to her mother, 28 January 1916, IOR:MSS Eur F177/18. Wilson became Deputy Chief Political Officer in Basra in January 1916. He had begun his career in the Indian Army but later transferred to the Political Service and served in southwest Persia and the Gulf. He had served as Assistant to David Lorimer at Ahwaz and, under Cox, as Assistant Resident at Bushire, from 1912–13. He did not marry until 1922. Bullard was Acting Consul in Basra in 1914 and then became Civil Adviser to the Military Government. He later became British Agent and Consul in Jeddah (1923–25) and subsequently British Minister there (1936–39). Born in 1885, he, also, did not marry until 1921.

66 Emily Lorimer to her father, 25 April 1912, MSS Eur F177/7.

67 Emily Lorimer to her mother, 28 January and 23 April 1916, MSS Eur F177/18–19.

68 Sir Reader Bullard, *The Camels must Go: An Autobiography* (London: Faber & Faber, 1961), ch. 1. Bullard returned Emily Lorimer's respect, and in his autobiography wrote, 'The list of unusual people who were recruited by Cox would be incomplete without mention of the Lorimers...Lorimer, an officer in the Indian Political, was also a philologist of note. Mrs Lorimer, also a philologist and formerly a don at Somerville, was a witty and entertaining woman.' (p. 92).

69 Emily Lorimer to her mother, 28 January 1916, MSS Eur F177/18. Dorothy Firman Van Ess was born in Wakefield Massachusetts and educated at Wellesley College. She was appointed to the Arabian Mission in 1909. Her husband, Rev. John Van Ess, was educated at Princeton Theological Seminary and appointed to the Mission in 1902.

70 Emily Lorimer to her mother, 18 December 1915, MSS Eur F177/18, and Elizabeth Monroe, *Philby of Arabia* (London: Faber & Faber, 1973), pp. 32–33, 55.

71 Kathryn Tidrick, *Heart-beguiling Araby* (Cambridge: Cambridge University Press, 1981), p. 163.

72 Sykes was a traveller and writer, with a military background. Clayton also started his career as an army officer, but then transferred to the Sudan Government Service and in 1914 became Director of Military Intelligence in Cairo. Hogarth later became Keeper of the Ashmolean Museum at Oxford, and President of the Royal Geographical Society.

73 Undated (December 1915) note by Cox, IOR:R/15/2/68. For a detailed political history of the Eastern Branch of the Arab Bureau, its administration and

relations with Cairo, see Busch, *Britain, India and the Arabs, 1914–1921* (Berkeley: University of California Press, 1971), ch. 2.

74   Emily Lorimer to her mother, 4 March 1916, MSS Eur F177/19.

75   Emily Lorimer to her mother, 18 March 1916, MSS Eur F177/19.

76   Bell's life and career as an explorer and writer is well known. Her papers are in the Gertrude Bell Archive at the University of Newcastle-upon-Tyne. She has been the subject of two major biographies and she has figured in both scholarly and popular studies of the period. The most recent biography is Janet Wallach's *Desert Queen: the Extraordinary Life of Gertrude Bell, Adventurer, Adviser to Kings, Ally of Lawrence of Arabia* (New York: Doubleday, 1996). The earlier one, H. V. F. Winstone, *Gertrude Bell* (London: Jonathan Cape, 1978) contains more detailed information on Bell's professional career, as a political officer in Mesopotamia. Winstone comments on the wide range of primary source material available on Bell: 'No life could ever have been better documented than that of Gertrude Bell. From early childhood to the end of her days she recorded every step, every significant event, in letters to her family and friends' (p. ix). Selections from Bell's letters were published, after her death, by her stepmother, Lady Florence Bell, in 1927 (*Letters of Gertrude Bell*, 2 vols, London: Ernest Benn) and by Elizabeth Burgoyne, in 1958 and 1961 (*Gertrude Bell: From her Personal Papers*, 2 vols, London: Ernest Benn). Bell's letters to her lover, Charles Doughty-Wylie, have been edited and published by Rosemary O'Brien (*Gertrude Bell: The Arabian Diaries, 1913–1914*, New York: Syracuse University Press, 2000). All these edited volumes of Bell's own testimony can be supplemented by the different perspectives of official India Office files and the papers of her contemporaries. Although much has been written about her travels, her personal relationships and her doomed love affairs, surprisingly little attention has been paid, in all these accounts, to the wider significance, in relation to gender and empire, of her political and professional status during the period in Mesopotamia and post-war Iraq.

77   Wallach, *Desert Queen*, pp. 24–25, and Winstone, *Gertrude Bell*, p. 19. General biographical information on Bell's early life and career is taken from these two biographies and Bell's own letters.

78   Janet Hogarth, quoted by Lady Florence Bell, *Letters of Gertrude Bell*, vol. 1, p. 11. Hogarth later published her account of Bell in *An Oxford Portrait Gallery* (London: Chapman & Hall, 1931).

79   Charles Hardinge, Baron Hardinge of Penshurst, was Viceroy from November 1910 to April 1916.

80   Winstone, *Gertrude Bell*, pp. 58–59, and Burgoyne, *Gertrude Bell*, vol. 1, p. 90.

81   See ch. 1.

82   Winstone, *Gertrude Bell*, vol. 1, p. 139.

83   Before their final defeat by 'Abd al-'Aziz Al Sa'ud in 1921, the Rashid confederacy were a powerful tribal force in central Arabia. For a detailed

history see Madawi Al Rasheed, *Politics in an Arabian Oasis: the Rashidi Tribal Dynasty* (London: I.B.Tauris, 1991).

84 IOR: L/PS/11/79, P.2221/14, IOR:L/PS/10/259 and Wallach, *Desert Queen*, pp.113–22.

85 Letter, 17 March 1914, Burgoyne, *Gertrude Bell*, vol.1, p.302.

86 Wallach, *Desert Queen*, pp.125ff.

87 D.G.Hogarth, 'Gertrude Bell's journey to Hayil', *Geographical Journal*, no70 (1927), pp.1–21.

88 Hogarth, 'Gertrude Bell's journey to Hayil', pp.15–16.

89 Mallet to the Foreign Secretary, Sir Edward Grey, 20 May 1914, IOR:L/PS/11/79.

90 The first book, *The Desert and the Sown*, an account of her 1905 Syrian expedition, was published in 1907 (London: William Heinemann) and *Amurath to Amurath* was published in 1911 (London: William Heinemann).

91 Both quoted by Wallach, *Desert Queen*, pp.79–80.

92 Bell, *The Desert and the Sown*, Preface, p.x.

93 Burgoyne, *Gertrude Bell*, vol.1, pp.296–97. Also reproduced in O'Brien, *Gertrude Bell*, pp.73–74. When Bell first met Doughty-Wylie, together with his wife Judith, he was British Consul in Konia. He was killed at Gallipoli in 1915. Colonel Gerald Leachman was a political officer who had travelled extensively in Arabia. He also joined the staff of the Mesopotamian administration in early 1915.

94 Hardinge to Sir Beauchamp Duff, Commander-in-Chief India, 11 February 1916, Hardinge Papers, Cambridge University Library, quoted by Busch, *Britain, India and the Arabs*, p.123.

95 India Office minute by Arthur Hirtzel, 29 May 1916, IOR:L/PS/10/576.

96 Wilson, *Loyalties*, pp.157–58.

97 Burgoyne, *Gertrude Bell*, vol.2, pp.39–40.

98 Winstone, *Gertrude Bell*, p.192. It is interesting, although perhaps understandable given the lack of archival materials, that Winstone makes only the briefest reference to Belle Cox in his book.

99 Ibid., p.192; also quoted by Philby's biographer, Elizabeth Monroe (*Philby of Arabia*, p.53).

100 Emily Lorimer to her mother, 5 August 1916, MSS Eur F177/20.

101 Wallach, *Desert Queen*, p.88.

102 See Introduction. In 1908 Bell was appointed first Honorary Secretary of the Women's National Anti-Suffrage League. After it merged with the Men's League to become the National League for Opposing Women's Suffrage in 1910, she also served for a time on the Executive Committee. In her commentary on Bell's letters, however, Elizabeth Burgoyne recalls that 'Much later, so her friend Janet Courtney [née Hogarth] told me, she was amused by her own attitude [to the suffrage campaign]; but for the time being, and with the campaign intensifying, she threw herself with

verve and conviction into the task of opposition'. Burgoyne, *Gertrude Bell*, vol. 1, p. 274.

103 Burgoyne, *Gertrude Bell*, vol. 1, p. 280.

104 Cromer to Curzon, 23 February 1912, MSS Eur F112/35.

105 Winstone, *Gertrude Bell*, p. 81.

106 Dorothy Van Ess, *Pioneers in the Arab World* (Grand Rapids, MI: Historical Series of Reformed Church in America, 1974), p. 98.

107 Burgoyne, *Gertrude Bell*, vol. 1, p. 127. One of her university friends, Mary Talbot, described Bell's viewpoint as 'unequivocal atheism' (Winstone, *Gertrude Bell*, p. 18).

108 Burgoyne, *Gertrude Bell*, vol. 2, pp. 39–40.

109 Gertrude Bell's job description, IOR:R/15/2/68.

110 Wallach, *Desert Queen*, pp. 181–82.

111 Most reports were forwarded to London under the signature of the Chief Political Officer, Sir Percy Cox. A close reading of the files, however, shows that Bell was the author of the majority of the administrative reports produced in 1916/1917, for example, 'Administration of Justice in the occupied territories of Iraq', 'The Shiahs and their position in Iraq', 'Note on Tribal Saiyids', 'The basis of Government in Turkish Arabia' (July 1916), IOR:L/PS/10/617.

112 Foreign Office to India Office, 20 January 1917, IOR:L/PS/10/576.

113 Minute by Hirtzel, 24 January 1917, IOR:L/PS/10/576.

114 Philip Graves, *The Life of Sir Percy Cox* (London: Hutchison & Co., 1941), p. 225.

115 Emily Lorimer to her mother, 10 December 1916, MSS Eur F177/21; IOR:L/PS/10/617, memo from Emily Lorimer to Cox, 14 August 1916.

116 Wilson, *Loyalties*, p. 73.

117 Emily Lorimer to her mother, 18 January 1918, MSS Eur F177/23.

118 Eleanor Franklin Egan, *The War in the Cradle of the World* (London: Hodder & Stoughton, 1918), pp. 131–32.

119 Ibid., p. 36.

5 Women and the 'New World Order': Anglo-American Perspectives on Colonialism, 1918–26

In their history of the Arabian Mission, published in 1926, Alfred De Witt Mason and Frederick J. Barny applauded the benefits of British colonial rule and the help it gave to the American missionaries:

> Surely whatever sins political or social may be laid to its charge, it is a fact that a greater degree of religious and intellectual liberty than is possible without it, follows the British flag all around the world. To that emblem and the authority it represents all mankind owe a debt of gratitude for the possibility, humanly speaking, of carrying the Gospel to millions of men, who but for the safeguard of Great Britain's friendliness to religious liberty, could never have been reached.[1]

Mason and Barny's rather generous summary epitomised and acknowledged the mutual sympathy and cultural similarities of British and American interests in the Middle East in the early part of the twentieth century. The British, as we have already seen, were equally grateful when the Americans contributed to the provision of badly needed medical and social services in the Gulf during the hard years of the Mesopotamia campaign. However, in spite of this shared sense of a Western civilising mission, and in spite of generally warm relations on a personal level, the political Anglo-American relationship in the area had always been at best cautious and at worst, on the part of the British at least, openly hostile.

In the immediate pre-war years, and during the war itself, the British had been constantly troubled by the missionaries' efforts to strengthen their influence in the Gulf region and, in particular, by their repeated attempts to penetrate inland. They were also uneasy about the Americans' increasing tendency, as they saw it, to meddle in the cultural and social life of the shaikhdoms. In 1916, for example, the Political Agent at Bahrain, Captain

149

Percy Loch, a successor of David Lorimer, had noted on file an exchange with the Americans over an unnamed local Muslim woman who had been abandoned by her husband, ill-treated by her own mother and subsequently given refuge by the missionaries.[2] When the mother demanded the daughter back, Loch had been afraid that there would be trouble because the missionaries were unwilling to return the young woman without a guarantee that she would not be ill-treated. The Reverend Dirk Dykstra who, with his wife, Winnie, was responsible for 'Evangelistic work' in Bahrain, had visited Loch to review the situation and to ascertain whether the mother had any rights to her daughter under Muslim law.[3] Loch subsequently persuaded the ruler of Bahrain, and the local Amir of Manama town, to prevent the woman's family from ill-treating her. Dykstra, however, also wanted a guarantee that the woman would be able to visit the missionaries whenever she chose to do so. Loch recorded that he had been obliged to warn Dykstra of a British assurance, made to the Shaikh some years earlier, that the Agency would not intervene on behalf of Bahraini women and would hand them over to the *shari'ah* courts for redress. Dykstra persisted and asked whether the Americans were bound by this agreement, adding that he would like to consult his wife, since the case concerned her more than it did him. After some further discussion, Loch noted, the Dykstras reluctantly agreed not to pursue the matter.[4]

The case was significant as an example of the attitudes and perspectives of the participants and the carefully constructed boundaries of imperial involvement in the Gulf shaikhdoms before the end of the First World War. The American missionaries were clearly determined in their pursuit of what they regarded as issues of social justice, and they were very clear about the relative positions and purpose of women's work in that mission and of women's spheres of influence.[5] In their attitude towards Arab women they were also clear about their own duty and right to bypass Islamic law and interpose Western values in cases of perceived injustice. The British were less concerned about the plight of the individual woman (and the social status of Arab women generally), or about establishing the truth of the allegations, and were more concerned about their relations with the ruler of Bahrain. At the end of his note, Loch concluded that he had recorded the incident 'especially as a case of the Missionaries admitting themselves bound by our agreements with the Shaikh'.[6]

Meanwhile, the missionaries were increasingly trying to pursue their earlier objective to break away from the coast and 'occupy Arabia'.[7] After the departure of Samuel and Amy Zwemer in 1913 to Egypt, to work and teach, the pursuit of the Arabian grail was taken up by Dr Paul Harrison and his wife Regina. Harrison was a graduate of Johns Hopkins Medical

School. Regina Rabbe Harrison was born in Catonsville, Maryland, and had trained at the Union Protestant Infirmary Training School for Nurses in Baltimore. The couple were married in November 1916 in Baltimore, and left for Bahrain together later in the same month.[8] The Harrisons were to be a continual source of irritation to the British for many years. They were initially the subject of suspicion because, in February 1915, the Military Censor's office in Karachi had intercepted a 'very anti-English' letter to Paul Harrison from his brother, which the officials reported to the Persian Gulf Intelligence Officer at Bushire.[9] Regina Harrison was also under suspicion because the British thought she might have pro-German sympathies.[10] Americans with German and Dutch names were a constant problem for the British because local officials were often unsure about the balance, or conflict, of loyalties produced by the family origin and the adopted nationality of many of the American women missionaries. The foreignness or 'otherness' of their names simply added to their mysteriousness, and to the perceived danger implicit in their activities.

In March 1917 Harrison wrote to Loch asking for authorisation to visit Qatif on the Saudi-controlled mainland coast, just north of Bahrain. Loch consulted both the Deputy British Resident at Bushire, Major Arthur Trevor, and Sir Percy Cox in Basra, and he eventually passed on to Harrison Cox's decision that there would be no objection to a visit but that the missionaries should not go further inland.[11] The British were at this time engaged in negotiations with the Saudis and were not about to endanger their own, carefully constructed, political supremacy in the region.[12] Subsequently, however, Loch found out that Harrison did intend to go inland and, if possible, to visit the central Saudi province of Najd. The trip, Loch discovered, was planned to be a 'fait accompli... only Mrs Dykstra gave it away at tea. I replied that our point of view, though we quite saw theirs, was that in case of trouble it was we who had to exact retribution or incur a serious loss of prestige'.[13] In June the position was further complicated by a request from 'Abd al-'Aziz Al Sa'ud for an American doctor.[14] Loch reported that he would rather send a British medical officer but since there was none available he had no choice but to allow Harrison to go, while at the same time warning him not to try anything relating to acquiring land for a new local base.[15] The British then heard that an Indian nurse from the Mission had been asked whether she would accept a permanent post at Qatif, and they became even more convinced that the Americans were attempting a *fait accompli*.[16] Trevor responded to Loch's report on the latest missionary activities with an order that he should warn Dykstra that 'Bin Saud is our ally and is helping in the war'. Any attempt to establish a permanent branch of the Mission in Saudi territory might easily result in trouble and the Mission would have to 'mind its Ps and Qs'.[17]

In December Loch reported to the Residency that Harrison had now been invited to visit the shaikhs of Qatar and Bahrain. Loch was also concerned about the return to Bahrain of another woman missionary, Jane Scardefield, who, during a previous posting there, had been known to hold 'strong pro-enemy views'.[18] Loch had heard rumours, admittedly unsubstantiated, that Scardefield had subsequently 'got into trouble at Kuwait or Basrah over expressing them too freely':

> I do not know if it is true. In any case I have met the lady and do not trust her at all. I propose to censor all her letters before they leave Bahrain. May I do so? I may mention that she has already been censured once for the scurrilous remarks regarding the censorship, in which she saw fit to indulge.[19]

The Assistant Political Resident, Maitland Rae, responded to Loch that the Resident, Colonel Trevor, knew Miss Scardefield personally and had no objection to her returning to Bahrain. Rae asked Loch to be more specific about the alleged pro-enemy views and 'scurrilous remarks', to which Loch responded that he could not, but that the censors had returned a letter to her, via his office, refusing to send it because it contained 'grossly insulting aspersions on the Postal Censors'.[20] Loch seems to have been particularly hostile to the women missionaries, over and above the official unease about missionary activity generally.

The Political Agent's growing anxieties were summarised early in the following year, 1918, in a memorandum addressed to the Deputy Political Resident at Bushire, in which he listed the visits to the mainland made by members of the Arabian Mission. Loch noted that he would prefer to have 'no such irresponsible persons visiting the neighbouring mainland' but had better make the best of it and establish a precedent 'for our being consulted before any journey is made'; Harrison's attitude to Britain, he thought, appeared to be quite friendly but some of the other missionaries were not 'friendly at heart', and those who were anti-British would have 'great opportunities for mischief owing to the influence the Mission exercise through their hospital, school, and, most difficult to discover or combat, the visits of the lady missionaries to the harems'. Loch recommended that the US Government should be warned that Britain 'holds a special position in the Persian Gulf'.[21]

Women, therefore, were at the centre of the British suspicion that the Americans might be a source of subversion, a suspicion that was fuelled by the supposed foreignness of those of German descent and by the secret and secretive contacts likely to be forged and maintained by the missionary women in areas forbidden to the British. That their own wives might also make contacts with local women does not seem to have occurred to the political agents and residents during this period. If they came out and stayed in the Gulf for any length of time, the British memsahibs mostly seem to have stayed firmly away from Arab women, repulsed and horrified, like Emily Lorimer, by the perceived squalor of local life. Gender became an issue in wartime and post-war Anglo–American relations, and a locus of dispute, precisely because of the missionary women's access to areas of Arab thought prohibited to British men and ignored by British women. In their attempts to prevent such contacts, the British authorities frequently resorted to the old, well-tried but unspoken, argument of sexual danger.

In March 1918, Loch was transferred to Kuwait, and a few weeks later the incoming Political Agent in Bahrain, George Mungavin, telegraphed Bushire to say that Harrison had again been invited to Qatar by the ruling Shaikh and intended to go there for two weeks; Harrison also wanted to take his wife as far as Darin, a town on an island offshore from Qatif, and leave her to stay with the shaikh's family during his absence. Mungavin wondered whether there would be any objection and added that personally he had no objection to the doctor's visit to Qatar but he did not 'fancy the idea of a white woman being left alone with natives'.[22] The First Assistant Resident at Bushire telegraphed his agreement: 'See no objection to Doctor's visit to Qatar as suggested but cannot permit lady's going there'.[23] In an undated note to Harrison, Mungavin added that: 'the more I think about it, the more I feel that it is not quite the thing for a white woman to be so far away with only natives … At first I thought it was all quite right but I am sure I should not have a moment's peace while she was away there all alone.'[24]

Until the end of the First World War, the British were able to use the specific circumstances of the political conflict and military uncertainty as a valid excuse to restrict the movements of the missionaries and maintain a delicate balance between their own imperial hold on the area, the missionaries' proactive and relentless attempts to penetrate inland, and the local rulers' requests for medical assistance from the Americans. The activities of missionary women were always at the centre of the picture, both as objects of interest and as convenient symbols of tension. Once the war was over, the shaikhs began to intensify their requests for medical assistance and the missionaries regarded themselves as free to respond and initiate their own contacts. Most significantly, the shaikhs began specifically to demand the visits of women doctors and nurses, with the result that the gender issue became even more entangled in the triangular inter-play of imperial relations in the area.

At the end of 1918, 'Abd al-'Aziz Al Sa'ud requested Dr Harrison to go urgently to Riyadh to treat the victims of an outbreak of influenza.[25] The British gave permission for Harrison to go, asking him at the same time to keep them 'fully posted regarding current developments'.[26] By now, however, the British had formulated new reasons to restrict the mission-aries from going further inland, and the Political Agent was instructed to write to Harrison and informally request him to make no visits without British approval, since: 'one result of the conclusion of peace will be a gradual extension of trade and communication generally with the interior of Arabia. With a suspicious and fanatical population this will naturally take time, and any untoward incident would set things back indefinitely.'[27]

The following February, the Saudi ruler wrote again to the Political Agent Bahrain, now Captain Norman Bray, asking for permission for Mrs Harrison to visit the eastern region of the country, Al Hasa province. Paul Harrison had just completed his trip to Riyadh and had set off back to Bahrain via Hasa, where he had interrupted his journey to treat more patients. 'Abd al-'Aziz warned Bray that Harrison would be delayed:

> I am grateful to him and he may require his wife to be with him during the time he will be in Hasa for the treatment of ladies as it is not concealed to you that the former cannot himself approach women in connection with treatment as it is forbidden by Shara and I would request you to allow her to proceed to him in Hasa.[28]

Alarmed by this letter, and by rumours that Harrison intended to stay in Hasa for three months, Bray immediately wrote to Harrison, asking him to deny that he had made arrangements, without official British permission, to stay in Hasa and, furthermore, to acquire land for a hospital.[29] Mrs Harrison did not, however, make the trip, and Paul Harrison returned to Bahrain in early March, agreeing to 'go nowhere' without the consent of the Political Agent.[30] Meanwhile, content to receive any political infor-mation the Harrisons might provide, the British were also intercepting the couple's private correspondence and, in February, Bray passed on to Baghdad a comment on Saudi political sympathies:

> Following extract from Harrison to his wife. Begins:- 'I wish you could hear all Ibn Saud says about President Wilson; he hopes that he will intervene between England and Germany. Ibn Saud is very anxious lest Germany's power should be too greatly curtailed. He does not care a rap about Turkey'.[31]

A year later, in February 1920, the latest British incumbent at the Bahrain Agency, Major Harold Dickson, reported receiving another letter from

'Abd al-'Aziz, this time saying that he would like Harrison, Mrs Harrison, and an Indian dentist to go to the Hasa oasis town of Hufuf.[32] Dickson, like his predecessors, was reluctant to agree but eventually the British gave permission for the Harrisons to go as far as Hufuf, although no further inland. Dickson was ordered to write to 'Abd al-'Aziz, asking him to 'refrain from extending invitation to Dr and Mrs Harrison to proceed beyond Hofuf without previous consultation' with British officials.[33] He also wrote to Harrison, telling him that personally he regretted not being able to allow the missionaries to travel beyond Hasa, but that they must not attempt to go to Riyadh and 'must not be too hard on the Baghdad authorities'. 'There is a good deal of method in their madness,' he added, 'and affairs in Arabia and Syria generally have much to do with their present apparently hard decision.' He concluded that he hoped Mrs Harrison was keeping fit and well and trusting she would not 'heap too many "CUSSES" on my poor head for preventing her plucking the forbidden fruit'.[34]

The image of the 'forbidden fruit' evokes a whole range of cultural and political ideas and perceptions, from the Orientalist exoticism and eroticism of nineteenth-century Western harem art and literature, to the literal and factual boundaries and hierarchies of imperial administration and diplomacy in the post-war Gulf. The idea and suspicion that women had access to unknown and yet tantalising – even threatening – spaces was to be a constant theme in both Anglo-American political relations and British colonial gender relations in the post-war years. In the months immediately after the Armistice in November 1918, the British were particularly nervous about the loyalty of the local rulers, the development of Arab nationalism and the security of their Middle Eastern economic and strategic interests. Any undercurrents of political unrest were carefully monitored and reported back, by political agents, to their regional and central government authorities in Baghdad, London and India. In April 1919, for example, the Deputy Political Resident, when reporting to Baghdad that Harrison had agreed to keep the British informed of his movements, also added that the Bahrain Agent was suspicious about the activities of other missionaries and that the 'ladies especially are intimate in the houses of several persons who are not too well affected to us'.[35]

The activities of the women missionaries in Bahrain were especially worrying for the British because of the latter's general uncertainty about the political loyalties of the Bahraini ruling family and, in particular, those of the ruler's still influential wife, 'Aisha bint Muhammad, and her associates. In his political diary for March 1920, Dickson reported that Shaikh 'Isa, 'though hale and hearty, is very old and leans more and more on the advice of his strong minded wife and her son, Abdullah'.[36] Although

Shaikh 'Isa was loyal, Dickson thought he had no actual affection for the British but simply knew on which side 'his bread is buttered'. His wife, who was much younger, was very ambitious and anxious for her son to succeed to the throne. Dickson described her as 'decidedly masterful' adding that she:

> Outwardly, rules the women of Bahrain only, and holds daily Majlis [open court] at which scores of disconsolate females come and lodge their complaints. Behind the scenes, however, she largely dictates Shaikh 'Isa's policy in company with Jassim [al-Chirawi]...Undoubtedly the triumvirate, Abdullah, Jassim and Abdullah's mother, are anti-foreign and so anti-British. Their eventual aim is to remove all British control and protection from the islands of Bahrain...Recent events in the world have been greatly responsible for existing ideas. The cry 'Rights of Small Nations' is quite commonly heard here...To the ordinary Arab of sense such ideas are utopian and ridiculous in the extreme, but not so to Shaikh Isa and family, whose ignorance of world affairs is colossal and whose mentality is of the simplest.[37]

This confident and patronising dismissal of local nationalist politics epitomised the ambivalence of the post-war British administrators in the region. While remaining generally optimistic and secure in their mission to govern or guide the emerging nations of the Arabian Peninsula region, they were nevertheless anxious to avoid any threats to their own imperial dominance. Their attitude to the American missionaries reflected this ambivalence. Although suspicious of the Americans' political ideas and close contacts with local people, the British were grateful for the social and medical work undertaken by the missionaries and they were also, as in previous years, keen to collect and use the political information reported to them by the Americans. The latter were equally relaxed about passing on information to the British, no doubt viewing this as a *quid pro quo* for gaining permission and support for further new medical enterprises. Paul Harrison's reports all found their way on to Arab Bureau files during the last two years of the war, and they were a source of detailed knowledge about local affairs in the Gulf shaikhdoms which would otherwise have been inaccessible to the British.[38] In April 1918, for example, Harrison wrote to the Political Agent in Bahrain, after a month-long visit to Abu Dhabi, where he had treated the ruler, Shaikh Hamdan bin Zaid Al Nahayyan. Harrison had also visited the smaller Trucial shaikhdoms and treated members of the ruling families and the local population. Harrison reported that Shaikh Hamdan was the most powerful ruler in the area and strongly loyal to the British. More generally, he reported on the political attitude of the local communities:

The need for medical services was everywhere extreme, and such services greatly appreciated... As to the political situation... On the surface nothing is met with but the most cordial loyalty to the British Government. But it is not difficult to see that, underneath, this loyalty is considerably tempered. In the first place the increase of British power is feared because it is felt that their ascendancy means the disappearance of slavery. This feeling however is pretty largely confined to the small upper class that are rich enough to own slaves... There is also wide-spread fear that the advent of the British would result in women's freedom from the domination of men to a very dangerous degree. I was not able satisfactorily to investigate the origin of this surprising feeling. On the other hand the people from the poorest to the richest have come to realize very keenly their economic dependence on British power... [39]

The irony of Harrison's statement about women's freedom cannot have been entirely lost on either the British officials or the missionaries themselves. Women's emancipation, along contemporary Western lines, had always been one of the declared motives of the missionary activity and, at the same time, one of the sources of contention with the British local authorities, who firmly believed in staying clear of such issues. The political attitude of the shaikhs, however, was of more interest to them. At the end of the war the British in the Gulf region were concerned with filling the imperial power vacuum left by the defeat of the Turks, securing the continuing loyalty and support of the independent, but British-protected, rulers of the Gulf and Arabian Peninsula states, and, subsequently, devising and laying down an administration in the newly created British Mandated territory of Iraq.[40] This latter administration was the subject of lengthy internal British Government discussions, as well as international post-war negotiations, both influenced to some extent by American declarations of support for Arab self-determination.[41] Regional American attitudes and missionary involvement in local politics were therefore carefully observed and monitored by British officials in all areas of the Gulf region and co-ordinated in the continuing British administrations in Baghdad and Basra.

After the capture of Baghdad, in the spring of 1917, Sir Percy Cox had been promoted to the post of Civil Commissioner in Mesopotamia, while nominally still retaining the position of Political Resident in the Persian Gulf.[42] Cox thus assumed overall responsibility for British political administration in the entire Arab Gulf region. Cox moved immediately to Baghdad and took with him a number of political officers from Basra, including Gertrude Bell, as Oriental Secretary and one of the few women allowed to travel to Baghdad. Belle Cox had remained in Basra. The Coxes' only son, Derek, who had seen little of his parents during his

childhood in England, and who was serving in France in the Royal Air
Force, was killed soon afterwards in August 1917. Cox later wrote to Lord
Curzon, hinting at the personal loneliness of both his and Belle's lives:

> The loss of our boy was a great blow to us, not so much in immediate effect
> because after three years of these continual tragedies around one, one's power
> to feel inevitably gets blunted or merged in the intense longing to see the
> vital issues through, but rather in its portent for us in the future. I have no
> ambition and never have had except to do the task set me as completely as
> I can; but I did look forward greatly if we had both come through the war,
> to being at home with my boy while he was at the University... My wife still
> lives at Basra; ladies are not allowed at Baghdad, except hospital nurses, so
> I only see her very rarely – twice during the past year – but she finds plenty
> to do distributing comforts, etc, in odd corners not reached by the ordinary
> organisations and prefers to be there than going home or to India.[43]

Early in 1918 Cox was recalled to London for government consultations,
and he was soon afterwards posted to the British Legation in Persia. The
Coxes left Mesopotamia, also taking Reader Bullard with them as tempo-
rary Oriental Secretary.[44] In Baghdad, Arnold Wilson was appointed as
Acting Civil Commissioner, with Gertrude Bell remaining in her post as his
Oriental Secretary, and becoming increasingly out of tune with Wilson's
high-handed imperialist views and more and more sympathetic to the
cause of Arab statehood. She wrote to one of her colleagues, Sir William
Willcocks, that she had 'grown to love this land, its sights and its sounds':
'I never weary of the East, just as I never feel it to be alien. I cannot feel
exiled here; it is a second native country. If my family were not in England,
I should have no wish to return.'[45]

Bell's personal and professional life in post-war Iraq, as the region
now became known, has been well-documented, as has her role in the
lengthy and often turbulent interdepartmental British government debate
on the formulation of policy in the post-war Middle East.[46] In February
1919 she produced a memorandum on 'Self Determination in Mesopotamia', and she subsequently attended the Paris Peace Conference, together
with Arnold Wilson, to discuss the future of the country.[47] At this stage, her
relations with Wilson were relatively placid. The memorandum generally
put forward the view that public opinion in Iraq was in favour of continuing British rule, but with an Arab governor under British protection.
In contrast to Wilson's static imperialism, however, Bell's sympathies and
convictions were continuing to change with the times. As one historian
of Iraq has written, Bell's great strengths 'lay in her flexibility and her
ability to adapt to changing circumstances'. While Wilson never really
accepted that nationalism was a 'force to be accommodated rather than

silenced, Gertrude Bell eventually came to realise that at least some concession must be made to the fact that people prefer to manage their own affairs'.[48] Returning to Baghdad via Cairo and Damascus, observing the political situation there, and meeting and talking to local Arabs, Bell's ideas 'turned almost one hundred and eighty degrees from where they had been before her trip'.[49] Converted by what she had seen in Syria to the principle of Arab self-government, she produced a report of her trip in which she now argued that the creation of an Arab state in Mesopotamia would be popular and practicable within a short period of years.[50]

From this date, Bell's sympathy for the Arab nationalist cause brought her into continual conflict with Wilson and the other British political officers in Baghdad, who were becoming more convinced of the need for the preservation of British strategic interests in the vicinity of the southern Persian oilfields. Their political disapproval was often conveyed in deeply misogynistic personal insults. Bell's biographer, Janet Wallach, writes that she was ignored in the political mess, where the men 'snidely referred to her walled house as Chastity Chase'. At the same time, in a letter to a friend, Wilson wrote that he was 'having some trouble with Miss Bell. On political questions she is rather fanatic.'[51] Nevertheless, Bell wrote to her stepmother in January 1920, reaffirming her new-found convictions:

> I pray the people at home may be rightly guided and realise that the only chance here is to recognise political ambitions from the first, not to try to squeeze the Arabs into our mould and have our hands forced…I wish I carried more weight…the truth is I'm in a minority of one in the Mesopotamian political service – or nearly – and yet I'm so sure I'm right that I would go to the stake for it. They must see; they must know at home. They can't be so blind as not to read such gigantic writing on the wall as the world at large is setting before their eyes.[52]

In April 1920, at the San Remo Conference, the colonial mandates for Iraq and Palestine were allocated to Britain. Syria and Lebanon went to France. While intended by the European powers to suggest at least temporary trusteeship, the mandates were interpreted by Arab nationalists as a ploy for the maintenance of colonial rule. In Iraq the situation was exacerbated by the failure of the British to set up any form of representative administration, and in the summer of 1920 rebellion broke out.[53] British reprisals under Wilson included a scorched-earth policy, in which insurgent villages were razed to the ground. Bell believed that Wilson's tactics were too harsh, but she was increasingly at odds with the British administration in Baghdad because of her Arab sympathies. Her relations with Wilson became correspondingly, and mutually, hostile.[54]

Characteristically, Bell herself remained confident that her policy was right, and when Sir Percy Cox paid a short visit to Baghdad in June 1920, she appealed to him for support:

> Sir Percy came after dinner and I gave him what I believe to be the correct view of the whole Arab situation, and how badly it has been handled for the last eight months. He was most understanding. Being with him has felt like getting on to a rock, after the wild upheavals of the last fortnight.[55]

In July, however, Wilson wrote to Cox, who had now arrived back at the India Office, suggesting to him that if he could 'find a job for Miss Bell at home I think you will be well advised to do so. Her irresponsible activities are a source of considerable concern to me here and are not a little resented by the Political Officers.'[56] By this time Wilson and the other political officers were solidly against Bell's sympathy for Arab independence and eventually she received a reprimand from the Secretary of State for India for not 'pulling together' while the future of Iraq hung in the balance.[57] By the autumn of 1920 the rebellion had been put down but thousands of Arabs and hundreds of British military and civilian officials had been killed. It had also cost the British a large amount of money and, in the domestic political atmosphere of post-war Britain, had proved to be very controversial. Even *The Times* criticised British policy in a leader article, telling its readers that the principal cause of the rising was that 'after the Arabs had been firmly promised that they should control their own affairs under advisory guidance, the British authorities proceeded to act as though we meant to take over the whole country lock, stock and barrel'.[58]

That women's views were not, in any sense, homogenous, or influenced by a specifically 'gendered' perspective on post-war politics, can be seen from the markedly different opinions of Emily Lorimer on Mesopotamian affairs at the end of the war and also during the rebellion. The Lorimers arrived in Britain in October 1918 and then stayed in Ireland and London until the end of 1919. In early 1920 they set off to Bombay, Loralai, Kashmir and Srinagar, finally ending up in Gilgit, where David Lorimer was Political Agent until his retirement in 1924. During their journey from Iraq to London and on their subsequent travels the Lorimers kept in touch with affairs in the Gulf and India, and also in Ireland. Emily's authoritarian and imperialist views seem, if anything, to have hardened during this period. In July 1918 she wrote to her mother from Vancouver reporting that she had heard from Reader Bullard how the administration in Iraq was progressing, and was amazed at how much work was being done to get the country 'into order and under cultivation, starting schools, running revenue, law courts etc etc. A contrast, rather, to German activities in Occupied Territories.'[59] It was a welcome contrast to Vancouver which, she said, was paralysed by striking tram workers and a generally irresponsible working class. Telling her mother about the strike, Emily complained that she would like to 'get the entire male population of Vancouver formed into Labour corps for Mesopotamia, let 'em do a little honest work for once'. 'No,' she concluded, 'democracy at close quarters isn't nice.' Nor, at the same time, were Catholicism and Irish nationalism, to both of which Emily continued to express a vituperative hostility, which must have coloured her entire world picture of colonialism. In May she had written to her mother to express her opinion on the current situation in Ireland:

> The news last night of the arrest of the Sinn Feiners on the eve of a new rebellion is the best thing we have heard for a long time…I wish the R.C. bishops had been lifted too…the present episode may be the beginning of some practical settlement without handing the country over to a lot of pro-Boer, pro-German, anti-British intriguers.[60]

Two years later, now in Loralai on the North West Frontier, while Gertrude Bell was observing the political and social changes in the former imperial territories, and changing her perspectives as she did so, Emily Lorimer's opinions were becoming more entrenched and more reinforced by a defensive and conservative view of herself as a member of the 'white' governing classes:

> I quite agree with Mother [David Lorimer's] that for the last 50 years the only people in Ireland with legitimate grievances against the British Govt have been the 'white people' like ourselves. All the world over that is the privilege of being English that England will let you down every time in favour of any alien sweep that comes along.[61]

Faced with the news of rebellion and slaughter in Mesopotamia in 1920, her reactions were perhaps predictable and they can best be summed up by her response to an article in the *Contemporary Review*, published by the renowned classical scholar, Gilbert Murray.[62] Murray was Regius Professor of Greek at Oxford from 1908 to 1936 and he had strong connections with Emily's old college, Somerville. In 1911 he and his wife had sent the Lorimers a copy of his book *The Rise of the Greek Epic* as a wedding present.[63] Murray was famous both as a classicist and an internationalist and, in the article, he had written about the inevitable hostility engendered in subject peoples when colonial rule is imposed on them and the misplaced confidence of imperial ruling classes in their right and ability to govern. He believed that the war had revealed the British as 'the supreme type and example of the determination of the White Man to rule men of all other breeds, on the ground that he is their superior'. 'Here and there,' he argued, 'peoples who have experience know that the British are better masters than most: but masters they are, and masters are apt to be hated.'[64]

Murray referred to the 1919 massacre at Amritsar, in northern India, where there had been 'a situation arising between governors and governed so acutely hostile that a British officer, apparently a good soldier, thought it right to shoot down without warning some hundreds of unarmed men'. In Ceylon, in 1915, large numbers of innocent people had been 'either shot or flogged and many more imprisoned owing to a panic in the government'. 'In Mesopotamia,' he went on, 'since the War, it is said that certain villages which did not pay their taxes and were thought to be setting a bad example were actually bombed from the air at night, when the population were crowded together in the enclosures.' Murray acknowledged that it was perhaps presumptuous of him to pass judgment while he was sitting at home in safety, but he concluded that actions such as these made it easy to see why the British were hated. Furthermore, they were blunders, not typical, and 'not necessary for maintaining empire', which, he believed, should be governed on the principles laid down by the great nineteenth-century political theorists, Richard Cobden, John Stuart Mill and Thomas Babington Macaulay:

> We hold our Empire as a trust for the governed, not as an estate to be exploited. We govern backward races that they may be able to govern themselves; we do not hold them down for our own profit, nor in order to use them as food for cannon. Above all, in our government and our administration of justice, we try to act without fear or favour, treating the poor man with as much respect as the rich man, the coloured man as the white, the alien as the Englishman. We have had the principles laid down again and again; they are mostly embodied in the Covenant of the League of Nations, on sale everywhere for a penny. We must live up to them.[65]

Emily Lorimer was appalled and, in June 1920, she wrote to her mother to express her rage. This long passage, quoted in full, illustrates Lorimer's emotional response to criticism of British rule around the world and, surprisingly for such an intellectually rigorous woman, shows a wilful misunderstanding of some of Murray's arguments:

> Did you see a disgraceful lie in the Contemporary Review? Accusing us in Mesopotamia of the most dastardly murder of Arab women and children. Punitive expeditions have to be undertaken against Arabs when they have been more than ordinarily murderous and since the economic spirit of the people at home insists on our troops there being reduced to ineffectiveness

and the country being run by aeroplanes it follows that the only thing to be done is sometimes to bomb a village from the air. This may be regrettable but is less so than the outrages that make it necessary (of course people at home know as little about the essential Arab as they do about the essential Sinn Feiner: thanks in part to the fact that no-one likes to harrow the feelings of the mothers and wives at home by telling them the unnameable things the Arabs did to our dead and dying). This disgraceful article accused our people, however, of deliberately waiting until they knew that the maximum number of women and children were collected in the compounds in order to murder as many of them as possible. You will say that no intelligent person will be taken in by a manifest piece of German or American or Sinn Fein propaganda; this ought to be true; but it isn't. The author of the cowardly, lying article is no less a man than Gilbert Murray. It makes one feel physically sick…If he has reason to think that even a single case of the kind had occurred by inadvertence, let him be a man and put on a topee and go out and see for himself. But to sit at home in safety and comfort, bought for him by other men's blood and write poetry and munch cabbages and stab in the back men who are trying to make the world safe for the weak and the oppressed while he '*dreams* noble things' at home. What right have he and his like to assume that men of his own race and breed, with their own standards and ideals will prove so false to all that Murray thinks holy?[66]

Gertrude Bell, meanwhile, wrote to her father in August, expressing the rather more humble and disheartened view that 'in the light of the events of the last two months there's no getting out of the conclusion that we have made an immense failure here'.[67] She later reflected, like Murray, that: 'At the back of my mind there's a firm conviction that no people likes permanently to be governed by another…it was a gross want of statecraft on our part to have let the idea crystallise that nationalism was anti-British'.[68]

In October 1920 Arnold Wilson was replaced by Sir Percy Cox, now appointed as High Commissioner in Iraq and posted to Baghdad to pick up the pieces and set up a new form of government which would 'give effect to the spirit in which His Majesty's Government regarded their responsibilities' under the mandate assigned to Britain in the peace negotiations.[69] Cox was accompanied by Lady Cox and by Philby, followed by Dora Philby and their young daughter. Bell was reconfirmed in her post of Oriental Secretary.

Bell's subsequent career and personal relations in Baghdad followed a now familiar pattern. She continued to perform her administrative duties and to define herself by them, almost exclusively, as a woman in a man's world. Her most successful and well-known accomplishments were her

1920 'Review of the Civil Administration of Mesopotamia', and her participation in the Cairo Conference in the spring of 1921, at which the throne of Iraq was given to Faysal bin Husayn. She was the only woman among 40 delegates. Through her multitude of contacts with local Arabs, she continued to provide the British with access to information about Iraqi politics and, after the installation of Faysal, she became the king's close confidante and advisor. The 'Review of the Civil Administration' was published officially as a parliamentary paper.[70] It included a digest of all the detailed information Bell had accumulated during her years in Mesopotamia: anthropological, historical and political material, together with an account of all aspects of the British administration. Arnold Wilson, in spite of his many differences with Bell, recalled it, in his memoirs, as an 'enduring record both of her literary gifts and unwearying and selfless energy in the service of the countries of her birth and her adoption'.[71] The report was highly praised in England but Bell was typically irritated by the acclaim:

> I've just got Mother's letter of December 15 saying there's a fandango about my report. The general line taken by the press seems to be that it's most remarkable that a dog should be able to stand up on its hind legs – i.e. a female write a white paper. I hope they'll drop that source of wonder and pay attention to the report itself, if it will help them to understand what Mesopotamia is like.[72]

Impatient at any suggestion that she was in some way different from her male colleagues, she also adopted many of their patronising attitudes towards the colonial wives and women of her acquaintance. Her assessment of Belle Cox continued to be one of sympathy but frustration. To Gertrude Bell, Lady Cox would never be more than a memsahib: senior but, nevertheless, still only a memsahib. In May 1921 Bell wrote about a garden party organised at the High Commission for four hundred people:

> The *nawab* (of our office) and I saw how things had to be planned out, arranged where Sir Percy should stand and how the carpets etc should be placed. Sir Percy was much pleased but Lady Cox's comment was that it was a pity we hadn't had all the trees washed, they were so dusty!...However, though she is no use for functions she has many negative qualities, as well as the positive one of being always extremely amiable to me.[73]

The following month Bell went to a ball organised by the Philbys, where she refused to dance but sat in the garden and talked to people. Balls, she wrote were 'a perfect mania' in Baghdad:

> They dance at the Club four times a week. It's accursed, I think. Men who are as hard worked as our officials can't sit up till one or two in the morning

and be in their office at seven or eight. It's the wives that do it, confound them – they take no sort of interest in what's going on, know no Arabic and see no Arabs. They create an exclusive (it's also a very second-rate) English society quite cut off from the life of the town. I now begin to understand why British Government has come to grief in India, where our women do just the same thing.[74]

The previous year, when the first girls' school opened in Baghdad, Bell had complained at the absence of British women from the official ceremony, noting that only 'four of our English women came, which was disgraceful; however A.T. Wilson has given them a sharp rap over the knuckles for it. When they are asked to an official function they must come, and be as pleasant as they can. They can play golf other days.'[75] After the capture of Baghdad, Bell, previously singularly lacking in interest in the lives or status of Arab women, had begun calling on the wives of local notables as a way of gaining easier access to their husbands, and she had begun to hold weekly tea parties. Gradually she had become interested and more knowledgeable about female Iraqi society, and when Humphrey Bowman was appointed as Director of Education in August 1918, with a remit to set up a school system, she had become sufficiently involved to suggest that girls should be included. Typically assuming herself to be an authority on the subject, she told Bowman, according to her American biographer Janet Wallach: 'We must give the girls an opportunity for self-expression...If only you knew the harems as I do, you would have pity upon the women. Nothing has been done for them – nothing.'[76]

Bell's perspective of harem life, and her definition of the type of Western domestic education which would be suitable for Arab girls, closely parallels the ideas of the American missionary women and reflects her own culturally inherited Orientalist ideas about women's status in the Arab world. What she actually wanted in the girls' schools were classes in domestic science, housecraft and hygiene. Janet Wallach concludes that Bell's influence in this area had a long-term effect and she describes the Iraq education system set up by Bowman as 'the best in the Arab world' and a 'unifying force in the country' with a radical concept of education for women.[77] The conclusion is debatable, however, and can be counterbalanced, for example, by Peter Sluglett's earlier study of post-war Iraq, which suggested that the declared British policy of educating Iraqis for independence should be seen in the context of the colonial power's overriding fear that education would lead to dissent and revolt.[78] Bell herself, in spite of her own public success and her self-identification as an independent working woman, firmly continued to believe in educating girls for domesticity, and her political and social views were always more influenced by her class loyalties

Gertrude Bell on a picnic with King Faysal I of Iraq (right foreground) and other British officials, early 1920s.

than her gender. Arab women remained a 'discovery', an object of phil-anthropy and an observable and manipulable group. In February 1920 she wrote to her friend Valentine Chirol describing her new interest:

> I really think I am beginning to get hold of the women here, I mean the women of the better classes. *Pas sans peine*, though they meet one more than half way. It means taking a good deal of trouble to go and see them and to have them to little tea parties at my home. Over and above the fact that I like seeing them and get to know a side of Baghdad which I could know no other way, I'm sure it's worth it. One comes and goes in the houses with intimacy and has a troop of female friends who vastly improve one's personal relations with the men. I am now going to try a more ambitious scheme and get the leading ladies to form a committee to collect among the rich families (themselves) funds for a small women's hospital for the better classes about which some of them seem keen.[79]

Meanwhile, Bell's relations with King Faysal eventually – and inevitably – became less close as the king found his own feet, and when Cox retired in 1923 she lost her long-standing power-base within the British admi-nistration. In the same year she founded the Iraqi National Museum, another genuine and lasting memorial to her influence in the country and a reflection of her former talents as an archaeologist. But she became increasingly more marginalised in the political world in which she had always primarily identified herself. In 1926 she took an overdose of sleeping pills and died, two days before her fifty-eighth birthday. Arnold Wilson, characteristically, reflected on her administrative abilities:

> She scorned publicity, and disliked the numerous journalistic tributes to her influence and skill; creative achievement, literary, cultural and political, meant everything to her. She lived to see her immediate hopes for the political future of Iraq on the road to fruition ... she was truly inspired to serve the countries alike of her birth and her adoption, with abilities and enthusiasms as rare as they were precious.[80]

Perhaps more appropriately, however, Sir Gilbert Clayton, speaking at the Royal Geographical Society, recalled her relationships with Arab leaders:

> I have had the privilege, and have the privilege, of the acquaintance of most of the leading Arab rulers and many of the chiefs in Arabia. I have never met one who has not either known Miss Bell personally or by repute, and I have never met one by whom she is not held in affection, in honour, and in reverence.[81]

Clayton's assessment hints at the class-based narrative of Bell's life and the ways in which her representation of it reflected the world order viewed through the eyes of the British imperial ruling élites. Bell identified with her male colonial colleagues and with male Arab politicians and leaders. The American missionary, Dorothy Van Ess, one of Bell's very few women friends, also recalled how much respect Bell inspired in local Arab male authorities, quoting one as saying that if 'the women of the Angleez are like her, the men must be like lions in strength and valor. We had better make peace with them.'[82] To the British political officers, the Van Esses themselves represented the acceptable face of American missionary activity, and they were praised not only for their outstanding and tireless medical and social work but also for their commitment to the British cause. John Van Ess was very friendly with Wilson, and Dorothy Van Ess later wrote that he and her husband 'saw eye to eye' on the situation in 1920 and their solutions would have been 'nearly identical. John considered Colonel Wilson the brains of Sir Percy Cox's administration.' She went on to describe how her husband and Gertrude would argue interminably about the future of Iraq, with Van Ess maintaining that the country was too diverse for premature unity. 'But Gertrude,' he would exclaim:

> You are flying in the face of four millenniums of history if you try to draw a line around Iraq and call it a political entity! Assyria always looked to the west and east and north, and Babylonia to the south. They have never been an independent unit. You've got to take time to get them integrated, it must be done gradually. They have no conception of nationhood yet.[83]

For many Americans, however, the end of the war brought the possibility of a much more radical sense of a new world order than that envisaged by the British governments in London, India and Baghdad and this divergence of political perspective continued to generate suspicion and rivalry. In the first place, the American experience of the war on the Mesopotamia front was very different from that of the British. In major ways the Americans were always on the sidelines but in some other respects they were left to pick up the pieces. Their view of the emerging new world order after the war, and the American and British roles in it, was consequently substantially different from that of the British administrators, politicians and military in the area. Fired by Woodrow Wilson's ideas and ideals of the American 'Project' in the post-war world, they embraced nationalism and republicanism with enthusiasm. This American historical perspective on post-war developments is summarised by Robert D. Kaplan in his account of American 'Arabist' involvement in the Middle East:

> While the British and French were drawing lines on the map and switching rulers around like chess pieces, the American Protestants were suffering alongside the victims of famine and massacre, which were the mundane consequences of World War I. While Britons like Lawrence, Philby and Miss Bell were falling in love with the Arabs, the missionaries were learning – more than they ever had before – what it actually felt like to be an Arab.[84]

Kaplan goes on to argue that, while the British were in the tents of kings and in the centres of power, the Americans were working in the hospices and soup kitchens. They were dealing, for example, with the consequences of famine in Syria among around 300,000 people blockaded by the Turks; they were the first to report to the world about the Armenian massacres; they worked under hostile conditions to provide relief; they sympathised with the Arab desire for self-determination, and they were not hampered by 'an imperial establishment with ulterior motives in the region'.[85] Howard Bliss, president of the Syrian Protestant College, the predecessor of the American University of Beirut, gave a speech at the Versailles Peace Conference on behalf of Arab nationalism.[86] Kaplan's judgment on the British is harsh, and conveniently ignores the huge British casualties and hardships and the immense wartime and post-war medical efforts undertaken by both British men and women. However, it reflects something of the post-war American pride and purpose in their newly defined role in the Arab world.

In 1920, Charlotte B. Kellien, a Canadian missionary doing educational work in Muscat, looked back on the consequences of the war and concluded that its effects had been an outpouring of patriotism and self-denial but, more importantly, a new sense of the brotherhood of humanity and an acknowledgement of world citizenship. As far as the American missionaries in the area were concerned, Kellien believed they should now return to preaching the gospel with renewed vigour.[87] The war, and its aftermath, provoked a serious and ongoing debate among the missionaries as to their purpose and methods, and was the main cause of the gradual change of balance between purely evangelical and social and medical work. In effect, the war changed for ever the *modus operandi* of the missionary enterprise and the relationship of the organisation and its individual members with the people in the Gulf. On the one hand the Americans became more culturally open-minded, and on the other they were more determined. However, they all recognised that their increasing emphasis on medical work was opening doors previously closed to them. Although the publicly stated long-term mission was still to bring people to Christianity, privately the failure to do so had encouraged the more practical project of bringing the Western, or rather the American, way of life to the Arab world.

In 1920, in an article entitled, 'Signs of the times in Arabia', Paul Harrison commented on colonialism and the significance of the colonial mandates and went on to describe with regret the 'marriage of western political control with Mohammedan desert fanaticism':

> But the situation is not changed by our opinions...The whole Arab race thus passes under the political domination of the West. We may regret it, or rejoice in it, but our mission remains the same, to plant the Kingdom of God in the hearts of the Arabs, whatever be the political forms under which their society is organized.[88]

Two years later John Van Ess echoed Harrison's words in a similar article about the British Mandate in Iraq, adding: 'We as Christians have a mandate for Mesopotamia but we cannot so easily unshoulder the burden'. Posing the question, what are the obligations of the reformed Church in Mesopotamia, he concluded that being an American was a special obligation. Every American admired 'what Britain has done for these backward races', but America was *persona grata* and trusted, liked and desired in these parts of Arabia.[89]

Faced with such determined American sympathy for national self-determination, and with the fervent belief in the special American project in the region, it was not surprising that British suspicion and hostility towards missionary activity increased in the post-war years. In the spring of 1920, Paul and Regina Harrison were finally given British permission to spend two months in Hasa. Although they were keen to go to into Najd, they were again refused this on the grounds that the political situation was too unsound and that 'Abd al-'Aziz Al Sa'ud was 'averse to having Europeans in his capital' and 'could not be responsible for their safety'.[90] The Political Agent in Bahrain, H.R.P. Dickson, reported that a certain lady missionary from Kuwait had written to 'Abd al-'Aziz to ask permission to visit him. 'Abd al-'Aziz had showed him the letter and 'expressed himself in no uncertain voice, of what he thought of such applicants, and asked that I inform His Majesty's Government that he definitely wanted no-one coming into his territories unless under Government auspices. He certainly wanted no ladies.'[91] Dickson concluded that though 'the medical side of the mission is worthy of the highest praise, I cannot but feel suspicious of the non-medical members of the mission'. The following month he re-emphasised the issues, recalling the British wartime prejudice about missionaries, particularly women, of German origin:

> We have our Anti-English agitators for ever at work. I fear I cannot acquit the American Missionaries altogether of innocence in this respect – To start with most of the members are of Dutch or German descent, hence they were pro-German during the war. Today their regular form of conversation is something as follows: 'America is the world power that counts, she won the war, Wilson is the greatest man in the world, he will see that the Allies don't ill treat the Germans or deprive the small nations of their rights etc.' Last but not least the whole mission is unpleasantly anti-English in the matter of the Irish question. It is scarcely to be wondered at, in view of the hostile attitude adopted by the American Press. I have the members of the Mission twice a week to tea and tennis, partly as a duty and partly to hear what they are talking about. Truly their ideas on Ireland are astonishing. The trouble is…they cannot keep their thoughts to themselves, they hold forth to Arabs regularly on world politics especially when they visit prominent people's Mijlis…My efforts to counteract propaganda and popularise things English are I am glad to say being most successful.[92]

The renewed missionary attempts to send women doctors and nurses into central Arabia illustrates the continuing emphasis placed by them on 'women's work'. The post-war issues of *Neglected Arabia* published a constant stream of propaganda about the status and predicament of Arab women. In 1919 Elizabeth Cantine, in an article on 'Arab Women and the War', reported that during her 16 years in Arabia she had not been in a single Arab home 'where the relations between a man and his wife were such as a Christian woman could endure. The wife is always more or less of a slave to be beaten or divorced at will.'[93] The same year, Eleanor Calverley, identifying herself as living 'in the midst of down-trodden

Moslem women', described 'the heartache and despair brought about in the lives of Arab women by the very religion which is said to exalt them': 'Polygamy, concubinage, easy divorce and the teaching that women are inferior to men and were created for their usage, all these things make misery the most common feature in the experience of Arab women'.[94]

In the 1920s some editions of *Neglected Arabia* were made up exclusively of articles by women and on women. Collectively, the female missionaries were sending back to their supporters enormous quantities of information. By the mid-1920s they were so convinced of the rightness and righteousness of their cause that they failed to see or recognise that Arab nationalism and parallel political developments were producing indigenous feminist movements grounded in Islam and in wider regional social changes. Recent studies of early-twentieth-century Middle Eastern feminist movements have shown that they relied to some extent on imported Western feminist discourses and that there was a complicated but dependent relationship between indigenous Arab nationalism and feminism and wider movements.[95] However, the missionary version, ever confident, claimed much more for itself. In 1926 Samuel and Amy Zwemer, having spent time both in Egypt and Persia, published their book on Muslim women.[96] They looked back on developments in post-war Turkey and Egypt and expressed satisfaction at the progress made in female education, symbolised by the throwing off of the veil: 'It is seventeen years since unveiled faces were first seen in Constantinople, and the fact that women students have now gained an entrance on the same footing as men to the University of Stamboul indicates how far they have travelled along the path of reform'.[97]

Reviewing the pioneering work of men and women in the Middle Eastern missions, and taking much more than their fair share of credit for what followed, they reflected that even they could not have imagined what their work would eventually lead to:

> Thus began the search for light and life. There was no thought in the minds of the early workers that by opening their simple homes to these veiled ladies and their babies, and by visiting them in the harems and zenanas, they were letting in the light that would later on demand and produce schools and colleges for women and, as a result, the Oriental Feminist Movement for full emancipation of women.[98]

Missionary women identified themselves primarily as the epitome of strong and liberated, American Christian Protestant, women whose objective was to bring less privileged women to the light. Arab women therefore became the essential 'Other' against whom they could measure themselves and gain and reinforce confidence in their own status, both domestic and international. The environment provided by colonial institutions was a useful tool in their objective but it was not the primary identifier in their lives. In contrast, Gertrude Bell and Emily Lorimer saw themselves as active representatives of the 'imperial power' and both identified themselves primarily as members of the imperial ruling class even though they had divergent views and reactions to the changing political environment of the post-war colonial world. Neither Bell nor Lorimer regarded 'women' or 'woman' as of special interest. While Lorimer, however, consciously represented herself as a wife, Bell always strove, at least in her public life, to transcend gender. Lorimer remained the upholder of imperial values, the believer in the British mission to manage Arab affairs. Bell came to believe strongly in Arab nationalism. It would be facile to speculate too far on the causes of her suicide, in which so much personal history must have been a factor. However her ultimate discarding by King Faysal of Iraq was an ironic and bitter consequence of the Arab struggle for independence, which she herself had come to support so strongly. Dorothy Van Ess heard about Bell's death while in Michigan, on furlough from Iraq, and she always regretted not being in Baghdad at the time. Bell, she thought, had been 'lonely and sad at feeling she was no longer necessary in councils of state':

> The king and government were becoming firmly established, but she was often profoundly disillusioned when she felt that Feisal and his ministers were falling short of her ideals for them. She was always a romantic and never a realist. Her work as Oriental Secretary during her last few years lived after her in the Museum of Antiquities in Baghdad which bore witness to her gifts as an archaeologist and a historian. Unlike Lady Hester Stanhope, to whom she has often been compared, Gertrude Bell never became an eccentric, nor sacrificed the personal dignity and integrity which characterized her to the end of her life. Beside the Bedouin's campfire, or in the King's palace in Baghdad, she remained what she was – a distinguished English gentlewoman.[99]

NOTES ON CHAPTER 5

1   Alfred DeWitt Mason and Frederick J. Barny, *History of the Arabian Mission* (New York: Board of Foreign Missions Reformed Church in America, 1926), p. 76.

2   File note by Loch, 7 December 1916, IOR:R/15/2/47.

3   Dykstra was born in the Netherlands and joined the Arabian Mission in 1906. Minnie Wilterdink Dykstra was born in Holland, Michigan, and appointed in 1907.

4   File note by Loch, 7 December 1916.

5   Unfortunately there is no missionary version of this specific case in the published reports in *Neglected Arabia*.

6   File note, 7 December 1916.

7   See ch. 3. Cantine and Zwemer's first attempt at expansion, once they had established themselves at Basra, had been directed towards inland Arabia and, in October 1892, they had told the Board of Trustees that 'if the Arabian Mission is to be true to its name and purpose, it must occupy Arabia'. *Arabian Mission Field Report*, no 3, July–September 1892, p. 7.

8   Rev. John Y. Broek, 'Dr. Harrison's Marriage', *Neglected Arabia*, no 99, October–December 1916.

9   Telegram from Karachi Censor to Persian Gulf Intelligence Officer, Bushire, 4 February 1915, IOR:R/15/2/81.

10 Even six years later, in 1923, the Political Resident (Trevor) was still referring, in letters to India, to Mrs Harrison as being 'of German origin' (Trevor to Government of India, 17 November 1923, IOR:R/15/2/81). See also ch. 6.

11 Loch to Harrison, 18 March 1917, IOR:L/PS/11/170, P.2048/1920. The title of this particular India Office file, 'American Missionaries at Bahrain: anti-British sentiments; attempts to get in touch with Ibn Saud' is indicative of the suspicion with which the British regarded the missionaries during World War I.

12 For a detailed political history of Anglo–Saudi relations during this period, see Busch, *Britain, India and the Arabs, 1914–1921* (Berkeley: University of California Press, 1971), pp. 215–66, and Gary Troeller, *The Birth of Saudi Arabia: Britain and the Rise of the House of Sa'ud* (London: Frank Cass, 1967), pp. 73–128.

13 Memo from Loch to Trevor, 11 April 1917, IOR:L/PS/11/170.

14 'Abd al-'Aziz Al Sa'ud to Loch, 24 June 1917, IOR:R/15/2/47.

15 Loch to Trevor, 4, 8 and 11 July 1917, IOR:R/15/2/47.

16 Loch to Trevor, 14 August 1917, IOR:R/15/2/47.

17 Trevor to Loch, 26 August 1917, IOR:R/15/2/47.

18 Loch to Deputy Political Resident Bushire, 3 December 1917, IOR:R/15/2/47. Jane Alice Scardefield was born New York City and educated at the Union Mission Training Institute. She was appointed in 1903 and retired in 1925.

19 Ibid.

20 Rae to Loch, 6 December 1917, and Loch to Deputy Political Resident, 29 December 1917, IOR:R/15/2/47.

21 Memo from Loch to J.H. Bill, Deputy Political Resident, 20 February 1918, IOR:R/15/2/81.

22 Mungavin telegram to Bushire, 25 May 1918, IOR:R/15/2/47.

23 Major M.E. Rae, First Assistant Resident in charge at Bushire, to Mungavin, 26 May 1918, IOR:R/15/2/47.

24 Mungavin to Harrison (May 1918), IOR:R/15/2/81.

25 Political Agent Bahrain to Baghdad, 16 December 1918, IOR:L/PS/11/170.

26 Political telegram from Baghdad to Bahrain, 16 December 1918, IOR:L/PS/11/170.

27 File note by Bill, 20 January 1919, IOR:R/15/2/47.

28 Bahrain Agency translation of letter from 'Abd al-'Aziz Al Sa'ud to Political Agent, 14 February 1919, IOR:R/15/2/81.

29 Bray to Harrison, 23 February 1919, IOR:R/15/2/81.

30 Political telegram from Bahrain to Baghdad, 24 February 1919, IOR:R/15/2/47; political telegram from Bahrain to Bushire, 12 March 1919, IOR:R/15/2/81; telegram from Bill to Baghdad, 17 April 1919, IOR:R/15/2/47.

31 Political telegram from Bahrain to Baghdad, 3 February 1919, IOR:L/PS/11/170.

32 Dickson to Civil Commissioner Baghdad, 2 February 1920, IOR:R/15/2/81. Postings and appointments in the period of the war and immediately afterwards were particularly fluid, and the frequent changeovers in Bahrain reflect this.

33 Political telegram from Baghdad to Bahrain, 3 February 1920, and Dickson to 'Abd al-'Aziz, 25 February, IOR:R/15/2/81: 'My advice is, should you have a really bad case in Riadh to write me an urgent letter asking for Dr Harrison only to go there for a few days only, but do not ask for his wife as Government will never let her go to Najd'.

34 Dickson to Harrison, 25 February 1920, IOR:R/15/2/81.

35 Telegram from Bill to Baghdad, 17 April 1919, IOR:R/15/2/47.

36 Bahrain Political Diary for month ending 31 March 1920, St Antony's College, Oxford, Middle East Centre: H.R.P. Dickson Papers, DN 2A/4/40-43.

37 Political Diary, March 1920. Jasim Chirawi was an influential local merchant and secretary to Shaikh 'Abdullah. For a detailed account of Bahraini politics during this period, see Mahdi Al-Tajir, *Bahrain 1920–1945: Britain, the Shaikh and the Administration* (London: Croom Helm, 1987).

38 IOR:L/PS/10/618, Mesopotamia: Miscellaneous Papers, including Arab Bureau Eastern Branch reports.

39 Harrison to Mungavin, Political Agent Bahrain, 27 April 1918, IOR:L/PS/10/618.

40 For an account of post-war administration and politics in Iraq and the Gulf, see Busch, *Britain, India and the Arabs*, and Peter Sluglett, *Britain in Iraq, 1914–1932* (London: Ithaca, 1976).

41 President Woodrow Wilson had made his 'Fourteen Points' speech to Congress on 8 January 1918, in which he expressed the view that the Middle East should not be divided among the belligerent powers and that peoples hitherto ruled by the Turks should become autonomous.

42 The actual day-to-day work at the Residency in Bushire continued to be carried out by a series of deputy political residents, including J.H.Bill and A.P.Trevor.

43 Cox to Curzon, 9 February 1918, quoted by Philip Graves, *The Life of Sir Percy Cox* (London: Hutchison & Co., 1941), pp.235–36. Belle Cox was awarded a DBE in 1923 in recognition of the hardship she had endured at Cox's side. Their only grandson was also killed in action in 1942. Percy Cox died in 1937 and Belle Cox, aged 90, in 1956. John Townsend, unpublished manuscript of the life of Sir Percy Cox.

44 Sir Reader Bullard, *The Camels Must Go: An Autobiography* (London: Faber & Faber, 1961), pp.101–3. Bullard returned to Iraq two months later and was posted to Mosul. In May 1920 he was appointed Military Governor of Baghdad.

45 Letter to Sir William Willcocks, January–February 1918, Elizabeth Burgoyne, *Gertrude Bell: From her Personal Papers, 1889–1914* (London: Ernest Benn, 1958), vol.1, pp.76–77.

46 See, for example, Janet Wallach's *Desert Queen: The Extraordinary Life of Gertrude Bell* (New York: Doubleday, 1996) and Victor Winstone's *Gertrude Bell* (London: Jonathan Cape, 1978), as well as Bell's own letters and also Busch, *Britain, India and the Arabs*, and Sluglett, *Britain in Iraq*.

47 Memorandum on Self-Determination in Mesopotamia, FO 371/4150. See also IOR:L/PS/10/755-764, P.4722/18 on the development of post-war British policy and administration.

48 Sluglett, *Britain in Iraq*, pp.32–33. After his resignation from government service in 1920, Wilson joined the Anglo–Persian Oil Company. In 1933 he became a Conservative Member of Parliament. His 1949 *Dictionary of National Biography* entry, by E.Bonham Carter, described him as 'a confirmed believer in the British Empire as a power to preserve peace and civilize backward races'.

49 Wallach, *Desert Queen*, p.242.

50 Gertrude Bell, 'Syria in October 1919', 15 November 1919, with covering note and dissenting comments by A.T.Wilson, addressed to India Office, 15 November, IOR:L/PS/18/B337.

51 Wallach, *Desert Queen*, pp.248–49.

52 Ibid., p.249.

53 The causes and progress of the 1920 rebellion have been the subject of several historical studies and are analysed by both Busch and Sluglett.

54 Wallach, *Desert Queen*, pp.252–78, and Winstone, *Gertrude Bell*, pp.217–28.

176 - PLAYING THE GAME

55 Letter, 20 June 1920, Burgoyne, *Gertrude Bell*, vol. 2, p. 142.

56 Quoted by Winstone, *Gertrude Bell*, pp. 217–18.

57 Private and personal telegram from Edwin Montagu to Bell, 6 August 1920, Bell Papers, University of Newcastle-upon-Tyne, quoted by Wallach, *Desert Queen*, p. 273.

58 *The Times*, 6 September 1920.

59 Emily Lorimer, Vancouver, to her mother, 7 July 1918, MSS Eur F177/24.

60 Emily Lorimer, Vancouver, to her mother, 19 May 1918, MSS Eur F177/24.

61 Emily Lorimer, Loralai, to her mother, 4 April 1920, MSS Eur F177/27.

62 Gilbert Murray, 'Satanism and the New World Order', *Contemporary Review*, 117 (1920), pp. 465–76.

63 Emily Lorimer to her father and mother, 27 September 1911, MSS Eur F177/6.

64 Murray, 'Satanism and the New World Order', p. 472.

65 Ibid, pp. 473–75.

66 Emily Lorimer, Loralai, to her mother, 13 June 1920, MSS Eur F177/28.

67 Burgoyne, *Gertrude Bell*, vol. 2, p. 159.

68 Letter, 12 June 1921, Burgoyne, *Gertrude Bell*, vol. 2, p. 220.

69 'Historical Summary of Events in Territories of the Ottoman Empire, Persia and Arabia affecting the British position in the Persian Gulf, 1907–1928', Committee of Imperial Defence, October 1928, IOR: L/PS/20/C247A, p. 31.

70 'Review of the Civil Administration of Mesopotamia', Parliamentary Papers, 1920, vol. 51, Cmd. 1061.

71 Lt Colonel Sir Arnold T. Wilson, *Loyalties: Mesopotamia, 1914–1917, a Personal and Historical Record* (London: Oxford University Press, 1930), p. xii.

72 Quoted by Wallach, *Desert Queen*, p. 292.

73 Letter, 8 May 1921, Burgoyne, *Gertrude Bell*, vol. 2, pp. 215–16.

74 Letter, 19 June 1921, Burgoyne, *Gertrude Bell*, vol. 2, pp. 220–21.

75 Letter, January 1920, Burgoyne, *Gertrude Bell*, vol. 2, p. 126.

76 Wallach, *Desert Queen*, p. 213.

77 Ibid., p. 213.

78 Sluglett, *Britain in Iraq*, pp. 273–91.

79 Gertrude Bell to Valentine Chirol, 12 February 1920, *Burgoyne*, Gertrude Bell, vol. 2, p. 127.

80 Wilson, *Loyalties*, p. 159.

81 Sir Gilbert Clayton, speaking during a discussion at the Royal Geographical Society, 4 April 1927, after a paper presented by D. G. Hogarth, 'Gertrude Bell's journey to Hayil', *The Geographical Journal*, no 70 (1927), pp. 1–21.

82 Dorothy Van Ess, *Pioneers in the Arab World* (Grand Rapids, MI: Historical Series of Reformed Church in America, 1974), p. 98.

83 Ibid., p. 113.

84 Robert D. Kaplan, *The Arabists: the Romance of an American Elite* (New York: The Free Press, 2nd edn, 1995), p. 63.

85 Ibid., p.67. *Neglected Arabia* reported in 1917 that missionaries had been carrying out relief measures in areas of great Armenian persecution and were now involved in the investigations (no 100, January–March 1917).

86 Kaplan, *The Arabists*, pp.63–72. Kaplan (p.67) says the American community in Syria was united in support of the Arab Nationalist cause.

87 Charlotte B. Kellien, 'Spiritual Patriotism', *Neglected Arabia*, no 112, January–March 1920, pp.6–8.

88 Paul Harrison, 'Signs of the Times in Arabia', *Neglected Arabia*, no 113, April–June 1920.

89 John Van Ess, 'The Mesopotamian Mandate', *Neglected Arabia*, no 124, January–March 1923.

90 Extract from Bahrain Diary, March 1920 (by H.R.P.Dickson), American Mission section, L/PS/11/170, P.2048/1920.

91 Ibid., March 1920.

92 Ibid., April and May 1920.

93 Mrs Cantine, 'Arab Women and the War', *Neglected Arabia*, no 108, January–March 1919.

94 Mrs Edwin Calverley, 'Beauty for Ashes', *Neglected Arabia*, no 110, July–September 1919.

95 There is a growing body of work on early Arab feminism, for example: Lila Abu-Lughod (ed.), *Remaking Women: Feminism and Modernity in the Middle East* (Princeton: Princeton University Press, 1998); Leila Ahmed, *Women and Gender in Islam* (New Haven, Yale University Press, 1992); Margot Badran, *Feminists, Islam and the Nation: Gender and the Making of Modern Egypt* (Princeton: Princeton University Press, 1995); Beth Baron, *The Women's Awakening in Egypt* (New Haven, Yale University Press, 1994); Parvin Paidar, *Women and the Political Process in Twentieth-Century Iran* (Cambridge: Cambridge University Press, 1995).

96 A.E. and S.M.Zwemer, *Moslem Women* (West Medford, MA: Central Committee on the Study of Foreign Missions, 1926). See ch.3 above.

97 Ibid., p.91.

98 Ibid., p.176.

99 Van Ess, *Pioneers in the Arab World*, p.120.

6 'Women called Wild': Travellers and Orientalists in the Inter-war Years

B ritish irritation with the American missionary project in the Gulf lasted until well into the 1920s and continued to focus, in particular, on the activities of Paul and Regina Harrison and their attempts to expand missionary influence into the Saudi provinces of central Arabia and along the coast into the smaller shaikhdoms of Dubai and the other Trucial states. An India Office Political Department file opened in 1921 described the 'further undesirable activities of Dr. Harrison' and discussed the Harrisons' ceaseless quest for new contacts in the Arabian Peninsula.[1] The Political Resident, A. P. Trevor, wrote to the Government of India that Harrison, although a 'very clever surgeon', had 'an inveterate tendency to mix himself up in political matters, and a strong anti-British bias' that appeared to be increasing. Trevor thought it would be 'highly undesirable' to allow Harrison to open a mission branch at Dubai and 'even dangerous to have him permanently on the Trucial Coast where we have no British Officer to check him'.[2] The Political Agent in Bahrain, Major Clive Daly, believed Harrison 'could do a lot of harm', and back in London, in the India Office, a Political Department official, D.T. Monteath, concluded that if

> it was undesirable to let Dr Harrison visit Ibn Saud, whose conduct is so reliable, it would seem even more undesirable that he should establish himself among the backward potentates of the Trucial Coast, or even remain in Bahrein where there is sufficient opportunity for pro-Arab and anti-British enthusiasm.[3]

In March 1922 the Harrisons left the Gulf for a long vacation in the United States, and the British heaved a sigh of relief. By November 1923, however, Trevor was again writing to the Government of India that, although the project for a missionary branch on the Trucial Coast had remained in abeyance since Harrison went on leave, the couple were soon expected back and, from information the Bahrain Agent had gathered from one of the members of the mission, it seemed that Harrison was 'returning "like a giant refreshed" eager for adventure in Central Arabia or Oman or both'. Trevor also reminded the government of an earlier assessment he had made about the Harrisons, that 'Dr. Harrison is thoroughly anti-British and Mrs Harrison, who is I believe of German origin, is even more so'.[4]

Regina Harrison was identified, and repeatedly described, by the British as a suspicious and troublesome character, although no evidence was ever put forward to justify such a conclusion. Her husband, although a larger-than-life character himself, was to some extent measured by his relationship with her. The Harrisons, and the established American missionary project, eventually came to be accepted by the British as an essential part of the local expatriate community, cautiously and gradually welcomed by the local rulers and their subjects and appreciated for providing a genuinely useful medical service. But in the decade after the First World War they were constantly perceived by the British as a potentially dangerous and subversive element in the region and any non-conformity or tendency to disobey British, written and unwritten, rules of political and social behaviour marked them out as dangerous.

On the margins of the missionary project there was also a small number of other women whose behaviour both worried the British and embarrassed the Americans. In the immediate post-war period, one was Frances Wakefield and another was Grace Strang. Frances Wakefield was a British woman, a doctor and member of the Church Missionary Society, who arrived in Bahrain in the spring of 1919 and made contact with the American missionaries. The local British authorities, clearly nervous, immediately telegraphed their superiors in Baghdad asking for information about her and, especially, about her true nationality. The Political Resident, meanwhile, explained to Wakefield that her hopes of travel in Arabia were 'inconsistent with our policy'.[5] The following month the British received a report from Cairo confirming that Wakefield was a British subject, formerly employed as a mechanic with the Egyptian Expeditionary Force, and that her 'bona fides is considered by the C.M.S. here to be beyond question, but they describe her methods as erratic and devious'.[6] In June British officials in Basra telegraphed Baghdad to say that Wakefield had arrived there and 'talks quite cheerfully about going into the desert with a view to seeing Ibn Rashid and is surprised that we are still under Military Law. She has offered, as a purely temporary measure, to help the Civil Surgeon here, but she is bent in getting in amongst the Bedouin'.[7]

Early the following year the Political Agent in Bahrain, H.R.P. Dickson, received a letter from the Amir 'Abd al-'Aziz Al Sa'ud who said he had been asked by a lady doctor, calling herself 'Hajiyah Narjis', for permission to visit Najd. The Saudi ruler was quite prepared to seek both male and female medical missionary assistance when it suited him but at this particular time he was nurturing diplomatic relations with the British. His letter said that he found Wakefield's request both socially and politically unaccceptable:

> You know the nature of the Arabs, they dislike to approach foreign ladies who are not related to them, and who are not accompanied by husbands, owing to laws and customs connected with religious and social life. Moreover, people may also come out with the object of travelling and something may happen which may displease the High British Government. Inshaallah should anyone desire to come over to the mainland, he should not do so without previous information from Government to me.[8]

Dickson also reported that 'Abd al-'Aziz had told him personally that he would like Wakefield to be prevented officially from going inland.[9] Meanwhile, the Political Agent in Kuwait reported that Wakefield was still in Kuwait, 'going about in Arab costume and arranging vainly with caravan owners to take her to interior'.[10] Wakefield was warned by Dickson not to persist in her attempts and Dickson reassured 'Abd al-'Aziz that he had acted accordingly.[11]

Frances Wakefield seems, after this, to have settled down in Kuwait, transforming herself from being politically undesirable to being 'harmless' but nevertheless still remaining outside imperial Gulf society. In November the new British Agent in Kuwait, J.C. More, told the Resident that:

> Dr (Miss) Wakefield has arrived back in Kuwait, after an absence of a couple of years, and has taken up her abode in her old house…She was viewed with a considerable amount of suspicion at first, but was eventually told she could come to Kuwait, and, with the exception of the last two years, she has been here ever since. She lives in a tiny little Arab house and normally dresses like an Arab woman – in fact I think she only puts on European clothes when she comes to see us, or goes to the American Mission. I believe she did once write to Ibn Sa'ud, under the name of Narjis Khatun (which is what she calls herself in Arabic), asking for permission to travel to Najd, but that was a long time ago. Since I have been here, however, she has not given any trouble – except to me personally, by occasionally coming to me with absurd rumours she has heard and by periodically wanting me to help her to go to Riyadh, or Hail, or somewhere like that. She is not a missionary, and she is not a practising doctor, and it is rather difficult to say what she is unless she is collecting material for a book, or something of that sort. Personally, I

think she is not quite 'all there', but is quite harmless, and I do not think there is much fear of her getting into trouble by trying to go inland without our knowledge.[12]

In December, More reported that Wakefield had finally left Kuwait to join some friends in Syria.[13]

While Frances Wakefield was marginalised as unconventional and not quite 'all there', a contemporary American traveller, Grace Strang, was perceived as equally, if not more, troublesome and unstable. Grace Orpah Strang was born in Jolly, Indiana, and received a Masters degree from the University of California in 1917. She was appointed to the Arabian Mission in 1922.[14] In May 1925 *Neglected Arabia* noted that she had been seriously ill and had been sent to India, to the Arcot Mission, where she was said to be recovering.[15] Two months later, however, she was reported by the British to have set sail from Bombay to Dubai and, after being told by the ship's officers that she would not be allowed to go ashore, had 'announced that she had received an inspiration that would compel her to land there'. When the ship arrived in Dubai, according to the Acting Political Agent George Mallam's account, Strang made some arrangement with one of the sailors and, during the night, slid down a rope over the ship's side when the gangways were up. The next morning the captain informed the Dubai police, who were at first unable to find her. However, they sailed along the coast to Sharjah and in the evening returned to the ship with Miss Strang 'dressed in Arab dress and accompanied by all her boxes. She was taken on board and the ship left for Bahrain.'[16]

Mallam asked the Resident to warn the Indian authorities not to issue tickets or passports for European passengers travelling to Dubai without permission but added that he had received a reassuring letter from Fred Barny, one of the most senior missionaries, currently stationed at the Baghdad Mission.[17] Barny had explained that Miss Strang had shown signs of serious illness the previous year but refused medical treatment on principle. The mission had sent her to India and told her not to return to the Gulf. Strang, however, said she refused to submit to the direction of the mission. She 'considered herself as having severed her connection with us and … intended to undertake religious work on her own responsibility'. Meanwhile the mission was expecting her formal resignation in due course and thought she would be going to Syria.[18] Major More, in Kuwait, wrote to the Resident in the same month to say that he thought she had been 'sent away from Kuwait to die' and was believed to be in the last stages of cancer, but that 'as she is something in the Christian Scientist line and will not allow any doctor to examine her or prescribe for her, this was more a guess than a diagnosis'; clearly, he added, she was much better when she had landed at Dubai.[19] At the India Office, Monteath again made a note on the file:

> Miss Strang...who managed to land at Debai in spite of the efforts of the authorities to prevent her, was formerly of the American Mission. Her triumph was short-lived. She is probably mentally as well as physically deficient and the Mission is in no way responsible for her escapade.[20]

Women like Wakefield and Strang were deliberately and consciously characterised as unstable and sick, both in mind and body, by the British and sometimes the American authorities. Their behaviour was at the very least unconventional, but without their own testimony it is hard to locate their own perceptions of reality or their motives and self-image. Some of their activities, such as dressing and living as Arabs, or attempting to travel into central Arabia, were simply politically and socially unacceptable in Gulf colonial society. Wakefield and Strang were at least in part motivated by religion but they were also, apparently, women who were not willing or able to live according to the rules and who sought independence through travel. In the late nineteenth and early twentieth centuries, many such women travellers were represented by others, or deliberately identified themselves, as wild or 'wayward'.[21]

Travel provided a route to freedom, or at least a route to a different and more independent way of living, for middle-class women of means who were not willing to conform to Victorian and early-twentieth-century family life. It offered a different geographical and cultural space in which there were alluring prospects of physical and emotional freedom, as well as intellectual stimulus. For British and American women, travel in the Orient, in contrast to travel in Europe, also promised a special status, fame or notoriety and the thrill of being a 'white woman among natives', rather than merely the wife or mother of the family.[22] On the other hand, the very 'waywardness' which drew women into independent travel also sometimes put them outside, or on the edge, of their own society and opened them up to ridicule and marginalisation. The lone woman traveller implicitly threatened the status quo, both at the domestic level of family life and also in the subtle, but carefully structured, hierarchy of colonial and imperial administration. British politicians and administrators in the Gulf in the early twentieth century were deeply, almost obsessively, concerned with the preservation of their power-base and with the avoidance of any interventions which might upset their perspective of the balance of colonial power in the Middle East. Women missionaries, indeed American missionaries of both sexes, were continually under suspicion because of their perceived tendency to overstep social and cultural boundaries.

Independent women travellers, with no respectable sponsors or organisations to protect and police them, were even more unsettling and each white female intruder into the Arabian desert provoked flurries of telegrams between political agents and files of reports in London and India.

Women travellers negotiated these obstacles in different ways. Some deliberately represented themselves as conformist in order to clear the way for further travels and neutralise the fear and objections put in front of them by the local colonial administrators. Women such as Gertrude Bell and, a decade later, Freya Stark, eventually chose to identify themselves as imperial or colonial servants, producing official reports, working within the local administrations and using the requirements of diplomacy to provide the validation for further travels. Bell, as we have seen, identified herself primarily as a government official, regarding her 'explorations' as of secondary importance. She nevertheless, like many of her male colleagues, gravitated towards imperial or colonial service partly because of her desire to travel and break away from the conventions of domestic life and society. Other women, such as Emily Lorimer and Violet Dickson, the wife of H.R.P. Dickson, were memsahibs who worked and travelled in the safety of partnership with political officer husbands. Some, like Dora Philby, were pulled along by the overwhelming personalities of their wandering husbands. A few, like Rosita Forbes, were simply irrepressible adventurers.

Joan (Rosita) Forbes published her book *Women Called Wild* in 1935.[23] It was an account of women she had met during a long career of travel, exploration and journalism in Asia, Africa and the Middle East. Its dust jacket described the book as 'Tales of strange ways and strange people', 'an epitaph for Wild Women, beset by the love of a man or a country, a religion or just an idea'. Its subject-matter ranged from slavery in Abyssinia (Ethiopia) and Arabia to stories of Chinese women fighting for Bolshevism, a woman camp-follower with the French Foreign Legion in southern Morocco, and the wife of a Kurdish chieftain who herself fought the Turks.[24] Its idiosyncratic title refers to the subjects of the book but it might just as well have been applied to its author and some of her female contemporaries.

Forbes was a prolific writer, but she identified herself primarily as a traveller and consciously referred to travel as the means through which she was able to find her true personality. In her *Who's Who* entry she describes her occupation as 'extensive travelling in most known countries', and at the beginning of her autobiography she wrote that 'searching for the beginning of me – as an individual, not as the daughter of a brilliant and much troubled father or the wife of a good-looking Highlander with whom for three preposterous years I was miserable – I find it aboard a tramp between Massawa and Suez'.[25] She was born in Lincolnshire in 1890, the eldest of six children. According to her autobiography, her father, Herbert Torr, was a Lincolnshire landowner from an old 'but generally unimportant family', a Cambridge-educated 'Liberal puritanical' with a profound sense of duty, and a social idealist who had worked in a 'slum mission'. Her mother was the daughter of a keen conservative, a Scottish businessman with Spanish ancestry. Forbes claimed that she herself was always conscious of being different from other people. She read voraciously while both she and her brother spent a lonely childhood without friends and, eventually, drifted into 'the inevitable unhappy marriage' to Colonel Ronald Forbes, 12 years older than herself.[26] With her husband she began her travels, to India and Australia; in 1917 they divorced. During the war she drove ambulances in France for the Société de Secours aux Blessés Militaires and was awarded two medals.[27] She went back to Paris at the time of the 1919 Peace Conference and afterwards set off to North Africa. In 1921 she met Colonel Arthur McGrath, an officer in Military Intelligence who had come to one of her lectures at the Royal Geographical Society, and she embarked on her second, unconventional but more enduring, marriage. 'Next to the sun', she wrote,

> horses have given me most joy and men least. I am not clever with men. I only get on with them when they will consent to be friends, linked in some hard-working purpose, generally international. Then I am content with them and – for a while – can establish a satisfactory personal relationship.[28]

Forbes's most famous journey, and the one which brought her to popular attention, was a camel trek in 1920 through the Libyan desert to the sacred 'forbidden' oasis of Kufra, which was outside Italian-occupied territory and under the authority of Sayed Idris el Senussi (later King Idris of Libya). Only one European expedition had been there before her.[29] In the tradition of earlier Victorian lady travellers, such as Lady Anne Blunt and Isabel Eberhardt, Forbes undertook the journey dressed as an Arab woman, but with the modern appendage of a hidden camera under her headdress. She was accompanied by an Egyptian scholar and explorer, Ahmad Hassanein Bey, to whose experience and knowledge, it must be added, she owed a considerable debt. After Kufra she continued through the desert into Egypt and the Siwa Oasis, charting a new route. She recorded her findings the following year in her best-known book, *The Secret of the Sahara*.[30]

Forbes's subsequent journeys were undertaken more openly, and more in the style of late-twentieth-century journalism, with cameramen and notebooks. In 1925 she travelled in Abyssinia, filming and photographing; she subsequently travelled to India, Persia, Afghanistan, Russian Central

Asia and South America. She interviewed political leaders and published her interviews in her many books and newspaper articles. She would have been a perfect television journalist had she been born half a century later.[31] Yet her popularist photo-journalism, and her flamboyant appearance and manner, gave an unfairly superficial impression of a woman who was in fact courageous and determined. Gertrude Bell, never one for sympathetic relationships with other forceful women, particularly rival travellers, thought Forbes was a dilettante. In September 1921 she recorded a second-hand account of Rosita's recent arrival in Egypt:

> I must...relate to you a tale of Mrs Rosita Forbes. The wife of one of our doctors here going home on leave observes a very elaborately clad lady get on to the ship at Port Said and take a long and intimate farewell with a party in a fez. After he leaves the lady looks so solitary that Mrs Sinderson strolls up, sits down by her and ventures a remark on the weather. Her interlocutor rejoins with: 'I suppose you know who I am!' 'Well' says Mrs. Sinderson innocently, 'I know your name is Forbes; I saw it on your hat-box.' Tableau!! She spoke to no one on the voyage; but at night, when the passengers wanted to give concerts, she sat at the middle table in the music room completely surrounded by books, foolscap and manuscript at which she never ceased to write busily.[32]

The Kufra expedition was a geographical triumph, however, and Forbes's books and travels were taken seriously enough to be discussed in the Royal Geographical and Central Asian Societies' journals. *Women Called Wild* was reviewed by Sir Percy Sykes, an imperial administrator and army officer as well as a noted scholar himself, who acknowledged that the book's account of the contemporary slave trade provided some 'valuable information'. Forbes, wrote Sykes, 'must have travelled more widely than any other living traveller, and from every field she has plucked an ear of wheat'. 'With the space at my disposal,' he concluded, 'I can only point out that this book of stories is "strong meat", which makes thrilling reading and proves the marked ability of the writer to probe deeply wherever she passes.'[33]

In the context of Gulf and Arabian history and travel, Rosita Forbes is most famous for her trip to southwest Arabia in 1922 and her attempt, in 1924, to go, either with or without Harry St.J.B. Philby, to the southern desert region of Arabia, known as the Rub' al-Khali or Empty Quarter, and to the Saudi capital to meet the ruler, 'Abd al-'Aziz Al Sa'ud. Both episodes are significant, for the sheer daring of their objectives and for the different perspectives from which they were constructed and described by Forbes herself and by British and Arab male observers.

In the first of these journeys, in 1922, Forbes set out to explore the southwest Arabian province of Asir and to visit its ruler, the Idrisi, a distant relative of the Senussi leaders she had encountered in Libya. Most importantly, the publicity surrounding the trip illustrates the respect given to Forbes by the male-dominated orientalist travel and exploration societies. Her account of the journey was published by the Royal Geographical Society in 1923, and is still a major primary source for historians of this little-known region.[34] After a turbulent crossing of the Red Sea, Forbes landed at the port of Jizan, in November 1922, with her companion, Kamel Fahmi, an Egyptian Railways inspector. Forbes recalled in her autobiography that both she and Fahmi were terribly seasick on the voyage and, in a later Foreign Office memorandum, a British diplomat in Cairo, Laurence Grafftey-Smith, noted that Fahmi was 'the man whom Rosita Forbes revived from collapse after sea sickness with a draught of Eau de Cologne, which they both mistook for brandy'. They had crossed from Suakin to Jizan 'in an open dhow and tossed about for fourteen days'.[35] Forbes's article presented a rare and detailed description of the port of Jizan, the capital, Sabya, the coastal towns of the Tihama plain, and the inland villages east and southwards. At Jizan the pair were met by the Idrisi Amir's son. The Idrisi would not, however, give Forbes permission to travel northwards, 'in spite of an argument lasting nearly nine hours and interrupted only by five cups of tea, each differently flavoured'.[36] Nevertheless, she gathered enough information to describe the society, religion and politics of Asir and illustrated her article with photographs. Finally, she presented a very good account of the political situation in southwest Arabia and the relations between the Idrisi, the Imam Yahya of Yemen and 'Abd al-'Aziz Al Sa'ud, with whom the Idrisi had just concluded an agreement and into whose country Asir would eventually be absorbed.[37]

Forbes has been given immense credit for her earlier trip across Libya, but in some ways her attempt to travel in southwestern Arabia was equally courageous. In 1922, Asir and Yemen were very much closed countries, apart from the Red Sea coastal strip where international merchants and trade had always flourished. The project was not, therefore, one to be undertaken lightly. Forbes was also well aware of the difficulties which would be put in front of her by the British, and possibly by the Italians, the two major European powers vying for influence in the Red Sea after the end of the First World War. In her autobiography she remarked that she had been forced to make preparations for the journey in secret 'for the British Government allowed no venturing off the edge of the known and safe map': 'All my life I have been in arms against the Lion's housekeeperly determination to prevent unofficial information creeping in among the labels in its storecupboards...In season and out of season I was told, "You cannot go! It is impossible." "Yes, I see – of course", I agreed, and went'.[38]

The British, for their part, watched Forbes closely and were not comfortable with her activities. In December 1922 Captain Muhammad Fazluddin, the locally appointed British political officer stationed at Hudaydah on the Red Sea coast, reported to his superior officers in Aden the arrival of 'the well-known traveller of the Libyan desert who went to Kufara in the winter of 1920–1921 – in a sambuk from Suakin', and said that Mrs Forbes was 'apparently not pleased' with the Idrisi's refusal to allow her to travel beyond the coast, or through northern Asir to Riyadh.[39] The Idrisi had, however, put one of his cars at her disposal. The First Assistant Resident at Aden, Major C.C.J. Barrett, replied immediately to Fazluddin saying that the British would not interfere in the case, as this was Idrisi territory, and they would not support Rosita's request against the Idrisi's wishes. 'For your personal information,' he added, 'the Resident considers it most undesirable that this lady should be travelling about Arabia at the present time.'[40]

Once she arrived at Hudaydah, Rosita decided she would try to go to inland Yemen, and she asked Fazluddin to help her arrange the trip. The British stuck to their policy of remaining unhelpfully neutral although the Resident took the precaution of discussing the matter with the local Yemeni Qadi in Aden, who assured him that the Imam would ensure Forbes's safety. 'I said,' the Resident reported, 'that Mrs Forbes is rather a remarkable lady and is a determined and headstrong person and it is just possible that she might proceed without permission.'[41] In a letter to Barrett, Fazluddin described the entire proceedings in a way which encapsulates Rosita Forbes's intrepid sense of purpose and confidence and the British officials' sceptical assessment of her motives. Forbes, according to Fazluddin, had demanded that he solve all her problems and she had asked him if he had heard of her. She had told him what a splendid success her book on Kufra had been and that she had received £10,000 for it; she also said that, after she had conceived the idea of going to Asir and Najd, publishers had offered her large sums of money. She said she thought the Idrisi was 'stupid' for stopping her and now she would write to the Imam. Fazluddin had warned her that the country was very unsettled and she had replied:

'But I can assume any disguise. I can colour my skin any colour. I can pretend to be a Moslem woman. I shall travel alone. I can say I am the second wife of some Shaikh'. That was her remark. It is useless arguing with a woman of such desperate nature, hence I merely tried to assuage her irritability by asking her to make herself comfortable here for a few days before something could be done.[42]

Having been willingly taken in by Rosita's own, disingenuous, deliberate and unashamed, portrayal of herself as a mercenary journalist, Fazluddin, however, appended to his report a list of questions which Rosita had asked him, and they reflect a much more erudite and well-informed interest in this little-known territory than the Aden officials would have liked to suggest. Forbes had asked about the system of taxation in Asir, about the rise to power of the Idrisi, his relations with 'Abd al-'Aziz Al Sa'ud, the location of Himyarite tombs, the link between Bedouin and townsfolk and, finally, 'Have you by any chance got Niebuhr's book here?'[43] When the Aden Resident reported back to the Government in London that the Idrisi had refused permission to Forbes to travel in the interior and that, following a further request from Forbes, 'Idrisi is being advised that he is entirely free to use his own discretion in the matter', the Colonial Office replied, approving Aden's action. On the India Office Political Department Minute Paper there is a note by an official: 'Well done the Idrisi! I hope he will continue obdurate'.[44]

Rosita Forbes's next Arabian travel project, two years later, was a plan to cross the Empty Quarter and meet 'Abd al-'Aziz Al Sa'ud. It brought her into contact with one of the other great Arabian adventurers of the period, Harry St. J.B. Philby. By 1924 Philby had resigned from British colonial service after increasing differences of opinion with colleagues in Baghdad and, from 1921, as Chief British Representative in Transjordan.[45] In Baghdad, Philby had worked closely with Gertrude Bell and, after the wartime restrictions on female spouses in the field were ended, Dora Philby, for a while, also spent more time there with her husband. Bell at first described her relations with the Philbys as cordial and after giving a dinner party for them, recorded that she liked Dora 'very much, and I'm very fond of him. As far as I'm concerned he is always admirable to work with.'[46] Before long, however, she was out of sympathy with Dora and, after dining with the Coxes a few months later, complained rather petulantly that:

> It was very friendly and pleasant – no, there was one exception. I find Mrs Philby quite markedly stand-offish. I've taken a good deal of trouble to be friends with her but it doesn't seem to be any good and I don't think I'll bother any more. What's the matter with her I can't imagine. It's conceivable, after all, that she just doesn't like me. I see very little of Mr Philby these days, but when I do see him he is quite pleasant.[47]

It was also 'conceivable' that Dora Philby resented Bell's open lack of sympathy for the wives of her colleagues. Always loyal, Dora had spent long months alone with her small children while Philby trekked around the Middle East. When he was appointed to Transjordan, Philby, according to his biographer, Elizabeth Monroe, 'cock-a-hoop…boarded the Royal Air Force plane bound for Amman…confident of his ability to gain acceptance, and leaving Dora alone to have her [third] baby, pay, pack and follow'.[48] Dora remained in Amman for a few months and then returned to London and a future life of intermittent separation, either from Philby or from her children. Early in 1923, for example, she returned to Amman with her two small daughters, leaving her son, Kim, behind in England at school. Back in Transjordan, the Philbys went on a tour to Petra, accompanied by Rosita Forbes and another well-known traveller, Bertram Thomas, and were immediately criticised by the British Air Officer Commanding in Amman for leaving their daughters alone with a nurse in the town.[49] Dora, like Belle Cox and hundreds of women in similar positions, was always to be torn between husband and children, and condemned if she failed to conform to conventional arrangements. Rosita, however, childless and well-established as an independent traveller, found the trip relaxing and afterwards wrote to the Philbys to thank them for giving her 'such a good time…it took off the ten years which Asir had added to my age. I've rarely laughed so much in my life.'[50]

Philby had wanted for a long time to cross the Rub' al-Khali, and it is an interesting insight into the personalities of both Philby and Forbes that both claimed credit for having planned the expedition. Philby's biographer, Elizabeth Monroe, suggests that Philby would have preferred to 'go it alone', but saw in Rosita, and her 'enviable capacity for wheedling money out of the popular press', a chance to raise financial support for the trip. 'For her,' wrote Philby in his autobiography, 'it was relatively easy. In those days of the Lawrence saga Arabia enjoyed a high priority in the publicity market. And any woman adventuring into so romantic and dangerous a country was worth her weight in gold.' Lord Burnham and the *Daily Telegraph* put up the sum of £4000: 'The details were arranged to the satisfaction of all concerned on the basis that Rosita should do all the publicity articles for the paper, while I should write the "serious" book on our travels'.[51] These distinctions, which reflect Philby's rather simplistic and typically self-obsessed assumption of certain gender roles, even in the area of scholarship and travel, were partly borne out by the writing careers of the two characters. But they do not do justice to Rosita's scholarship, which was always hidden under a veneer of stereotyped 'feminine' superficiality. Rosita's main objective, in any case, seems to have been to meet

The Philbys with Rosita Forbes and Bertram Thomas, Petra, 1923.

'Abd al-'Aziz Al Sa'ud rather than to cross the desert, and she had been using Philby for some months to try to obtain permission to go to Riyadh. In May 1923 she wrote to Philby referring to a meeting at the India Office, before which she had apparently promised him she would put forward his views on the political situation in Transjordan:

> I had two solid hours with Sir J. Shuckburgh and told him the state of affairs in Palestine and Transjordan. I've also seen most members of the Govt... Now, please, I have done all that which I should have done with regard to Palestine, Transjordan and your views thereon without even mentioning that I met you. Therefore will you please fulfill the dreadful task you promised... and send a messenger to Ibn Sa'ud with a most persuasive epistle asking him to let me go in to Riadh next winter. Tell him he is the only great Arab leader whom I don't know... of course you know much better than I do what to say, and please do make it impossible for him to refuse. I am sure you can. I do terribly want to see Central Arabia and I could easily go in with a caravan from Damascus... and if you will seriously help me in this – you are the only person who can – I shall be grateful as long as I live!!!! True statement but sounds exaggerated.[52]

Forbes had a wide and influential range of acquaintances and never lost an opportunity to use her contacts to her own advantage. However, she was never inclined to wait too long for official permission and, in July, she was writing again to Philby to encourage him to go ahead with the arrangements, telling him that she was 'thrilled to hear you are in touch with Sa'ud again, but why, oh why, wait for the Colonial Office permission? They are so terribly slow!'[53] Meanwhile, still without an answer, she embarked on a lecture tour of the US and wrote to Philby again, from New York, in February 1924, to express her impatience, and at the same time to give him a prescient and accurate appraisal of the potential power and influence of the Saudi ruler. 'It is the "dream of my life" at present to go to Riadh,' she told him, 'for more and more I feel Ibn Sa'ud is the big figure in Arabia – I *must* see him somehow.' Her lecture tour, she said, was 'a horrible job of solid hard work – lecturing about five times a week, with immense distances to travel in between and one is always talking to ignorance so abysmal that they don't even know what an Arab is'. Nevertheless, she needed the money for the Riyadh trip and 'when people are particularly idiotic, I think that they are supplying me with the means of going to Nejd'.[54]

In October 1924 Forbes formally applied to the Colonial Office for permission to travel overland to the Gulf, telling them that she was going on behalf of an American Film Syndicate to make a film in Persia and to photograph some Phoenician ruins in Bahrain.[55] However, the Colonial Office had received information 'from a secret and reliable source' that her real intention was to join forces with Philby and to carry out the joint expedition into southern Arabia with a view to crossing the Rub' al-Khali. Colonial Office officials, therefore, gave her their standard warning that, in view of the unsettled conditions in Central Arabia, the British Government considered it 'undesirable' for British travellers to go there.[56] Eventually Forbes and Philby decided to set off in secret and separately, she going via Syria and Iraq and he via Marseilles. They would then meet up in the Gulf. Rosita wrote a conspiratorial letter to Philby confirming the plan: 'Yes, all is well arranged now. But we mustn't be seen together so will you lunch *here* on Monday.'[57] She left England to an immediate chorus of official criticism and suspicion. In Baghdad, Gertrude Bell, always identifying herself with colonial authority, even when disagreeing with its policy, voiced the general government frustration. In October she wrote to her father that:

> Rosita Forbes proposes to come out via Syria and go down the Persian Gulf whence she and Mr. Philby intend to visit Ibn Sa'ud. The FO, again all agog and rightly, are doing their best to stop Rosita Forbes. I do pray that it won't end in her landing up here to stay. She is a first-class busybody. Ibn Sa'ud has now gone to Mecca where she can scarcely follow him. Mr Philby and Rosita Forbes do seem to be unnecessary additions to our burdens![58]

In the event, Forbes landed at Bushire, with a cine-cameraman, and stayed with the 'kindly' Resident, Lieutenant-Colonel Francis Prideaux, and his wife, while waiting to hear from Philby who eventually telegraphed her to meet him in Aden. 'By this time,' she recalled, 'secrecy was in shreds. Whitehall knew all about our intentions. So did Fleet Street. In contiguous columns, the London dailies published our photographs – in Arab dress. We were described as "romantic figures". This was the culmination of my disgust.'[59]

By the time Forbes and Philby reached Aden, the 'kindly' Resident had warned his counterpart there of their plans.[60] In a flurry of inter-departmental telegrams the British discussed the project and plotted their response. When the travellers arrived they were interviewed, separately, by the Resident, and both were told not to proceed with their journey.[61] The record of the two interviews shows how Forbes and Philby were using each other's names and motives for their own ends. Philby told the Resident he had always wanted to make the trip but he had no money, as he was not a 'cinema star'. When he heard that Rosita, who was working for a film company, was planning a trip, he thought he could join her. Forbes, on the other hand, said she could not understand the attitude of the government and that she was 'engaged in perfectly legitimate cinema business and considered Mr Philby had made a mess of his affairs. He was always anxious to visit the Hadramaut and saw a chance of getting the necessary funds as she was going there.' She then asked whether the Colonial Office could be persuaded to reconsider their position and the Resident replied that 'it was his duty to carry out orders not to question them'. Forbes responded that she would go to Abyssinia instead.[62] Forbes recalled in her autobiography that she listened to the General 'wide-eyed and receptive': 'You get back to England and enjoy yourself', said Scott, 'buy yourself some more of those big hats I've seen you wearing'.[63] Forbes left Aden the same day on a cargo boat to Djibouti. The following year she wrote to Philby that it was 'the wrong moment for the Rub al Khali and it will be very difficult for either you or me to get into Arabia "agin the Govt". We are too well known.'[64] In an India Office political file, an official noted: 'The lady has now passed out of our ken, and is unaccompanied by Mr Philby. In an outburst of feminine irritation she announces her intention of renouncing allegiance to His Majesty; this is surely an impossible course so long as she remains the wife of a British subject.'[65]

When Forbes reached Addis Ababa, in February, the British represent-ative there reported to the Colonial Office that she was working for the 'Britannia Film Company', and that in his opinion her activities were 'perfectly harmless'.[66] A week later he reassured London that her

Dora Philby wearing a dress presented to her by King 'Abd al-'Aziz Al Sa'ud, Kuwait, 1935.

cameraman, Arnold Jones, had previously accompanied the Prince of Wales on his travels. Mrs McGrath, he added, 'gave proof of much tact and good sense during her short stay here. She showed no disposition to mix in matters which did not concern her.'[67]

Rosita Forbes had absolutely no scruples about telling officials whatever story would enable her to achieve her travel goals. Moreover, she knew, and could persuade, an impressively wide range of 'establishment' officials to support her projects. Although her Saudi plans were obstructed by the local British authorities and the Colonial Office in London, two further incidents show the extent to which she established her reputation as a respected, knowledgeable and influential traveller and journalist during the following decade. In the autumn of 1935 Mussolini invaded Abyssinia and Italy became the focus of international hostility and sanctions in the League of Nations. A British intercept of a telegram, only recently made publicly available, from the Italian Ministry of Foreign Affairs in Rome to the Italian Embassy in London, reveals that the Italians were concerned about a report that Forbes might write hostile articles in the newspapers:

> The well-known traveller and writer, Rosita Forbes (Mrs Arthur McGrath), is said to be preparing a journalistic campaign hostile to us with regard to the Italo-Ethiopian question. Please report whether the above writer is now in London. If she is, it would be advisable to let her be approached and to ascertain the possibility of winning her over to our cause.[68]

In the same year Forbes planned a visit to India, Afghanistan and Soviet Central Asia, and she applied to the India Office for assistance and permission. The India Office Political Department file on her project illustrates the way in which Forbes was now able to use her 'establishment' contacts and 'friends in high places' to achieve her objectives. Official Government of India policy, enshrined in printed Army Orders, did not generally allow European women to travel along the North West Frontier, although certain places, for example the Khyber, were allowed under certain conditions, and visitors were able to go to Kabul where the India Office said they could give Forbes an introduction to the Chargé d'Affaires, Lieutenant-Colonel W. K. Fraser-Tytler.[69] The Under-Secretary of State at the India Office, however, was R. A. Butler and he discussed Rosita's trip with her 'over the luncheon table' and told her he would write to 'friends in Burma and India who might look after her on her proposed journey'. He minuted his colleagues at the India Office to say that:

> I feel sure that she will write on her return in the popular press … besides an occasional flight into more intellectual regions, and I think that she had much better go to India on our encouragement and with our help judiciously given, and thus give her impressions gained through more friendly spectacles … It is, of course, understood that while meandering about India she is not under our control and that the introductions are purely personal. We must, however, have some knowledge of her movements when she reaches Afghanistan and starts to enter Russia, if that can be achieved. I am sure she is a very courageous explorer.[70]

Butler wrote to Fraser-Tytler in Kabul telling him that he had known Rosita for many years and she had 'recently completed the most courageous tour of exploration in Dutch and British Guiana'. He was 'convinced of her immense courage and her sense of humour'; she was accustomed to travelling alone, knew the Nepalese Minister and had been 'courting for a long time Maisky, the Soviet Ambassador, who will, I am pretty certain, give her facilities once she reaches Russian territory'. Butler added that he had admired her previous adventures and he thought Rosita had 'a strange knack of getting where she wants in the end, and we had much better help and advise her from the beginning'. Fraser-Tytler replied the following month to say that he would be honoured to receive Forbes and would probably waive the rule that no woman could travel in Afghanistan without a male escort.[71] He later discovered that the Afghan Government had withdrawn permission for Rosita to travel because they had acquired some of her articles and were 'alarmed by her vivid but critical style'.[72] Finally the Afghans agreed to allow her to go, but on condition that she did not publish anything about Afghanistan without it being submitted to the British Government first. Fraser-Tytler reported that Forbes now intended to travel round Afghanistan in a lorry 'so as to get in touch with the people', a proposal which filled him with 'profound misgivings'.[73]

On her return to Kabul, Rosita drafted three articles and gave them to Fraser-Tytler, who made some suggestions for amendments. He reported to the India Office in April 1936 that:

> We had a little difficulty when she got back from Kandahar, as she was annoyed with the Afghans for not letting her have an audience with the King and rather wanted to say what she thought about them. The result was a struggle between that charming person Rosita McGrath and that insatiable journalist and publicity hunter Rosita Forbes. On the whole I think Rosita McGrath won but once she [is] away from this roof and beyond the Oxus Rosita F. may get the upper hand. She was, as I've said, most entertaining and charming, but I think it would have been fairer if she'd told you before she left that she was under contract with the D.T. [*Daily Telegraph*] to write up Afghanistan. However if she had she'd never have got into this country![74]

Forbes continued on to Bukhara and Samarkand, crossing the Hindu Kush in a lorry. On her return to London she submitted the drafts of her articles to the India Office and the officials there discussed them. Mainly they seem to have been concerned not to offend the Afghan Government and not to present it as being too pro-British (which they thought would embarrass it). At the same time, they were not willing to allow any public suggestion that there might be trouble on the frontier. In one article ('Kabul and the New Afghanistan'), for example, Rosita had referred to 'the natural opposition of a democratic people to an autocracy which imprisons without trial suspected political opponents'. The India Office suggested she change the wording to 'opposition of a democratic people to interference by the central authority'. Walton remarked that although Rosita made a note of the edit, he would not be surprised if she failed to change it, since she said she disliked suppressing the truth and she had told the Afghan ministers she intended to say it, 'and that they appeared to acquiesce, saying that it was better to imprison people than to kill them'.[75]

Walton also wrote to Forbes to ask whether she would tone down her mention of 'war' since 'India (including the frontier) is at present one of the few bright spots in the public mind in regard to foreign and Imperial affairs, and to foresee an early prospect of disturbances (which we sincerely hope will not materialise) might tend to take the gilt off the gingerbread'. Rosita wrote back to say she had amended the articles accordingly: 'Am I not a SAINT?'[76] In the same month, however, she gave a talk on her travels to the Royal Central Asian Society in which she criticised the lack of social legislation in India and said she had found women working 17 hours a day in the jute mills in Calcutta.[77] In her autobiography she wrote: 'I am persistently tactless. I tell too much of what I see. I say too much of what I think.'[78]

Forbes had a real interest in ordinary people and the reality of their lives and, to some extent, she wrote about them and 'produced' the information for a popular readership in the traditional, easily read genre of women's popular travel writing. When she travelled in the Middle East or Asia her books and articles were imbued with the female Orientalist imagery and perceptions of her Western predecessors in the region. Forbes often explicitly identified herself as being outside the male hierarchies of knowledge and power, and she continually emphasised her very 'female' or 'feminine' personal and close contacts with non-Western women and men. Yet travelling in these regions and in this period would have been virtually unthinkable without extensive 'establishment' connections. Forbes, in any case, always had a fascination for the society of international statesmen and rulers and she both assiduously pursued them and used them for her own ends. The British colonial and imperial authorities tried to control her and, to a certain extent, succeeded because she wanted to be part of their circle. They, on the other hand, could not always hide their admiration for her. She was perpetually elusive and, as her fame grew, British officials resigned themselves to the fact that they could never be sure what she would actually do. She travelled all over the world, never really stopping until her death in Bermuda in 1967. In an apt metaphor for the fascination, freedom and unconventionality of travel, she described herself as a 'gypsy' 'seeking the sun'.[79] She was flamboyant, prone to exaggeration and a 'popular' journalist and writer. Nevertheless, she was awarded gold medals by the French and Dutch Geographical Societies, and a silver medal by the Royal Society of Arts. During the Second World War she lectured for the War Office.

While Forbes was planning trips on the North West frontier and Central Asia, Philby was still trying to revive his Rub' al-Khali expedition plans. Elizabeth Monroe claims that by the early 1930s he had abandoned all thought of Rosita 'as a companion, or indeed as a serious contributor to the science of desert exploration'.[80] Yet Philby was in many ways just as much of an outsider as Rosita, and he was continually under a cloud of suspicion in British government eyes because of his ambiguous motives, loyalties and activities. Eventually he settled permanently in Saudi Arabia and worked for the Saudi government. In 1930 he converted to Islam after which he was given a *jariya*, Miriam bint 'Abdullah Hasan, by King 'Abd al-'Aziz, who looked after his house in Mecca for many years. Philby casually wrote to Dora to tell her. In his diary he described the position of the *jariya* as a slave girl 'until she produces a child, when she automatically becomes free and can go on living with the man'.[81] Miriam bint 'Abdullah did not give Philby a child but later, in 1945, he was to marry a Saudi wife, who bore him two sons. Dora, who had known about his Saudi liaisons, only found out much later, in 1955, about the two children and that her own son, Kim, also knew about his father's other family. Continually in debt, Dora nevertheless remained loyal and supportive throughout Philby's life and in 1935, accompanying her husband on one of his many journeys, she became the first woman to cross Arabia from sea to sea by car. In Kuwait, en route, the Philbys stayed with the Political Agent, Lieutenant-Colonel H.R.P. Dickson and his wife Violet.

Harold Richard Patrick Dickson was born in 1881, in Syria, where his father was British Consul, and he grew up speaking Arabic and spending holidays with bedouin tribes in the desert. After an Oxford education and military service in Ireland, he joined the Indian Army in 1908. During the first year of the First World War he was posted to Mesopotamia and was then transferred from the military to the political service, serving as Political Officer under Cox until 1919, when he was appointed to Bahrain as Political Agent. In 1921 he returned to Iraq as advisor to the *Mutassarif* (Governor) of the Hilla district.[82] Violet Dickson was born Violet Penelope Lucas-Calcraft in 1896, and was one of three daughters of an estate manager employed by a Lincolnshire landowner. Her own account describes her childhood as happy and easy, a country upbringing among ponies and other animals, hunting and trapping with her father on the estate. She was educated by a Swiss governess and then at a local school until 1910 when, after the death of her father, she moved to Switzerland with her mother and younger sister and continued her education in a school at Vevey. On the outbreak of war she returned to England and worked in a bank in Lincoln. In 1918 she moved to London to train as a dispatch-rider in the Women's Royal Air Force but her training was interrupted by the Armistice. Determined to use her French language skills, she applied for an overseas banking post and joined the Marseilles branch of Cox & Co.[83]

Violet Dickson's autobiography, *Forty Years in Kuwait*, opens with a memorable account of her first meeting with her future husband:

> I was working at Cox's Bank on the Cannebière in Marseilles during the autumn of 1919 [1920] when Captain H.R.P. Dickson of the 29th Lancers, Deccan Horse, Indian Army, came in to enquire if there was any mail for him. He had arrived by train from London, he told me, and was joining a ship which was to take him back to the Persian Gulf via India. As there were

no letters for him, he spent a short time talking to me over the counter, and asked me my name. I was naturally flattered by the interest shown by the handsome young officer, but when he walked out of the Bank I assumed that was the last I should ever see of him. Imagine my surprise, therefore, when about a week later I received a cable from him from Port Said asking me to marry him and go out to join him in the Persian Gulf. The prosaic and unromantic interior of a Bank would hardly be thought of as the setting for a meeting which would lead a young English girl to travel to the East, and to make her home there for the next forty-five years. But it was in such workaday surroundings that I met my future husband, whose love for Arabia and the Arabs I was to share throughout our married life.

It was a tremendous decision for me to have to make, and my hesitation was natural, but in the end it was short-lived. After some heartsearching and some consultation with kind friends in Marseilles, I decided to throw in my lot with my handsome suitor; I would cable 'Yes'. Our marriage was to last for thirty-nine years, and I never had cause to regret the decision.[84]

Having accepted Harold Dickson's proposal, Violet travelled to Bombay and the couple were married. After four 'idyllic' days at the Taj Mahal Hotel they left for the Gulf and travelled, via Basra, upriver by paddle steamer to Kut and then Baghdad, where they stayed with Philby and Dora Philby. In her autobiography Violet Dickson describes a dinner party with Gertrude Bell and five senior Arab officials. The conversation was mostly in Arabic and she was unable to understand much except that Bell made a loud remark in English that it was 'such a pity that promising young Englishmen went and married such fools of women':

As Harold had been one of her 'promising young Englishmen' in Mesopo-tamia during the war, I felt most uncomfortable and was glad when the party was over. Gertrude Bell was devoted to Sir Percy [Cox] and was often in and out of his house; but she was not interested in women's conversation and had no interest in any of the ladies in Baghdad at that time. She seemed to me rather aloof and unprepossessing…Jack Philby…has described her as follows: '…She lived on a man's plane; she was a little contemptuous of her own sex'. She has gone down in history as a very remarkable woman, but I did not at that point appreciate her great talents as a scholar and her courage as a traveller.[85]

Bell only recorded that the evening was 'a real success'.[86] As far as Violet Dickson was concerned, however, Bell had certainly pre-judged her. This spirited young woman had taken a huge step in the dark by agreeing to marry a man she had only just met, and to go with him to Iraq, and she was certainly no ordinary memsahib. Bell, as usual, failed to recognise any merits in colonial wives. If Dickson showed a lack of confidence at this stage of her career it was hardly surprising, and the dinner party episode is a good example of the suspicion and hostility which sometimes faced newcomers to colonial posts, from both the opposite and their own sex. Political and intellectual rivalry and jealousy were part of the game. The Dicksons, however, were to become perhaps the most famous Orientalist couple of the twentieth century, following in a tradition set by the Blunts a generation earlier. Violet Dickson's life, like that of Gertrude Bell, deserves to be the subject of exclusive and extensive studies and doubtless will be in the future. In the meantime, her memoirs, her husband's publications and papers, and the official British Colonial Office and India Office archives are major sources for her life and work.[87]

Clearly an independent and courageous young woman, Dickson nevertheless recreated herself, as partner and helpmate, as soon as the couple were married. In her autobiography she wrote that she 'realised from the beginning' that she had to 'share Harold's interest in the country and its people' and she sat with him as often as possible when he talked to the bedouin who visited him officially, and 'tried to get to know them'.[88] From the beginning of their relationship, Violet accompanied Harold on travels and visits, often spending time with the women of a household while her husband talked with the men. Although at first, she seems to have found her visits difficult and embarrassing, she very quickly made Arab women friends and took to wearing Arab dress, which she said Harold liked her to do.[89] In 1922 the couple heard that they might be posted to Bahrain and that there was even a possibility that Cox might try to 'fix up a post' for Harold as agent to 'Abd al-'Aziz Al Sa'ud, tempting Violet with the thought that 'then we might go and live with him in Central Arabia... eight days or more inland by camel from Bahrain! I should simply love that, so would Harold'.[90]

In the event the Saudi posting did not materialise, although Harold was sent to Bahrain in September 1922 for a few months as Liaison Officer with 'Abd al-'Aziz during boundary negotiations with Kuwait and Iraq. The Dicksons then took leave in Switzerland where their son was born. The child was named Hanmer Yorke Warrington Saud but the vicar was 'diffident' about 'Saud', which he thought was not a Christian name, and so wrote 'Sand' on the baptism certificate.[91] The Dicksons were subsequently posted to India, where Harold became Private Secretary to the Maharajah of Bikaner, until 1928 when he was appointed Secretary to the Political Resident at Bushire and they returned to the Gulf. In May 1929 he was appointed Political Agent Kuwait, a post which he held until his retirement in February 1936. After retirement he joined the Kuwait Oil Company as their Chief Local Representative, and the Dicksons stayed together in Kuwait until Harold's death in 1959.

During their years together in Kuwait Violet supported and assisted Harold, both as the wife of the official British Agent, the memsahib, and as Orientalist collaborator in the compilation of two huge and detailed studies of Arab life, published under Harold's name. The first book, *The Arab of the Desert*, was published in 1949, and consisted of 650 pages of information on topics ranging from bedouin life, marriage and divorce, to the tent and its furnishings, morality in the desert and town, wild animals and birds and, not least, the camel. It included numerous drawings done by Violet. The manuscript was edited by Emily Lorimer and was one of the last of her many literary accomplishments. The Lorimers had returned to England after David Lorimer's retirement from the Indian Political Service in 1924 and had then embarked on a new joint career of travel, anthropology, scholarship and journalism. In 1934 they went together to the Karakoram and Emily acted as correspondent for *The Times* in Kashmir as well as writing a book of her own about the expedition, *Language Hunting in the Karakoram*, which was published in 1939. She died in 1949, the year in which *The Arab of the Desert* finally reached publication. Her editing work on the Dicksons' book, mainly done in the difficult conditions of wartime and post-war Britain, as Harold acknowledged, made the entire enterprise possible.[92]

The second Dickson book, *Kuwait and Her Neighbours*, was published in 1956 and also included numerous contributions by Violet, particularly in the section relating to a visit made by the couple to Riyadh in 1937, where she described the details of their journey from Kuwait and her own visits to the women's quarters of the royal family.[93] After receiving frequent invitations from King 'Abd al-'Aziz, the Dicksons set off on their trip in October 1937, by car, with two guides and two drivers. Both of them wore Arab dress, in Violet's case a *burqa* and '*aba*. On the road from Kuwait to Riyadh, Harold took 'copious notes of the country lying on both sides, using a cavalry sketching-board, a compass and the hodometer readings of the car. He also had with him his field-glasses and rifle.' Violet took photographs.[94] In Riyadh, while Harold discussed the 'Palestine question' with the king, Violet visited the royal ladies, including four of the king's wives and his sister, Shaikha Nura bint 'Abd al-Rahman al Faysal Al Sa'ud, who, Violet recalled, tried to persuade her to convert to Islam so that she could accompany the Saudi women to the Holy Places. At Princess Nura's palace she also met King 'Abd al-'Aziz himself, with his eldest son Amir Sa'ud .[95] Violet was clearly very impressed by the king's sister and, in a postscript to the visit, Harold noted that his wife,

> who had been most affectionately received by the royal ladies on three occasions, had been particularly attracted by the Lady Nura, whom she

described as one of the most charming and lovable women she had ever met, with all the magnetism and nobility of her great brother, and clearly one of the most important personages in the whole of Arabia, sharing in the King's most intimate councils.

Nura bint 'Abdul Rahman, he added, 'was undoubtedly one of Arabia's fairest, greatest and most famous daughters of all time, her name being rivalled only by that of the mighty King Ibn Sa'ud.'[96]

Like other travellers and the American missionaries before them, the Dicksons were attracted to and intrigued by central Arabia, the desert and the idea of the 'innocent but noble' bedouin. In her memoirs, Violet wrote that Harold had formed a 'deep and lasting affection for the desert Arab whose ideas of honour and chivalry appealed to him most strongly'. For her it had been a slow process to get to know the desert and its people, and it was some time before she had felt at ease. However, gradually her friendships with Arab men and women had increased because of her involvement in Harold's plans to publish his account of 'every aspect' of bedouin life. Harold, she recalled, 'was happiest when he could spend his time among the *badu* questioning them about their history and their way of life', and she was able to help him in his fact-finding by going into the segregated women's quarters, watching the cooking, and learning about all the details of women's private life. Together, they spent extensive time camping in their own desert tent, and Violet was to continue the habit after her husband's death.[97]

The Dicksons' studies on bedouin life were romanticised and 'Orientalist', sometimes seeming to have more in common with the Victorian language of Charles Doughty or Richard Burton than the mid-twentieth century of the oil men and the creation of Arab nation states. In one passage in *The Arab of the Desert*, Harold described the 'bedouin woman' as

> nearly all charm, the natural charm of an unspoiled daughter of Eve, who knows nothing of the world...She has very much of the child about her... She is prone to sudden storms of rage and will sulk without apparent reason. She is full of jealousy, and will love and hate with passion and ferocity, yet she can be the gentlest of beings and is capable of great sacrifice.[98]

In a critical study of English writers on Arabia, published in 1978, the same year as Edward Said's *Orientalism*, Caroll Pastner aptly summed up the tone and perspective of Harold Dickson's work:

> The tone of *The Arab of the Desert* reflected romantic affection for the Bedouin. Their camp, for Dickson, was an escape into domesticity, a pristine, timeless sphere set apart from the demands of the world beyond the desert. The image of the delightful, childlike Bedouin woman was part of a nostalgic and patronizing portrait of a people.[99]

The Arab of the Desert and *Kuwait and Her Neighbours* now seem dated and anachronistic, part more of a Victorian past than the recent post-imperial era. Violet Dickson, however, spent more than thirty years in Kuwait after Harold's death, and her views and perspectives developed, as did her relations with her many Kuwaiti friends. In her autobiography she noted the changes sweeping Arabia and the destruction of much of the old tribal life, and she describes them, still in romantic prose but with a realism that is markedly different from the patronising Western vision of the pre-oil Arabian economies which permeates the writing of some of her male contemporaries:

> I have enjoyed so many happy days and nights among my badawin friends during these last seven years. Does the distant hum of a plane up in the sky, hardly visible, disturb or spoil one's pleasure? Perhaps the tribes from the deep south even enjoy it, reminding them, as it does, of the singing sands of the great Empty Quarter, which most of them have left, never to return. Life is too good here in Kuwait they will tell you; they will never return there. The ugly great water-tanker that comes rattling along, bringing distilled water from the distillation plants of Kuwait or Shaiba, does not worry them; it only gives them joy – especially the women whose task it once was to fetch and carry the heavy water-skins from well or pool. Now, with pleasure, they see that water-carrying has become men's work, and they rejoice.[100]

After Harold died, Violet Dickson remained in Kuwait until a few weeks before her own death, at the age of 94, in 1991. She was evacuated from Kuwait just after the Iraqi invasion. Her life, her own writing and her contributions to her husband's books are now rightly regarded as important in their own right. Yet Violet's role in the couple's anthropological information-gathering was clearly delineated as being the specifically female part of the venture. She investigated Arab women's lives and customs, and she concerned herself with supposedly feminine subjects such as the flora and fauna of the desert. Her writings, like those of Rosita Forbes, 'produced' Arabia for a home audience and with a specifically female voice. However, Violet Dickson was different from Rosita Forbes and the wayward missionary women cited earlier in this chapter in one important respect. Like Emily Lorimer, she was a memsahib and, though unconventional, she travelled, at least for the early part of her life, with her husband, who in turn was, or had been, a British official. They were an acceptable imperial 'couple'. In spite of immersing herself in Arab life to an unusual extent, Violet Dickson did not attempt to cross frontiers, real or imaginary, or undertake any projects 'forbidden' by the British authorities. Rosita Forbes and the missionary women, on the other hand, flouted convention and persisted with their travels in spite of opposition from the male colonial authorities, consistently and deliberately putting themselves outside the traditional boundaries of colonial society. The contrasting activities and perceptions of these travelling women illustrate the wide range of female voices in the imperial landscape of pre-war Arabia.

NOTES ON CHAPTER 6

1   IOR: L/PS/11/170.
2   Trevor to the Government of India, 30 December 1921, IOR:L/PS/11/170. Lt Colonel Arthur Prescott Trevor became Political Resident in November 1920 and held the post until April 1924. He had succeeded David Lorimer at Bahrain in November 1912 and for a time acted as Deputy Resident in the Gulf during Cox's absence in Baghdad in 1915–17. In 1913 Emily Lorimer had told her mother that her husband's successor in Bahrain was 'looked on as one of the strongest and best men in the Department, thoroughly sane and reliable if not flashy'. Correctly predicting his future career pattern, she added, 'They talk of him as Sir Percy's possible successor in Bushire'. Emily Lorimer to her father and mother, 22 January 1913, MSS Eur F177/10.
3   Daly to Trevor, 11 December 1921, and India Office minute by D. T. Monteath, 17 February 1922, IOR:L/PS/11/170.
4   Trevor to Government of India Foreign and Political Department, 17 November 1923, IOR:L/PS/11/170.
5   Political telegram from Bushire to Baghdad, 6 April 1919, IOR:R/15/2/47.
6   General Allenby, Cairo, to Baghdad, 1 and 27 May 1919, IOR:R/15/2/47.
7   Political telegram from Basra to Baghdad, 3 June 1919, IOR:R/15/2/47.
8   'Abd al-'Aziz Al Sa'ud to Political Agent Bahrain, 17 February 1920, IOR:L/PS/11/170.
9   Dickson to Chief Commissioner Baghdad, 25 February 1920, IOR:L/PS/11/170.
10 Political Agent Kuwait to Baghdad, 26 February 1920, IOR:L/PS/11/170.
11 Dickson to 'Abd al-'Aziz Al Sa'ud, 26 February 1920, IOR:R/15/2/81.
12 J. C. More, Political Agent Kuwait, to Political Resident, 25 November 1924, IOR:R/15/5/98.
13 More to Political Resident, 27 December 1924, IOR:R/15/5/98.
14 Alfred DeWitt Mason and Frederick J. Barny, *History of the Arabian Mission* (New York: Board of Foreign Missions Reformed Church in America, 1926), p. 247.
15 *Neglected Arabia*, no 132, January–March 1925.
16 Acting Political Agent Bahrain, Captain George Mallam, to Colonel F. B. Prideaux, Political Resident, 17 May 1925, IOR:R/15/2/81.
17 The Rev. Fred Barny, one of the joint authors of the *History of the Arabian Mission*, was born in Basel, Switzerland, and educated at the New Brunswick

and Princeton Theological Seminaries. He was appointed to the Arabian Mission in 1897.

18 Mallam to Prideaux, 17 May 1925, and Rev. J.Barny to Mallam, 16 May 1925, IOR:R/15/2/81.

19 More to Prideaux, 18 May 1925, IOR:L/PS/11/170.

20 Minute by D. T. Monteath, India Office Political Department, IOR:L/PS/11/170.

21 Jane Robinson's 1990 guide to women travellers (*Wayward Women: a Guide to Women Travellers*, Oxford: Oxford University Press, 1990) uses the adjective for her title.

22 For analyses of the genre of women's travel writing and the colonial context, see: Sara Mills, *Discourses of Difference: An Analysis of Women's Travel Writing and Colonialism* (London and New York: Routledge, 1991); Mary Louise Pratt, *Imperial Eyes: Travel Writing and Transculturation* (London and New York: Routledge, 1992); Billie Melman, *Women's Orients: English Women and the Middle East, 1718–1918* (Basingstoke: Macmillan, 1992).

23 Rosita Forbes, *Women Called Wild* (London: Grayson & Grayson, 1935).

24 Dustjacket of *Women Called Wild* on 1935 India Office Political Department file on travellers, IOR:L/PS/12/4306.

25 Rosita Forbes, *Gypsy in the Sun* (London: Cassell, 1944), p.9; *Who Was Who, 1961–1970*.

26 Forbes, *Gypsy in the Sun*, p.10ff.

27 Biographical note on Forbes by Dorothy Middleton in *Dictionary of National Biography*, 1961–1970, pp.376–77.

28 Forbes, *Gypsy in the Sun*, pp.61–62.

29 This was Gerhard Rohlfs in 1879. *Dictionary of National Biography*, 1961–1970, p.377.

30 Rosita Forbes, *The Secret of the Sahara: Kufara* (London: Cassell, 1921).

31 Some of Forbes's films are preserved by the Women Film Pioneers Project at Duke University, Durham, NC.

32 Gertrude Bell, letter, 25 September 1921, Elizabeth Burgoyne, *Gertrude Bell: From her Personal Papers, 1889–1914* (London: Ernest Benn, 1958), vol.2, p.248.

33 Percy Sykes's review of *Women Called Wild*, *Journal of the Royal Central Asian Society*, no23 (1936), p.174.

34 Rosita Forbes, 'A visit to the Idrisi territory in 'Asir and Yemen', *Geographical Journal*, no62 (1923), pp.271–78.

35 Forbes, *Gypsy in the Sun*, p.73; Foreign Office file note by Grafftey-Smith, 1 January 1927, FO 141/796/16420.

36 Forbes, 'A visit to the Idrisi territory in 'Asir and Yemen', p.275.

37 Asir became a province of Saudi Arabia in 1930.

38 Forbes, *Gypsy in the Sun*, pp.72–73.

39 Memorandum by Captain M.Fazluddin to the British Resident in Aden, 6 December 1922, IOR:R/20/A/3047A.

40 C.B. (Barrett), First Assistant Resident, Aden, to Captain M.Fazluddin, 11 December 1922, IOR:R/20/A/3047A.

41 Aden Residency File Note addressed to First Assistant Resident, signed B.R. (Reilly), 13 December 1922, IOR:R/20/A/3047A.

42 Fazluddin to Barrett, 13 December 1922, IOR:R/20/A/3047A.

43 A reference to the great Danish traveller, Carsten Niebuhr, and his book *Travels Through Arabia*, first published in English in 1792.

44 Telegram from Aden Resident to Secretary of State for the Colonies, 11 December 1922, and Colonial Office reply, 14 December; India Office note by EGB, 28 December, IOR:L/PS/11/222.

45 See Elizabeth Monroe, *Philby of Arabia* (London: Faber & Faber, 1973), chs 5–6.

46 Gertrude Bell letter, 7 February 1921, Burgoyne, *Gertrude Bell*, vol.2, p.204.

47 Gertrude Bell letter, 22 May 1921, Burgoyne, *Gertrude Bell*, vol.2, p.217.

48 Monroe, *Philby of Arabia*, p.113.

49 Ibid., pp.127–28.

50 Rosita Forbes to H.StJ.B. and Dora Philby, 4 March 1923, St Antony's College Middle East Centre, Oxford, Philby Papers, GB165-0229. Kim Philby was to achieve notoriety in adulthood as a Soviet spy.

51 H.StJ.B.Philby, *Arabian Days: An Autobiography* (London: Robert Hale, 1948), p.241; Monroe, *Philby of Arabia*, p.141.

52 Rosita Forbes to Philby, 20 May 1923, Philby Papers, GB165-0229. Sir John Evelyn Shuckburgh was Secretary of the India Office Political Department and at the time seconded to the Colonial Office as Assistant Under Secretary of State. He was transferred to the Colonial Office in 1924.

53 Forbes to Philby, 6 July 1923, Philby Papers, GB165-0229.

54 Forbes, New York, to Philby, 6 February 1924, Philby Papers, GB165-0229.

55 Note of Colonial Office interview by Sir John Shuckburgh with Forbes, 22 October 1924, IOR:L/PS/11/251.

56 Secretary of State for the Colonies to Aden Resident, 3 January 1925, IOR:R/20/A/4998.

57 Forbes to Philby (undated, 1924), Philby Papers, GB165-0229.

58 Gertrude Bell to her father, 29 October 1924, Burgoyne, *Gertrude Bell*, vol.2, pp.357–58.

59 Forbes, *Gypsy in the Sun*, p.110.

60 Prideaux to Aden Resident, General Thomas Scott, 27 December 1924, IOR:R/20/A/4998.

61 Note to Resident (Scott) by CB (Barrett) on interviews with Philby and Mrs McGrath, 8 January 1925, IOR: R/20/A/3047B.

62 Note on interviews with Philby and Mrs McGrath, 8 January 1925.

63 Forbes, *Gypsy in the Sun*, p.110.

64 Forbes to Philby, 30 July 1925, Philby Papers, GB165-0229.

65 File Note by J.P.Gibson, 2 February 1925, IOR:L/PS/11/251.

66 Claud Russell, Addis Ababa, to Secretary of State for the Colonies, 9 February 1925, IOR:L/PS/11/251.

67 Russell to Secretary of State, 16 February 1925, IOR:L/PS/11/251.

68 'Most Secret' telegram from Ministry of Foreign Affairs, Rome, to Italian Embassy, London, 22 November 1935, intercepted by British Government, PRO: HW 12/197. This is a series of intercepts of foreign diplomatic communications released by the Public Record Office in 1999.

69 J.C.Walton, India Office, minute to R.A.Butler, 22 July 1935, enclosing copy of 'Indian Army Orders: Rules regulating the visits of European ladies to places situated in the tribal areas of the North West Frontier', June 1935, IOR:L/PS/12/4306. The Rules delineated in detail the areas women were allowed to visit, and the conditions under which they could travel, for example 'with a responsible male escort', only at certain times, and only on main roads.

70 R.A.Butler, minute to Walton, 25 July 1935, IOR:L/PS/12/4306. Richard Austen ('RAB') Butler was Under-Secretary of State at the India Office from 1932 to 1937. He later became Chancellor of the Exchequer (1951–55), Home Secretary (1957–62) and Foreign Secretary (1963–64). Walton responded that he also thought the India Office should help Forbes because ten years earlier they had been obliged to prohibit her journey across Arabia because of the circumstances prevailing at the time.

71 Butler to W.K.Fraser-Tytler, 31 July 1935, and Fraser-Tytler to Butler, 15 August 1935, IOR:L/PS/12/4306.

72 Fraser-Tytler telegram to Government of India Foreign Department, 25 February 1936, IOR:L/PS/12/4306.

73 Ibid.

74 Fraser-Tytler to J.C.Walton, 11 April 1936, IOR:L/PS/12/4306.

75 J.C.Walton to L.Collier, Foreign Office, 19 May 1936, IOR:L/PS/12/4306.

76 Draft letter from Walton to Rosita McGrath, 19 May 1936, IOR:L/PS/12/4306, and Rosita McGrath to J.C.Walton, 24 May 1936, IOR:L/PS/12/4306.

77 'Rosita Forbes on Central Asia', *Great Britain and the East*, 28 May 1936.

78 Forbes, *Gypsy in the Sun*, p.370.

79 Ibid., ch.1.

80 Monroe, *Philby of Arabia*, p.175.

81 Ibid., pp.150–53, 171.

82 *Who was Who*, 1951–1960, p.305, and Preface by Harold Dickson to his book, *The Arab of the Desert: a Glimpse into Badawin Life in Kuwait and Sa'udi Arabia* (London: George Allen & Unwin, 1949).

83 Violet Dickson, *Forty Years in Kuwait* (London: George Allen & Unwin, 1971), Prologue, pp.11–13. Dickson described her autobiography as having been written from memory and from letters, and it is occasionally factually inaccurate.

84 Dickson, *Forty Years in Kuwait*, Prologue, pp.12–13. The Dicksons met and married in 1920, and not 1919, according to their *Who's Who* and

Dictionary of National Biography entries. Harold Dickson was posted to Iraq in 1921.

85 Dickson, *Forty Years in Kuwait*, pp. 23–24.

86 Gertrude Bell, letter, 17 January 1921, Burgoyne, *Gertrude Bell*, vol. 2, p. 199.

87 Harold Dickson's papers are at St Antony's College, Oxford, Middle East Centre.

88 Dickson, *Forty Years in Kuwait*, p. 89.

89 Ibid., pp. 35–36: 'Harold used to like to see me in Arab gowns, and in the evenings I would change into a long Arab dress, which at least gave me a little variety in my wardrobe'.

90 Violet Dickson to her sister, 21 August 1922, quoted in *Forty Years in Kuwait*, pp. 51–52.

91 Dickson, *Forty Years in Kuwait*, p. 55.

92 Dickson, *The Arab of the Desert*, p. 11. Emily Overend Lorimer, *Language Hunting in the Karakoram* (London: George Allen & Unwin, 1939).

93 Harold Dickson, *Kuwait and her Neighbours* (London: George Allen & Unwin, 1956).

94 Violet Dickson, 'Our trip to Riyadh by car', in Dickson, *Kuwait and Her Neighbours*, pp. 371–85.

95 Violet Dickson, 'A call on the Royal Ladies', in Dickson, *Kuwait and Her Neighbours*, pp. 395–404.

96 Dickson, *Kuwait and Her Neighbours*, pp. 414–15.

97 Dickson, *Forty Years in Kuwait*, pp. 95–96.

98 Dickson, *The Arab of the Desert*, p. 57.

99 Caroll McC. Pastner, 'Englishmen in Arabia: Encounters with Middle Eastern women', *Signs*, no 4 (1978), pp. 309–23 (p. 321).

100 Dickson, *Forty Years in Kuwait*, pp. 218–19. Compare, for example, the writings of Wilfred Thesiger's romantic nostalgia and regret at the intrusion of so-called 'modern life' into the desert.

7 The 'Beach Pyjama Incident', 1933: Oil, the Arabian Gulf Air Route and the 'Opening up' of the Coast

In the decade before the Second World War, three major economic changes in the Gulf region began to have an effect, both on local society and on international perspectives towards the area. The decline of the pearling industry in the 1930s initially devastated the economies of the small Gulf states, in particular Bahrain. At the same time, however, the immediate impact and future potential of the discovery of oil, and the development of worldwide air routes and other communication networks, started to expose the shaikhdoms to a much larger number of Western influences and pressures. In a phrase which itself expresses all the traditional Western perspectives of regional backwardness and isolation, ripe for colonial development and exploitation, the Gulf began to be described as being 'opened up'.[1]

Oil, the commodity which was to change the face of the Arabian Peninsula and the Gulf, began to be exported from wells in Bahrain in 1933, and from Saudi Arabia in 1939. The British had depended heavily on oil from neighbouring Persia for their First World War effort, and prospecting on the Arabian side of the Gulf began as early as 1923. However, the major American and British oil companies were slow to realise the extent and potential of the Arabian fields and in the 1930s less than five percent of world oil was supplied by the Middle East.[2] Although no-one could have imagined the effects that oil would have on the region's long-term economic and political development, in the short term the 1930s saw the first impact of the industry with the arrival of oil men, negotiators, geologists and technicians, and the beginnings of much larger expatriate communities. At the same time, the development of the Arabian Gulf coast as the main air route between Europe, India and further East resulted in an influx of travellers, many of them women, and posed new problems for already embattled British officials in the Gulf shaikhdoms. In 1933 an incident in Sharjah illustrated the extent of their anxiety.

Since the opening of the air route, Sharjah had become a refuelling base and it had a famous rest house with bath and showers. It was also becoming increasingly common for passengers stopping overnight there to visit the town, and sometimes the ruler. In March 1933 the Political Agent in Bahrain, Lieutenant-Colonel P. G. Loch, reported to the Resident that a female Imperial Airways passenger had been seen going into the town wearing casual clothing, described as 'beach pyjamas'. Loch also wrote to the Imperial Airways Rest House superintendent at Sharjah asking him to discourage passengers from entering the town.[3] The Resident, Lieutenant-Colonel Trenchard Craven Fowle, replied by express letter on 1 April: 'I quite agree with your views as to the undesirability of Imperial Airways passengers wandering about Shargah town – especially women'; and he wrote both to the ruler and to Imperial Airways headquarters in London asking for the practice to be stopped. To the latter he expressed outward concern about the danger to women:

> I have just received a communication from the Political Agent, Bahrain, that passengers at Shargah have begun going into the town, one lady passenger doing so clad in beach pyjamas. However suitable the latter garb may be in its right place, that place is obviously not Shargah … It must be remembered that the people of Shargah have not up to now been accustomed to having strangers, especially ladies, wandering about their bazaars, and it is of course most desirable from the point of view of the Company, as well as from my point of view, that any risk of passengers being molested should be avoided.[4]

Having apparently put the onus of responsibility firmly on the company and its passengers, Fowle then addressed a rather different letter to the ruler of Sharjah, Shaikh Sultan bin Saqr Al Qasimi, reminding him of his own position:

> As you are aware the people of your town, though friendly to us, are not accustomed to strange Europeans wandering about in their bazaars, and if by any unfortunate chance one of the passengers was insulted or molested by some bad character, or Bedouin from the desert, it would be a serious matter, and one for which I would have to hold you, O Shaikh, entirely responsible.

Fowle reminded the ruler of the clause in the Sharjah Air Agreement, signed by himself and the British in 1932, to the effect that neither company employees nor passengers would be allowed to enter the town of Sharjah without the Shaikh's permission.[5] The British, Fowle said, had assumed this clause would be needed because an influx of visitors would be undesirable from the ruler's point of view. Nevertheless, it was now apparent that the

Shaikh was rather enjoying the visitors. 'It is clearly undesirable,' wrote Loch, 'that passengers should wander about Shargah, both from the point of view of incidents arising and of the Shaikh becoming spoilt.'[6] Imperial Airways were anxious to preserve their position on the coast and were only too willing to comply with the government's requirements. They ordered the station superintendent at Sharjah to ensure that the 'utmost discretion' was exercised when dealing with local people. At the same time, however, their London office presented a rather different picture of the situation at Sharjah, noting that, from weekly reports received from their station superintendent, it seemed that his relationship with the Shaikh was 'very cordial and indeed the people at Shargah seem to have accepted the Company and its aircraft, staff and passengers in a much more amiable way than might have been expected'.[7]

The British administrators in the Gulf were clearly concerned to preserve not only sexual propriety but also the status quo. The ruler of Sharjah was reassured, in the usual patronising tone and with scant regard for the obvious success of the airline stopover, that 'later on, when your people have become accustomed to the coming and going of travellers, we can consider the matter again'; in other words, when the British authorities, rather than the ruler himself or Imperial Airways, felt the time was suitable for social intercourse, the rules could be relaxed.[8] When the incident was reported to the India Office Political Department in London, one of its senior officials recorded a deeper underlying government concern:

> In connection with Shargah, reference may be made to…the beach pyjama incident. The correspondence speaks for itself. It is obviously quite undesirable that European ladies should wander about Shargah in beach pyjamas and it is to be hoped that the Resident's letter to the Sheikh of 30th March and his representations to Imperial Airways will secure that passengers shall not be allowed to enter the town. This is incidentally desirable from quite another point of view, for it will help us to keep a check on the activities of concession hunters, etc. We have just heard that the Iraq Petroleum Company have applied for visas for the Trucial Coast for a representative and, while these have been refused, communication between passing passengers and the Sheikh such as appears to have been taking place since the opening of the air station would obviously make it much more difficult for us to exercise the control we desire.[9]

As the Sharjah 'incident' showed, the development of civilian airlines in the 1930s, and the increased opportunities they provided for travel, created an entirely new situation for the British administrators in Arabia and the Gulf. Although a few individual and well-known independent women travellers and writers such as Rosita Forbes and Freya Stark continued to carry out expeditions, and to venture into the desert, many more people were now simply passing through the area and stopping off for brief encounters. Furthermore, the parallel development of the oil industry was beginning to bring in entirely new groups of people, including women doctors, nurses and industry wives, who were all outside the British political and diplomatic class and much more difficult to control.

Neither Fowle nor Loch, respectively Political Resident in the Gulf and Political Agent in Bahrain, were particularly open-minded or flexible about the changes going on around them. Fowle had been appointed Resident in 1932 and had previously served as a Political Officer in Mesopotamia during World War I, followed by postings in southern Persia, where Emily Lorimer privately referred to him as 'Chicken'.[10] Philby was also rather dismissive of Fowle's abilities and later, in his autobiography, described Fowle as 'an intelligent but uninspired person who always said the commonplace thing in a commonplace way and scorned every form of enthusiasm for any cause or thing'.[11] Although fluent in Arabic and knowledgeable about Arab culture and society, Fowle nevertheless still held a strong conviction that he represented the British civilising mission in a still 'semi-barbaric' land.[12] Loch, the Political Agent in Bahrain, on one occasion described conditions on the Trucial Coast as being 'not unlike those on our own border in the fifteenth century – indeed I have found a study of early Scottish history invaluable in helping me to understand their somewhat mediaeval ways'.[13] Yet, faced with the dilemma of allowing social interchange between local people and travellers from the 'civilised' world, neither man was able to see the illogicality of his position, or to recognise and acknowledge the changes which were taking place in imperial and colonial politics. The British authorities in the Gulf, already confronted by economic rivals in the region, now also realised that their ordered male world was facing an influx of potentially disruptive women. A series of 1930s India Office Political Department files illustrate the interest taken by the British Government, and the protocol put in place to monitor non-official female travellers and residents in the Arabian Gulf.[14] One of these was Lady Dorothy Mills.

In December 1931 the Passport Office in London sent a report to the India Office concerning a meeting with Lady Mills, who was planning to visit Egypt and the western Arabian region of Hijaz and then travel on to Aden and along the southern coast of Arabia to the Gulf. Mills had personal introductions to the Saudi Governor of Jeddah, and to the British representative there, Andrew Ryan. The passport officers reported that she had been given a visa for Egypt and the Hijaz, but not for Yemen and Oman, and she had been warned to adhere to the advice of British representatives and made to sign an undertaking to keep in close touch with local British authorities.[15] Mills was an aristocrat, the daughter of the Earl of Oxford, and an experienced traveller. In 1923 she had been the first Englishwoman to visit Timbuktu and she had subsequently undertaken expeditions to Liberia and Portuguese Guinea. She was a Fellow of the Royal Geographical Society and an Honorary Member of the Portuguese Geographical Society and she had already published numerous books about her travels.[16] Mills had told the Passport Office that she wanted to go to Arabia for pleasure and to collect material for another book. In a note which typifies the response of the India Office bureaucrats, J.C. Walton, Secretary of the Political Department, passed the information on to the Government of India, identifying her as 'Lady Dorothy Mills (who is, I understand, an authoress of sorts)'. The words 'an authoress of sorts' replaced a previous phrase, 'an authoress of no great merit', which had been crossed out and amended.[17]

Two years later, the same India Office file records the extensive time and official paperwork taken up by the case of another woman writer, Winifred Howard-Clitty. Clitty was an author of children's books and was looking for bedouin tales, and for information on pearl fishing, for some new stories she was working on. She told the passport officials that she was a friend of a well-known and influential Bahraini businessman, Yusuf Kanoo, who had promised to give her information about the pearl industry, and she was given a visa for travel to Kuwait, Bahrain and Saudi Arabia, although not to the interior. In December 1933, however, Fowle wrote to the India Office, saying that her 'threatened arrival' had caused 'no little concern to the Rulers and the Political Agents of Bahrain and Kuwait'. She had, in fact, only met Yusuf Kanoo casually for a few hours when travelling in the Gulf a few years earlier and now she was proposing to stay with him; he 'by no means relished the prospect, and of course it was most undesirable that a European lady ... should stay with an Arab', even though Yusuf Kanoo himself was 'a most respectable citizen' and a recipient of the C.I.E. (Companion of the Order of the Indian Empire).[18] Even worse, continued Fowle, Clitty was also planning to stay in Kuwait with an oil-company agent, Mohamed Yatim, who had 'an unenviable reputation in the Gulf of being a notorious drunkard and evil liver, and in Kuwait actually resides in the prostitutes' quarter.' The Political Agent in Kuwait, Harold Dickson, had told Clitty that she must stay with the American Mission, or somewhere else approved of by him. Fowle concluded his letter with a request that in future, before visas were given to women travellers to the Gulf, he should be consulted first.

After discussions with the India Office and the Foreign Office, the Passport Office agreed to refer all requests for visas from British women to the Resident, as was already the practice with foreign women travellers. Clitty was in fact a British subject, married to an American.[19] The remaining papers in the official archives, however, reveal the shifting perspectives and conflicting narratives of the Clitty episode. In January 1934, Loch telegraphed Fowle from Bahrain to say that Mrs Clitty, now arrived at Basra, had been visited at the rest house there 'by an Arab from Kuwait who remained with her for some three hours, and, it is said, told her stories. She subsequently did a good deal of typing.' Loch gathered that she was 'socially not of the type which should be permitted to come to Bahrain'.[20] Meanwhile, the American Mission in Kuwait agreed to put her up with one of their women, Miss Van Pelt, who would 'not allow Mohamed Yatim in her house, or let Mrs. Howard-Clitty go out with him'.[21] In March, Fowle wrote to the Secretary of State to give him an account of Clitty's visit to the Gulf, and the background to it. According to Fowle's version, in 1931 and before her marriage, Clitty (as Miss Winifred Howard) had already visited Bahrain and Kuwait. On the boat from India she had met Mohamed Yatim, the confidential agent of Major Frank Holmes, the leading oil negotiator at Kuwait. She also briefly met Yusuf Kanoo at Bahrain. At Kuwait she asked for an interview with the Shaikh, which was refused. On this more recent trip the American missionary, Miss Van Pelt, who was to put her up, backed out, and both Holmes and Kanoo expressed reluctance to meet her:

> The Political Agents at Kuwait and Bahrain reported that both Shaikhs were distinctly perturbed at the proposal of an unattached European lady coming to reside in their Principalities under the conditions contemplated by Mrs. Howard-Clitty, who has now, I believe, left Basrah for Europe – where she probably intends, so it is reported, to write the inevitable article, and perhaps the equally inevitable book, considered necessary by most tourists to this part of the world. Both articles and book may have an anti-British tinge as Mrs. Howard-Clitty is reported to be disgruntled on account of the restrictions which had, in the circumstances explained above, to be placed on her travels in the Gulf.[22]

The papers on the case kept at the Bahrain Agency show the same hostility and disapproval from Loch and from Dickson in Kuwait, but they vindicate, to some extent, Clitty's claims that she had been offered hospitality by Yusuf Kanoo. The file contains copies of Clitty's correspondence with Kanoo after her visit in 1931, telling him about her marriage and her plans for her next trip. Kanoo had, in fact, written to her in November 1931, in response to a letter of thanks for his hospitality during this first visit:

It is very good of you to give so much expression to what little hospitality I could offer you. I feel I ought to have done much more for such a good person like you, but it is a pity your stay here was only for a couple of hours. Surely, I hope, you will have another chance of visiting Bahrain and give me the pleasure of your much longer stay...[23]

In February 1933, Kanoo wrote to her again to say that he was assuming she would now bring her husband too 'and show him our country. You are both welcome at my place.' When Clitty wrote back in August to say that she would be coming alone because her husband was an engineer and away at sea, Kanoo replied that he would be very pleased to meet her.[24] Meanwhile Harold Dickson reassured Loch from Kuwait that he would certainly do his best to prevent her from getting to Bahrain, 'if she ever gets here, which, I hope, I shall succeed in preventing'. At the same time Dickson reported to Fowle that he had talked to the ruler of Kuwait, and while he did not 'definitely say that he objected to the lady's presence in Kuwait, I could clearly see that he did not at all like the idea of her putting up with Mr. Mohamed Yatim.' Dickson concluded that 'British "prestige" forbids that she puts up with a young Arab man living alone, and in the evil quarter mentioned by me'.[25] Kanoo, meanwhile, told Loch that his reply to Clitty's request to stay with him had not been serious, but was simply expressed 'in the usual polite Arab way'.[26] In February 1934, Loch telegraphed Fowle to report that Clitty was leaving Basra by car for Haifa and then Greece:

She is said to be hysterical and possibly consumptive. It is understood that some of her draft articles for the Press are of an undesirable type. She regards the Arab as the highest form of man and is very angry at not being permitted to go to Kuwait. Her intention is said to be to give her impressions in a series of articles in the Press (possibly under a pen-name, which I do not know) and in a novel. It seems possible that she may try to pillory the Political Department.[27]

Consciously or unconsciously appropriating Victorian discourses of female hysteria, just as his predecessors had done in relation to some of the women missionaries, Loch dismissed Clitty and passed the responsibility to the government in London. He suggested that they should keep an eye out for her and consider the possibility of warning the press, 'or of taking other action', not specified. In a note at the end of the file he concluded:

I recently had an opportunity of finding out the views of a lady who stayed in the Rest House with Mrs Howard Clitty in Basra, though she did not attempt to get to know her personally. I gather that she formed a poor opinion of her and thought it would be unwise, if it were possible to avoid it, to allow her to come to a place like Bahrain.[28]

The episode was a miniature representation of wider colonial fears and prejudices, illustrating, on a political level, British concern about preserving diplomatic and economic supremacy, and, on a social level, the class, gender and racial bigotry exemplified by Fowle's and Loch's anxiety about the behaviour of Clitty, her personal background and character, and her relations with Arab men. As in India, fear of sexual impropriety was both a real and imagined factor in the preservation of imperial authority and control. Winifred Clitty was a symbol of changing attitudes to the Middle East and to the notion of the Gulf as a British fiefdom, in which permission to travel and to fraternise with the natives was to be sought from paternalist and increasingly outmoded official bureaucracies. Furthermore, the new wave of women travellers challenged preconceived colonial ideas about who was, and who was not, suitable to represent Britain in the Orient.

The subtle differences in attitude among officials in postings across the region are illustrated by the case of another British woman, Kathleen Palmer Smith, who had been working as a governess in Tehran, for the family of the former British minister, Sir Robert Clive. In 1935 Fowle wrote to the Foreign Office because Palmer Smith was planning to visit the American missionary doctors Marion Wells Thoms and her husband Sharon, in Bahrain.[29] As with Winifred Clitty, Fowle complained about the fact that visas for travel to the Gulf Arab states were being issued without reference to the local political officers, or in other words, himself: 'In such States there are no hotels appropriate for the accommodation of English women and they should not be allowed to visit such States with the object of residence unless the Political Agent can arrange suitable accommodation for them'.[30]

Fowle complained that Miss Palmer Smith's arrival had caused embarrassment to Loch, to the British Government and to the American missionaries. However, in this case, it appears that he was thought by at least some other officials to have overstepped the mark, and he subsequently received a reprimand from the incumbent British minister in Tehran, Hughe Montgomery Knatchbull-Hugessen. The minister wrote to the Foreign Office complaining that such instructions should not be necessary, pointing out that Miss Palmer Smith was 'an entirely respectable lady with adequate private means who is well known to the staff of this Legation', and adding that he thought her arrangements with the missionaries should be a private one between her and them.[31] Whether the reprimand was an acknowledgement that Fowle was seen elsewhere as being over-zealous and bureaucratic, or simply a reflection of the fact that some women were judged to be suitable and decent, and others not, the exchange indicated a rather more sophisticated outlook in at least some other more urban and cosmopolitan diplomatic postings.

Both the Clitty case and the case of Kathleen Palmer Smith illustrated the shifting hierarchies within British perceptions of imperial authority and social acceptability. On the sidelines of both episodes, the American missionaries appeared, and were identified, as figures of authority and substance, in stark contrast to their previous characterisations as disruptive and difficult interlopers in the region. In both affairs they were portrayed as the potential providers of respectable accommodation and, by inference, as the upholders of moral standards; in the case of Palmer Smith they were additionally linked with both the Political Agent in Bahrain and the British Government as a group facing embarrassment from the activities of troublesome women. These references indicate the subtle way in which the missionaries, long established in the Gulf, and now recognised and respected as providers of education and healthcare, had eventually become almost part of the establishment themselves. In fact, far from being sympathetic to the new wave of economic migrants and entrepreneurs, many of whom were, like themselves, American, the missionaries adopted a rather ambivalent attitude to the new arrivals.

In an article published in *Neglected Arabia* in 1936, the Reverend B.D. Hakken argued that the arrival of the oil industry had presented a new and difficult problem for the missionaries.[32] The effects on Bahrain society and its economy had already been enormous. The oil operations had brought changes in infrastructure and had provided local employment and relieved some of the poverty caused by the slump in the pearl industry. At the same time it had brought in more Europeans and Americans with their wives and children. The mission had established a close relationship with the oil company and supplied medical services in return for much-needed cash. Furthermore, Hakken thought, the American and European employees of the company on the whole were 'a fine lot of men' and had treated the Arabs well. However, the fact that the oil men did not attend services gave the Arabs the wrong idea:

> The fact that even before their advent, the English were not good attendants does not enter into the picture, for the Arabs recognize that the English are a different people, but coming face to face with the knowledge that there are Americans who are not religious is a strange and wholly unaccountable thing for them. This awakening has not helped our work.

Actively or unconsciously, both missionaries and British officials were reinventing the missionary presence and realigning themselves in the face of the new arrivals. When the question of missionary visits to Saudi Arabia,

Qatar and the Trucial Coast, and the related issue of visas was raised by Loch in the 1930s, it was now with a sense of resignation that the British could no longer prevent them from visiting Saudi Arabia, 'which is an independent State, nor... Qatar, especially if the Shaikh issues... an invitation'.[33] By 1936 both Loch and Fowle had accepted that conditions in Qatar and the Trucial Coast had so changed that it was now unreasonable to make the missionaries pay for a visa for every visit, although Fowle noted that in the case of 'evangelical personnel' the British could definitely refuse permission on the grounds that the individuals would not be welcomed by the shaikhs and were not involved in 'humanitarian' work.[34]

In 1933, in this changing atmosphere, the first missionary women finally made it to Riyadh. The group consisted of Dr Louis and Mrs Elizabeth Dame, Josephine Van Peursem and an Indian Christian nurse, Grace Davis, who had been trained in the Americans' Arcot Mission. They also took with them a former slave named Medina, 'a black woman and mission helper of many years standing'.[35] In a letter written to the Board of Foreign Missions, Josephine Van Peursem remarked on the cordial hospitality offered to them by King 'Abd al-'Aziz, adding that both she and Mrs Dame had been 'adopted as members of the family as far as social position is concerned'. She reported that at the king's weekly *majlis*, for his women relatives, the missionary women were seated next to the king's three full sisters by his own mother, and ahead of the other nine. The king had introduced them as the only Christians he would invite to Riyadh, saying that they 'were real true Christians, missionaries, whose purpose is to spread their religion, and that we were doing everything we did in the service of God... That he admired us for our noble lives, zeal and honesty.'[36] Elizabeth Dame's own account of the visit referred back to the appointment of Amy Zwemer, 37 years earlier, which had been seen as an experiment and doubted by some, and noted that 'another red-letter day' had been added to the mission history 'in the penetration of the first women missionaries to Central Arabia':

> Our greatest interest of course was in the women. We found them very responsive and were met with friendliness and cordiality on every hand, whether from members of the royal family, wives of retainers, servants or slaves. We felt when we left that we were leaving real friends, for our intimate association had deepened our acquaintanceship to friendship even in the short space of three months.[37]

While the perceived danger from American missionary women had by now largely evaporated, independent travellers continued to give the Gulf officials more anxiety. Since the early 1930s the British authorities had also been defensive about the potential influx of non-diplomatic wives. In June 1934, for example, Imperial Airways headquarters in London wrote to the British Consul-General at Bushire to ask whether their station super-intendent at Sharjah could have his wife to stay with him in the winter months, arguing, quite reasonably, that if it could be allowed, 'it would make our representative happier, and he has sufficient experience of the Gulf and its inhabitants not to abuse the trust'.[38] Fowle replied in the negative, saying that since the airport had opened at Sharjah things had gone very smoothly, far more so than he anticipated, and he was therefore reluctant to do anything likely to 'increase the risks of any incident occurring' or 'augment the complications when any incident had occurred'.[39] Furthermore, if at any time there was trouble at Sharjah, the fact that there was a woman in residence, who might have to be evacuated, would just increase the difficulties. More specifically, Fowle continued: 'I cannot guarantee that some unpleasant incident would not arise in regard to Mrs. Janes, such as her being insulted by some uncouth Bedouin from the interior or by an impertinent townsman.' Any such incident would require retribution and lead to bad relations with the Shaikh. With a startling failure to recall the problems raised by the 'beach pyjama incident', Fowle admitted that women passengers passed through the shaikhdom, but explained that they arrived late in the evening, departed the next morning and did not stay in the town; living permanently there would be a different proposition. Characteristically, Fowle added that the question was his responsibility and, although the Shaikh had said there was no objection, this would not help in the event of an 'incident':

> I quite appreciate the desire of the Company to make your Shargah repre-sentative happier, and as a married man myself I think it distinctly hard that Janes should be separated for long periods from his wife. The remedy, however, appears to be in the Company's hands. They can either send a bachelor to Shargah, or – for married men – make it a short service post.

In a covering letter to the India Office, Fowle added that allowing Mrs Janes to go to Sharjah might create an awkward precedent if other places on the Trucial Coast, or Qatar, were subsequently 'opened up'. Eventually, he predicted, the Trucial Coast would no doubt become suitable for women to live in, 'but for the present it is not'.[40] Clearly understanding the *quid pro quo* required for expanding its business activities in the region, Imperial Airways replied to Fowle, thanking him for giving such a clear exposition of why Mrs Janes would not be allowed, and accepting his view that it would be 'inadvisable'.[41]

In the next few years, pressure from the airline and the oil companies for accommodation for families became increasingly more of an issue. In

September 1936, for example, Fowle telegraphed the India Office about a report that a party of oil-concession men (managers, drillers and geologists) was being sent to Bahrain and had been enquiring in London about houses. By this time, Fowle was willing to accept that wives could be permitted, as long as the company had satisfied the Political Agent in Bahrain that suitable accommodation was available and had obtained the latter's written agreement.[42] He also said that the same understanding might apply to Kuwait, although Dickson had said there was now no spare accommodation for European women. However, women 'should not, repeat not in any case be allowed to go to Qatar or Trucial Coast'. The India Office wrote accordingly to the Kuwait Oil Company and to Petroleum Concessions Limited, who were both starting operations on the coast from headquarters in Bahrain, and they also wrote to the Passport Office.[43] The companies accepted the terms, but at the beginning of October the India Office wrote again to say that it had discussed the matter of Bahrain with Fowle who, in fact, did not 'take so serious a view of it as Colonel Loch'.[44] Fowle's view now was that it was the company's responsibility to make sure that suitable accommodation was available before allowing ladies to go to Bahrain, and that the government should not take responsibility for certifying accommodation as 'suitable'. On 3 October the Secretary of State for India telegraphed both political agents, in Bahrain and Kuwait, to say that 'Fowle considers that position … is quite satisfactory … He would deprecate Political Agent taking any responsibility for certifying accommodation as adequate and would prefer to leave onus on Company.'[45]

In response to pressure from London, Fowle was beginning to unbend. In general terms, permission was gradually being given for more women to travel, even if, as individuals, they were subjected to close scrutiny, and sometimes ridicule, in the process. Officials such as Fowle and Loch, and to a lesser extent Dickson, were still expressing views that referred back to ideas inherited from the Indian Rebellion (the 'Indian Mutiny') in 1857 when the arrival in India of increasing numbers of women in the years preceding the disturbances had led the British to conclude that the female presence was inevitably disruptive in the masculine world of empire.[46] However, in metropolitan Britain these assumptions were being increasingly challenged.

In 1932 the *Contemporary Review* published an article written jointly by Professor Ernest Barker and Freya Stark, in which women's roles in imperial and colonial service were re-appraised.[47] Barker was Professor of Political Science at Cambridge; Freya Stark was, by then, an experienced traveller who had just begun to write for publication. The article was written in two sections, the first part by Barker and second part by Stark, and it was described by Barker as being the result of conversations between the two which had taken place in an Italian hill town the previous autumn.[48]

In the introduction to the article Barker acknowledged the fact that it was recognised that a woman should go overseas with her husband, although he added that 'when you think of it, it is a thing for wonder and admiration. She pays a heavy price' – since, when children are born, the children go home and the mother and wife either follows them and loses her husband, or vice versa. Nevertheless, she 'pays the price quietly; and we take the payment for granted'. The second general assumption, in Barker's view, was that the Englishwoman living overseas with her husband was 'one of the barriers – subtly, unconsciously, but all the more powerfully – to ready understanding and easy sympathy between the Englishmen who work abroad and the people of the land in which they work'. Barker went on to argue that the fault 'lies with the man rather than with the woman'. Englishmen, he thought, more than French, Spaniards or Italians, had a strong sense of 'race', which itself was a 'sadly abused word':

> We cherish an ideal of race purity; we hold to an ideal of uncontaminated whiteness...there is wisdom and moral prudence about it if we keep it as a control on ourselves. But we extend it; and we make it a sort of control on our women-folk. Starting with an idea of chivalry, which is not necessarily the highest tribute to them, we desire to keep them fenced and protected; we want them to live the English life, with all its amenities and sanctities, apart from the outer world.

Barker deprecated the tendency towards a colonial 'enclave' of English social life and secluded English womanhood, which he likened to a conservatory, 'useful for plants...not necessarily useful for human beings'. He also apportioned some blame to women themselves, for colluding in this segregation:

> On top of this comes the action of the Englishwomen themselves. Women have a gift for creating 'society', with its gatherings, its rules, its round of activities, its codes. The active genius of Englishwomen has been busy in this way. Wherever they have settled, they have organised a whole system of social life, partly for themselves, but mainly for the leisure hours of their men... But the more the impulse works, the more it accentuates the tendency towards an *enclave*. The development of social life is also the development of social distinctions. Women, who are the great creators of social etiquette, may also be the creators of social barriers.

Introducing Stark's section of the article, Barker commented that he agreed entirely with what she had to say: women were already doing social work during working hours and there was no reason why they should not do more of it, as long as men were prepared to drop some of their masculine taboos and cease to regard women as either coquettes 'for hours of rest' or nurses for when they were ill. Woman, he concluded, should instead be

> the companion and fellow-worker...She has an instinct for social work as well as the social round...it will be a genuine liberation of the gifts and capacities of the Englishwoman serving the Empire abroad. Nor will it only be her liberation. It will be a new and singularly effective way of conciliation and sympathy between the English stock and native peoples. When women understand one another, the battle is won, and the way is easy for men.

Stark's piece continued in the same vein. She pointed out that the British Empire of Disraeli, 'so large and strong and unassailable that it overshadowed the acquiescent world with no effort of its own', was long gone, and so had the static prosperity which accompanied it. The ideas which underpinned it had altered, and 'outward forms, following in their clumsy dangerous way', were also changing:

> The whole thing moves like a stream of lava...the heaving, wrinkled surface threatens at any moment to crack and break...That it should move – that at any rate it does so – is now obvious to all: to keep it from doing so destructively is our concern. Meanwhile the process, disturbing our easy tenure, makes us revise our tools and methods.

Stark went on to call for the empire to be organised on a broader basis, bringing in other professional people from trade, industry or journalism:

> If we are still to lead in the world, we shall soon need every resource that we can muster...In this connection we have one asset which is unique to our race. This is the British woman. No other has had quite the same training or developed quite the same qualities. She has been formed by a discipline, now centuries old, of hardship abroad or separation at home, which has combined with a Puritan tradition of self-control to weave as it were a steel thread into the very fibres of her character. After nearly three hundred years of such training in all quarters of the globe, it is now taken as a matter of course that our women can bear danger and responsibility, discomfort of climate and loneliness, almost as well as their menfolk. We take it for granted.

Stark asserted that other countries' colonies could not claim to have this type of woman, and other countries' colonies did not send their children home. It was, she thought, considering the strengths of the British colonial woman, 'depressing to notice that our unpopularity in foreign lands appears to coincide with her appearance'; and it was not her fault. Men alone, 'homeless, clubless', 'naturally mingle with the people they live among, and become known and liked', they spread influence and enhanced imperial prestige. Nevertheless, echoing the missionary arguments, Stark thought that in places where women were alone, they could sometimes give better service than men, because of their access to local homes. 'The harm is done when she is so numerous that she can make a little world of her own.'

On a practical level, Stark suggested that women should be better trained in languages and customs, and that women would probably like this. Recalling a stay in the house of a local shoemaker and his wife, when she was studying Arabic in Baghdad, she described how she was told by friends and family that it was 'not done' and that she would be a social outcast because of the intolerance, stupidity and narrow-mindedness of the average official's wife. This was unfair, she decided:

> After a little hesitation, not surprising in the circumstances, the slandered ladies were perfectly charming and showed an admirable independence in being nice to me. I was not of the flock. I was outside the enclosure...I was not surprised by sidelong glances from some among the virtuous but less imaginative matrons. What did surprise me was to discover how many of these ladies, whom the highbrow considers to be completely taken up by bridge, would have liked to join me and nibble at the Herb of Understanding outside the official railings.

With hindsight, Stark probably underestimated the outrage she caused by this incident in the winter of 1929, when she went to Iraq to improve her Arabic before setting off on further travels in the region. At the time she had written to her friend, Venetia Buddicom, about the reactions of the local British community:

> My dear, you can't imagine...what a mutual shock my first contact with proper conventional civil service society has caused. No one else (respectable) appears ever to have settled in a shoemaker's home on the banks of the Tigris, nor has anyone succeeded in living in Baghdad on two rupees a day. One lady has asked me if I am not 'lowering the prestige of British womanhood' by sitting in school among the Iraqi girls...For a time, except for one or two people who were really very nice all through, I felt rather like an outcast; the men nearly all disapproved and looked on uneasily if their wives were nice to me – apparently expecting something explosive to happen every second. The East must have rather a distorting effect on people's perspectives.[49]

To her mother, Flora, she expressed her disappointment and scorn at the conventional social mores of the colonial community:

What a blessing that Paradise isn't run by our Civil Service, or so few of us would get in…I am surrounded by a kind of frost, and Mrs Drower [the wife of the Legal Advisor to the Iraq Ministry of Justice] tells me that all the men disapprove of me. It makes me feel like a kind of pariah from my own kind, and awfully disgusted, because after all I really have done nothing and, beyond wishing to talk as much Arabic as I can, and regretting that we can't be less superior and more polite, I am not even pro-native, certainly as much of an imperialist as any of the people here. But Mrs Sturges told me today that one can't be friends with the natives and British both; and so what is to be done? It seems to me an almost unbelievable idiocy.[50]

Stark nevertheless persisted in her view that languages were an important part of colonial life, and in the *Contemporary Review* article she lamented the fact that women were not encouraged more to study them. Young brides, she had observed, arrived in overseas postings 'all keen' to learn the language, and if they were somewhere remote, they tended to succeed and become 'useful' members of the empire. However, if they were part of a larger community, they needed real character and perseverance to do it and to avoid being sucked into domestic and social routine. Those who tried to do more risked being thought eccentric or even unpatriotic:

What might be accomplished in a positive way is beyond the scope of this article; nor do I wish to be accused of 'feminism' or any 'ism' at all. All I plead is that we should be encouraged to devote some time and energy to the study of not doing harm…In all the world there is a right and a wrong way of saying things, unfortunately not everywhere the same. The London manner in Timbuctoo is often very unsatisfactory. Our men are taught with great care to study the Timbuctoo manner if that is where they happen to be sent. Our women may do so if they like, but it is not a fashionable thing to do. I think it would be to the interest of the Empire if we made it as fashionable as possible.

This joint male/female-authored article presented an entirely different view from the defensive and hostile attitude of Fowle, Loch and other British officials in the Gulf. Neither Barker nor Stark raised issues of Arab nationalism or attempted to question or re-appraise the strategic or economic basis of the British presence in the region, but they did attempt to redefine the potential roles of women and they convincingly argued against the dangerous exclusivity of the imperial, or colonial, project as a masculine preserve. Stark also accurately delineated the distinction between the social pressures of large expatriate communities, such as those in India, and the smaller, more remote, postings such as the Gulf, where talented women like Emily Lorimer could clearly have more freedom to participate.

224 - PLAYING THE GAME

Stark herself was both a violator of boundaries, real and imagined, and at the same time a collaborator in colonial administration. Like Bell before her, she managed to combine an outstanding career as an explorer with a successful period of employment in government. Born in 1893 in Paris, and brought up in Devon, at the age of eight she moved with her sister and their half-Genoese mother to live in Asolo in northern Italy, the town which became her base, between travels, for the rest of her life. From 1912 until the outbreak of the First World War she read history at Bedford College, London, and during the First World War she served first, briefly, as a government censor and then trained as a nurse, finally serving in a hospital on the Italian front. Like Bell and Emily Lorimer, she was a voracious reader and taught herself Latin at the age of 13, reading the whole of Caesar's *Wars* from beginning to end with the help of a dictionary.[51] By adulthood she spoke fluent Italian and good French and German. In true Orientalist tradition, she said that her inspiration to travel was a copy of *Arabian Nights* given to her as a child.[52] In Italy after the war, in April 1920, she followed the discussions of the victorious Allied powers in neighbouring San Remo, where the colonial mandates for Syria and Lebanon were assigned to France, and for Iraq and Palestine to Britain. Soon afterwards she began to learn Arabic. She took lessons from a Capuchin monk, also in San Remo, for whose teaching she had to walk for an hour to the railway station several times a week. She later claimed that she could not remember exactly what inspired her to take up the language, but she thought that 'the most interesting things in the world were likely to happen in the neighbourhood of *oil*'.[53] Using the biblical parable of Martha and Mary, she recalled in her autobiography that she 'studied Arabic with the hope that at some time it might lead me out of the endless Martha lane into some sort of fairyland of my own'.[54]

Stark was a prolific and gifted writer and photographer, and before her death, at the age of 100, in May 1993, she had published around thirty books, including four volumes of autobiography and six of letters, and numerous articles.[55] Like Gertrude Bell she has also been the subject of several biographies which have analysed her life and achievements.[56] Her travels and her professional life cover a considerably larger geographical and chronological space than the scope of this book. However, her appearance and activities in the Arabian Peninsula in the 1930s, and her own and other's people's representation of them, are significant in the overall development of the British imperial outlook in the decade before the Second World War, as well as in the changing perspectives on Western women's involvement in the area. Furthermore, although accounts of her life and travels are numerous, her own, by definition, are self-representing, and the biographies by other authors tend to rely heavily on Stark's own writings and other individuals' personal reminiscences. None of them have examined in depth the official government files.

Freya Stark's first travels in the Middle East were in the winter of 1927, when she visited Lebanon and Syria. Two years later she passed through Lebanon again, en route to Baghdad, where her lodging with the shoe-makers' family caused so much offence to the local British community. With Baghdad as a base, she made three unaccompanied journeys into Iran between 1929 and 1931, and subsequently established herself as a writer with the publication of an account of her experiences in *The Valley of the Assassins*. In the 1930s, however, she made two separate journeys into Arabia. The first, in 1934–35, was a trip into the hinterland of southern Arabia, the Hadhramaut, in an attempt to reach Shabwa, an ancient centre of the Arabian incense trade, never before visited by Europeans; the second, in 1937–38, was also into the Hadhramaut, this time with the distinguished archaeologist Gertrude Caton Thompson.

Stark set out on the first Arabian trip in January 1935, after spending a few weeks in Aden studying the local Arabic and successfully persuading the British authorities there to give her letters of introduction to the local rulers. In the southern Arabian port of Mukalla she stayed as a guest of the local sultan, and wrote that it was 'a rather nice feeling that I am just now the only European for at least 200 miles either way along this coast and goodness knows how many miles northward'. She later said that she wanted 'space, distance, history and danger' but that she was also 'interested in the living world'.[57] From Mukalla she travelled inland, accompanied by guides, stopping in villages, taking photographs and talking to local men and women, and ever conscious that she was in a kind of European travellers' race to be first to reach the fabled city. Before leaving Aden she had written to her old friend Venetia Buddicom, to say that she was 'just in time, as everyone is now going to the Hadhramaut, but no one has yet been to Shabwa'.[58] Six days' journey inland, however, she caught measles and was confined for days at a fort called Masna'a. Eventually she was able to travel onwards as far as Shibam in the Wadi Hadhramaut, where her illness recurred. She wrote again to Buddicom that she was fortifying herself with Nietzsche in moments of weakness:

> You can imagine my sorrow at this illness, my Beduin and all waiting ready. And now a last dramatic touch has added itself to my bitterness – a horrid stunting German who has already written a *cheap* book about this country, is here again, making for *Shabwa*! I am helpless. I think I may be able to go there in ten days or so but not before, and meanwhile he is getting Beduin

and all. No one here likes him and everyone is trying to stop him (and I am meanly letting them do so – but he does not deserve any sympathy: he has told such lies in self-boasting). I know it is vulgar to want just to be the first, but yet it is bitter when one has come so far, and but for this illness I would have been there five days ago.[59]

The German was Hans Helfritz, who did actually reach the outskirts of Shabwa but was driven away by its inhabitants almost immediately. In March Freya was airlifted out of the Hadhramaut by the RAF and taken to a hospital in Aden, from where she eventually sailed to Italy. Her difficulties and rescue aroused intense irritation among British officials at Aden, and she was warned by the Resident that she would not be allowed to undertake any further journeys. She wrote to her mother to express her frustration at the damage the episode may have done to women's travel and exploration: 'I suppose I have dished women's chances of going alone for at least half a generation. This is the really sad part about it all – and I can hardly bear to think about it.'[60]

It was left to Harry St. John Philby to finish the job. Stimulated by the publicity surrounding Stark's trip and fired, as in the past with Rosita Forbes, by rivalry with a woman traveller, Philby set off in 1936 and reached Shabwa. His own exploits in politically sensitive territory brought him into conflict with the British Government but inspired mixed feelings in Stark:

> Philby has gone and taken Shabwa on his way from Najran. I find I do not grudge it him: I feel much more as if we were all colleagues rather than rivals, and I think that is what one ought to feel (though not about little German worms). Anyway Aden is all fuming because he came down with an armed escort and penetrated British territory without asking or even mentioning his intentions. I think this was tactless, but of course he may not have felt sure of bringing it off and then it is rather difficult to talk of one's plans beforehand. What is much more deplorable is that I rather fear he has done it by car: I hope for a refutation of this, but it sounds bad.[61]

Stark, in the end, received praise and admiration for her journey and for her account of it, *The Southern Gates of Arabia*, which became a best-seller. The Royal Scottish Geographical Society awarded her with their Mungo Park medal. She later commented: 'I hear Philby hates me, only because I wrote a book'.[62] The British Government was only too happy to receive any information on the activities and loyalty of the Hadhramaut tribes in the inland region where the boundary with Yemen was as yet undetermined.[63] Nevertheless, with the local British administration in southern Arabia, Stark had been identified as troublesome, notably with female vulnerability through illness as the defining attribute.

In the autumn of 1937 Stark set off again into the Hadhramaut in the company of Gertrude Caton Thompson, and a geologist, Elinor Gardner.[64] The trio began their journey in Mukalla, as Freya had done two years earlier, where they stayed with the British Resident, Harold Ingrams, and his wife Doreen, whose own joint survey work in the Eastern Aden Protectorate was eventually to earn them the Royal Geographical Society's gold medal.[65] Any suggestion, however, that women travellers would, or should, collaborate more sympathetically with each other, or share similar perceptions and motivations, was dispelled by both Stark's and Caton Thompson's later accounts of the expedition. Stark's views were summarised in a letter written to her publisher, John Murray, from Shibam in December 1937:

> I am becoming such an Anti-Feminist...I do much prefer dealing with men. We do nothing but fuss over our health and talk about tinned food, and the one day we had a little discomfort in the way of sitting in Ba Obaid's quite nice room with only about four people and ten million flies to bother – why they just *wilted* and then turned upon me for not keeping the inhabitants of the country away! (Elinor Gardiner was already sickening but Miss Caton Thompson is really *hopeless* as a traveller though a marvellous archae-ologist – but so anxious not to take any of my suggestions that she won't even look at a perfectly good site if I have mentioned it.)... *What* a way to travel! I have come to the conclusion that there is a deep cleavage in human beings which the East and West represents – those who wish to *be* and those who wish to *do*: the experts, occidentals, and certainly archaeologists belong to the latter: but the proper traveller is the former and thinks it a waste to move from his own home if nothing happens *inside* him as a result. I mean something fundamental, like a chemical change when two substances come into contact. But to sit here and mix with none and just feel how far you are from Europe is a dreary business.[66]

All three women suffered from minor ailments from the start of the expedition, and in December Stark had to be evacuated from Shibam to hospital in Aden for a week. Caton, as she was known to her friends and acquaintances, later recalled that she and Gardner were 'much relieved when she had gone', allowing them time to recover from their own fevers and sore throats without dissention while Freya was away.[67] A month later, however, Stark was back and ill again, with suspected pneumonia, and the women, now at Huraydah, were forced to contact the nearest British authorities, at Say'un, to ask for medicine and possibly evacu-ation. Harold Ingrams, after visiting the women himself, recommended that Freya should be evacuated to hospital in Aden again, but when the plane duly arrived she refused to go. The British officials in Say'un and

A woman carrying water at Mukalla and two girls at Huraydah, photographed by Freya Stark during her travels in southern Arabia, 1938.

Aden exchanged increasingly irritated telegrams: 'Presume you are aware Stark woman refused evacuation and apparently surprised at suggestion of it and is still chez vous. Pike [the American geologist whose aeroplane had been used] not unnaturally fed up...'[68]

Quite unaware Stark situation and consider she has behaved very badly. An urgent letter from Miss Gardiner stating pneumonia took me [to] Hureda where she told me a doctor or Aden hospital were only alternatives. Stark herself pressed for doctor and gave me no indication in visit of five minutes that she would refuse evacuation. I deeply regret trouble Pike has had. As to future illness you are prepared definitely disclaim all future responsibility which seems to me very difficult especially for me. Consider she ought to be ordered away as health is continuously unsatisfactory.[69]

In March 1938 Caton Thompson and Gardner left southern Arabia for Cairo and Stark carried on alone in search of the incense route and determined to visit Husn al-Ghurab in an attempt to establish beyond question whether it was the Himyaritic town of Cana, the centre of the incense trade. Caton and Gardner delivered a letter from Stark to the Agent at Say'un announcing Stark's intention to continue. A few days later the local British Agent telegraphed Aden to say that Stark had fallen ill again and asked for a car. However, the car had been met on the way by another messenger to say that she was better and did not require it. 'As you can imagine,' he added, 'I find all this rather trying and if she persists in further exploits propose to forbid them if I can catch her as she is quite unfit. Trust you agree.'[70] Forty-five years later, Gertrude Caton Thompson, then 90 years old, published her own autobiography and gave her version of events. She described Stark as quarrelsome, imperious and unscrupulous and added that Stark had been called a 'bloody bitch' by the RAF pilot who had tried to track her down when she was first ill, a phrase which Caton Thompson thought was 'moderate in the circumstances'.[71] On the other hand, Caton acknowledged, Stark's 'gruelling' solo journey had produced some new information about rock carvings and fortifications, and 'her careful descriptions' of the lands she passed through were 'excellent, reinforcing what was already known, and supplementing the bits that were not'. Whether the results of the journey warranted the difficulties, however, she was unsure. As far as the British officials in the Aden Government were concerned, Harold Ingrams, she recalled, was 'incensed' at Freya's 'unauthorised escapade and said he would never have allowed it'.[72]

In a talk to the predominantly male Royal Central Asian Society in 1935, and published in the society's journal, Stark had forcefully and mockingly defended herself against criticism that her place as a woman was with a husband rather than alone in the desert:

'What is the *use* of your travels?' I was asked this once in Persia by an Englishwoman who evidently disliked me…She herself, she said, was fully occupied in looking after her husband: she could spare no time to wander

.   in the hills. Just then, she said – it was the end of August – she had begun
to rear a little flock of Turkeys for his Christmas dinner and this would keep
her busy for the rest of the year. I was amused, and of course agreed that it
would not do for her to abandon the turkeys and search for mediaeval
castles as I did; but, on the other hand, I pointed out in my own defence that
it would be useless for *me* to devote myself to such things as turkeys when
there was no husband to eat them when they grew up. To marry one merely
to provide domestic occupation seemed unsuitable; and to devote oneself
to the Christmas dinners of other people's husbands might lead to a lot of
trouble.[73]

Like Gertrude Bell in her earlier years, Stark, in the 1930s, represented
herself as an independent traveller, taking on the masculine world of
empire and expanding the boundaries of traditional female participation.
However, as long as she continued to project herself as being outside and
uncontrollable by British colonial authority, she received only guarded
admiration and support, even when producing useful political information as a result of her travels. Freya herself reciprocated the suspicion,
and in 1979 she told her biographer, Molly Izzard, that her policy
towards British authority had been to 'Start well away from them and
don't ask for anything!'[74] On the other hand, she claimed at the same time
to have been sensitive to British imperial political aspirations and to the
delicacy of local diplomatic relations, unlike the flamboyant Rosita Forbes
who, Stark said, had a tendency to embarrass the British wherever she went.

In fact, like Bell before her, Freya Stark recreated herself a few years
later when she became an employee of the British Government. On the
outbreak of the Second World War, Stark was employed by the Ministry
of Information as a Middle Eastern expert and worked for British Government in Aden. In 1940 she was sent to Yemen with a collection of
propaganda films to counter Axis influence. On the Colonial Office file
relating to Stark's appointment, Sir John Shuckburgh noted that Stark
had travelled extensively in the Middle East and written several 'very
attractive' books about her experiences. 'I have known her for a good
many years past,' he wrote, 'and, apart from admiration for her qualities,
have every confidence in her judgment. Unlike most "Arab" enthusiasts
that I have come across, she never allows her enthusiasm to outrun her
common sense.'[75]

As her *Contemporary Review* article makes clear, Stark shared with
both Emily Lorimer and Gertrude Bell a strong sense of Britain's imperial
role and of her own identity as a contributor to the imperial project.
Her American biographer Jane Geniesse concludes that Stark 'believed
profoundly in the British Empire. The British more than any other colonial

power, she was convinced, should be the messengers of enlightened governance, just as she believed peace and security along the routes to India were best guarded by a firm British hand.'[76] Stark herself told Molly Izzard that the British Empire 'as far as empires go, was the best rule of life after Christianity'. 'Christianity teaches love your brother as yourself; the Mandate says you rule and teach a people to rule itself, then give it its freedom. That is practical Christianity…It was a Christian empire, with the minimum of human beings running it, a very closely knit band of brotherhood.'[77]

In much the same way, Emily Lorimer also continued to believe in the fundamental humanity and benevolence of the British Empire, and, like Stark, she believed in the right and duty of women to participate and contribute. Unlike Stark, she was not averse to devoting herself to turkeys and Christmas dinners, and she always regarded her marriage and her partnership with her husband as the anchor and true centre of her life. Nevertheless, she increasingly argued for more freedom for women to fulfil themselves outside the domestic sphere. As the Second World War approached, Emily continued to work with Lock on their joint studies of society and languages on the North West Frontier but she also returned to her earlier intellectual and scholarly interests in German literature and culture. In 1931 she published a translation of Ernst Kantorowicz's monumental life of the medieval ruler Frederick II.[78] Closely monitoring the contemporary European political scene, she became more and more alarmed about the rise of Nazism and obsessed with the fear that the evil nature of Hitler's political programme was being underestimated in Britain. While submitting articles to *The Times* about her Kashmir trip, she also began sending the newspapers pieces about Nazi propaganda and in 1939 she published a Penguin special, *What Hitler Wants*. In an article in the magazine *Time and Tide* she said that she thought *Mein Kampf* the 'most evil, the most untruthful, the most demoralizing book ever written'. 'It screams and screeches violence, brutality, hate and terror, just as Hitler screams them in his speeches.'[79] During the war, again like Stark, she was employed by the Ministry of Information to write articles which drew on both her Middle East and Asian knowledge and her German expertise, and she fell easily into the spirit of the work. A piece for translation into Arabic and then for distribution in southern Yemen compared German repression in Czechoslovakia with the benefits of British administration in Aden. Entitled 'The Two Protectorates', it argued that more than a century of British involvement in South Arabia had brought medical care, education and a peaceful environment for trade and economic growth.[80]

The war reinforced Emily Lorimer's view that women should be given more encouragement to use their talents and energies outside, as well as inside, the home. In the autumn of 1941 she wrote a scathing letter to *Time and Tide* about women and war service and the numbers of young women who were eager to join female branches of the armed forces but whose husbands told them it would be too tough. She thought it was amazing that in the 1940s young people were reverting to this preposterous 'early-Victorian attitude', which simply disguised 'the possessive vanity of the young male who instinctively objects to his wife's having in life any duty or interest that is not centred in him'. In the meantime, 'if for lack of woman-power, Hitler were to make good his invasion, would the shirking, sheltered wife not find the Nazis rather too tough a crowd?'[81] Three years later she wrote to Ernest Bevin, then Minister of Labour and National Service, to argue for government measures to liberate women from domestic chores, including a wages for housework plan which would enable a direct payment to women to be used for domestic help while the recipient returned to professional life.[82]

The Second World War completed a political process started in the 1930s and precipitated the gradual dismantling of Britain's predominantly masculine imperial power. In 1947 India became independent, and although the British remained in the Gulf for another two decades, it was a markedly different place from the 'British lake' visited by the Curzons in their imperial progress of 1903. Western women remained on the margins of Western involvement in the Arabian Peninsula, but the changes of the 1930s and 1940s brought an influx of professional female teachers, doctors and nurses, as well as the wives of diplomats and business people, and provided the impetus for a wider acceptance, or at the very least a toleration, of women in the increasing internationalisation of the region. Meanwhile Arabia and 'the Orient' continued to exert a fascination over many of the people who travelled there even for short periods. Emily Lorimer had lived in the Gulf for less than ten years and on the borders between India and the Gulf for another five but she remained interested in the region for her entire life. In the 1930s and 1940s, when she had time to spare, she often reviewed, almost uniformly enthusiastically, the travel books of her 'Arabist' contemporaries, Philby, Bertram Thomas and other less well-known writers. In May 1948, at the anniversary general meeting of the Royal Asiatic Society, she and Lock were jointly awarded the Burton Memorial Medal. The Society's President, Lord Scarbrough, commented that the Lorimers had travelled further afield in the Muslim world than Sir Richard Burton himself. Among their many achievements, Emily's work on the *Basra Times* during the

First World War was cited. She herself responded modestly and somewhat disingenuously:

> I cannot easily tell you how deeply gratified I am that you have reckoned
> my good man not unworthy to be named in the illustrious company of such
> holders of the Burton Medal as Arnold Wilson, Harold Ingrams and St.John
> Philby. But if it is not ungracious, I should like to protest most vigorously
> against being mixed up in the business. I have always loved the simple vow
> of the Roman matron on her wedding day: 'Wherever you are Gaius, why,
> I'm there too.' And I must frankly admit that if my Gaius had wanted to
> collect butterflies, or whales, to dig for gold, to prospect for oil...I should
> have done my best to be of modest use to him. It was just my luck that his
> hobbies were languages, folk-lore and anthropology, which interested me
> vastly more, though I knew not one word of any Eastern tongue.[83]

It was a surprisingly self-effacing comment from a woman whose intellectual ability, learning and energy were a perfect and vital match for
her husband's own scholarship and diplomatic skills, and whose life and
writings illustrate so vividly the complexities of Western women's imperial
involvement in the Arabian Gulf region.

NOTES ON CHAPTER 7

1   Alexander Frater, in his book *Beyond the Blue Horizon: On the Track of
     Imperial Airways* (London: William Heinemann, 1986) includes an anecdote
     which epitomises this feeling of the region being 'opened up'. When the
     Marquess of Londonderry, Secretary of State for Air, made a brief stop in
     Bahrain in 1934, he commented on the improvement in communications: 'We
     landed at midday, and I enjoyed a short walk in the sun, under a cloudless
     sky, with Colonel Loch, the Political Agent, and Mrs Loch. They told me
     what a vast difference the coming of Imperial Airways had made to their
     lives. They were within a week of London instead of five weeks. They were
     in the world instead of out of it' (pp. 112–13).

2   Middle East oil exploration began in 1901 in Iran, and oil was discovered
     there in 1908, followed by Iraq (1923–27), Bahrain (1931), Saudi Arabia
     and Kuwait (1938) and Qatar (1940). The Persian oilfields were controlled
     until 1951 by the British Government with a 51 percent stake in the Anglo-
     Persian Oil Company (later British Petroleum, or BP). Kuwait's oil, after
     lengthy bidding and adversarial negotiations, started off in British and
     American hands through the Kuwait Oil Company (KOC), a consortium of BP
     and Gulf Oil; however, although the 1938 discovery indicated massive reserves,
     production was held up until after World War II. Iraq's oil industry, until

nationalisation was completed in 1972, was managed by the Iraq Petroleum Company (IPC), a consortium of British, Dutch, French and US companies. In Bahrain and Saudi Arabia, until the 1970s, the major player was Standard Oil of California (SoCal), a subsidiary of the present-day American company Exxon (Esso) and its partners and associated companies (most importantly the Arabian American Oil Company [Aramco]). See Anthony Sampson, *The Seven Sisters: The Great Oil Companies and the World They Made* (London: Hodder & Stoughton, 1975) and Daniel Yergin, *The Prize: The Epic Quest for Oil, Money and Power* (New York: Simon & Schuster, 1991).

3   Loch to Political Resident, 20 March 1933, and to Station Superintendent, Imperial Airways Rest House, same date, IOR:L/PS/12/3807.

4   T.C.Fowle to General Manager, Imperial Airways Ltd, London, 28 March 1933, IOR:L/PS/12/3807.

5   Fowle to Shaikh Sultan b.Saqr, Ruler of Sharjah, 30 March 1933, IOR:L/PS/12/3807. Air agreements were concluded by the British with all the Gulf Shaikhdoms, allowing for landing facilities for the services. The Sharjah Air Agreement was signed in July 1932.

6   Loch to Fowle, 20 March 1933, IOR:L/PS/12/3807.

7   H.Burchall, Imperial Airways, London, to Fowle, 4 April 1933, IOR:L/PS/12/3807.

8   Fowle to Ruler of Sharjah, 30 March 1933, IOR:L/PS/12/3807.

9   Minute by J.G.Laithwaite, India Office Political Department, 8 May 1933, IOR:L/PS/12/3807.

10   In August 1916, for example, Emily Lorimer wrote to her mother asking whether she had read Chicken's book (Trenchard C.Fowle, *Travels in the Middle East: Being Impressions by the Way in Turkish Arabia, Syria and Persia* [London: Smith, Elder & Co.,1916]), 19 August 1916, MSS Eur F177/20.

11   H.StJ.B.Philby, *Arabian Days: An Autobiography* (London: Robert Hale, 1948), p.135.

12   Rosemary Said Zahlan, *The Origins of the United Arab Emirates: a Political and Social History of the Trucial States* (London: Macmillan, 1978), p.174.

13   Lt Colonel G.Loch 'The Persian Gulf', *Journal of the Royal Central Asian Society*, no25 (1938), quoted in Said Zahlan, *Origins of the United Arab Emirates*, p.232.

14   For example: IOR:L/PS/12/4252 and 4340, 'Travellers: Persian Gulf, Arab States, Arabia'; IOR: L/PS/12/4336, 'Travellers. Women: miscellaneous visits abroad'; IOR:L/PS/12/3807 and 3868, 'Persian Gulf: question of residence of European women on the Trucial Coast' and '...question of residence of European women in Bahrain and Kuwait'.

15   Passport Office memoranda on interviews with Lady Dorothy Mills, forwarded to the India Office, 17 December 1931, IOR:L/PS/12/4252.

16   *Who was Who*, 1951–1960.

17 Draft letter from J. C. Walton, India Office, to E. B. Howell, Foreign Secretary to the Government of India, 18 December 1931, IOR:L/PS/12/4252.

18 Fowle to the India Office, 20 December 1933, IOR:L/PS/12/4252. For Yusuf Kanoo, see also ch. 4.

19 Patrick Roberts, Foreign Office to J. G. Laithwaite, India Office, 20 February 1934, IOR:L/PS/12/4252.

20 Loch to Fowle, 8 January 1934 (incorrectly dated 1933), IOR:L/PS/12/4252.

21 Political Agent Kuwait (Dickson) to Fowle, 1 February 1934, IOR:L/PS/12/4252.

22 Fowle to Secretary of State for India, 27 March 1934, IOR:L/PS/12/4252.

23 Yusuf Kanoo to Winifred Howard, 6 November 1931, IOR:R/15/2/594.

24 Kanoo to Winifred Clitty, 13 February 1933, and Clitty to Kanoo, 13 August 1933, and reply, 10 September, IOR:R/15/2/594.

25 Dickson to Loch, and Dickson to Fowle, 29 November 1933, IOR:R/15/2/594.

26 Loch to Fowle, 9 December 1933, IOR:R/15/2/594.

27 Loch to Fowle, 26 February 1934, IOR:R/15/2/594.

28 File note by Loch, 20 February 1934, IOR:R/15/2/594.

29 Loch to Fowle, 30 December 1934, IOR:L/PS/12/4252.

30 Fowle to Foreign Office, 20 January 1935, IOR:L/PS/12/4252.

31 H. M. Knatchbull-Hugessen, Tehran, to Sir John Simon, 6 February 1935, IOR:L/PS/12/4252.

32 Rev. B. D. Hakken, 'A new phase in Mission history', *Neglected Arabia*, no 177, October–December 1936.

33 Loch to Fowle, 24 May 1934, IOR:R/15/2/853.

34 Loch to Fowle, 14 November 1936, and Fowle to Loch, 12 December 1936, IOR:R/15/2/853.

35 *Neglected Arabia*, no 166, October–December 1933.

36 Ibid., p. 9.

37 Mrs L. P. Dame, 'A trip to central Arabia', *Neglected Arabia*, no 167, January–March 1934.

38 A. Fletcher, Imperial Airways, to E. H. Gastrell, British Consulate General Bushire, 7 June 1934, IOR:L/PS/12/3807.

39 Fowle to Burchall, Imperial Airways, 19 August 1934, IOR:L/PS/12/3807.

40 Fowle to G. Laithwaite, India Office, 19 August 1934, IOR:L/PS/12/3807.

41 Burchall to Fowle, 27 August 1934, IOR:L/PS/12/3807.

42 Fowle to Secretary of State for India, 23 September 1936, IOR:L/PS/12/3868.

43 M. Clauson, India Office, to J. W. Stafford, Passport Office, 26 September 1936, to S. H. Longrigg, Petroleum Concessions Ltd, same date, and to H. T. Kemp, Kuwait Oil Company, 30 September 1936, IOR:L/PS/12/3868.

44 Clauson to Longrigg, 1 October 1936, IOR:L/PS/12/3868.

45 Secretary of State for India to Resident and to Political Agents, Bahrain and Kuwait, 3 October 1936, IOR:L/PS/12/3868.

46 There is a substantial body of writing on Western women and their role in the causes and events of 1857. See, for example, Kenneth Ballhatchet, *Race,*

Sex and Class under the Raj: Imperial Attitudes and Policies and their Critics,
1793–1905 (London: Weidenfeld & Nicolson, 1980) and, more specifically,
Penelope Tuson, 'Mutiny narratives and the imperial feminine: European
women's accounts of the Rebellion in India in 1857', *Women's Studies*
International Forum, no 21 (1998), pp. 291–303.

47   Professor Ernest Barker and Freya Stark, 'Women and the Service of the
Empire', *Contemporary Review*, no 141 (1932), pp. 54–61.

48   This presumably refers to Stark's home at Asolo in northern Italy. Stark was
friends with both Ernest Barker and his wife Olivia and had stayed at their
house in London in early 1931 after a riding accident. In her autobiography
she recalled that they 'not only kept me with kindness, but were able to
provide all the books I most wished to read'. She also referred to Barker as
having 'placed' some of her work in the *Contemporary Review*. Freya Stark,
Beyond Euphrates: Autobiography 1928–1933 (London: John Murray, 1951),
pp. 183–184, 194–195.

49   Stark to Venetia Buddicom, from Baghdad, 6 January 1930, in Caroline
Moorehead (ed.), *Over the Rim of the World: Freya Stark Selected Letters*
(London: John Murray, 1988), pp. 49–50.

50   Stark to her mother, 17 December 1929, in Moorehead (ed.), *Over the Rim*
of the World, pp. 47–48.

51   Caroline Moorehead, *Freya Stark* (Harmondsworth: Penguin Books, 1985),
pp. 22–23.

52   Jane Robinson, *Wayward Women: a Guide to Women Travellers* (Oxford:
Oxford University Press, 1990), p. 29.

53   Freya Stark, *Travellers Prelude: Autobiography 1893–1927* (London: John
Murray, 1950), p. 276. She added, 'This was 1921 and the forecast has been
accurate up to this day'. At San Remo Britain and France also concluded a
secret agreement (which became public later the same year) to share Middle
Eastern oil production between them. Stark's American biographer, Jane
Fletcher Geniesse, says that Stark was enthralled by the places she heard
reported on from the conference. Geniesse, *Passionate Nomad: The life of*
Freya Stark (New York: Random House, 1999), pp. 4–5.

54   Stark, *Travellers Prelude*, p. 324. Emily Lorimer also sometimes referred to
women whom she regarded as boring and unadventurous as 'Marthas'.

55   Stark's travel writings include *The Southern Gates of Arabia: A Journey in the*
Hadhramaut (London: John Murray, 1936) and *The Valley of the Assassins*
(London: John Murray, 1934), both of which have become classics. Several
volumes of her photographs have also been published. For a select list, see
bibliography. Stark's photograph collection is at St Antony's College Oxford,
Middle East Centre Archive, and her personal papers are at the Harry
Ransom Humanities Research Center, University of Texas at Austin.

56   The most recent is Geniesse, *Passionate Nomad*. Also interesting are
Caroline Moorehead, *Freya Stark* and Molly Izzard's rather more analytical

and challenging *Freya Stark: A Biography* (London: Hodder & Stoughton, 1993).

57 Moorehead (ed.), *Over the Rim of the World*, p.102; Stark to Venetia Buddicom, 17 January 1935, ibid, p.106.

58 Stark to Buddicom, 23 December 1934, Moorehead (ed.), *Over the Rim of the World*, p.102.

59 Stark to Buddicom, 22 February and 9 March 1935, Moorehead (ed.), *Over the Rim of the World*, pp.115–17.

60 Stark to her mother, 3 April 1935, quoted in Geniesse, *Passionate Nomad*, p.184.

61 Stark to Buddicom, 20 September 1936, Moorehead (ed.), *Over the Rim of the World*, p.126.

62 Stark to Mrs Lionel Smith, September 1937, Moorehead (ed.), *Over the Rim of the World*, pp.136–37.

63 George Rendel, Foreign Office, to Sir Cosmo Parkinson, Colonial Office, 30 May 1935, enclosing letter from Stark, 15 April 1935, CO 725/31/1.

64 Gertrude Caton Thompson (1888–1985) was an archaeologist and authority on African history who had excavated in Egypt and Rhodesia (Zimbabwe). She was a Fellow of Newnham College, Cambridge.

65 The Royal Geographical Society Founder's Medal was awarded jointly to Harold and Doreen Ingrams in 1940.

66 Stark to John Murray, 3 December 1937, Moorehead (ed.), *Over the Rim of the World*, pp.141–42.

67 Gertrude Caton Thompson, *Mixed Memoirs* (Gateshead: Paradigm Press, 1983), p.187.

68 Political Secretary Aden to Residency Agent Say'un, 28 January 1938, IOR:R/20/C/180.

69 Residency Agent Say'un to Political Secretary Aden, 29 January 1938, IOR:R/20/C/180.

70 Residency Agent Perim(?) to Political Secretary Aden, 11 March 1938, IOR:R/20/C/180.

71 Caton Thompson, *Mixed Memoirs*, p.189.

72 Ibid., p.195.

73 Freya Stark, 'In defence of travel', *Journal of the Royal Central Asian Society*, no23 (1936), pp.104–10.

74 Izzard, *Freya Stark*, p.48.

75 File note by J.E.Shuckburgh, 12 March 1940, CO 725/74/15.

76 Geniesse, *Passionate Nomad*, p.6.

77 Izzard, *Freya Stark*, p.50.

78 Ernst Kantorowicz, *Frederick the Second, 1194–1250*, translated by E.O.Lorimer (London: Constable & Co., 1931).

79 Review by Emily Lorimer of a translation of *Mein Kampf* by James Murphy, *Time and Tide*, 1 April 1939, MSS Eur F177/75.

80 MSS Eur F177/76.

81 Letter to *Time and Tide*, 11 October 1941, MSS Eur F177/84.

82 Emily Lorimer, 'The birth rate and the status of women', typescript article sent to Ernest Bevin, 30 June 1944, MSS Eur F177/71.

83 *Journal of the Royal Asiatic Society* (1948), report of Anniversary General Meeting, 13 May 1948, and speech by Emily Lorimer to Royal Asiatic Society, 13 May 1948, MSS Eur F177/91.

Postscript: Completing the Story

The story of Western women in the Arabian Gulf is only just beginning to be told. In many ways this book, and the making of it, is about the process of recovering hidden histories. When I began the research it seemed that there was likely to be very little material on the activities and attitudes of Western women in the Gulf region. Certainly there appeared to be very little in the official archives of imperial government and administration. It soon became clear, however, that underneath the surface of conventional mainstream and 'malestream' history and politics, there was plenty of information on Western women's involvement in the imperial and colonial projects in this part of the Middle East. Some of it was easily accessible; some of it required detective work and persistence to discover. My original fears that – outside the obvious sources relating to well-known travellers such as Gertrude Bell or Freya Stark – there would be little to work with, were very quickly dispelled. I concluded that the major problem was not that the material was lacking but that historians had either not wanted to find it or had not looked in the right direction – more probably the former. It was apparent that women, and women's participation in the imperial and colonial life of the Arabian Peninsula, were not part of the agenda of conventional history.

Many of the women in this book deserve biographies to themselves. Other women, some of them outstanding, for whom there was simply no space or time in this book, deserve further research. Doreen Ingrams, Marjorie Belgrave, Miriam Bullard and the wives of dozens of other successive political residents, governors, agents and advisors, all form a list which grows with every new source which turns up. Much more can, and should, be done to locate papers on women's involvement in the Western relationship with the Arabian Gulf region, by searching both in government archives and also outside, in the alternative narratives of the women themselves and in the extra-government organisations and arenas in which they lived and recorded their lives. At the same time, the response of local women and men to the Western female presence is almost completely unexamined territory, and remains an essential but elusive alternative narrative for any future overview of female participation in the complex colonial and imperial relationships of the period. Many individual stories have still to be told, and a collective picture is only just emerging.

In the context of contemporary debates on the theory and practice of imperialism, it became clear during this search for women's stories that the old readings of empire as an essentially masculine political enterprise, in which women were relegated to distinct and carefully circumscribed passive or caring roles on the social fringes, simply would not stand up. Most historians now recognise that women's responses to empire, and their levels of participation in imperial and colonial life were much more complex and wide-ranging. The Gulf and Arabian Peninsula was no exception, even if the numbers of women involved were much smaller than in imperial India or colonial Africa. Emily Lorimer, for example, represented herself as an intellectual, politically educated and active participant and supporter of the political imperial mission. While she described many of her female contemporaries as confined by the stereotypical boundaries of domestic concerns, she determinedly constructed an identity for herself as a brash and unequivocal imperialist. Her colleague in First World War Basra, Gertrude Bell, represented herself primarily as a colonial government servant, yet came to identify much more closely with Arab nationalist politics than most of her contemporaries, male or female; and the American Protestant missionary women in the Gulf in the early twentieth century all viewed themselves as active and working members of their own particular mission to the East. Although, in its own way, this was just as Orientalist and imperialist as that of the British, it brought them much more closely and positively into contact with local social and economic realities and with the everyday lives of men and women in the Gulf shaikhdoms. By the 1930s, the perspectives and activities of those women involved in the life of the Gulf, and the attitudes of women newly arrived or passing through, were very different from the early 1900s and yet shared many of the same certainties.

For all of these women, empire played an essential part in the construction of their personal, female, identities, and they were united by their common belief in the Western civilising mission. Nevertheless, although Western imperialism clearly provided a fundamental consistency to their lives, there were many dissimilarities and contradictions in their interpretations of it. Women's individual views of themselves and their roles seem to have been informed as much by nationality, religious conviction, social class and, not least, by the changing political and economic circumstances of the First World War and inter-war years. There was never one, female, unitary, response to empire, but a wide range of perspectives based on a similarly wide range of social and cultural domestic backgrounds. None of them were overwhelmingly influenced by gender in any exclusive sense. On the other hand, there is no doubt that Western women's positions and images within the hierarchies of empire and imperialism were to a large extent constrained and defined by domestic standards of female behaviour, both public and private. While Western women all aspired to play some part in the imperial project, the further they departed from conventional gender roles the more difficult their lives became. Independent women travellers such as Rosita Forbes, or women on the fringes of the missionary project such as Frances Wakefield and Grace Strang, were often categorised, and thus marginalised and obstructed, by the British male imperial authorities as being at worst deviant, unstable and hysterical, and at best difficult and unfeminine. Those women who succeeded most comfortably in the imperial environment were the semi-conformists such as Violet Dickson and Emily Lorimer, who managed a measure of independence and intellectual freedom while remaining protected by their partnerships with their political officer husbands and by their efficient performances as 'incorporated' memsahibs, wives and helpmates. The extent to which the civilising, feminising and velvet-glove roles of women in the empire were both a construction of the male imagination and, moreover, a vital political imperative in the management of empire, is clearly illustrated in the archives by the accounts of recurring struggles between nonconforming women and the male imperial authorities.

Finally, it must be acknowledged that power and status are negotiated, defined and redefined in terms of hierarchical relationships with others. The Protestant Christian missionary women, in particular, defined their emancipated female status partly through a comparison with the perceived inferior and servile lives of Muslim Arab women. Almost all of the women in this study were empowered to some extent by their vision of Arab women as enslaved and downtrodden. By viewing Arab women as less emancipated than themselves, Western women in the Gulf were able to enhance their own status in ways which were often simply not available to them in the domestic society of metropolitan Britain or America. At the same time, their consistent belief in the imperial mission allowed them to negotiate more powerful public roles and personal self-images within the overseas structure of imperial authority.

The women who recounted the stories of their own lives, in the form of diaries, letters and published writings, were particularly active in the business of self-representation. Historians are limited not only by the perspectives of the sources available to them, but also by their scope. The history of Western women in the Arabian Peninsula in the period between 1890 and 1939 is dominated by a small number of highly articulate and energetic individuals whose writings are most easily available for analysis. As a group they portray a vivid and active engagement with imperial politics and a startling contrast to the traditional stereotype of the passive and silent female characters they themselves so often caricature. The next stage in the opening up of the history of Western women's involvement in the region will require a painstaking and time-consuming search for the stories of those women, both Western and Eastern, whose lives were not publicly prominent but whose perspectives and relationships reflected the wider social and cultural reach of empire. In the meantime, the accounts of Mary Curzon, Gertrude Bell, Emily Lorimer, Eleanor Calverley, Rosita Forbes and many others all broaden the picture of the British presence in the Gulf, and bring a whole new body of information to the study of the social and political history of the region.

Bibliography

I – PRIMARY SOURCES

(1) Archival and Manuscript Sources

    (a) Oriental and India Office Collections in the British Library

India Office Records
The British Library's Oriental and India Office Collections (OIOC) include the most important archival sources on the modern history of the Arabian Peninsula outside the region itself. They cover the period of British involvement from the earliest East India Company contacts, in 1600, to the late 1940s and the end of British imperial rule in India. The most useful series are the records of the British Political Residency and Agencies in the Persian Gulf (IOR:R/15) and the records of the India Office Political Department (IOR:L/PS):
IOR:R/15/1, Records of the Political Residency Bushire, 1763–1947
IOR:R/15/2, Records of the Political Agency Bahrain, 1900–1947
IOR:R/15/3, Records of the Political Agent's Court at Bahrain, 1913–1948
IOR:R/15/4, Records of the Residency Agency, Trucial Coast, c 1825–1947
IOR:R/15/5, Records of the Political Agency Kuwait, 1904–1947
IOR:L/PS, Records of the India Office Political and Secret Department:
Includes the *Gazetteer of the Persian Gulf, Oman and Central Arabia*, by John Gordon Lorimer, 2 vols, 1908–1915, Calcutta: Superintendent Government Printing (IOR:L/PS/20/C91); the *Gazetteer* has also been reprinted and published by Archive Editions (Farnham Common, 1986).

India Office Records: European Manuscripts Collection
These are personal papers of individuals who worked, lived or travelled in India or the surrounding British territories during the period of Empire. They include:
MSS Eur F111 & F112. Papers of George Nathaniel Curzon, Marquis Curzon of Kedleston
MSS Eur F306. Papers of Lady Mary Curzon
MSS Eur F177. Papers of Emily Overend Lorimer
MSS Eur D922 & D1168. Papers of David Lockhart Robertson Lorimer

    (b) Public Record Office

Foreign Office (FO) correspondence and files and Embassy and Consular Archives
Colonial Office (CO) correspondence and files

244 — PLAYING THE GAME

(c) Personal Papers at St Antony's College Oxford, Middle East Centre Archive

Papers of Lt Colonel Harold Richard Patrick Dickson (1881–1959), GB 165-0085
Memoirs of Dr C. Stanley Mylrea (b.1876), GB 165-0214
Papers of Harry St. John Bridger Philby (1885–1960), GB 165-0228
John Townsend, unpublished manuscript of the life of Sir Percy Cox, GB 165-0286

(d) United States National Archives: State Department Records

Consular reports from Arabian posts from the 1920s onwards are a useful source of information from the American perspective.

(e) American Arabian Mission Archives: *Neglected Arabia*

The complete run of field reports and journal of the Arabian Mission, from 1892–1962, were re-printed and published, in eight volumes, in 1988 (Farnham Common: Archive Editions).

(2)   Published Primary Sources: Autobiography, Memoirs, Travel Writing and Missionary Accounts

Allison, Mary Bruins, *Doctor Mary in Arabia: Memoirs by Mary Bruins Allison, MD*, edited by Sandra Shaw, Austin: University of Texas, 1994.
Barker, Ernest and Freya Stark, 'Women and the Service of the Empire', *The Contemporary Review* 141, 1932, pp. 54–61.
Belgrave, C. Dalrymple, 'Bahrain', *Journal of the Central Asian Society* 15, 1928, pp. 440–45.
Bell, E. M., *Flora Shaw (Lady Lugard DBE)*, London: Constable, 1947.
Bell, Gertrude, *The Desert and the Sown*, London: William Heinemann, 1907.
— *Amurath to Amurath*, London: William Heinemann, 1911.
— *Letters of Gertrude Bell*, 2 vols, selected and edited by Lady [Florence] Bell, London: Ernest Benn, 1927.
Bent, James Theodore and Mabel Virginia, *Southern Arabia*, London: Smith Elder & Co., 1900.
Billington, Mary, *Woman in India*, London: Chapman & Hall, 1895.
Blunt, Lady Anne, *Bedouin Tribes of the Euphrates*, London: John Murray, 1879.
— *A Pilgrimage to Nejd, the Cradle of the Arab Race*, 2 vols, London: John Murray, 1881.
Bradley, John (ed.), *Lady Curzon's India: Letters of a Vicereine*, London: Weidenfeld and Nicolson, 1985.
Bullard, Sir Reader, *The Camels Must Go: an Autobiography*, London: Faber and Faber, 1961.

Burgoyne, Elizabeth, *Gertrude Bell: from her Personal Papers*, 2 vols, London: Ernest Benn, 1958–61.

Burton, Richard Francis Burton, *Personal Narrative of a Pilgrimage to Al-Medinah and Meccah*, 3 vols, London: Longman & Co., 1855–56.

Calverley, Eleanor T., *My Arabian Days and Nights*, New York: Thomas Y. Crowell Company, 1958.

Caton-Thompson, Gertrude, *Mixed Memoirs*, Gateshead: Paradigm Press, 1983.

Chamberlain, Houston Stewart, *The Foundations of the Nineteenth Century*, 2 vols, London and New York: John Lane, 1911.

Curzon, George Nathaniel, *Lord Curzon in India. Being a Selection from His Speeches as Viceroy and Governor-General of India, 1898–1905*, London: Macmillan & Co., 1906.

— *Subjects of the Day: Being a Selection of Speeches and Writings*, ed. Desmond M. Chapman-Huston, London: George Allen & Unwin, 1915.

— *Tales of Travel*, London: Hodder and Stoughton, 1923.

Dickson, H.R.P., *The Arab of the Desert: a Glimpse into Badawin Life in Kuwait and Saudi Arabia*, London: George Allen & Unwin, 1949.

— *Kuwait and Her Neighbours*, George Allen & Unwin, 1956.

Dickson, Violet, *Forty Years in Kuwait*, London: George Allen & Unwin, 1971.

Doughty, Charles M., *Travels in Arabia Deserta*, 2 vols, Cambridge: Cambridge University Press, 1881.

Egan, Eleanor Franklin, *The War in the Cradle of the World: Mesopotamia*, New York and London: Harper & Bros., 1918.

Forbes, Rosita, *The Secret of the Sahara: Kufara*, London: Cassell, 1921.

— 'A visit to the Idrisi territory in 'Asir and Yemen', *The Geographical Journal* 62, 1923, pp.271–78.

— *Women called Wild*, London: Grayson & Grayson, 1935.

— *Gypsy in the Sun*, London: Cassell & Co., 1944.

— *Appointment with Destiny*, London: Cassell & Co., 1946.

Fowle, Trenchard C., *Travels in the Middle East: Being Impressions by the Way in Turkish Arabia, Syria and Persia*, London: Smith, Elder & Co.,1916.

Freeth, Zahra, *Kuwait was My Home*, London: George Allen & Unwin, 1956.

Harrison, Paul W., 'Economic and Social Conditions in East Arabia', *The Moslem World* 14, 1924, pp.163–71.

— *Doctor in Arabia*, New York: John Day Company, 1940.

Henderson, Edward, *This Strange Eventful History: Memoirs of Earlier Days in the UAE and Oman*, London: Quartet Books, 1988.

Hogarth, David George, *The Penetration of Arabia: a Record of the Development of Western Knowledge Concerning the Arabian Peninsula*, London: Lawrence and Bullen, 1904.

— 'Gertrude Bell's journey to Hayil', *The Geographical Journal* 70, 1927, pp.1–21.

Hogarth, Janet, *An Oxford Portrait Gallery*, London: Chapman Hall, 1931.

Jersey, M.E., 'The Hindu at Home', *The Nineteenth Century: a Monthly Review* 25, January-June 1889, pp.653–66.

Kaye, Sir John, *A History of the Sepoy War in India, 1857–1858*, 3 vols, London: W.H. Allen, 1864–76.

Lane, Edward William, *An Account of the Manners and Customs of the Modern Egyptians*, 2 vols, London: 1836.

— *The Thousand and One Nights*, 3 vols, London: C.Knight & Co., 1839–41.

Loch, Lt Colonel G., 'The Persian Gulf', *Journal of the Royal Central Asian Society* 25, 1938, pp.349–64.

Lorimer, Emily Overend, *Frederick the Second, 1194–1250*, London: Constable & Co., 1931 (translated from Ernst Kantorowicz, *Kaiser Friedrich der Zweite*, Berlin, 1927).

— *Language Hunting in the Karakoram*, London: George Allen & Unwin, 1939.

— *What Hitler Wants*, Harmondsworth: Penguin Special, 1939.

— *What the German Needs*, London: George Allen & Unwin, 1942.

Malcolm, Sir John, *Sketches of Persia, from the Journals of a Traveller in the East*, 2 vols, London: John Murray, 1828.

Mason, Alfred De Witt and Barny, Frederick J., *History of the Arabian Mission*, New York: Board of Foreign Missions, Reformed Church in America, 1926.

Max-Müller, Georgina, *Letters from Constantinople*, London, 1897.

Moberley, F.J., *History of the Great War based on Official Documents: the Campaign in Mesopotamia*, London: Committee of Imperial Defence Historical Section, 1923.

Montgomery, Helen B., *Western Women in Eastern Lands: An Outline Study of Fifty Years of Woman's Work in Foreign Missions*, New York: Macmillan Co., 1910.

Moorehead, Caroline (ed.), *Over the Rim of the World: Freya Stark Selected Letters*, London: John Murray, 1988.

Muir, Sir William, *The Life of Mahomet and History of Islam, to the Era of the Hegira*, 4 vols, London, 1858–61.

Murray, Gilbert, 'Satanism and the New World Order', *Contemporary Review* 117, 1920, pp.465–76.

Niebuhr, Carsten, *Travels through Arabia and other Countries in the East*, trans. Robert Heron, 2 vols, Edinburgh: R. Morison & Son, 1792.

O'Brien, Rosemary, *Gertrude Bell: the Arabian Diaries, 1913–1914*, New York: Syracuse University Press, 2000.

Palgrave, William G., *Narrative of a Year's Journey through Central and Eastern Arabia (1862–1863)*, 2 vols, London: Macmillan, 1865.

Philby, H.St.J.B., *Arabian Days*, London: Robert Hale, 1948.

— *Forty Years in the Wilderness*, London: Robert Hale, 1957.

Sommer, Annie Van and S.M.Zwemer, (eds), *Daylight in the Harem: a New Era for Moslem Women. Papers on present-day reform movements, conditions and methods of work among Moslem women read at the Lucknow*

Conference, 1911. Edinburgh and London: Oliphant, Anderson & Ferrier, 1911.

Stark, Freya, *The Valley of the Assassins*, London: John Murray, 1934.

— 'Two months in the Hadhramaut', *The Geographical Journal* 87, 1936, pp. 113–26.

— 'In defence of travel', *Journal of the Royal Central Asian Society* 23, 1936, pp. 104–10.

— *The Southern Gates of Arabia: a Journey in the Hadhramaut*, London: John Murray, 1936.

— *Baghdad Sketches*, London: John Murray, 1937.

— *Seen in the Hadhramaut*, London: John Murray, 1938.

— 'An Exploration in the Hadhramaut and Journey to the Coast', *The Geographical Journal* 93, 1939, pp. 1–17.

— *A Winter in Arabia*, London: John Murray, 1940.

— *Traveller's Prelude: Autobiography, 1893–1927*, London: John Murray, 1950.

— *Beyond Euphrates: Autobiography 1928–1933*, London: John Murray, 1951.

— *The Coast of Incense: Autobiography, 1933–1939*, London: John Murray, 1953.

— *Dust in the Lion's Paw: Autobiography, 1939–1946*, London: John Murray, 1961.

— *Freya Stark Letters,* ed. Lucy Moorehead, Salisbury: Compton Russell, 1974 (vol. 1, 1914–1930), 1975 (vol. 2, 1930–1935), 1976 (vol. 3, 1935–1939).

Van Ess, Dorothy, *Pioneers in the Arab World*, Grand Rapids MI: Historical Series of Reformed Church in America, 1974.

Van Ess, John, *Meet the Arab*, New York: John Day Company, 1943.

Wilson, Lt Colonel Sir Arnold T., *Loyalties: Mesopotamia, 1914–1917, a Personal and Historical Record*, London: Oxford University Press, 1930.

— *S.W. Persia. Letters and Diary of a Young Political Officer, 1907–1914*, London: Oxford University Press & Readers Union Limited, 1942.

Zwemer, A. E. and S. M., *Moslem Women*, West Medford MA: Central Committee on the Study of Foreign Missions, 1926.

Zwemer, Samuel M., *Arabia the Cradle of Islam: Studies in the Geography, People and Politics of the Peninsula with an Account of Islam and Mission Work etc.*, Edinburgh and London; New York: Oliphant, Anderson & Ferrier, 1900.

Zwemer, Samuel M. and James Cantine, *The Golden Milestone: Reminiscences of Pioneer Days Fifty Years Ago in Arabia*, New York: Fleming H. Revell Company, 1938.

II — SECONDARY PRINTED WORKS

Abu-Lughod, Lila, *Writing Women's Worlds: Bedouin Stories*, Berkeley: University of California, 1992.

— (ed.), *Remaking Women: Feminism and Modernity in the Middle East*, Princeton NJ: Princeton University Press, 1998.

Adams, Pauline, *Somerville for Women: an Oxford College, 1879–1993*, Oxford: Oxford University Press, 1996.

Ahmed, Leila, 'Western Ethnocentrism and perceptions of the Harem', *Feminist Studies* 8, 1982, pp. 521–34.

— *Women and Gender in Islam: Historical Roots of a Modern Debate*, New Haven and London: Yale University Press, 1992.

Abdul-Aziz, Moudi M., *King Abdul-Aziz and the Kuwait Conference, 1923–1924*, London: Echoes, 1993.

Abdullah, M. Morsy, 'Changes in the economy and political attitudes, and the Development of culture on the coast of Oman between 1900 and 1940', *Arabian Studies* 2, 1975, pp. 167–78.

— *United Arab Emirates: a Modern History*, London: Croom Helm, 1978.

Alangari, Haifa, *The Struggle for Power in Arabia: Ibn Saud, Hussein and Great Britain, 1914–1924*, Reading: Ithaca Press, 1998.

Alghanim, Salwa, *The Reign of Mubarak Al-Sabah, Shaikh of Kuwait, 1896–1915*, London: I.B. Tauris, 1998.

Al Rasheed, Madawi, *Politics in an Arabian Oasis: the Rashidi Tribal Dynasty*, London: I.B. Tauris, 1991.

Al-Qasimi, Muhammad, *The Myth of Arab Piracy in the Gulf*, London: Croom Helm, 1986.

Al-Sayegh, Fatma, 'American missionaries in the UAE region in the twentieth century', *Middle Eastern Studies* 32, 1996, pp. 120–39.

Al-Tajir, Mahdi, *Bahrain 1920–1945: Britain, the Shaikh and the Administration*, London: Croom Helm, 1987.

Altorki, Soraya, *Women in Saudi Arabia: Ideology and Behavior among the Elite*, New York: Columbia University Press, 1986.

Amos, Valerie and Pratibha Parmar, 'Challenging imperial feminism', *Feminist Review* 17, July 1984, pp. 3–19.

Badran, Margot, *Feminists, Islam and the Nation: Gender and the Making of Modern Egypt*, Princeton NJ: Princeton University Press, 1995.

Ballhatchet, Kenneth, *Race, Sex and Class Under the Raj: Imperial Attitudes and Policies and their Critics, 1793–1905*, London: Weidenfeld & Nicolson, 1980.

Barker, A.J., *The Neglected War: Mesopotamia, 1914–1918*, London: Faber & Faber, 1967.

Baron, Beth, *The Women's Awakening in Egypt: Culture Society and the Press*, New Haven and London: Yale University Press, 1994.

Barr, Pat, *The Memsahibs*, London: Hamish Hamilton, 1976.

Baykan, Aysegül C., 'The Turkish Woman: an adventure in feminist historiography', *Gender and History* 6, 1994, pp. 101–16.

Bolt, Christine, *Victorian Attitudes towards Race*, London: Routledge & Kegan Paul, 1971.

Bowie, Fiona, Deborah Kirkwood and Shirley Ardener (eds), *Women and Missions: Past and Present. Anthropological and Historical Perceptions*, Providence and Oxford: Berg Publishers, 1993.

Brantlinger, Patrick, *Rule of Darkness: British Literature and Imperialism, 1830–1914*, Ithaca and London: Cornell University Press, 1988.

Burrowes, Robert D., *Historical Dictionary of Yemen*, Lanham MD and London: Scarecrow Press, 1995.

Burton, Antoinette, 'The white woman's burden: British feminists and 'the Indian Woman', 1865–1915', in Chaudhuri and Strobel (eds), *Western Women and Imperialism: Complicity and Resistance*, Bloomington: Indiana University Press, 1992.

— *Burdens of History: British Feminists, Indian Women and Imperial Culture, 1865–1915*, Chapel Hill and London: University of North Carolina, 1994.

Busch, Briton Cooper, *Britain and the Persian Gulf, 1894–1914*, Berkeley and Los Angeles: University of California Press, 1967.

— *Britain, India and the Arabs, 1914–1921*, Berkeley: University of California Press, 1971.

Bush, Julia, *Edwardian Ladies and Imperial Power*, London: Leicester University Press, 2000.

— 'British Women's Imperial Politics and the South African War (1899–1902)', *Women's History Notebooks* 7 (2), Summer 2000, pp. 2–9.

Callan, Hilary and Shirley Ardener (eds), *The Incorporated Wife*, Beckenham: Croom Helm, 1984.

Callaway, Helen, *Gender, Culture and Empire: European Women in Colonial Nigeria*, London: Macmillan, 1987.

Callaway, Helen and Dorothy O. Helly, 'Crusader for Empire: Flora Shaw/Lady Lugard' in Chaudhuri and Strobel (eds), *Western Women and Imperialism: Complicity and Resistance*, Bloomington: Indiana University Press, 1992.

Cannadine, David, *Ornamentalism: How the British Saw their Empire*, London; Allen Lane, 2001.

Carr, E. H., *What is History? The George Macaulay Trevelyan Lectures delivered in the University of Cambridge, January–March 1961*, London: Macmillan & Co., 1961.

Chambers, Iain and Lidia Curti (eds), *The Post-Colonial Question: Common Skies, Divided Horizons*, London: Routledge, 1996.

Chaudhuri, Nupur and Margaret Strobel (eds), *Western Women and Imperialism: Complicity and Resistance*, Bloomington: Indiana University Press, 1992.

Cohn, Bernard S., 'Representing authority in Victorian India' in Hobsbawm and Ranger (eds), *The Invention of Tradition*, Cambridge: Cambridge University Press, 1983.

— *Colonialism and its Forms of Knowledge: the British in India*, Princeton NJ: Princeton University Press, 1996.

Cooper, F and A. Stoler, 'Tensions of empire: colonial control and visions of rule', *American Ethnologist* 16, 1989, pp. 609–21.

Cottrell, Alvin J. (ed.), *The Persian Gulf States: a General Survey*, Baltimore and London: Johns Hopkins University Press, 1980.

Crawford, Elizabeth, *The Women's Suffrage Movement: a Reference Guide, 1866–1928*, London: Routledge, 1999.

Davies, Charles L., *The Blood-Red Flag: an Investigation into Qasimi Piracy, 1797–1820*, Exeter: University of Exeter Press, 1997.

Doumato, Eleanor Abdella, *Getting God's Ear: Healing in Saudi Arabia and the Gulf*, New York: Columbia University Press, 2000.

Donnell, Alison and Pauline Polkey (eds), *Representing Lives: Women and Auto/biography*, Basingstoke: Macmillan, 2000.

Evans, Richard J., *In Defence of History*, London: Granta, 1997.

Fernea, Elizabeth, 'Ways of seeing Middle Eastern women', *Women: A Cultural Review* 6, 1995, pp. 60–66.

Flemming, Leslie A., 'American missionaries' ideals for women in North India, 1870–1930' in Chaudhuri and Strobel (eds), *Western Women and Imperialism: Complicity and Resistance*, Bloomington: Indiana University Press, 1992.

Foucault, Michel, *History of Sexuality, vol. 1, An Introduction*, London: Allen Lane, 1979 [translated from *La Volonté de Savoir*, Paris 1976].

— *The Archaeology of Knowledge*, London: Tavistock, 1977.

Frater, Alexander, *Beyond the Blue Horizon: On the Track of Imperial Airways*, London: William Heinemann, 1986.

Geniesse, Jane Fletcher, *Passionate Nomad: the Life of Freya Stark*, New York: Random House, 1999.

Gilmour, David, *Curzon*, London: John Murray, 1994.

Gordon, Peter and David Doughan, *Dictionary of British Women's Organisations, 1825–1960*, London: Woburn Press, 2001.

Graham-Brown, Sarah, *Images of Women: the Portrayal of Women in the Photography of the Middle East, 1860–1950*, London: Quartet Books, 1988.

Graves, Philip, *The Life of Sir Percy Cox*, London: Hutchison & Co., 1941.

Guha, Ranajit, 'On some aspects of the historiography of colonial India', *Subaltern Studies* 1, 1982, pp. 1–7.

Haggis, Jane, 'Gendering colonialism or colonising gender? Recent women's studies approaches to white women and the history of British colonialism', *Women's Studies International Forum* 13, 1990, pp. 105–15.

— 'White women and colonialism: towards a non-recuperative history' in Clare Midgley (ed.), *Gender and Imperialism* (1998).

— '"A heart that has felt the love of God and longs for others to know it": conventions of gender, tensions of self and constructions of difference in offering to be a lady missionary', *Women's History Review* 7, 1998, pp. 171–92.

Hall, Catherine, 'Politics, post-structuralism and feminist history', *Gender and History* 3, 1991, pp. 204–10.

— 'Histories, empires and the post-colonial moment' in Chambers and Curti (eds), *The Post-Colonial Question: Common Skies, Divided Horizons*, London: Routledge, 1996.

Hall, Stuart, 'When was 'the post-colonial'? Thinking at the limit' in Chambers and Curti (eds), *The Post-Colonial Question: Common Skies, Divided Horizons*, London: Routledge, 1996.

Halliday, Fred, '"Orientalism" and its critics', *British Journal of Middle Eastern Studies* 20, 1993, pp. 145–63.

Harrison, Brian, *Separate Spheres: the Opposition to Women's Suffrage in Britain*, London: Croom Helm, 1978.

Hatem, Mervat, 'Through each other's eyes: Egyptian, Levantine-Egyptian, and European women's images of themselves and of each other (1862–1920)', *Women's Studies International Forum* 12, 1989, pp. 183–98.

Heilbrun, Carolyn, *Writing a Woman's Life*, New York: Ballantine Books, 1988.

Hill, Patricia R., *The World their Household: the American Woman's Foreign Mission Movement and Cultural Transformation, 1870–1920*, Ann Arbor: University of Michigan Press, 1985.

Hobsbawm, Eric, and Terence Ranger (eds), *The Invention of Tradition*, Cambridge: Cambridge University Press, 1983.

Howell Georgina, 'Gertrude of Arabia', *The Sunday Times Magazine*, May 1997.

Hunt, Nancy Rose, '"Single ladies on the Congo": Protestant missionary tensions and voices', *Women's Studies International Forum* 13, 1990, pp. 395–403.

Hunter, Jane, *The Gospel of Gentility: American Missionaries in Turn-of-the-Century China*, New Haven & London: Yale University Press, 1984.

Hutchison, William R., *Errand to the World: American Protestant Thought and Foreign Missions*, Chicago IL: University of Chicago Press, 1987.

Hyam, Ronald, *Empire and Sexuality: the British Experience*, Manchester: Manchester University Press, 1990.

Izzard, Molly, *Freya Stark: A Biography*, London: Hodder & Stoughton, 1993.

James, Liz, '"This is me!": autobiography and the construction of identities' in Stanley (ed.) 'Lives and Works: Auto/Biographical Occasions', *Auto/Biography* 3, 1994, pp. 71–82.

Johnson-Odim, Cheryl and Margaret Strobel, *Expanding the Boundaries of Women's History: Essays on Women in the Third World*, Bloomington and Indianapolis: Indiana University Press, 1992.

Kabbani, Rana, *Europe's Myths of the Orient: Devise and Rule*, London: Macmillan, 1986.

Kandiyoti, Deniz (ed.), *Gendering the Middle East: Emerging Perspectives*, London: I. B. Tauris, 1996.

Kaplan, Robert D., *The Arabists: the Romance of an American Elite*, New York: The Free Press, 2nd Edition, 1995.

Keddie, Nikki R. and Beth Baron (eds), *Women in Middle Eastern History: Shifting Boundaries in Sex and Gender*, New Haven and London: Yale University Press, 1991.

Kelly, J. B., *Britain and the Persian Gulf, 1795–1880*, Oxford: Oxford University Press, 1968.

Knapman, Claudia, *White Women in Fiji, 1835–1930: The Ruin of Empire?*, Sydney: Allen & Unwin, 1986.

Lawton, John, 'A lifelong journey [Freya Stark], *Aramco World* 44, July/August 1993, pp. 2–7.

Lewis, Reina, *Gendering Orientalism: Race, Femininity and Representation*, London and New York: Routledge, 1996.

Mabro, Judy, *Veiled Half-Truths: Western Travellers' Perceptions of Middle Eastern Women*, London: I. B. Tauris, 1991.

McClintock, Anne, *Imperial Leather: Race, Gender and Sexuality in the Colonial Context*, New York and London: Routledge, 1995.

MacMillan, Margaret, *Women of the Raj*, London: Thames & Hudson, 1988.

Marshall, Brian, 'European travellers in Oman and Southeast Arabia 1792–1950: a bibliographical study', *New Arabian Studies* 2, 1994, pp. 1–57.

Mason, Philip, *The Men who Ruled India*, London: Guild Publishing, 1985.

Melman, Billie, *Women's Orients: English Women and the Middle East, 1718–1918: Sexuality, Religion and Work*, London: Macmillan, 1992.

Midgley, Clare (ed.), *Gender and Imperialism*, Manchester: Manchester University Press, 1998.

Mills, Sara, *Discourses of Difference: An Analysis of Women's Travel Writing and Colonialism*, London and New York: Routledge, 1991.

Mohanty, Chandra, 'Under western eyes: feminist scholarship and colonial discourses, *Feminist Review* 30, Autumn 1988, pp. 61–88.

Monroe, Elizabeth, *Philby of Arabia*, London: Faber & Faber, 1973.

Moorehead, Caroline, *Freya Stark*, Harmondsworth: Penguin Books, 1985

Moyse-Bartlett, H., *The Pirates of Trucial Oman*, London: Macdonald, 1966.

Nair, Janaki, 'Uncovering the zenana: visions of Indian womanhood in English-women's writings, 1813–1940' in Johnson-Odim and Strobel, *Expanding the Boundaries of Women's History: Essays on Women in the Third World*, Bloomington and Indianapolis: Indiana University Press, 1992.

Nicolson, Nigel, *Mary Curzon*, London: Weidenfeld & Nicolson, 1977.

Nourallah, Riad Atef, 'The Blunts' road to the Mu'allaqat', *Arabian Studies* 8, 1990, pp. 105–35.

Paidar, Parvin, *Women and the Political Process in Twentieth-Century Iran*, Cambridge: Cambridge University Press, 1995.

Pastner, Caroll McC., 'Englishmen in Arabia: encounters with Middle Eastern women', *Signs: Journal of Women in Culture and Society* 4, 1978, pp. 309–23.

Peirce, Leslie, *The Imperial Harem: Women and Sovereignty in the Ottoman Empire*, Oxford: Oxford University Press, 1993.

Peterson, J. E., *Historical Dictionary of Saudi Arabia*, Metuchen NJ and London: Scarecrow Press, 1993.

Polkey, Pauline (ed.), *Women's Lives into Print: the Theory, Practice and Writing of Feminist Auto/biography*, Basingstoke: Macmillan, 1999.

Pratt, Mary Louise, *Imperial Eyes: Travel Writing and Transculturation*, London and New York: Routledge, 1992.

Ramusack, Barbara, 'Cultural missionaries, maternal imperialists, feminist allies: British women activists in India, 1865–1945' in Chaudhuri and Strobel (eds), *Western Women and Imperialism: Complicity and Resistance*, Bloomington: Indiana University Press, 1992.

Reynolds, Kimberley and Nicola Humble, *Victorian Heroines: Representations of Femininity in Nineteenth-Century Literature and Art*, London: Harvester Wheatsheaf, 1993.

Riley, Denise, *'Am I that name?' Feminism and the Category of 'Women' in History*, Basingstoke: Macmillan, 1988.

Rich, Paul, *The Invasions of the Gulf: Radicalism, Ritualism and the Shaikhs*, Cambridge: Allborough Press, 1991.

Robinson, Jane, *Wayward Women: a Guide to Women Travellers*, Oxford: Oxford University Press, 1990.

Rumaihi, M. G., *Bahrain: Social and Political Change since the First World War*, London: Bowker, 1976.

Said, Edward, *Orientalism, New York & London*: Routledge & Kegan Paul Ltd., 1978; reprinted with an afterword, Harmondsworth: Penguin, 1995.

— *Covering Islam: How the Media and Experts Determine How We See the Rest of the World*, London: Routledge & Kegan Paul, 1981.

— *Culture and Imperialism*, London: Chatto & Windus, 1993.

Sampson, Anthony, *The Seven Sisters: the Great Oil Companies and the World They Made*, London: Hodder & Stoughton, 1975.

Schick, Irvin Cemil, 'Representing Middle Eastern women: feminism and colonial discourse', *Feminist Studies* 16, 1990, pp. 345–80.

Scott, Joan Wallach, *Gender and the Politics of History*, New York: Columbia University Press, 1988.

Sharpe, Jenny, *Allegories of Empire: the Figure of Woman in the Colonial Text*, Minneapolis: University of Minnesota Press, 1993.

Sheridan, Dorothy, 'Getting on with Nella Last at the Barrow-in-Furness Red Cross Centre: romanticism and ambivalence in working with women's stories', *Women's History Notebooks* 5, 1998.

Sluglett, P., *Britain in Iraq, 1914–1932*, London: Ithaca, 1976.

Spivak, Gayatri Chakravorty, 'Subaltern Studies: deconstructing historiography', *Subaltern Studies* IV, Delhi, 1985, pp. 330–63.

— 'Can the Subaltern speak?' in Patrick Williams and Laura Chrisman (eds), *Colonial Discourse and Post-Colonial Theory*, London: Harvester Wheatsheaf, 1993.

— *A Critique of Postcolonial Reason: Toward a History of the Vanishing Present*, Cambridge MA and London: Harvard University Press, 1999.

Stanley, Liz, *The Diaries of Hannah Cullwick: Victorian Maidservant*, New Brunswick: Rutgers University Press, 1984.

— 'British feminist histories: an editorial introduction', *Women's Studies International Forum* 13, 1990, pp. 3–7.

— 'Recovering women in history from feminist deconstructionism', *Women's Studies International Forum* 13, 1990, pp. 151–57.

— *The Auto/biographical I: the Theory and Practice of Feminist Auto/biography*, Manchester: Manchester University Press, 1992.

— (ed.) 'Lives and Works: Auto/Biographical Occasions', *Auto/Biography* 3, 1994.

Strobel, Margaret, *European Women and the Second British Empire*, Bloomington: Indiana University Press, 1991.

Tidrick, Kathryn, *Heart-Beguiling Araby*, Cambridge: Cambridge University Press, 1981.

Tinkler, Penny, 'Introduction to Special Issue: Women, Imperialism and Identity', *Women's Studies International Forum* 21, 1998, pp. 217–22.

Troeller, Gary, *The Birth of Saudi Arabia: Britain and the Rise of the House of Sa'ud*, London: Frank Cass, 1967.

Tucker, Judith (ed.), *Arab Women: Old Boundaries, New Frontiers*, Bloomington: Indiana University Press, 1993.

Tuson, Penelope, *The Records of the British Residency and Agencies in the Persian Gulf*, London: Foreign and Commonwealth Office, 1979.

— *Sources for Middle East Studies*, London: The British Library, 1984.

— *The Queen's Daughters: an Anthology of Victorian Feminist Writings on India, 1857–1900*, Reading: Ithaca Press, 1995.

— 'Mutiny narratives and the imperial feminine: European women's accounts of the Rebellion in India in 1857', *Women's Studies International Forum* 21, 1998, pp. 291–303.

Tuson, P. and E. Quick, *Arabian Treaties, 1600–1960*, 4 vols, Farnham Common: Archive Editions, 1992.

Vassiliev, Alexei, *The History of Saudi Arabia*, London: Saqi Books, 1998.

Vicinus, Martha (ed.), *Suffer and be Still: Women in the Victorian Age*, Bloomington: Indiana University Press, 1972.

Wallach, Janet, *Desert Queen: the Extraordinary Life of Gertrude Bell, Adventurer, Adviser to Kings, Ally of Lawrence of Arabia*, New York: Doubleday, 1996.

Ware, Vron, *Beyond the Pale: White Women, Racism and History*, London: Verso, 1992.

Weeks, Jeffrey, *Sex, Politics and Society: the Regulation of Sexuality since 1800*, London: Longman, 2nd edition, 1989.

Winder, R. Bayley, *Saudi Arabia in the Nineteenth Century*, London: Macmillan, 1985.

Winstone, H.V.F., *Gertrude Bell*, London: Jonathan Cape, 1978.

Yapp, Malcolm, 'British Policy in the Persian Gulf' in Alvin J. Cottrell (ed.), *The Persian Gulf States: a General Survey*, Baltimore and London: Johns Hopkins University Press, 1980.

Yegenoglu, Meyda, *Colonial Fantasies: Towards a Feminist Reading of Orientalism*, Cambridge: University Press, 1998.

Yergin, Daniel, *The Prize: the Epic Quest for Oil, Money and Power*, New York: Touchstone, 1991.

Young, Robert, *White Mythologies: Writing History and the West*, London: Routledge, 1990.

— *Colonial Desire: Hybridity in Theory, Culture and Race*, London: Routledge, 1995.

Zahlan, Rosemarie Said, *The Origins of the United Arab Emirates: a Political and Social History of the Trucial States*, London: Macmillan, 1978.

Index